STUDY GUIDE

to accompany

BASIC ECONOMICS, Second Edition

STUDY GUIDE

to accompany

BASIC ECONOMICS, Second Edition

by

Edwin G. Dolan

The Dryden Press
901 North Elm Street
Hinsdale, Illinois 60521

How to Use This Study Guide

This study guide to <u>Basic Economics</u>, Second Edition is intended for use as an integral part of your learning program for the first course in economics.

The text, your instructor's lectures, and the study guide each cover the same ground, but they cover it in different, complementary ways. The text is the most comprehensive of the three in its coverage, but because of physical limitations on its size it can usually only offer one or two illustrations of each theory, and one or two examples of each type of problem. Your instructor's lectures and class discussions cannot cover the material as extensively as the text, but they offer new points of view, applications of economic theory to this week's problems of economic policy, and -- perhaps most valuable of all -- a chance for you to ask questions.

This study guide complements both the text and the lectures. It provides the repeated, additional illustrations, examples, and problems you need to become proficient in the more technical aspects of economics. It provides learning objectives that help you focus on the key concepts presented in the text. And it provides questions and sample test items that will not only prepare you for examinations, but will show you what questions you should be asking in class.

Different students will use this study guide in different ways, but here are my own suggestions for using each section.

WHERE YOU'RE GOING

As you approach each new chapter, begin with the text. Read the section entitled "What You Will Learn in This Chapter," and check the terms for review. Then skim quickly through the chapter looking at headings, key ideas, graphs, and new vocabulary items. All this will give you an overview.

Now turn to the "Where You're Going" section in this study guide, and carefully read through the learning objectives listed there. As you read through the chapter carefully for the first time, keep this list of learning objectives handy, and check them off as you go along. By the end of your first careful reading of the chapter, you should have at least a good preliminary grasp of each objective.

CHAPTER SYNOPSIS

The chapter synopsis is not a shortened substitute for the chapter in the text. It covers all the main ideas of the text, but many important propositions are simply asserted, without the detailed evidence or argument used to back them up in the text. The synopsis makes an excellent review after you have read the text carefully, and that is what it is intended for. If there are points in the synopsis that you do not understand, go back to the full treatment in the text.

WALKING TOUR

The "Walking Tour" sections of this study guide provide a further review of what you have learned from the text, but this time in a form that makes you an active participant. The word "active" is important. You will be wasting your time and the money you spent on this study guide unless you carefully cover the answers given in the margin and <u>think</u> about each question before you look at the answer.

When you come to graphical or numerical problems, actually work the problems yourself before checking the answers. Once you have filled in the blanks and solved the problems, the completed walking tour section will make a useful supplementary review when exam time comes around.

SELF TEST

When you have read the chapter carefully and worked through the other sections in the study guide, you are ready for the self test. The items in the self test are real examination items from real tests given at real colleges and universities. They are carefully coordinated with the Basic Economics text, and selected to represent a range of difficulty. Answers to all items and explanations where necessary are given at the end of each chapter. Don't take the self test too early in your program of study for each chapter. It is most useful when you have the material pretty well in hand. If you find yourself missing more than five items per self test, you should study more before using these sections of the study guide.

WHEN EXAM TIME COMES

When exam time comes, the best thing for you to do would probably be to read page by page through the whole text and all of your lecture notes. But let's be realistic--unless economics is the only course you are taking, you just may not have time to do that much studying during midterm or finals week. That is when this study guide can be most valuable of all. Sit down with the study guide and pick up a pen or pencil with a color you have never used in the book before. Read through each chapter of the study guide including the "Walking Tour" and "Self Test" sections, which you by now will have completed. As you go along, use your colored pen or pencil to highlight every definition, concept, or problem-solving technique that you have not yet completely mastered. Then use your time selectively to go back over the text and your lecture notes for those selected topics. You can then approach your exam with confidence.

TABLE OF CONTENTS

CAREERS IN ECONOMICS

Keith D. Evans

California State University, Northridge

Prepared with the cooperation of the National Association of Business
Economists and the Society of Government Economists

I. The General Value of an Economics Degree

In describing the qualities essential to a good economist, John Maynard Keynes, himself a master at the profession, remarked:

> He must study the present in the light of the past for the purpose of the future. No part of man's nature or his institutions must lie entirely outside his regard.[1]

As you begin the study of economics, you will quickly become aware of the breadth Keynes refers to. There seem to be no limits to the reaches of economic inquiry; it encompasses both the far-reaching and the everyday. Your first exam may well include a question relevant to today's newspaper headlines. At the same time, economics is very much a part of everyday life. Indeed, a discussion with a local merchant concerning the price of an item for sale may lead you to the conclusion that many people think an understanding of economics comes intuitively, with being born; however, it is not a subject to be left to common sense alone.

The trained economist is a valuable and respected member of many organizations-- be they private businesses, public utilities, governments, or universities--and the career opportunities for an economist are primarily limited only by the resourceful- ness of employers and employees. The following sections will show you how an economics major can prepare you for a wide variety of careers as an economist or how training in economics can help prepare you for a professional career in a related field such as law.

Every effort has been made here to provide you, the beginning economics student, with the latest information concerning career opportunities in economics. Major assistance toward this objective was provided by the National Association of Business Economists (NABE). NABE secretary-treasurer, David L. Williams, sup- plied the latest salary surveys of its membership, as well as other publications of his association. In addition to data supplied by the NABE, attitudes, opinions, and experiences of successful, currently employed business and government econ- omists were solicited by means of a questionnaire that was sent to a significant number of randomly selected members of the NABE and the Society of Government Economists. (This will be referred to below as the Dryden questionnaire to dis- tinguish it from the NABE salary survey.)

Even if your career interests lie in other directions, the analytical training that is emphasized in an economics major can generally make you more adaptable to changing employment opportunities after graduation. As one member of the National Association of Business Economists put it when asked about the value to his career of his college major in economics, "Some theoretical micro and macro concepts proved useful; however, more often than not my training in analyzing and researching subjects was used."

---

1. John Maynard Keynes, Essays in Biography, ed. Geoffrey Keynes (New York: W. W. Norton & Company, 1963).

Further, there are definite benefits to you in having a better understanding of how our private enterprise economy works and in having a basis for comparing it with other, more centrally planned, economies. Often people have indicated that in their first career job they literally got lost in a maze--they didn't have perspective as to where they fit in and what relationship their job had with any larger picture. A background in economics can ease that shock. The analytical training, with specific applications to real-life situations, makes it easier to come to grips with the events of the world around us.

One respondent to the Dryden questionnaire put it this way: "My work in economics prepared me well for career advancement and flexibility because of the emphasis my economics study placed on cause and effect relationships, on the link between incentives and resultant actions, all of which have helped me develop a rational and productive way of generating results-oriented thinking." Another replied that the most useful part of his training in economics was the "flexibility, perspective, and ability to deal with intangibles and uncertainty." Still another successful career economist reflected on the importance of his economics degree this way: "It taught me the ability to think and to reason."

You cannot possibly learn all you will need to know in four years of college; but in pursuing a degree in economics you can learn how to think well. With that ability your opportunities are immensely varied and exciting.

II. What Kinds of Career Opportunities are Available to an Economics Major?

It is not enough to say to yourself that you will study economics because in doing so you can learn how to think well, and thinking well is essential to a career as an economist. Choosing a course of study in college is more likely to lead to a successful career if you discover what subjects are of interest to you and in what subjects you do well. So it follows that if you enjoy and do well in courses in economics and business administration, you are very likely to enjoy a career as an economist.

But what are your opportunities as an economics major? What type of work might you actually do as an economist? In general, and depending upon the amount of education you ultimately receive, your future lies in three areas--working in one of a wide variety of positions in private business; serving in a local, state or national governmental agency; or teaching economics at the college and university level. In fact, many economists combine their primary work in one of these fields with part-time work in another. It is not at all unusual for a business economist to teach part-time or for a professor to also be a consultant to business or government.

Economics as an academic subject goes back more than a century and a half. In practical terms, economists found their theories influencing federal government decisions more and more as the Depression of the 1930s occupied world-wide attention. It was not until after World War II, however, that private businesses began to realize the extent to which economic theory might be applied in solving business problems and in formulating business policies. Despite this relatively late start, almost three-fourths of those people who are now called economists by the Bureau of Labor Statistics work in the private business sector. They are employed by manufacturing firms, transportation companies, utilities, banks, institutions with financial interests, communications organizations, insurance firms, investment brokerages, retailing companies, and more.

Those business organizations large enough to warrant their own economists employ them directly. Other, smaller, firms hire the services of economic consultants as needed. Regardless of their size, businesses are aware that government policies and subsequent actions will have an economic effect. One function of the business economist is to analyze and interpret government policies in light of their effect on the economy in general and the specific firm in particular.

In its booklet Business Economics Careers the National Association of Business Economists states that "the business economist's primary function is to apply economics to business problems." To do this requires the ability to understand the economic implications of events taking place in the world, to project how those external events might affect the functioning of the business in question, to prepare guidelines for the decision makers in the organization, and to be able to communicate concepts, principles, and conclusions in a clear, effective, and concise manner. Possessing these qualities prepares a business economist for work in many fields.

The NABE stresses that business economists follow no set patterns. The most successful, established economists have high job mobility because their ability to interpret national and international events in light of their economic impact on a particular sector of business makes them especially adaptable to changing business requirements. For example, while a bank economist might specialize in short-term and long-term forecasts of the markets for money and credit and an industrial economist might devote more attention to economic methods of forecasting company sales, each is essentially using economic knowledge to project how events occurring outside of the organization will affect the organization itself and how best to plan for the future of the business. A consulting economist, while often providing general economic forecasts to a number of companies, finds the greatest success in becoming a specialist in some field. His or her particular expertise is then recognized and sought out.

The main function of an investment economist might be to help relate the economic outlook to investment analysis and portfolio decisions, while an insurance company economist might provide special guidance related to investing the company's funds and marketing its insurance policies. Again, each economist uses the knowledge he or she has acquired to forecast how external events will act upon the particular business involved and how economic and business principles apply to the internal operation of the firm.

Work as a trade association economist involves a variety of activities. Such a person might provide analysis of current national economic problems affecting business, prepare testimony and testify before Congressional committees, write articles for trade and professional journals, forecast economic trends, serve as a spokesperson for industry and business in public speeches or as an advisor to government and industry groups, and do consulting within the trade association.

Government economists may perform essentially the same tasks as those who work in business as far as forecasting the outcome of economic conditions is concerned. The emphasis, however, may well be on formulating policy rather than reacting to policy changes, as the governmental agency can be in a position to initiate economic changes. The government economist may be called upon to do research on major policy issues, to draft speeches for legislators and government officials, and to help determine the purpose and scope of Congressional hearings.

Academic economists concentrate upon the understanding and improvement of economic theory. In teaching theory, they stress how economies function and how a knowledge of economics applies to business and government decision making and to decisions people have to make as individuals. In addition, academic economists may devote some time to research, writing, and consulting with business firms, government agencies, or private individuals.

The Dryden questionnaire asked members of the National Association of Business Economists and the Society of Government Economists to reflect on the value of their college education and on what advice they might have for people just beginning the study of economics. Of those whose major was economics, more than two-thirds of each group reported that their college study had been very useful to them in their first full-time job; and from the vantage point of their ultimate career, more than half still felt their college education was useful in carrying out the duties of their present occupation. What courses did they feel were of such lasting value? Both business and government economists most frequently mentioned courses in micro-economic and macroeconomic theory, econometrics (the application of statistical techniques to obtain quantitative estimates of relationships suggested by economic analysis), money and banking, forecasting, international economics, and those courses which provided specific applications of economic theory to the decision-making process or which had applications to public policy.

Respondents also emphasized the importance of courses involving the economic and business applications of statistics and accounting, as well as the study of related business institutions, especially financial ones. Important, too, were courses on how to use computers and how to program them. Mathematics courses were emphasized as having been helpful. Along with the reference to applied statistics there was continual mention of such courses as analytical geometry, calculus, and linear algebra.

One necessary skill for an economist, whether academic, business, or government, cannot be overlooked or overemphasized, and that is the ability to make the results of his or her work understandable to a wide range of people. To be useful, economic analyses and forecasts must be understood by those who make the decisions for the business or government agency. Because of that, an economist must be able to write and speak clearly and be able to state sophisticated economic ideas in a way that can be understood, even by people with less economic knowledge. Recognizing this necessity to make their work clear and usable to other people, both the government and business economists placed high value on courses that improved their written and oral communication skills.

The NABE advises potential business economists to strive to be generalists, rather than specialists, and the Business Economics Careers booklet recommends some familiarity with as many as possible of the major fields of economics and business administration. In addition to those areas mentioned by the respondents to the Dryden questionnaire, economics and business administration also is concerned with economic and business history, national income and public finance, business cycles and government stabilization policies, corporate finance and industrial organization, marketing and consumer behavior, labor and collective bargaining, purchasing and personnel policies, and economic development and comparative economic systems.

Some of those who answered the Dryden questionnaire had not majored in economics at the undergraduate level. Many of them said they had benefitted from the broad-based liberal arts education they acquired before pursuing economics and business study while earning advanced degrees.

Frank Endicott, retired placement director at Northwestern University and author of an annual job outlook report for college graduates, offers some advice for liberal arts majors, however. The November 13, 1978, issue of U.S. News and World Report quotes him as saying, "Any liberal arts major in this job market would be foolish not to take some courses in economics, accounting, computer science, or other marketable skills."

It should, perhaps, be added that the course of study guidelines presented here must be taken in the spirit in which they have been given--as suggestions from practicing professional economists. When you are planning your particular course of study to fulfill the requirements of your college or university and to satisfy your unique interests, these guidelines cannot, and should not be expected to, replace the need for personal faculty advisement.

How important is an advanced degree? For an academic economist it is a necessity. The master's degree is the minimum qualification for teaching at the community college level, and the Ph.D. is required for most university teaching.

According to the Dryden questionnaire, 80 percent of the government economists who responded indicated that they consider an advanced degree very important, and 11 percent consider one moderately important. Of that number, 56 percent specified a Ph.D. as the required degree, while an additional 25 percent specified a master's degree.

Business economists surveyed by the Dryden questionnaire placed less importance on an advanced degree. Only 57 percent rated it as very important, and 25 percent as moderately important. Those responses were much more evenly distributed regarding which advanced degree is of the most importance. Almost 30 percent favored the M.B.A. (Master of Business Administration), while another group of equal size suggested pursuing either an M.A. or an M.S. degree in economics or business administration. Only 35 percent considered a doctorate essential.

These differences undoubtedly reflect the attitudes of different employers in different businesses and governmental agencies. Again, they are presented here as guidelines which can be one source of help to you as you make your own career decisions.

III. Where Are Economists Working and
What Are Their Average Salaries?

The 1978 NABE Salary Survey

Probably the best source of information regarding current employment and earnings of economists is the latest salary survey (1978) of its membership conducted by the National Association of Business Economists (NABE). This survey consisted of 1,402 usable responses from 50 percent of its membership and hence can be considered a representative sample of that membership. The median base salary for NABE members in 1978 was $33,000. (This means half the NABE members earned $33,000 or more, and half less than $33,000.) Table 1 indicates the percentage distribution of base salary by income class developed from the NABE survey.

Table 1.
Percentage Distribution of
Base Salary by Income Class

Base Salary (Thousands of dollars)	Total (percent)	New York (percent)	Other (percent)
Under 20	9.3	7.0	9.8
20-24.9	12.3	11.0	12.6
25-29.9	15.0	10.3	16.2
30-34.9	17.8	15.8	18.2
35-39.9	12.1	10.7	12.5
40-44.9	9.5	11.8	8.9
45-49.9	6.9	7.4	6.8
50-54.9	4.9	6.2	4.6
55-59.9	2.5	4.0	2.1
60 and over	9.7	15.8	8.3
Median	$33,000	$37,750	$32,400
Mode (most commonly mentioned salary)	30,000	30,000	30,000

Note that over half (57 percent) reported annual base incomes between $20,000 and $40,000 and that almost 10 percent received base salaries in excess of $60,000. While the median base salary of New York City area respondents significantly exceeded that of the median for all respondents to the survey, the percentage of New York respondents to the total continued its decline in recent NABE surveys. These economists represented 19.4 percent of the total number of respondents in 1978, down from 20.9 percent in 1976 and 22.7 percent in 1974. Moreoever, the difference between the total median salary and the New York median had narrowed from the $6,000 salary margin that existed in both the 1976 and 1974 surveys.

In general, how sensitive was the base salary to geographical location? Tables 2 and 3 provide some answers.

Table 2.
Salary by Major City

	Number Reporting	Base-Median	Gross Median
Atlanta	14	$31,500	$32,000
Boston	43	34,000	37,000
Cleveland	35	36,000	42,000
Chicago	82	35,750	38,800
Dallas/Houston	60	34,150	36,550
Detroit	36	33,500	37,000
Los Angeles	60	35,500	39,504
New York City	272	37,750	40,630
Philadelphia	46	33,000	36,000
Pittsburgh	27	38,000	41,000
San Diego	*	33,000	37,000
San Francisco	50	31,100	33,800
Washington, D.C.	107	37,500	39,000
Other	561	30,500	34,600

*Distribution withheld.

Table 3.
Base Salary by Region

Region	Number Reporting	Median
New England	110	$32,000
Middle Atlantic	404	35,500
East North Central	261	33,000
West North Central	59	31,020
South Atlantic	185	33,900
East South Central	24	27,750
West South Central	106	29,977
Mountain	33	27,000
Pacific	180	31,800
Foreign	40	36,530

Gross median income in the table includes what the NABE defines as additional primary and secondary professional income of those responding to their salary survey. Additional primary income includes cash bonuses, income from profit-sharing plans, and so on, before deductions. Secondary professional income includes gross cash income from royalties, directors' and other fees, honoraria, and the like.

Note that among major cities, gross median incomes were highest in Cleveland, Pittsburgh and New York City and that they were lowest in Atlanta and San Francisco. However, the NABE found intercity salary differences to have narrowed significantly based upon comparisons of their 1976 and 1978 salary surveys.

Table 3 indicates that economists working abroad earned the highest salaries. Within the United States the highest median salary was reported in the Middle Atlantic states (New York, New Jersey, and Pennsylvania), while the lowest reported median salary was in the mountain states (Montana, Idaho, Wyoming, Colorado, New Mexico, Arizona, Utah, and Nevada).

How significant was the amount of additional compensation (additional primary and secondary professional income) received by respondents to the 1978 NABE salary survey? Half of all respondents received additional compensation related to their primary employment. The median amount of additional income was $4,500, or 13.6 percent of the median base salary (1977 additional income as a percentage of early 1978 base salary).

Professional income from secondary employment was reported by almost one-third of all respondents. The median secondary income amounted to $2,500, or 7.6 percent of the median base salary.

How do the incomes of men and women in the economics profession compare? Tables 4 and 5 provide some answers. While both the median base salary and median additional compensation amounts were significantly greater in each category for men than for women, the percentage of women in the 1978 survey was 9.5 percent, compared to only 7.2 percent in 1976. Moreover, the women's median base salary of $25,000 represented an 11.1 percent increase over the 1976 salary survey figure, whereas the overall median base salary for all respondents increased by 10 percent between 1976 and 1978.

Table 4.
Base Salary--
Male and Female

	Number Responding	Median Amount
Male--Total	1,269	$34,000
New York	232	39,000
Other	1,037	33,000
Female--Total	133	$25,000
New York	40	32,300
Other	93	24,000

Table 5.
Additional Compensation--
Male and Female

	Number Responding	Median Amount	Mode
Additional primary income			
Male	650	$5,000	$5,000
Female	60	2,750	3,000
Professional secondary income			
Male	407	3,000	2,000
Female	30	1,500	500

Which industries (or other types of job-location classifications) paid the highest salaries? See Tables 6 and 7. Although shrinking as a proportion of total respondents (from 10.5 percent of the respondents in 1974 to 5.9 percent in 1978), economists in the securities and investments area were again the most highly paid. Their median base salary of $43,000 represented a 13.2 percent increase over the $38,000 reported in 1976, when they also ranked first. Economists in the mining, consulting, banking, insurance, transportation, and nondurable manufacturing industries followed in the top rankings in 1978.

While economists in the real estate area were the lowest paid, their sample was extremely small and may not be truly representative of salary conditions in that classification. Other economists earning comparatively low salaries were those employed in academia and in government.

Table 7 indicates that the combined medians for 1977 additional primary income and professional secondary income were again highest in the securities and investments industry, followed by transportation, mining, and publishing. Note that although base salaries for academic economists are low, opportunities for professional secondary income are higher for academics than for any other group of economists. The classifications with the lowest combined median additional incomes were communications and utilities and trade associations.

What of differences in compensation by areas of responsibility? Respondents to the 1978 NABE salary survey were asked to indicate which of twelve areas of responsibility best described their jobs. The results are indicated in Table 8, with median base salaries of these job responsibilities listed in descending order. While there were some changes in the top end of the median base salary distribution in 1978 compared withe the 1976 and 1974 salary surveys, the lowest median base salaries continued to be paid to those respondents who described their jobs as that of statistician, econometrician, or teacher.

To what extent does the amount of compensation depend upon the size of firm and the number of persons supervised by an economist? The 1978 NABE salary survey again indicated that there appears to be no correlation between the size of firm (measured in terms of number of employees) an economist works for and the amount of salary received. The 1976 and 1974 surveys also indicated that no apparent correlation existed.

Table 6.
Base Salary by Income Class by Industry of Employment
Percentage Distribution, Medians and Modes
(Thousands of Dollars)

	Under 20	20–24.9	25–29.9	30–34.9	35–39.9	40–44.9	45–49.9	50–54.9	55–59.9	60 and over	Median	Mode	Number Responding
Durable Manufacturing	3.3	11.2	17.2	23.7	14.9	9.3	7.5	3.2	2.3	7.4	33.0	30.0	215
Nondurable Manufacturing	4.3	12.3	11.1	19.1	13.6	15.4	6.2	5.0	2.5	10.5	35.0	30.0	162
Retail and Wholesale Trade	10.7	21.4	3.6	28.6	10.7	7.1	3.6	10.7	3.6	0	31.5	30.0	28
Banking—All Types	8.5	9.4	16.6	14.9	11.1	9.8	8.5	6.4	3.4	11.4	35.0	50.0	235
Securities and Investments	8.4	7.3	4.8	7.3	10.8	14.5	6.0	4.8	4.8	31.3	43.0	40.0	83
Insurance	7.3	9.8	9.8	17.1	14.5	2.4	7.3	4.9	9.8	17.1	35.0	30.0	41
Communications and Utilities	13.1	16.7	11.9	19.0	9.5	10.7	3.6	6.0	3.6	5.9	31.6	22.0	84
Publishing	14.3	14.3	19.0	4.8	0	19.0	4.8	9.5	0	14.3	34.4	20.0	21
Transportation	6.5	16.1	6.5	19.4	6.4	6.4	9.7	16.1	3.2	9.7	35.0	30.0	31
Mining	---	---	---	18.7	18.7	12.5	12.5	12.5	---	---	39.5	32.0	16
Construction*	---	---	---	---	---	---	---	---	---	---	31.5	23.7	7
Real Estate*	---	---	---	---	---	---	---	---	---	---	25.5	20.0	8
Consulting	8.6	8.6	13.3	14.3	12.4	6.7	11.4	6.7	2.9	15.1	36.0	30.0	105
Nonprofit Research Organizations	12.2	7.3	22.0	22.0	24.4	4.8	4.8	---	---	---	31.5	35.0	41
Trade Associations	8.3	16.7	11.7	18.3	18.3	8.3	5.0	3.3	---	10.0	32.8	30.0	60
Government	13.0	11.6	24.7	18.2	9.1	9.1	14.3	---	---	---	30.0	47.5	77
Academic	25.2	16.5	26.2	17.5	3.9	5.8	2.9	---	---	---	25.7	25.0	103
Other	14.1	16.5	12.9	18.8	14.1	5.9	2.4	5.9	1.2	8.2	30.6	30.0	85

*Distribution withheld.

Table 7.
Additional Compensation by Industry of Employment

Industry	Additional Primary Income		Professional Secondary Income	
	Number of Respondents	Median	Number of Respondents	Median
Durable Manufacturing	126	$5,000	41	$2,400
Nondurable Manufacturing	100	5,000	36	2,400
Retail and Wholesale Trades	15	4,000	11	2,000
Banking	142	3,550	90	2,000
Securities and Investments	60	9,000	20	3,500
Insurance	18	3,500	10	1,506
Communications and Utilities	32	1,500	21	2,000
Publishing	14	5,000	9	4,200
Transportation	11	8,000	8	2,500
Mining	8	6,750	*	3,500
Construction	*	*	*	*
Real Estate	*	2,600	*	2,000
Consulting	69	6,000	32	2,000
Nonprofit Research Organizations	9	2,800	19	4,000
Trade Associations	16	1,035	18	3,000
Government	*	3,000	19	2,000
Academic	37	3,000	81	5,000
Other	39	3,000	16	3,500

*Distribution withheld

Table 8.
Compensation by Area of Responsibility

	Base Salary			Additional Primary Income			Professional Secondary Income		
	Number Reporting	Median	Mode	Number Reporting	Median	Mode	Number Reporting	Median	Mode
General Administration--Economist	163	$42,500	$30,000	88	$6,500	$3,000	63	$3,000	$2,000
Economic Advisor	158	40,000	40,000	87	5,000	1,000	58	2,000	1,000
Financial Administration	64	39.750	26,000	34	5,100	4,000	20	3,750	3,000
Research Administration	90	38,500	30,000	40	3,500	2,500	33	2,000	2,000
General Administration	66	36,000	25,000	29	6,000	5,000	24	4,800	2,000
Corporate Planning	209	35,000	30,000	125	5,000	1,000	44	2,000	2,000
Financial Analyst	60	30,250	22,000	32	3,100	5,000	6	1,750	100
Economic Analyst	278	28,000	21,000	126	2,800	5,000	75	1,500	2,000
Marketing Research	83	27,300	30,000	41	4,000	5,000	15	2,000	1,500
Teaching	81	25,000	25,000	33	3,000	1,000	62	5,000	5,000
Econometrician	34	24,450	40,000	11	2,500	1,000	8	3,000	3,000
Statistician	11	24,180	17,300	3	1,000	365	5	1,500	500
Other	105	34,000	30,000	61	5,000	1,000	28	3,000	5,000

However, as Table 9 demonstrates, the size of the operation managed does corre-late directly not only with the median base salary of the economist but also with the median amount of additional primary income received.

Table 9.
Primary Compensation by Number of Persons Supervised

Number Supervised	Base Salary		Additional Primary Income	
	Number Reporting	Median	Number Reporting	Median
None	355	$26,000	140	$ 2,500
1 to 3	504	31,888	261	4,000
4 to 9	301	38,000	168	5,000
10 to 24	128	44,000	74	6,000
25 and over	114	52,800	67	10,000

How important is the amount of education received with respect to the size of the economist's income? Table 10 provides some rather definite answers.

Table 10.
Primary Compensation by Education

Highest Degree Obtained	Base Salary		Additional Primary Income	
	Number Reporting	Median	Number Reporting	Median
Bachelor's	161	$30,500	87	$5,000
Master's	614	30,550	306	3,750
Ph.D.	455	37,500	226	5,000
All but dissertation	165	33,000	85	4,875
No degree	*	34,000	*	3,200

*Distribution withheld.

Eighty-eight percent of the respondents to the 1978 NABE survey reported additional education beyond the bachelor's degree, with about one-third having completed the Ph.D. Those with Ph.D. degrees had the highest median base salary, 23 percent greater than the median base salary of respondents possessing only a bachelor's degree. Moreover, those who had completed all requirements for the Ph.D. but the dissertation had a median base salary some 8 percent higher than respondents holding only a bachelor's degree. NABE salary surveys continue to indicate that there is little difference in median base salary between holders of bachelor's and master's degrees, although the proportion of respondents holding only a bachelor's degree fell from 13.5 percent in 1976 to 11.4 percent in 1978.

How much is the economist's compensation based upon years of work experience? Not surprisingly, Table 11 suggests that a direct correlation exists between both median base salary and median additional primary income and years of professional experience. Note that respondents with ten to fourteen years experience surpassed the $33,000 median base salary of all respondents (from Table 1), and they also

Table 11.
Primary Compensation by Years of Professional Experience

Years	Base Salary			Additional Primary Income		
	Number Reporting	Median	Mode	Number Reporting	Median	Mode
0 to 4	287	$22,900	$20,000	94	$2,000	$ 1,000
5 to 9	340	30,000	30,000	141	2,000	2,000
10 to 14	275	35,200	30,000	155	5,000	5,000
15 to 19	170	39,000	50,000	91	6,000	5,000
20 to 24	114	42,125	35,000	72	7,150	5,000
25 and over	216	45,000	50,000	70	7,000	10,000

surpassed the $4,500 median additional primary income. While not indicated in Table 11, the NABE reported that Ph.D. holders with zero to four years' experience earned a median base salary of $29,000. This was significantly above the $22,900 median base salary received by all respondents with zero to four years' work experience.

Finally, how rapidly have the salaries of NABE survey respondents risen since the inception of such studies? Table 12 provides some interesting results. Note that salary data are in _nominal_ terms (that is, they are _not_ adjusted for inflation).

Table 12.
NABE Salaries: Growth Pattern 1964-1978

Year	Number Reporting	Median Base Salary	Median Additional Primary Income	Approx. percent Annual Increase in Median Base Salary
1964	445	$16,800	Not reported	
1968	553	19,600	Not reported	4.2
1972	993	25,000	$3,000*	6.9
1974	1,072	27,000	4,000*	4.0
1976	1,159	30,000	4,000*	5.6
1978	1,402	33,000	4,500*	5.0

*For year prior to survey data.

A number of surveys have been done comparing starting salaries of candidates with bachelor's degrees in economics with the salaries of graduates in other fields. Generally, economists earn more than majors in any other social science discipline, and more than humanities majors. It is especially interesting to compare economics majors with majors in other business related disciplines. Economics majors consistently receive better starting salary offers than general business majors. Accounting majors, on the other hand, generally earn more.

These patterns vary according to type of employer, as the following table (taken from The College Placement Council's Salary Survey) demonstrates. Salaries for economists are highest in manufacturing industry, and lowest in nonprofit organizations. Within the federal government, economists' starting salaries are actually higher than those of accounting majors, although accountants earn more in private business.

When looking at the table, the numbers on the top line following each "Functional Area" indicate the range of starting salaries. The number below it indicates the median starting salary offered.

Table 13.
Bachelor's Degree Candidates
(Data Combined for Men and Women)
Monthly Salary Offers by Functional Area and Employer

Functional Area	Business	Manufacturing /Industrial	Type of Employer Government-- Federal	Government-- Local/State	Non-Profit Organizations
Accounting/Auditing	$1,315-$1,080 $1,207	$1,350-$1,083 $1,222	$1,150-$ 875 $1,063	$1,175-$ 918 $1,058	$1,200-$ 750 $ 975
Business Administration	$1,250-$ 800 $ 985	$1,475-$1,000 $1,214	$1,115-$ 850 $ 980	$1,216-$ 700 $ 929	$1,200-$ 628 $ 891
Communications	$1,167-$ 650 $ 898	$1,560-$ 880 $1,249	$1,178	$ 909	$ 961
Community and Service Organizations Work	$ 841	$1,022	$ 885	$1,083-$ 741 $ 912	$1,167-$ 600 $ 839
Engineering	$1,550-$1,135 $1,315	$1,692-$1,400 $1,545	$1,491-$1,138 $1,344	$1,385-$1,092 $1,231	$1,600-$1,167 $1,427
Finance and Economics	$1,292-$ 850 $1,074	$1,400-$1,100 $1,238	$1,250-$ 875 $1,066	$1,005	$ 939
Manufacturing and/or Industrial Operations	$1,633-$ 850 $1,114	$1,670-$1,170 $1,441	$1,354	$1,035	$1,333
Marketing--Consumer Products/Services	$1,208-$ 800 $ 984	$1,433-$ 980 $1,177	$1,026	$1,029	$ 909
Marketing--Industrial Products/Services	$1,333-$ 933 $1,126	$1,525-$1,000 $1,274	$1,142		
Personnel/Employee Relations	$1,083-$ 775 $ 962	$1,550-$1,000 $1,262	$1,008	$1,032	$ 922
Research--Nonscientific	$1,013	$1,600-$ 918 $1,271	$1,039	$ 922	$ 804
Research--Scientific	$1,057	$1,700-$1,200 $1,468	$1,410-$ 833 $1,061	$1,300-$ 833 $1,015	$1,100-$ 641 $ 859

References

College Placement Council. CPC Salary Survey. Bethlehem, Pennsylvania, July 1979.

Endicott, Frank S., Endicott Report: Trends in the Employment of College and University Graduates in Business and Industry, 1979. Placement Center, Northwestern University, Evanston, Illinois, 1978.

National Association of Business Economists. Salary Characteristics 1978. Cleveland, Ohio.

National Association of Business Economists. Salary Survey 1976. Cleveland, Ohio.

National Association of Business Economists. Salary Survey 1974. Washington, D.C.

IV. What Is the Employment Outlook for Economists in the 1980s?

Before launching into some "fearless forecasts" about the employment outlook for economists in the 1980s, it might be well to include a bit of caveat emptor. Let the buyer, whether of tangible goods or intangible ideas, beware. Even the U.S. Department of Labor, in its Occupational Outlook Quarterly, hedges all of its predictions with this statement:

> Common assumptions are that there will be no war,
> that unemployment will not exceed a specific level,
> and that our system of government will not change.[1]

With this recognition that all forecasts are fallible, we will attempt to show the current thought regarding the employment outlook for economists in the decade ahead.

The 1980-81 Occupational Outlook Handbook, Bureau of Labor Statistics Bulletin 2075, will be published in the spring of 1980. The January 21, 1980, issue of U.S. News and World Report excerpts portions of the report, which predicts that a boom in white-collar work lies ahead. The Labor Department projects that more than half of an estimated 66.4 million job openings between 1978 and 1990 will be in the professional, technical, managerial, sales, and clerical fields. Compared with the latest available estimate of 130,000 economists employed in 1978, the forecast projects average annual openings of 7,800 jobs, or 6 percent of the existing number of employed economists. This 6 percent figure compares with a projection of average annual openings of 4.3 percent for industrial engineers, 3.8 percent for mechanical engineers, 6.5 percent for statisticians, 4.3 percent for chemists, and 4.3 percent for systems analysts.[2]

If career decisions are to be made in a thoughtful way, it must be recognized that not all types of economists face the same projected outlook. Colleges and universities employ about 10 percent of the total number of economists, and government agencies another 10 percent; the projections of the Bureau of Labor Statistics refer most pertinently to the approximately three out of four economists whose jobs are located in private industry or research organizations.

For this majority of economists, the Bureau of Labor Statistics' projection of the demand for economists through the mid-80s can be considered encouraging for students in college today. The 1980-81 edition of the Occupational Outlook Handbook reinforces the prediction made previously by the Bureau in its 1978-79 publication that employment of economists will grow faster than the average for all occupations. The 1978-79 edition declared that

---

1. John P. Griffin, "The Job Outlook in Brief, Based on the Occupational Outlook Handbook, 1978-79 Edition." Occupational Outlook Quarterly, U.S. Department of Labor (Washington, D.C.: Government Printing Office, Spring 1978), p. 3.

2. Percentages figured from tables provided in "Tomorrow's New Jobs: Where You Can Find Them," U.S. News and World Report, January 21, 1980, p. 66.

private industry and business will continue to provide
the largest number of employment opportunities for
economists because of the increasing complexity of the
domestic and international economies and the increased
reliance on quantitative methods of analyzing business
trends, forecasting sales, and planning purchases and
production operations. Employers will seek those well-
trained in econometrics and statistics. In addition,
the increasing need for business economists to assist
lawyers, accountants, engineers, and other professionals
in solving problems should stimulate employment growth. [3]

In its discussion of specialties within the field of economics, the Occupational Outlook
Handbook projects that those who are prepared in the fields of environment, energy
and natural resources, health, and transportation can look forward to attractive job
opportunities. The report also recognizes that economists may move from one specialty
to another and that job opportunities may change over fairly short periods of time.
For this reason the handbook suggests that "a strong background in economic theory
and econometrics provides the tools for acquiring any specialty within the field." [4]

The outlook for those who seek careers as academic economists is not as bright
in an era when higher education faces enrollments declining from the peaks that were
reached in the late 1960s and early 1970s. An article by Charles E. Scott in the
May 1979 American Economic Review concludes that academic employment for economists
will be lower than during the boom period of the 1960s. [5] Scott's projection is similar
to that of the Bureau of Labor Statistics, which predicts that colleges and universities
are not expected to increase the numbers of economists employed by any significant
number.

Barbara B. Reagan, an authority on women economists in academia, addresses
the question of opportunities for women economists as members of college and university faculties in an article also published in the May 1979 American Economic Review.
The conclusion of her study shows that

> evidence of affirmative action in economics departments
> is sparse over the last four years....Improved oppor-
> tunities will be needed to avoid discouragement of new
> (i.e., women) Ph.D. candidates. [6]

Because of the relative difficulty of obtaining satisfactory employment in an academic
setting, many people who might otherwise have directed themselves toward a career
in higher education are now accepting nonacademic jobs. That puts graduates with
bachelor's degrees in a position of competing not only with others of similar academic
background and level, but also with those who possess more advanced degrees. For

3. U.S. Department of Labor, Bureau of Labor Statistics, Occupational Outlook
    Handbook, 1978-79 edition (Washington, D.C.: Government Printing Office),
    pp. 520-521.
4. Ibid., p. 521.
5. Charles E. Scott, "The Market for Ph.D. Economists: The Academic Sector,"
    American Economic Review 69 (May 1979): 141.
6. Barbara B. Reagan, "Stocks and Flows of Academic Economists," American
    Economic Review 69 (May 1979): 143.

this reason, the Spring 1978 <u>Occupational Outlook Quarterly</u> summarizes its prediction for economists by stating:

> Employment [is] expected to grow faster than average.
> Master's and PhD. degree holders may face keen competition for college and university positions but can expect good opportunities in nonacademic areas.
> Persons with bachelor's degrees [are] likely to face keen competition. [7]

These indicators are in harmony with several NABE Dryden questionnaire respondents who believe that the best preparation for many of today's careers in economics begins with an undergraduate degree in economics and continues through to the degree of Master of Business Administration.

---

7. U.S. Department of Labor, Bureau of Labor Statistics, <u>Occupational Outlook Quarterly</u> (Washington, D.C.: Government Printing Office, Spring 1978), p. 29.

References

Griffin, John P. "The Job Outlook in Brief, Based on the Occupational Outlook Handbook, 1978-79 Edition," U.S. Department of Labor. Washington, D.C.: Government Printing Office, Spring 1978, p. 3.

Reagan, Barbara B. "Stocks and Flows of Academic Economists." American Economic Review 69 (May 1979):143.

Scott, Charles E. "The Market for Ph.D. Economists: The Academic Sector." American Economic Review 69 (May 1979):141.

"Tomorrow's New Jobs: Where You Can Find Them." U.S. News and World Report, January 21, 1980, p. 66.

U.S. Department of Labor, Bureau of Labor Statistics. Occupational Outlook Handbook, 1978-79 edition. Washington, D.C.: Government Printing Office, pp. 520-521.

U.S. Department of Labor, Bureau of Labor Statistics, Occupational Outlook Quarterly. Washington D.C.: Government Printing Office, Spring 1978, p. 29.

V. Some Tips on Preparing a Resume

While this section will present some ideas on preparing a resume, it should be noted here that the value of a resume, as well as what form it should take, is a controversial subject. Some employers place great importance on the resume; others do not. (Roughly half the respondents to the Dryden questionnaire consider the resume very important, while the other half consider it only of moderate importance or not important at all.)

A local college placement office should be very useful to you not only in helping you write a resume but in showing you how to tailor your resume to a particular firm. In fact, it is best to visit your college placement office well before your senior year in order to take full advantage of the many services such centers usually offer today. They have many publications available for your use, and you will be better off selecting from their supply rather than buying without direction one of the many guides currently on the market.

The Dryden questionnaire asked those economists who do interviewing for their companies what they would suggest to improve the quality of a potential employee's resume. Perhaps the most prominent comment was that the resume should be suited to the particular job being applied for; you cannot prepare one general resume, send it to fifty different companies, and expect a high percentage of positive responses.

The respondents to the Dryden questionnaire, people who receive resumes in their current work and act upon what they read in them, offer these additional pointers for you to consider when preparing your resume: Be brief and relevant and indicate your career objectives. The person who reads your resume may have as little as forty-five seconds to devote to what you have prepared and to make a decision about asking you to come in for a personal interview. Your resume should be neat, well organized, and clearly and simply written. Career accomplishments should be highlighted. If you have had some work exprience while in college that is not directly related to your career goals, some respondents feel that it should still be emphasized, because it shows exposure to the "real world." Even if it is not specifically related to the job being applied for, you have been in a situation where you were trained for the work you did, and every bit of experience helps in your future career. A number of respondents feel that extracurricular college activities should be included.

Negative reaction was given by the Dryden respondents to the use of "canned, prepackaged resumes." The stress seems to be on presenting yourself as a unique individual seeking a specific job. One word of caution was mentioned by several people in exactly the same words: "Don't write a 'cute' resume."

While it still remains an area of some disagreement, the value of a resume might be summarized this way: A good resume may or may not earn you a personal interview, depending upon the importance the particular company's interviewer assigns the resume. But a poorly prepared resume may well close the door to any further contact.

Reference

Warrington, Dr. Donald L. Guide to Effective Resume Development. New York: Metropolitan Life Insurance Company, 1978. (Dr. Warrington is director of career placement services at the University of Nebraska in Omaha.)

VI. How to Make the Job Interview
Work to Your Advantage

Unlike the resume, about which a divergence of opinion exists, the job interview was considered extremely important by everyone responding to the Dryden questionnaire. Because of that, you should be in contact with your college placement office well before you are ready to start interviewing for a career job. In addition to providing written information, college placement offices are increasingly making available video-taping equipment as an aid to you in preparing for job interviews. You can participate in a mock interview which will be video recorded and then watch the tape with a placement counselor who will offer constructive criticism.

June Hillman, a career counselor in the Office of Career Planning and Placement at California State University, Northridge, emphasizes that body language is a key element in any job interview. She stresses that a lasting impression of a candidate is formed within the first five minutes of an interview. Her staff works with students to teach them how to bring out their own positive attributes. Their efforts attempt not to create a stilted image but rather to show each student how to present his or her own best image.

In offering advice about job interviews, respondents to the Dryden questionnaire had a number of common themes. These items, mentioned by many of the respondents, are listed here as advice from people who actually conduct interviews as part of their jobs.

1. Be honest about your goals and experience. Don't claim to have experience you don't have. Try to have in mind what your goals are.

2. Research the employer before you arrive at the interview. (Some placement offices are extremely helpful here, because often employers send information about themselves.)

3. Emphasize the basic applicability of your economic skills to the firm or organization you hope will hire you. Show you have the ability to apply your knowledge of economics to the particular work that interests you.

4. Show interest in opportunities for personal growth and advancement.

5. Demonstrate an ability to communicate well orally and to get along well with people. In the process, try to be relaxed. Many respondents placed a heavy emphasis on being relaxed during the interview.

6. Don't brag. As one person put it, "Maintain a balance between 'can do' and 'can learn.'"

7. Emphasize your ability to write analytically. Take some evidence of analytical writings in economics, especially for a research-type job.

8. There is a difference of opinion about asking questions. Some respondents feel you should have ready a list of questions to ask. Others indicate it is best to let the interviewer initiate much of the conversation. Your own best judgment in the situation will have to prevail.

9. Avoid a "packaged" appearance. As with the resume, interviewers are looking for a unique individual to fill a specific job.

10. As one respondent put it, "Wear the tribal costume of the company being interviewed."

11. Don't appear uncertain or indecisive.

12. Listen!

In a brochure advising students about the employment interview, Dr. Frank S. Endicott, director of placement (emeritus) of Northwestern University, lists fifteen reasons why candidates receive rejection replies after their interviews. These reasons are definitely worth considering as you prepare for your career interviews.

1. Lack of proper career planning--purposes and goals ill defined--needs direction.

2. Lack of knowledge of field of specialization--not well qualified--lacks depth.

3. Inability to express thoughts clearly and concisely--rambles.

4. Insufficient evidence of achievement or capacity to excite action in others.

5. Not prepared for the interview--no research on company--poor presentation.

6. No real interest in the organization or the industry--merely shopping around.

7. Narrow location interest--unwilling to relocate later--inflexible.

8. Little interest and enthusiasm--indifferent--bland personality.

9. Overbearing--overaggressive--conceited--cocky--aloof--assuming.

10. Interested only in the best dollar offer--too money conscious.

11. Asks no or poor questions about the job--little depth and meaning to questions.

12. Unwilling to start at the bottom--expects too much too soon--unrealistic.

13. Makes excuses--evasive--hedges on unfavorable factors in record.

14. No confidence and lack of poise--fails to look interviewer in the eye-- immature.

15. Poor personal appearance--sloppy dress--lacks sophistication.

When you near graduation, you will likely wonder how important your college transcript will be to an interviewer. In the Dryden questionnaire, the transcript was considered an "important" part of the evaluation of job candidates by slightly more than half of the economists responding. A little more than one-third considered the transcript to be "moderately important," while the rest paid little or no attention to the transcript.

Those who did find the transcript of at least moderate importance looked at overall GPA first and, to a somewhat lesser extent, the grades in certain key courses second. The "reputation of the college or university" was important to only a small number of the responding economists.

VII. Useful Publications for Economics Majors

The following is offered as a representative, but abridged, list of publications that you should find useful in your studies of economics and in pursuit of a career involving those studies.

I. General Reference Material

A. Dictionary of Business and Economics. Christine Ammer and Dean S. Ammer. New York: Free Press, 1977. A remarkably thorough and complete compilation of definitions of terms and concepts commonly encountered in business and economics courses. Also contains some biographical sketches of famous past and present-day economists.

B. The McGraw-Hill Dictionary of Modern Economics: A Handbook of Terms and Organizations, 2d ed. Similar in scope to the Ammer's Dictionary of Business and Economics, this book perhaps gives somewhat greater emphasis to a description of some 225 private, public and nonprofit organizations concerned with economics and marketing.

C. The Student Economist's Handbook. Ralph L. Andreano, Evan Ira Farber, Sabron Reynolds. Cambridge, Mass.: Schenkman Publishing Company, 1967. A comprehensive guide to sources of information in government documents, professional books and journals, and periodicals which are readily available, reliable, and easy to use. "How to" chapters on using statistics, libraries, government documents, and other sources of information concerning research in economics are included. Contains an annotated bibliography of major statistical sources. The book is out of print now but should be available in college libraries.

II. Resume Writing and Interviewing Tips

Many books covering these topics are currently available. Your college or university placement office or library, as well as your local public library, should contain a representative sample of them. Here are three that come highly recommended.

A. Guide to Effective Resume Development. Donald L. Warrington. New York: Metropolitan Life Insurance Company publication T.16958 (3-78). A "no frills" twenty-page brochure which is concise but thorough. Contains an appendix of "action words."

B. How to Write Better Resumes. Adele Lewis. Woodbury, New York: Barron's Educational Series, 1977. A very thorough discussion of finding a job. Includes sections on what to include in a resume, samples of resumes for over 100 different careers, samples of covering letters, a guide to finding work, and suggestions for following through and keeping records.

C. Job Hunting Guide: Office Manual of the Employment Management Associ-
    ation. John D. Erdlen. Boston: Herman Publishing, 1975. Among other
    things, this book provides tips for writing resumes and cover letters, as
    well as samples of each, advice on making interviews more successful, and
    a directory section that contains a list of employment agencies and a list of
    executive search consultants.

III. Government Publications

The following are published by the U.S. government (or are based upon a
federal publication). They contain a wide variety of regularly published statistics pertaining to such areas as national income accounting, money supply
data, employment information, population trends, and so on. Most of the
following also contain helpful interpretative articles regarding trends and
correlations of the various data as well.

A. Economic Report of the President. Transmitted to the Congress in January
    of each year, together with the Annual Report of the Council of Economic
    Advisors. For sale by the Superintendent of Documents, U.S. Government
    Printing Office, Washington, D.C., 20402.

B. Federal Reserve Bank of St. Louis Review. Published monthly by the
    research department of the Federal Reserve Bank of St. Louis. No charge
    for subscriptions. For information write: Research Department, Federal
    Reserve Bank of St. Louis, P.O. Box 442, St. Louis, Missouri 63166.
    This rather independent research department often publishes articles crit-
    ical of current monetary and fiscal policy.

C. Federal Reserve Bulletin. Published monthly under the direction of the
    Board of Governors of the Federal Reserve System. For information write:
    Division of Support Services, Board of Governors of the Federal Reserve
    System, Washington, D.C. 20551.

D. Monthly Labor Review. Published monthly by the Bureau of Labor Statis-
    tics of the U.S. Department of Labor. For information write: Superinten-
    dent of Documents, Government Printing Office, Washington, D.C. 20402.

E. Survey of Current Business. Published monthly by the Bureau of Economic
    Analysis of the U.S. Department of Commerce. For information write:
    Superintendent of Documents, U.S. Government Printing Office, Washington,
    D.C. 20402.

F. The U.S. Fact Book. The American Almanac for (current year). An un-
    abridged edition of the U.S. Bureau of the Census' The Statistical Abstract
    of the United States. Published annually by Grosset & Dunlap, New York.
    If the book is not available in your book store, it should be possible for
    you to order it from that store.

IV. Newspapers and Magazines

These selected newspapers and magazines concentrate in whole or in part upon
the reporting and interpretation of current business and economic news. All
are highly readable.

A. <u>Barron's National Business and Financial Weekly</u>. Published every Monday by Dow Jones & Company. For information write: Barron's, 200 Burnett Road, Chicopee, Massachusetts 01012. Student subscription discount available.

B. <u>Business Week</u>. Published weekly, except for one issue in January, by McGraw-Hill. Student discount may be available on some campuses. For information write: Business Week, McGraw-Hill Building, 1221 Avenue of the Americas, New York, New York 10020.

C. <u>Challenge, the Magazine of Economic Affairs</u>. Published bimonthly by M. E. Sharpe. For information write: Challenge, 901 North Broadway, White Plains, New York 10603. Leading economists write articles aimed at readers with little formal training in economics. These articles largely contain applications to current problems and policies.

D. <u>The Economist</u>. Published weekly. For information write: The Economist Newspaper Limited, P.O. Box 190, 23a St. James's Street, London SW1A 1HF, England. Student subscription discount available. This entertaining British publication frequently contains criticisms of U.S. economic policies.

E. <u>Fortune</u>. Published fortnightly by Time, Inc., 541 North Fairbanks Court, Chicago, Illinois 60611. Student subscription discount may be available on some campuses.

F. <u>Newsweek</u>. Published weekly. Student subscription discount may be available on some campuses. For information write: Newsweek, Newsweek Building, Livingston, New Jersey 07039.

G. <u>Time</u>. Published weekly. Student subscription discount may be available on some campuses. For information write: Time, Inc., 541 North Fairbanks Court, Chicago, Illinois 60611.

H. <u>U.S. News and World Report</u>. Published weekly except two issues combined into one at year-end. Student subscription discount may be available on some campuses. For information write: U.S. News and World Report, Inc., 2300 N Street, N.W., Washington, D.C. 20037.

I. <u>Wall Street Journal</u>. Published daily except Saturdays, Sundays, and general legal holidays. Student subscription discount available. For information write: Wall Street Journal, 200 Burnett Road, Chicopee, Massachusetts 01021.

V. Selected Professional Economic and Business Journals.

The following is a small sample from the rather large number of journals whose intended readership consists primarily of professional economists or of professionals in related fields. While many articles may be too technical for the beginning economics student, each journal contains writing well within the grasp of the interested student who has completed one school year's study of microeconomic and macroeconomic principles. Journals of selected <u>regional</u> professional economic associations have also been included.

A. American Economic Review. Published quarterly by the American Economic Association, along with its annual Proceedings of the annual meetings published in May. Student subscription discount available. For information write: Secretary, C. Elton Hinshaw, 1313 – 21st Avenue South, Nashville, Tennessee 37212. Students should find the Proceedings issue especially useful, as it usually contains broad coverage of selected economists' views on current economic issues and government policies.

B. The American Economist. Journal of the International Honor Society in Economics, Omicron Delta Epsilon. Published semiannually in Spring and Fall. For information write: Dr. William D. Gunther, Department of Economics, P.O. Drawer AS, University of Alabama, University, Alabama 35486.

C. Business Economics. Published quarterly by the National Association of Business Economists. Student subscription discount available. For information write: National Association of Business Economists, 28349 Chagrin Blvd., Suite 201, Cleveland, Ohio 44122.

D. Economic Inquiry. Journal of the Western Economic Association. Published quarterly. Student subscription discount available. For information write: Western Economic Association, Executive Office, Department of Economics, California State University, Long Beach, California 90840.

E. Harvard Business Review, "a bimonthly journal for professional managers, is a program in executive education of the Graduate School of Business Administration, Harvard University." For information write: Harvard Business Review, Subscription Service Department, P.O. Box 9730, Greenwich, Connecticut 06835.

F. Journal of Business. Published quarterly by the Graduate School of Business of the University of Chicago. Student subscription discount available. For information write: Journal of Business, University of Chicago Press, 5801 Ellis Avenue, Chicago, Illinois 60637.

G. Journal of Economics Literature. Published quarterly by the American Economic Association along with the American Economic Review . This publication is a must for any economics researcher. It usually contains a survey article of the latest developments in a field of economics and also provides reviews of recently published economics books, an annotated listing of new books, contents of selected current economic and business professional journals, and a classification by economics area of articles and abstracts of selected articles in current economic and business journals, among other things. See American Economic Review.

H. Journal of Law and Economics. Published twice a year by the University of Chicago Law School. Student subscription discount available. For information write: Editor, Journal of Law and Economics, University of Chicago Law School, 1111 East 60th Street, Chicago, Illinois 60637.

I. Journal of Political Economy. Published bimonthly by the University of Chicago Press. Student subscription discount available. For information write: The University of Chicago Press, 5801 Ellis Avenue, Chicago, Illinois 60637.

J. Quarterly Journal of Economics. Published quarterly by John Wiley & Sons, Inc., and by the President and Fellows of Harvard College. For information write: Journal Department, John Wiley & Sons, 605 Third Avenue, New York, New York 10016.

K. Atlanta Economic Journal. Published quarterly by the Atlantic Economic Society. For information write: John M. Virgo, Atlantic Economic Society, Box 618, Worden, Illinois, 62097.

L. Southern Economic Journal. Published quarterly by the Southern Economic Association and the University of North Carolina. For information write: Vincent J. Tarascio, Managing Editor, Southern Economic Journal, Hanes Hall 019-A, Chapel Hill, North Carolina, 27514.

M. Nebraska Journal of Economics and Business. Published quarterly by the College of Business Administration of the University of Nebraska-Lincoln. For information write: Nebraska Journal of Economics and Business, Bureau of Business Research, 200 CBA, University of Nebraska-Lincoln, Lincoln, Nebraska 68588.

CHAPTER ONE
AN OVERVIEW OF THE MARKET ECONOMY

WHERE YOU'RE GOING

Here is what you will be able to do when you have mastered this chapter:

--Explain why scarcity is the central concept of economics.

--Identify the objectives, alternative activities, and constraints present in all situations of economic choice.

--Distinguish between the two kinds of economic decision making known as pure economizing and entrepreneurship.

--Apply the concept of opportunity cost to familiar economic decisions of the kind you make yourself.

--Distinguish between normative and positive elements in discussions of economic policy.

--Explain the meaning and significance of the following additional terms and concepts:

> Production possibility frontier.
> Homogeneous.
> Margin, marginal.
> Scientific prediction.
> Empirical.
> Econometrician.
> Efficiency.
> Distributive justice.
> Market justice.
> Ideology.

In addition, after mastering the appendix to this chapter, you will be able to:

--Associate pairs of numbers with points on a graph, and read common economic graphs.

--Determine the slope of a line or curve drawn in a graph.

--Use graphs efficiently and effectively as a study aid.

--Construct graphs of your own on the basis of verbal instructions.

CHAPTER SYNOPSIS

Reading this synopsis is not a substitute for reading the chapter, but it should help you to recall the main points. If there are any you feel unsure of, refer to the full discussion in the text.

Scarcity is the central concept of economics. Economic scarcity is a subjective concept that means not having as much of something as one wants. As such, scarcity cannot be measured by any objective, physical standard.

1

The fact of scarcity makes it necessary for people to choose among alternative uses for their limited time and resources. All of the great variety of choices that people make every day can be described in terms of three features: objectives, alternative activities, and constraints. Economic objectives can usually be described in terms of maximizing or minimizing something. Alternative activities are the different ways that might be used to achieve the objectives. Constraints are limits on the ability of the decision maker to achieve the desired objectives in full.

Choosing what to eat in a restaurant is a classic example of economic choice in which each of these three elements can be easily identified: Your objective is to maximize your dining satisfaction. Your alternative activities are represented by the various dishes that appear on the menu. And your pursuit of dining satisfaction is constrained by the size of your budget.

Objectives, alternative activities, and constraints are present in all situations of economic choice, but they are not always equally well defined or inflexible. In the simplest case, all of the elements of the problem at hand are known with certainty. Economic decision making then becomes a matter of choosing precisely the pattern of activities from among the available alternatives that will best serve the given objectives, subject to the known constraints. This kind of decision making is known as pure economizing. In practice, however, not all economic decisions are so clear-cut. Often people must search out the available alternatives or invent new ones and must make risky decisions without knowing all of the constraints they face. The activities of exploration, experimentation, alertness to new opportunities, guesswork, and risk-taking are the entrepreneurial elements in economic decision making.

In a world of scarcity, economic objectives can never be attained without cost. The key to understanding how cost enters into economic decision making is the concept of opportunity cost, which means the cost of doing something expressed in terms of the loss of the opportunity to pursue instead the best alternative activity with the same time or resources. The production possibility frontier is a simple graph that makes it easy to visualize the concept of opportunity cost. It shows that there is always a tradeoff between one economic activity and another--for example, using more of the nation's resources for higher education means bearing an opportunity cost in terms of lost production of other goods and services. The magnitude of the opportunity cost is shown by the slope of the production possiblity frontier.

Much of this course will be devoted to problems of economic policy. Should the government cut taxes in an attempt to combat a coming recession? Should gasoline prices be controlled, or should they be permitted to seek their own level in the market? Should special measures be taken to protect the elderly from the effects of inflation? Systematic thinking about policy issues like these requires a three-step chain of reasoning somewhat like the following:

1. If Policy X is followed, Outcome Y will result.
2. Outcome Y is a good (or bad) thing.
3. Therefore, hurrah (or ugh) for Policy X.

The first proposition in this three-step chain of reasoning is a proposition of positive economics or scientific prediction. It is an objective prediction in the form "If A occurs, then B will occur, other things being equal." The second statement is a proposition in normative economics, that is, a subjective evaluation of the predicted result in terms of personal values. The third statement, which reaches a conclusion as to the desirability of the policy itself, combines positive and normative economic reasoning.

It can be seen, then, that disputes about economic policy can arise from two distinct sources. On the one hand, economists may disagree about what the actual outcome of the policy will be. On the other hand, they may disagree about what outcomes are in fact desirable. Disagreements of the second sort arise because of the differing importance that people attach to such values as efficiency, distributive justice, and market justice. Meaningful debate about economic policy thus requires at a minimum, that it be clear to all participants whether the issue being debated is primarily one of positive or normative economics.

WALKING TOUR

You have read the chapter at least once and have reviewed the synopsis. Now you are going to walk through the material step by step, filling in the blanks and answering the questions as you go along. After you have answered each question, check yourself by uncovering the answer given in the margin. If you do not understand why the answer given is the right one, refer back to the proper section of the text.

Scarcity and Choice in Economics

In economics, scarcity is an [objective/subjective] concept.   subjective
That means that it is properly measured in terms of [objective
physical standards/human wants].   human wants

    Because people cannot have as much of everything as they
want, they must make choices. Every situation of economic
choice involves three elements: _____, _____,   objectives
and _____. For example, when you are studying   alternatives
                                                                           constraints
for final exams, you face an economic problem in which these
three elements are as follows:

   1. Objectives: _____   good grades
   2. Alternatives: _____   study time on
                                                                              various courses
   3. Constraints: _____   total study time

    Economic decision making under conditions where objectives,
alternatives, and constraints are all fully known is called
_____. In many situations, however, the de-   pure economizing
cision maker may have to be alert to new alternatives, invent
new activities, and take risks. This is the _____   entrepreneurial
element in economic decision making.

    The cost of attaining any chosen economic objective is the loss
of the opportunity to do something else instead with the same
time or resources. Cost measured in this way is known as
_____ cost. In a production possibility frontier dia-   opportunity
gram, such as that shown in Exhibit S1.1, opporunity cost is
indicated by the _____ of the frontier at any given point.   slope
For example, at Point A on the diagram, the opportunity cost

Exhibit S1.1

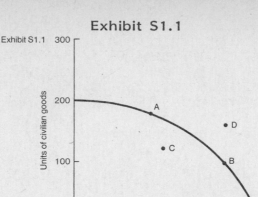

Exhibit S1.1

per unit of civilian goods is approximately _____ units of
military goods. At Point B, the opportunity cost per unit of
civilian goods is approximately _____ unit of military goods.

    When the economy is operating at a point like A or B, it is
producing _____. If it is producing at a point like
C, it is producing _____. A point such as D is
_____ given the quantities of resources and the
technology available.

    In economics, the effects of making a small increase or de-
crease in some economic activity are referred to by use of the
term _____. For example, the cost of producing
one additional barrel of oil is the marginal cost of oil.

Economic Science and Economic Policy

Any discussion of economic policy can be put in the form of a
three-step chain of reasoning as follows:

1. If Policy X is followed, Outcome Y will result.
2. Outcome Y is a good (or bad) thing.
3. Therefore, hurrah (or ugh) for Policy X.

The first step in this chain of reasoning is known as a/an
_____. Such a statement has the form of a
prediction that if A occurs, then B will occur under [all/
specified] conditions. When economists make scientific predictions, they are said to be practicing _____
economics.

    Methods of resolving disputes over matters of positive
economics by looking at evidence based on observations of
past experience are known as _____ methods.
Economists who specialize in the statistical analysis of empir-

---

Answer column (right margin):

two

one

efficiently

inefficiently

impossible

marginal

scientific predic-
tion

specified

positive

empirical

---

ical economic data are known as _____.   econometricians

The second step in the three-step chain of reasoning given
above is a statement in _____ economics. Among   normative
the important value standards used in normative economics are:

                                                                   efficiency
_____
_____ justice   distributive
_____ justice   market

Appendix: Working with Graphs

Learning how to work with graphs begins with learning how
to associate points on a graph with pairs of numbers. Exhibit
S1.2, for example, represents graphically the records kept
by a small rental firm of the number of cars rented per day
on each of three dates and the rental price per car on that
date.   Use a graph to fill in this table:

Date	Number of Cars	Price	
July 1, 1969	_____	_____	10, 5
July 1, 1974	_____	_____	7, 11
July 1, 1979	_____	_____	5, 15

A further examination of the firm's records shows that on
December 31, 1973, eight cars were rented at a price per
car of $7. Add this point to the graph, and label it accor-
dingly. It lies [above/below/on] a straight line drawn through   below
the three points given in the table. On the basis of the data
given in the graph, including the point that you have added,
it can be said that for this firm, the number of cars rented
per day tends to decrease as the price [increases/decreases].   increases

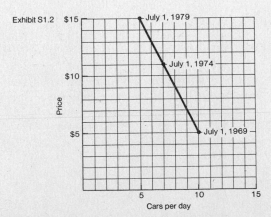

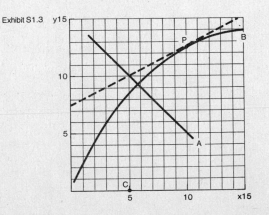

5

It is also important to be able to determine the slope of a line or curve in a graph. Turn your attention to Exhibit S1.3. Line A in that exhibit has a slope of _____. The curve B has a slope, at Point P, of approximately _____. Now draw a line from Point C with a slope of 4. This new line passes through Line A at a point having an x value of _____ and a y value of _____.

-1

0.5

7

8

Suppose you were asked to draw a graph representing the following proposition: as the quantity of fertilizer used per acre (x) increases, other things being equal, the yield of corn (y) tends to increase, rapidly at first, and then less rapidly. Your graph would look most like [A/B/C] in Exhibit S1.3.

B

SELF TEST

These sample test items will help you check how much you have learned. Answers and explanations can be found at the end of this chapter. Scoring yourself: One or two wrong -- on target. Three to five wrong -- passing, but you haven't mastered the chapter yet. Six or more wrong -- not good enough; start over and restudy the chapter.

True or False

Indicate whether each statement is true or false as it stands. If it is false, explain why in a few words.

T F   1.   When you are choosing what to eat for lunch, the list of items on the menu would best be interpreted as your constraints.

T F   2.   The decisions necessary to start a new business are likely to be more entrepreneurial in nature than those necessary for the conduct of a going concern.

T F   3.   Ignoring the particular talents of individuals when assigning them to specific tasks would tend to make the economy operate outside the production possibility frontier.

T F   4.   The use of a controlled experiment to establish the truth of a scientific prediction in economics is an example of the empirical method in operation.

T F   5.   The term "marginal," as used in economics, refers to something of little or no importance to the outcome of the economic event in question.

T F   6.   The statement "Other things being equal, it is better to suffer a little inflation than a lot of unemployment" is an example of positive economics.

T F   7.   Of all the points on the production possibility frontier, only one can be considered to represent an efficient division of labor.

T F   8.   The concept of market justice is at least approximately conveyed by the phrase "value for value."

T F 9. Two people will not be able to agree on their choice of an economic policy unless they agree both on the positive and on the normative issues under-lying the policy choice.

T F 10. Positive economics discusses what is, normative economics what ought to be.

Multiple Choice

1. Scarcity would cease to exist as an economic problem if
   a. everyone were willing to accept a monastic standard of living.
   b. everyone in the world enjoyed as high a material standard of living as the average worker in the United States.
   c. the population of the planet Earth were reduced to a tenth of its present size and stabilized at that number.
   d. none of the above.

2. A good example of the alternative activities available to you in planning your education is
   a. your opportunity cost budget.
   b. the list of courses in your college's catalog.
   c. the twenty-four hours of each day.
   d. the salary you would like to earn in your first job after graduation.

3. The opportunity cost of taking a course in biology rather than a course in economics would not include
   a. the cost of any special lab supplies needed for the biology course.
   b. the need to spend three hours a week in biology lab in addition to the three hours of lecture which each course requires.
   c. the cost of the biology text.
   d. a possible reduction in your grade point average, assuming the biology course to be harder than the economics course.

4. The discovery of a low-cost method for extracting huge quantities of oil from garbage would
   a. permit the economy to reach a point now outside the production possibility frontier.
   b. permit the economy to move from a point inside the production possibility frontier to one on it.
   c. tend to straighten the curvature of the production possibility frontier.
   d. best be represented by a movement along the current production possibility frontier.

5. If a production possibility frontier is drawn with "cars" on the horizontal axis and "other goods" on the vertical axis, the opportunity cost of cars, in terms of other goods, is represented graphically by
   a. the slope of the frontier at any point.
   b. the reciprocal of the slope of the frontier at any point.
   c. the distance to any point on the frontier from the vertical axis.
   d. the distance to any point on the frontier from the horizontal axis.

6. An improvement in the efficiency of the division of labor in an economy would best be represented on a production possibility frontier diagram as
   a. a movement along the frontier to a higher point.
   b. a movement along the frontier to a lower point.
   c. an outward shift of the entire frontier.
   d. a movement toward the frontier from an interior point.

7. If you pay $20 for a season pass to the campus film society, which shows ten films each season and charges a regular admission or $2.50, the marginal cost to you of going to any one performance is
   a. $2.50
   b. $2.00
   c. $0.50
   d. zero

8. Which of the following is not a proposition of positive economics?
   a. Unemployment averaged 5.8 percent of the labor force in 1979.
   b. Other things being equal, interest rates tend to rise when the rate of inflation rises.
   c. If most workers prefer to work during the day rather than during the night, employers are likely to have to pay higher wages to get night shift workers.
   d. It is likely that we would all be happier if federal policy makers paid more attention to econometric forecasts in formulating their economic policy and less attention to the next election.

9. If I think inflation is bad and price controls will make it worse and you think inflation is good and price controls will stop it, then
   a. we will agree that price controls should be tried.
   b. we will agree that price controls should not be tried.
   c. you will think price controls should be tried and I will not.
   d. I will think price controls should be tried and you will not.

10. The phrase that best expresses the idea of distributive justice is
    a. value for value.
    b. from each according to ability, to each according to need.
    c. an eye for an eye, a tooth for a tooth.
    d. to each his own.

Note: The remaining questions in this section cover the appendix on working with graphs.

11. Draw a graph with "number of students in college" on the horizontal axis and "tuition, dollars per year" on the vertical axis. On this diagram, the statement "The higher the tuition, the fewer students in college, other things being equal" would best be represented by
    a. a line with a slope greater than zero.
    b. a line with a slope of zero.
    c. a line with a slope less than zero.
    d. a vertical line.

12. Draw a diagram with x on the horizontal axis and y on the vertical axis. Put in Point A at x = 3 and y = 4. Put in Point B at x = 4 and y = 6. A straight line connecting A and B would have a slope of
    a. 1/2.
    b. 2.
    c. −1/2.
    d. −2.

13. You are shown a graph with "hours spent studying per week" on the horizontal axis and "student's grade point average" on the vertical axis. The relationship between studying and grades is shown by a line that first rises, reaches a maximum, and then falls. The best interpretation of this graph in words would be that
   a. you can't hurt your grades by studying more.
   b. it's not worth studying; you can get bad grades whether you study or not.
   c. grades depend more on native intelligence than on studying.
   d. up to a point you can improve your grades by studying but if you study so much you don't have time to get a good night's sleep, your grades may suffer.

14. You are shown a graph on which two points, A and B, are marked. Point B lies below and to the right of Point A. A straight line connecting A and B would have a slope of
   a. less than zero.
   b. less than 1.
   c. greater than 1.
   d. insufficient information given for an answer.

15. You are shown a graph with the horizontal axis labeled in years from 1974 to 1980 and the vertical axis labeled "total dollar value of food stamps distributed per year." A curve drawn on the diagram has a positive slope throughout. The best interpretation of this graph in words is that
   a. food stamps recipients were better off in 1980 than in 1974.
   b. poor people ate more food in 1980 than in 1974.
   c. more people were eligible for food stamps in 1980 than in 1974.
   d. none of the above is a valid interpretation in the absence of additional information.

ANSWERS TO CHAPTER 1 SELF TEST

True or False

1-F; they are your alternative activities.
2-T.
3-F; inside.
4-T.
5-F; it refers to the effects of a small increase or decrease.
6-F; it is a normative statement.
7-F; all points on the frontier are efficient.
8-T.
9-F; they could disagree on both and still agree on the policy.
10-T.

Multiple Choice

1-d.
2-b; a and c are constraints, d is an objective.
3-c; presumably the economics course also requires a text.
4-a.
5-a.
6-d.
7-d; once you have the ticket, an additional movie costs nothing.
8-d.
9-b.
10-b.
11-c.
12-b.
13-d.
14-a.
15-d; a is a normative statement, and to know if b or c were true, you would have to know the price of food and the allowance per person.

CHAPTER TWO
THE PRICE SYSTEM AND THE MARKET ECONOMY

WHERE YOU'RE GOING

Here is what you will be able to do when you have mastered this chapter:

--Explain how the price system functions as a mechanism for transmitting information in a market economy.

--Explain how the market system also provides the incentives necessary to insure that people will make effective use of the information they receive via the price system.

--Explain why the third function of markets, distributing income, cannot be entirely separated from the first two.

--Identify transactions costs in everyday economic situations and explain how they can prevent markets from operating perfectly efficiently.

CHAPTER SYNOPSIS

Reading this synopsis is not a substitute for reading the chapter, but it should help you to recall the main points. If there are any you feel unsure of, refer to the full discussion in the text.

Markets are all of the various arrangements that people have for trading with one another. In the U.S. economy, markets play a central role in coordinating economic activity by performing three major functions: transmitting information, providing incentives, and distributing income.

In order to put scarce resources to their best use, people must know what the best uses are. The most important source of information in a market economy is the price system. Changes in relative prices act as signals about relative scarcities that are broadcast widely to economic decision makers all over the globe. If the price of some good or service rises relative to the prices of other goods and services, that is the signal that the good or service in question is becoming relatively more scarce. If the relative price of a good or service falls, that is a signal that it is becoming relatively more abundant. Decision makers are able to act on the basis of the scarcity information contained in relative prices even when they do not know the details of the circumstances that caused the change in price in the first place.

At the same time the price system transmits information throughout the economy, it provides incentives to make effective use of that information. When the price of a good goes up relative to the prices of other goods, users have an incentive to eliminate nonessential uses or look for substitutes. The price increase also provides profit incentives to producers to increase the quantity of the good available. In their efforts to increase output, producers in turn bid up wages, which act as incentives for workers to take jobs in the industry.

As a by-product of providing incentives, markets distribute income to the individuals who respond to market signals by putting their resources to the indicated best use. The distributional function of markets is a source of controversy, both over how fair the distribution of income is and over the degree to which redistribution policies interfere with the information transmission and incentive functions of markets.

Although markets, as a rule, tend to move resources toward their best uses, they do not always function perfectly. The sources of friction that prevent markets from operating perfectly are called transactions costs. They include the costs of gathering information, finding the right people to do business with, negotiating terms, drawing up contracts, guarding against involuntary default and foul play, and so on. Because of transactions costs, some exchanges that could benefit all parties and improve economic efficiency never get carried out.

How seriously transactions costs interfere with the efficient use of resources often depends on the structure of property rights that underlie the market system. For the most part, efficient functioning of the market system requires well-defined private property rights. (The problem of overuse of ocean fishing grounds provides a classic illustration of the problems that arise in the absence of private property rights.) Occasionally, however, private ownership of property may increase transactions costs. (A classic example concerns the problem of negotiating a right of way for a road across the property of many individual landowners.)

WALKING TOUR

You have read the chapter at least once and have reviewed the synopsis. Now you are going to walk through the material step by step, filling in the blanks and answering the questions as you go along. After you have answered each question, check yourself by uncovering the answer given in the margin. If you do not understand why the answer given is the right one, refer back to the proper section of the text.

The Functions of Markets

The three main functions performed by markets are:

1. _____
2. _____
3. _____

transmitting information
providing incentives
distributing income

Of all the various channels for transmitting information in the market economy, the most important is _____.

the price system

Increasing scarcity of a good or service is signalled by a [rise/fall] in its price relative to the prices of other goods and

rise

services. Increasing abundance is indicated by a [rise/fall] in the relative price.

fall

It is important to understand that relative prices, not absolute prices, are what count in transmitting information. For example, if the price of copper goes up from $1 per pound to $1.10 per pound while all other prices go up by 10 percent, the price of copper relative to the prices of other goods [has/has not] changed; no signal is given that copper is more

has not

or less scarce than before. If the price of lumber goes up from $0.50 per board foot to $0.75 per board foot while all other prices go up by 10 percent, the relative price of lumber has _____. Users will react by using [more/less]

increased; less

lumber and by using [more/less] brick. If the price of corn
goes up from $2.00 per bushel to $2.15 per bushel while all
other prices go up by 10 percent, the relative price of corn
has _____. Cattle producers will respond by using
[more/less] corn and [more/less] of other feed grains.

more

decreased
more; less

    Profits, an important source of incentives in a market
economy, account for a very [large/small] percentage of all
income earned. They have an importance out of proportion to
their magnitude because they are the incentive provided to
_____ for coordinating the contributions of
workers and other resource owners.

small

entrepreneurs

    The distribution of income in a market economy is fair
according to the standard of _____ justice but not
necessarily fair according to _____ justice.

market
distributive

    The market system does not always function with perfect
efficiency because of _____. One of the
most important transactions costs is that of acquiring
_____. How serious a problem transactions costs are
in any particular circumstance often depends on the structure
of _____ that underlie the market system.

transactions costs

information

property rights

SELF TEST

These sample test items will help you check how much you have learned. Answers
and explanations can be found at the end of this chapter. Scoring yourself: One
or two wrong -- on target. Three to five wrong--passing, but you haven't mastered
the chapter yet. Six or more wrong -- not good enough; start over and restudy the
chapter.

True or False

Indicate whether each statement is true or false as it stands. If it is false, explain
why in a few words.

T F   1.   Markets exist wherever a list of prices for a good or service is made
            available to all potential buyers.

T F   2.   Market prices provide users with at least an approximate guide to the
            opportunity costs of the things they buy.

T F   3.   If the price of oil goes up by 80 percent while the prices of other goods
            and services, on the average, go up by 100 percent, the relative price
            of oil has decreased.

T F   4.   The profit motive is no longer as relevant in our complex corporate
            economy as it was in the days of the butcher and the baker.

T F   5. An increase in the relative price of a good provides an incentive to use and produce more of it.

T F   6. The greater the reliance we place on the market to provide incentives, the less able the market is to distribute income.

T F   7. The market distributes income fairly, but only according to the standard of distributive justice.

T F   8. One function that real estate brokers perform in the housing market is to reduce transactions costs of buyers and sellers.

T F   9. Private property rights always reduce transactions costs to a minimum.

T F   10. The cost of labor and energy used to mine gold is an example of a transactions cost in a market economy.

Multiple Choice

1. The importance of bargaining in a bazaar economy is an indication that
    a. profits are very high.
    b. profits are very low.
    c. information is very abundant.
    d. information is very scarce.

2. Which of the following is not an example of a market?
    a. The New York Stock Exchange.
    b. The system of contacts between drug users and pushers.
    c. The United States Senate.
    d. The Sefrou bazaar.

3. Adam Smith wrote that the "invisible hand" of the market led the "butcher and baker" to promote an end (consumer satisfaction) which was no part of their intention. His point was
    a. that participants in the market system often operate with minimal information.
    b. that the profit motive gives sellers an incentive to do what buyers want.
    c. that the merchants of his day were selfish and greedy.
    d. that a knowledge of economic science, as set forth in The Wealth of Nations, would improve the management of the small businesses on which prosperity ultimately depends.

4. The price system provides incentives
    a. to businesses, through the profit motive.
    b. to workers, through different wages for different jobs.
    c. to consumers, through the relative prices of goods.
    d. all of the above.

5. The distributional function of markets is best regarded as
    a. a matter of normative economics to be kept quite distinct from the positive information and incentive functions.
    b. a necessary evil which, however, interferes only slightly with the other functions of markets.
    c. closely linked to the other functions of markets and arguably inseparable from them.
    d. an illusion.

6. The distributional function of markets is a source of controversy because
   a. the question of the fairness of distribution is a sensitive normative issue.
   b. there is little empirical evidence on the distribution of income.
   c. it is not known whether the market really has much to do with distribution.
   d. different economists have different definitions of what constitutes a market.

7. A method of redistributing income that avoids the danger of upsetting incentives and information is
   a. taxation.
   b. manipulating prices through controls and subsidies.
   c. manipulating wages through controls and subsidies.
   d. none of the above.

8. If rents on urban housing are held down to make it easier for the poor to afford a decent place to live,
   a. builders may receive false signals about where to put new housing.
   b. renters may have an incentive to pass up good jobs in small towns.
   c. owners may have insufficient incentive to maintain the buildings.
   d. all of the above.

9. During the mid-1970s, salaries of engineers lagged behind other salaries because the winding down of the space program created an engineer surplus. This illustrated
   a. the fact that the market doesn't always work.
   b. the fact that markets can't be counted on to distribute income.
   c. the market at work guiding people in their choice of occupations.
   d. a need for more investment in engineering education.

10. If there were no price controls of any kind on oil, natural gas, or other energy sources,
    a. the distribution of income would be different than if controls were in force.
    b. users would lack the necessary information to choose the right fuel for the right job.
    c. users would lack the necessary incentive to choose the right fuel for the right job.
    d. none of the above.

11. Most if not all imperfections in the market system can be traced to
    a. greed.
    b. the invisible hand.
    c. private property.
    d. transactions costs.

12. The costs of finding people to do business with, negotiating terms, drawing up contracts, and guarding against involuntary default or foul play are known as
    a. opportunity costs.
    b. marginal costs.
    c. transactions costs.
    d. information costs.

13. If there were no transactions costs, the question of whether to permit smoking on airplanes could most efficiently be settled by
    a. majority vote of the passengers.
    b. a fixed rule set by the airline.
    c. an auction of smoking rights or of rights to seats in the no smoking section.
    d. an on-the-spot decision by the flight crew.

14. In general, transactions costs are minimized by
    a. private property ownership.
    b. public property ownership.
    c. often a, but sometimes b.
    d. neither a nor b--transactions costs have nothing to do with the form of property ownership.

15. Governments often have the power to force property owners to sell land at an established "fair market value" for purposes such as road or powerline construction. This practice is usually justified as an attempt to
    a. give landowners an incentive to sell by raising the value of their land.
    b. improve efficiency by lowering transactions costs.
    c. redistribute income from landowners to consumers.
    d. provide taxpayers with accurate information about the true cost of the project to be undertaken.

ANSWERS TO CHAPTER 2 SELF TEST

True or False

1-F; wherever exchange takes place.
2-T
3-T
4-F; it is still relevant.
5-F; to produce more and use less.
6-F; the two go together.
7-F; market justice.
8-T
9-F; often, but not always.
10-F; these are ordinary production costs.

Multiple Choice

1-d
2-c
3-b
4-d
5-c
6-a
7-d
8-d
9-c
10-a
11-d
12-c
13-c
14-c
15-b

CHAPTER THREE
SUPPLY AND DEMAND -- THE BASICS

WHERE YOU'RE GOING

Here is what you will be able to do when you have mastered this chapter:

--State the law of demand and explain the importance of the concept of effective demand and the "other things being equal" assumption.

--Distringuish between changes in quantity demanded, represented by movements along a given demand curve, and changes in demand, represented by shifts in entire demand curves.

--Interpret movements along and shifts in supply curves.

--Explain the meaning of market equilibrium, and show why equilibrium occurs at the price and quantity represented graphically by the intersection of the supply and demand curves.

--Show how equilibrium prices and quantities are affected by given changes in supply or demand.

--Explain the meaning and significance of the following additional terms and concepts:

    Normal good.
    Inferior good.
    Substitutes.
    Complements.
    Shortage.
    Surplus.

CHAPTER SYNOPSIS

Reading this synopsis is not a substitute for reading the chapter but it should help you to recall the main points. If there are any you feel unsure of, refer to the full discussion in the text.

According to the law of demand, the quantity of a good demanded by buyers tends to increase as the price of the good decreases and tends to decrease as the price increases, other things being equal. Demand, as used in this context, means effective demand--the quantity purchasers are both willing and able to buy at the particular price. The "other things being equal" assumption in the law of demand covers the prices of other goods and services, buyers' tastes and incomes, and expectations about the future.

The law of demand can be represented graphically in the form of a downward-sloping demand curve showing how the quantity demanded changes in response to changes in price, other things being equal. A change in the price of the good in question, other things being equal, produces a movement along the demand curve. This is called a change in the quantity demanded. A change in income, in tastes, in the prices of other goods, or in expectations produces a shift in the entire demand curve. This is called a change in demand.

The supply curve for a good is a graphical representation of the relationship between the price of a good and the quantity of the good that sellers are willing to supply. Supply curves normally slope upward, indicating that an increase in the price of the good, other things being equal, induces suppliers to sell a larger quantity. The effects of the change in the price of a good, other things being equal, are represented by a movement along the supply curve (a change in the quantity supplied). The effects of changes in other economic conditions, such as technology, the prices of other goods, or the prices of inputs used in production of the good in question, are represented by shifts in the entire supply curve (a change of supply).

A market is said to be in equilibrium if the separately formulated plans of buyers and sellers mesh exactly when tested in the market place. Graphically, the equilibrium price and quantity correspond to the intersections of the supply and demand curves. At any price higher than that indicated by the intersection of the curves, there will be a surplus, or excess quantity supplied, of the good. A surplus puts downward pressure on the price, returning the market to equilibrium. At any price lower than the equilibrium price, there will be a shortage, or excess quantity demanded, of the good. A shortage puts upward pressure on the price, returning it to the level where supply and demand curves intersect.

WALKING TOUR

You have read the chapter at least once and have reviewed the synopsis. Now you are going to walk through the material step by step, filling in the blanks and answering the questions as you go along. After you have answered each question, check yourself by uncovering the answer given in the margin. If you do not understand why the answer given is the correct one, refer back to the proper section of the text.

The Law of Demand

According to the law of demand, the quantity of any good
demanded tends to increase as the price _____,   decreases
other things being equal. Demand curves thus normally have
_____ slopes.   negative

A change in the quantity demanded means a [shift in/
movement along] the demand curve. A change in demand   movement along
means a [shift in/movement along] the demand curve. Consumer   shift in
income is one of the "other things" held equal in the statement
of the law of demand, so a change in consumer income is said
to cause a _____. If an increase in consumer   change in demand
income causes an increase in demand for the good, it is said
to be a/an _____ good. If an increase in income   normal
causes a decrease in demand for the good, it is said to be
a/an _____ good.   inferior

The prices of other goods are also held equal in the
statement of the law of demand. If an increase in the price
of Good X causes a decrease in the demand for Good Y, the
two goods are said to be _____. If an increase in   complements

the price of Good X causes an increase in the demand for Good
Y, the two goods are said to be _____ .

substitutes

Supply

Supply curves normally have _____ slopes. This
indicates that an increase in the price of a good tends to
induce sellers to increase the [supply/quantity supplied] of
the good in question. Changes in technology, input prices,
or the prices of other goods are potential causes of changes
in [supply/quantity supplied].

positive

quantity supplied

supply

The Interaction of Supply and Demand

When the plans of buyers and sellers of a good exactly mesh,
so that the quantity supplied and the quantity demanded at the
prevailing price are equal, the market is said to be in
_____ . At any price higher than the equilibrium
price, there will be a [shortage/surplus] of the good. Inventories of the good will tend to [grow/shrink] and the price will
tend to [rise/fall]. At any price below the equilibrium price,
there will be a [shortage/surplus], and the inventories will
tend to [grow/shrink]. This will put [upward/downward]
pressure on the price until equilibrium is restored.

equilibrium
surplus
grow
fall
shortage
shrink; upward

Supply and demand curves can be used to represent the
effects of changing supply and demand conditions. Exhibit
S3.1, which shows hypothetical supply and demand curves
for oak floowing, provides an exercise. As the diagram is
drawn, the equilibrium price is _____ per board foot,
and the equilibrium quantity is _____ million board
feet (mbf) per year. Suppose that a boom in home construction

$1.20
160

Exhibit S3.1

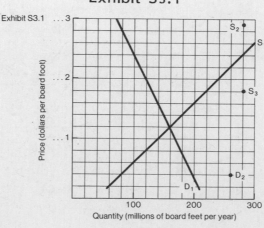

Exhibit S3.1 ...3

Price (dollars per board foot)

Quantity (millions of board feet per year)

20

occurs, raising the demand for oak flooring. This would properly be represented in the exhibit as an [upward/downward] shift in the [demand/supply] curve. Draw in the new demand curve so that it passes through the point D_2 and has the same slope as the original demand curve. The new equilibrium price is _____. Next suppose that a strike against a major producer of oak flooring cuts the supply. This would best be represented by the supply curve shifting so that it passes through [S_2/S_3] with the same slope as before. After this takes place, the new equilibrium price will be _____ per board foot and the equilibrium quantity will be _____ mbf.

upward
demand

$1.60

S_2
$2
180

     The preceding example assumed that the price of flooring was free to vary in response to changes in supply and demand. The next example, given in Exhibit S3.2, assumes a controlled price for the product, which this time is house paint. Initially the supply and demand curves are in the positions S and D_1, respectively, giving an equilibrium price of _____ per gallon. After that price is established, the government imposes a price ceiling preventing it from rising any further. Now the boom in housing construction comes along, shifting the demand curve to D_2. Without the price ceiling, this increase in demand would push the price up to _____ per gallon. With the price ceiling in effect, however, there is a shortage of _____ million gallons at the $14 price. One likely result of the price ceiling is the emergence of a black market in house paint. Producers receive only the controlled price of $14, but buyers lucky enough to have their orders filled resell the product to less fortunate buyers for whatever the market will bear. As the exhibit is drawn, the black market price could rise as high as _____ per gallon.

$14

$18
30

$22

Exhibit S3.2

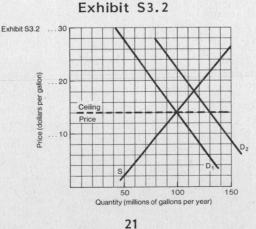

SELF TEST

These sample test items will help you check how much you have learned. Answers and explanations can be found at the end of this chapter. Scoring yourself: One or two wrong -- on target. Three to five wrong -- passing, but you haven't mastered the chapter yet. Six or more wrong -- not good enough; start over and restudy the chapter.

True or False

Indicate whether each statement is true or false as it stands. If it is false, explain why in a few words.

T F 1. Effective demand means not the quantity that purchasers want to buy but the quantity they are willing and able to buy.

T F 2. The law of demand relates changes in the quantity demanded to changes in relative prices.

T F 3. There can be no exceptions to the law of demand unless consumers behave irrationally.

T F 4. The term "change in demand," by convention, is used to refer to a movement along a demand curve.

T F 5. If the quantity of pork consumed increases when the price of chicken increases, both pork and chicken must be normal goods.

T F 6. An inferior good cannot be a substitute for a normal good.

T F 7. On a supply and demand diagram, market equilibrium is indicated by the intersection of the supply and demand curves.

T F 8. Economists say there is a shortage of a good when there is less than the usual quantity supplied, regardless of the price.

T F 9. When an excess quantity of a good is supplied, an accumulation of unsold inventories of that good is likely to result.

T F 10. According to the theory of supply and demand, gasoline lines are most likely to occur when price controls are in force.

Multiple Choice

1. The "other things being equal" clause in the law of demand covers
   a. consumer incomes.
   b. the prices of other goods.
   c. consumer tastes and preferences.
   d. all of the above.

2. A rise in the price of coffee is likely to have which of the following effects on the market for tea?
   a. A movement up along the tea demand curve.
   b. A movement down along the tea demand curve.
   c. A leftward shift in the tea demand curve.
   d. A rightward shift in the tea demand curve.

3. If consumer incomes go up while the prices of new cars remain unchanged, which of the following is most likely?
   a. An upward movement along the demand curve for cars.
   b. A downward movement along the demand curve for cars.
   c. A rightward shift in the demand curve for cars.
   d. A leftward shift in the demand curve for cars.

4. Assuming gasoline and tires to be complementary goods, the effect on the tire market of an increase in the price of gasoline (other things being equal) would best be described as
   a. an increase in the demand for tires.
   b. a decrease in the demand for tires.
   c. an increase in the quantity of tires demanded.
   d. a decrease in the quantity of tires demanded.

5. If the price of leather rises, other things being equal, which of the following would be the most likely effect?
   a. An upward shift of the shoe supply curve.
   b. A downward shift of the shoe supply curve.
   c. An upward movement along the shoe supply curve.
   d. A downward movement along the shoe supply curve.

6. Market equilibrium
   a. is represented graphically by the intersection of the supply and demand curves.
   b. is the condition under which the plans of buyers and sellers exactly mesh when tested in the market.
   c. is the condition under which neither buyers nor sellers have an incentive to change their plans.
   d. includes all of the above.

7. Using QS to indicate quantity supplied and QD to indicate quantity demanded, which of the following circumstances would be likely to produce an upward movement of the price?
   a. QS = 100, QD = 200.
   b. QS = 100, QD = 100.
   c. QS = 200, QD = 100.
   d. Not enough information is given for an answer.

8. An increase in the cost of raising hogs, other things being equal, would be likely to affect the price of bacon via
   a. an upward shift of the supply curve.
   b. an upward shift of the demand curve.
   c. a downward shift of the supply curve.
   d. a downward shift of the demand curve.

9. An increase in the price of beef increases the demand for pork. Restoration of equilibrium in the pork market will require
   a. an upward shift of the supply curve.
   b. a downward shift of the supply curve.
   c. a movement up along the supply curve.
   d. a movement down along the supply curve.

10. Suppose intercity bus travel to be an inferior good. An increase in consumer incomes, other things being equal, is likely to cause which of the following?
    a. A shift in the demand curve and a higher price.
    b. A shift in the supply curve and a higher price.
    c. A shift in the demand curve and a lower price.
    d. A shift in the supply curve and a lower price.

11. If the steelworkers' union negotiates a new contract with sharply higher wages, we would expect, once a new equilibrium is reached in the steel market,
    a. a shortage of steel.
    b. a decrease in the demand for steel.
    c. a decrease in the price of steel
    d. a decrease in the quantity of steel demanded.

12. During a recent visit to Moscow, an American tourist noticed long lines outside every butcher shop. The most reasonable conclusion to be drawn from this observation is that
    a. meat is very expensive in the Soviet Union.
    b. citizens of the Soviet Union are insatiable carnivores.
    c. the clerks in Soviet stores work very slowly.
    d. meat is subject to price controls in the Soviet Union.

13. If the equilibrium price of natural gas is $2.50 per thousand cubic feet and a price ceiling is imposed at $3.00 per thousand cubic feet, the likely result will be
    a. a surplus.
    b. a shortage.
    c. a depletion of inventories.
    d. none of the above.

14. According to supply and demand analysis, the likely effect of a minimum wage law would be
    a. a shortage of jobs for low-skill workers.
    b. a shortage of workers to fill low-skill jobs.
    c. increased incomes for all low-skill workers.
    d. decreased incomes for all low-skill workers.

15. If the equilibrium price of sugar is 15 cents per pound and the government imposes a minimum price of 20 cents per pound, the likely result will be
    a. a shortage of sugar.
    b. a surplus of sugar.
    c. a depletion of sugar inventories.
    d. none of the above.

ANSWERS TO CHAPTER 3 SELF TEST

True or False

1-T
2-T
3-F; but such exceptions are rare.
4-F; a shift in the demand curve.
5-F; the conclusion is that the goods are substitutes.
6-F; it can be and usually is.
7-T
8-F; shortage means a smaller quantity supplied than demanded at a given price.
9-T
10-T

Multiple Choice

1-d
2-d
3-c
4-b
5-a
6-d
7-a
8-a
9-c
10-c
11-d
12-d
13-d
14-a
15-b

CHAPTER FOUR
THE ROLE OF GOVERNMENT IN THE ECONOMY

WHERE YOU'RE GOING

Here is what you will be able to do when you have mastered this chapter:

--Contrast the important characteristics of government as an economic agent with those of private firms and individuals.

--Identify five major economic functions of government and give examples of each.

--Contrast the federal government with state and local governments in terms of sources of revenues and types of expenditures.

--Use supply and demand analysis to determine the incidence of simple taxes under given conditions.

--Discuss overall tax incidence for the United States in terms of the concepts of <u>progressive</u> and <u>regressive</u> taxes.

--Use supply and demand analysis to explain the potential incentive effects of various taxes.

--Explain the meaning and significance of the following additional terms and concepts:

<u>Government purchases of goods and services.</u>
<u>Transfer payments.</u>
<u>Public goods.</u>
<u>The Laffer curve</u>
<u>Marginal tax rate.</u>

CHAPTER SYNOPSIS

<u>Reading this synopsis is not a substitute for reading the chapter, but it should help you to recall the main points. If there are any you are unsure of, refer to the full discussion in the text.</u>

As an economic actor, government differs from private firms and individuals in a number of ways. First, it can legitimately apply force in economic affairs by using its powers of taxation and regulation. Second, most of its services are provided to users without direct charge. And third, the government's political decision making process differs considerably from decision making in the private sector.

Federal, state, and local units of government use their considerable powers to perform five major economic functions. The first is the provision of <u>public goods</u>-- goods or services that cannot be provided to one citizen without at the same time being provided to all and that, once provided to one citizen, can be provided to others at no additional cost. The second function is the transfer of income in cash or in kind. Economic stabilization is the third function, and it includes all policies through which the government promotes full employment, price stability, and economic growth. A fourth major function is the regulation of private business, sometimes in pursuit of narrowly economic objectives and sometimes of social objectives. The fifth economic function of government is the administration of justice.

In addition to classification by function government expenditures can also be classified by type of program. For the federal government, the largest single category of expenditure is income security, followed by national defense. The largest single category of state and local expenditure is education, followed by public health and highways.

Sources of revenue also differ according to level of government. The federal government gets the largest share of its revenues from the individual income tax, with the next largest share coming from social insurance contributions. The largest source of revenue for state governments is the sales tax, and the largest source for local governments is the property tax.

For purposes of economic analysis, it is usually more important to know the actual incidence of a tax--that is, who bears its economic burden--than to know who is legally responsible for making the tax payment. Supply and demand analysis can be used to determine the incidence of any given tax, provided the shapes and positions of the supply and demand curves are known. As a general rule, the steeper the supply curve relative to the demand curve, the greater the share of the burden borne by sellers, and the steeper the demand curve relative to the supply curve, the greater the share of the burden borne by buyers.

The overall incidence of taxes can be categorized as progressive or regressive. A progressive tax takes a larger percentage of income from people whose incomes are high, whereas a regressive tax takes a larger percentage of income from people whose incomes are low. Of the major taxes used in the United States, the personal income tax is substantially progressive, while the social security tax and state and local taxes are regressive. On balance, the U.S. tax system as a whole is neither markedly progressive nor markedly regressive.

Economists today are paying increasing attention to the incentive effects of taxes. Traditionally, for example, income and payroll taxes were considered to have few if any major incentive effects--people were thought not to vary the quantity or quality of their work effort in response to differences in the tax rates they faced. Today, this view is being challenged. Studies of European tax systems, which generally impose higher marginal tax rates on workers than does the U.S. tax system, indicate that incentive effects increase as tax rates rise. The Laffer curve indicates that, at least hypothetically, incentive effects can, beyond some point, cause total tax revenues to fall as tax rates are increased.

WALKING TOUR

You have read the chapter at least once and have reviewed the synopsis. Now you are going to walk through the material step by step, filling in the blanks and answering the questions as you go along. After you have answered each question, check yourself by uncovering the answer given in the margin. If you do not understand why the answer given is the right one, refer back to the proper section of the text.

What Does Government Do?

Government purchases of goods and services in the United

States are currently equal to about _____ percent of gross   20

national product. If payments made by government to individ-

uals not in return for goods or services currently supplied--

that is, _____ --are included, the total is   transfer payments

about_____ of GNP. Compared to the advanced   one-third

27

industrial countries of Western Europe, the size of the government sector in the United States is thus relatively [large/small].

small

Government at federal, state, and local levels uses this share of GNP to perform five major functions, which involve:

1. _____

public goods

2. _____

income transfers

3. _____

stabilization

4. _____

regulation

5. _____

administration of justice

Another way to classify government activities is by type of program rather than by function. Different levels of government are responsible for different programs; for example, defense is the responsibility of the _____ government while the largest program for state and local governments is

federal

_____.

education

Who Pays for Government?

The largest source of revenue for the federal government is the _____ tax. For state governments, the largest is the _____ tax, and for local governments,

personal income

sales

the _____ tax.

property

Economists are more interested in who bears the true economic burden of various taxes than in who has the legal obligation to make the tax payments. This is known as the problem of _____. Supply and demand analysis can be used to determine the incidence of any tax, provided the shapes and positions of the curves are given. For example, you can use Exhibit S4.1 to determine the incidence of a 5 cent per box tax on matches collected from manufacturers. Initially, the equilibrium price is _____ cents per box. Imposition

tax incidence

6

Exhibit S4.1

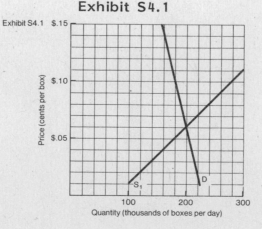

Exhibit S4.1

Price (cents per box)

$.15

$.10

$.05

S_1

D

100   200   300

Quantity (thousands of boxes per day)

of the tax can be represented by an [upward/downward] shift   upward
in the supply curve by _____ cents. Draw in the new supply   5
curve, using the same slope as in S_1, and label it S_2. The new
equilibrium price is _____ cents per box. Of this, sellers   10
keep _____ cents per box, and the government collects   5
_____ cents. The price to consumers has gone up by   5
_____ cents as a result of the 5 cent tax, and the price   4
received by sellers has gone down by _____ cents. The   1
burden of the tax is thus distributed unequally between buyers
and sellers. If the slope of the demand curve had been flatter,
indicating that buyers were more sensitive to the price of
matches, then consumers would have borne a [larger/smaller]   smaller
share of the burden of the tax. They also would have borne
a smaller share of the tax if the slope of the supply curve
had been [flatter/steeper].   steeper

Many important issues in the economics of taxation concern
the incidence of income and payroll taxes. The percentage of
each added dollar of a worker's income that goes for taxes is
called the _____ for that worker. Often the   marginal tax rate
marginal tax rate varies according to income. For example, a
tax which imposed a marginal rate of 30 percent on a worker
with a $10,000 annual income and a marginal rate of 50 percent
on one with a $30,000 annual income would be known as a
_____ tax, whereas one that applied a higher mar-   progressive
ginal tax rate to workers with relatively low incomes would be
a _____ tax. On balance, taking federal, state and   regressive
local taxes into account, the U.S. tax system, for the broad
middle range of incomes, is [progressive/regressive/neither].   neither

Traditionally, even very high marginal income tax rates
were thought to have negligible incentive effects, because the
supply curve of labor was thought to be quite [steep/flat].   steep
However, recents studies of responses to taxation in Europe,
where marginal tax rates are generally [higher/lower] than in   higher
the United States, indicate that, beyond a point, incentive
effects can become substantial. When incentive effects are
taken into account, increases in marginal tax rates will
[always/not always/never] produce increases in total tax   not always
revenues.

SELF TEST

These sample test items will help you check how much you have learned. Answers and explanations can be found at the end of this chapter. Scoring yourself: One or two wrong -- on target. Three to five wrong -- passing, but you haven't mastered the chapter yet. Six or more wrong -- not good enough; start over and restudy the chapter.

True or False

Indicate whether each statement is true or false as it stands. If it is false, explain why in a few words.

T F   1. Because government uses force to collect taxes, it is immune to the realities of supply and demand as expressed through the price system.

T F   2. Military pay expenditures are included in government purchases of goods and services.

T F   3. Government purchases of goods and services as a percentage of GNP reached an all time peak during World War II.

T F   4. The United States is a world leader in terms of total government expenditures as a percentage of GNP.

T F   5. The "spillover" effect is one characteristic of public goods.

T F   6. National defense continues to be the largest single category of federal expenditure, as it has been since World War II.

T F   7. The income tax is the most important tax at the federal level but is relatively unimportant for state and local government.

T F   8. Supply and demand analysis indicates that sellers are usually able to pass the entire burden of sales taxes along to buyers.

T F   9. The federal income tax and social security tax are progressive, whereas state and local taxes are regressive.

T F   10. According to the Laffer curve, an increase in tax rates can sometimes result in a decrease in tax revenues.

Multiple Choice

1. During the 1970s, total government purchases of goods and services averaged about what percentage of GNP?
   a. 10 percent.
   b. 20 percent.
   c. 30 percent.
   d. 40 percent.

2. Which of the following least fits the concept of a public good?
   a. National defense.
   b. Immunization against epidemic disease.
   c. Public housing construction.
   d. Enforcing highway safety rules.

3. Which of the following is part of the economic stabilization function of government?
   a. Promoting full employment.
   b. Regulating electric utility rates.
   c. Providing public education.
   d. Prosecuting white-collar crime.

4. Which of the following takes the largest share of state and local government expenditure?
   a. Public education.
   b. Public welfare.
   c. Highways.
   d. Law enforcement.

5. Which of the following is most important as a source of federal tax revenue?
   a. Individual income taxes.
   b. Corporate income taxes.
   c. Social insurance contributions.
   d. Property taxes.

6. Supply and demand analysis suggests that sales taxes
   a. are borne entirely by consumers.
   b. are borne entirely by retailers.
   c. are borne entirely by wholesalers.
   d. are usually borne jointly by buyers and sellers.

7. Other things being equal, the share of a sales tax borne by buyers tends to be larger
   a. the steeper the supply curve and the flatter the demand curve.
   b. the flatter the supply curve and the steeper the demand curve.
   c. the steeper either the supply or demand curve.
   d. the flatter either the supply or demand curve.

8. Which of the following taxes is the most progressive?
   a. Local sales taxes.
   b. The social security payroll tax.
   c. The federal income tax.
   d. All of the above are regressive.

9. The traditional view that the income tax has no important incentive effects is based largely on
   a. the fact that this tax has not been an important source of revenue until the last few years.
   b. the belief that the labor supply curve was nearly vertical.
   c. the belief that the labor supply curve was nearly horizontal.
   d. a belief in the Laffer curve.

10. The Laffer curve is best characterized as
    a. traditional theory now largely abandoned.
    b. an idea widely supported by empirical evidence but with little theoretical plausibility.
    c. an idea with considerable theoretical plausibility but supported only by fragmentary empirical evidence.
    d. the fundamental theoretical basis of federal tax policy today.

11. Supply and demand analysis suggests that the division of the social security payroll tax into two parts, one nominally paid by employers and the other by employees,
    a. makes no difference to the true incidence of the tax.
    b. relieves workers of about half the burden of the tax.
    c. makes the tax more regressive than it otherwise would be.
    d. makes the tax more progressive than it otherwise would be.

12. If a person earning $30,000 a year pays $10,000 in income taxes and a person earning $31,000 pays $10,500 in income taxes, the marginal income tax rate for that income level is approximately
    a. 10 percent.
    b. 33 percent.
    c. 50 percent.
    d. 66 percent.

13. In the United States and major European countries,
    a. marginal income tax rates are higher than average income tax rates.
    b. average income tax rates are higher than marginal income tax rates.
    c. average income tax rates and marginal income tax rates are about equal.
    d. there is too much variation from country to country to justify any of the generalizations given above.

14. European experience suggests that which of the following would not be a likely result of increased marginal tax rates?
    a. Pressures for a shorter work week.
    b. Increased absenteeism.
    c. A growing "underground economy."
    d. A growing shortage of workers willing to take low-skill jobs.

15. European experience suggests that excessively high tax rates may interfere with which of these other objectives of government?
    a. A strong national defense.
    b. Redistribution of income from the rich to the poor.
    c. Economic growth.
    d. Regulation of private industry.

ANSWERS TO CHAPTER 4 SELF TEST

True or False

1-F; partially, but not totally, immune.
2-T
3-T
4-F; most European countries are much higher.
5-T
6-F; income security is now higher.
7-T
8-F; the burden is divided between the two.
9-F; social security tax is regressive too.
10-T

Multiple Choice

1-b
2-c; the others are at least mixed public goods.
3-a
4-a
5-a
6-d
7-b
8-c
9-b
10-c
11-a
12-c
13-a
14-d
15-c

CHAPTER FIVE
THE CIRCULAR FLOW OF INCOME AND PRODUCT

WHERE YOU'RE GOING

Here is what you will be able to do when you have mastered this chapter:

--Trace the circular flow of income and product through an economy made up of households, firms, governments, and foreign countries.

--Identify and give examples of the factors of production: labor, capital, and natural resources.

--Distinguish between stocks and flows and give examples of each.

--Explain why national product is always equal to total expenditure when both planned and unplanned expenditure are taken into account.

--Explain the meaning of aggregate supply and aggregate demand and explain how the economy reacts when the two are not equal.

--Explain what injections and leakages are and why total injections are always equal to total leakages.

--Explain why national product is always equal to national income.

--Explain the meaning and significance of the following additional terms and concepts:

> Macroeconomics.
> Microeconomics.
> Aggregate.
> Fixed investment.
> Inventory investment.
> Investment.
> Net taxes.
> Deficit.
> Surplus.
> Net exports.

CHAPTER SYNOPSIS

Reading this synopsis is not a substitute for reading the chapter, but it should help you to recall the main points. If there are any you feel unsure of, refer to the full discussion in the text.

Macroeconomics is the branch of economics devoted to the study of unemployment, inflation, and economic growth. The circular flow of income and product is a useful tool for visualizing important macroeconomic relationships among the major sectors of the economy: households, firms, government, and the foreign sector. In the circular flow, physical goods and services travel in one direction while flows of funds in payment for those goods and services travel in the opposite direction. For purposes of macroeconomic analysis, we concentrate on the flows of funds.

Households receive income in the form of <u>factor payments</u> for the labor, capital, natural resources, and entrepreneurial talents that they contribute to firms. They allocate the income they receive among consumption expenditures (a flow of funds into product markets), saving (a flow of funds into financial markets), net taxes (a flow of funds to government), and imports (a flow of funds to the foreign sector).

Firms receive revenue from product markets in return for the goods and services they sell, and they make factor payments to households. Firms also borrow funds in financial markets and use these funds to make investment expenditures (a flow of funds to product markets). Some investment funds are spent to purchase imported capital goods (a flow of funds to the foreign sector).

Federal, state, and local government units collect taxes from households and make transfer payments to households. The difference between taxes and transfers is <u>net taxes</u> (a flow of funds from households to government). Governments use these funds for purchases of goods and services (a flow of funds to product markets). Some government expenditures are made to purchase imported goods or services (a flow of funds from government to the foreign sector). If government purchases exceed net taxes, the government runs a <u>deficit</u> and borrows from financial markets (a flow of funds from financial markets to government). If net taxes exceed government purchases, the government has a budget <u>surplus</u> that it can use to pay off past borrowing (the repayments appear as a flow of funds from government to financial markets).

The foreign sector receives revenue from sales of goods imported into the United States and makes purchases of goods exported from the United States. Imports thus appear as a flow of funds into the foreign sector and exports as a flow of funds into domestic product markets. Exports minus imports equal <u>net exports</u>. If net exports are positive, the foreign sector borrows funds from U.S. financial markets to pay for the exports not paid for by earnings from goods imported into the United States. (This appears in the circular flow as a flow of funds from U.S. financial markets to the foreign sector.) If net exports are negative, U.S. importers borrow from the foreign sector (a flow of funds from the foreign sector into U.S. financial markets).

The total output of goods and services in the domestic economy is known as <u>national product</u>, or, alternatively, as <u>aggregate supply</u>. The total of all planned expenditures--consumption plus planned investment plus government purchases plus net exports--is known as <u>aggregate demand</u>. Because production and expenditure plans are not coordinated in advance, aggregate supply does not always equal aggregate demand. The difference is made up by unplanned inventory investment: if planned expenditures exceed national product, inventories decline, and if planned expenditures fall short of national product, inventories accumulate. National product is thus always equal to total expenditure; that is, to total planned expenditure plus unplanned inventory investment. Producers react to unplanned inventory investment by reducing output and/or prices, thus causing the circular flow of income and product to contract. They react to unplanned inventory disinvestment by increasing output and/or prices, thus causing the circular flow of income and product to expand.

A second important equality in the circular flow is the equality of <u>injections</u> and leakages. Injections are all expenditures on domestic goods and services other than household consumption expenditures--that is, the total of investment, government purchases, and exports. Leakages are the part of household income not devoted to purchases of domestic consumer goods (saving, taxes, and consumer imports) plus expenditures of firms and governments not made for domestic goods and services (imports by firms and government). Thus, total injections (investment plus government purchases plus net exports) equal total leakages (saving plus taxes plus total imports). Note, however, that these totals do not need to match up item by item. For example, saving can exceed investment, with the difference offset by a government budget deficit or positive net exports.

35

WALKING TOUR

You have read the chapter at least once and have reviewed the synopsis. Now you are going to walk through the material step by step, filling in the blanks and answering the questions as you go along. After you have answered each question, check yourself by uncovering the answer given in the margin. If you do not understand why the answer given is the right one, refer back to the proper section of the text.

The Structure of the Circular Flow

In economics, it is important to distinguish carefully between stocks and flows. For example, the number of radios that a factory produces per month would be a _____, while   flow
the number of radios in the warehouse awaiting shipment on any given date would be a _____. The distinction be-   stock
tween stocks and flows applies to quantities measured in dollars as well as to those measured in physical units. For example, your consumption expenditures measured in dollars per month would be a _____, while the funds you   flow
have accumulated in your bank account as of a certain date would be a _____.   stock

Two of the most important components of the circular flow of income and product are the total of all wages, rents, interest, and profits earned by households, known as
_____, and the total value of all goods and   national income
services produced by the economy, known as _____.   national product
National product is alternatively known as _____.   aggregate supply

The sum of consumption, planned investment, government purchases, and net exports—that is, total planned expenditure—is known as _____. When aggregate supply   aggregate demand
and aggregate demand are equal, the economy is said to be
_____. If aggregate demand is not equal   in equilibrium
to aggregate supply, the difference must be made up by [planned/unplanned] inventory investment. For example, if   unplanned
total planned expenditure exceeds national product, there will be unplanned inventory [accumulation/depletion]. If aggregate   depletion
supply exceeds aggregate demand, there will be unplanned

_____.   inventory accumu-
                                                                                                                                lation
Unplanned inventory changes act as a signal to producers that the production plans they have formulated are not meshing with the expenditure plans of households, firms, government, and the foreign sector. If unplanned inventory accumulation takes place, producers are likely to react by [cutting/raising]   cutting

36

prices and/or output until inventories fall to the desired level. Similarly, producers will tend to raise prices and/or output when inventory changes indicate an excess aggregate [supply/ demand].

demand

Whether the circular flow is in equilibrium or not, national product must always be equal to total expenditure. This can be demonstrated by filling in the missing totals in the following table:

Output resulting from producers' plans:		[1]_____
Shirts	$70,000	
Tennis rackets	80,000	
Drill presses	50,000	
Expenditures resulting from buyers' plans		
Total consumption expenditure		[2]_____
Shirts	70,000	
Tennis rackets	90,000	
Total planned investment expenditure		[3]_____
Fixed investment	50,000	
Planned inventory investment	0	
Total planned expenditure (aggregate demand)		[4]_____
Total unplanned inventory investment		[5]_____
Summary		
National product		[6]_____
Total expenditure		[7]_____
Planned	[8]_____	
Unplanned	[9]_____	

Answers: [1] $200,000 [2] $160,000 [3] $50,000 [4] $210,000 [5] -$10,000
[6] $200,000 [7] $200,000 [8] $210,000 [9] -$10,000

When government and a foreign sector are added to the circular flow, the equality between national product and total expenditures (planned plus unplanned) is retained. The concepts of injections and leakages are useful to the analysis of such an economy. Class each of the following transactions as an injection or a leakage (from the point of view of the U.S. economy):

You pay $1 sales tax on a purchase of a dress. — leakage

An accounting firm buys a new U.S.-made typewriter. — injection

The city of Chicago has a street paved. — injection

A private school buys an imported school bus. — leakage

A U.S. worker deposits $25 in a savings account. — leakage

37

A French firm buys a U.S.-built computer.   injection
When both planned and unplanned investment are taken into
account, injections must equal leakages. This [means/
does not mean] that saving must match investment, government   does not mean
purchases must match net taxes, and imports must match
exports. For example, suppose net exports for some economy
are $500 and the government deficit is $1,000. It follows that
saving must [exceed/fall short of] total investment by   exceed
_____. If saving and planned investment are equal, then $1,500
unplanned inventory investment will be _____. Beginning   -$1,500
from this position, a $250 increase in government transfer pay-
ments, other things being equal, would bring total unplanned
inventory investment to _____. This unplanned inventory   -$1,750
depletion could be eliminated by an increase in [imports/exports]. imports

SELF TEST

These sample test items will help you check how much you have learned. Answers and explanations can be found at the end of this chapter. Scoring yourself: One or two wrong -- on target. Three to five wrong -- passing, but you haven't mastered the chapter yet. Six or more wrong -- not good enough; start over and restudy the chapter.

True or False

Indicate whether each statement is true or false as it stands. If it is false, explain why in a few words.

T F   1. Labor, capital, and natural resources are known as factors of production.

T F   2. The total value of automobile inventories as of September 1, 1979, is an example of a stock.

T F   3. National income and national product are equal only if saving and investment are left out of the picture.

T F   4. Fixed investment refers to investment in nonportable forms, such as structures and improvements to land.

T F   5. If a firm produces 5,000 radios in a month and sells only 4,000 of them, it is said to engage in inventory investment.

T F   6. Aggregate demand means the total value of all goods and services produced by the economy.

T F   7   If national income is $2,000 billion and aggregate demand is $2,100 billion, some unplanned inventory disinvestment must be taking place.

T F   8. The term net taxes means taxes paid to government minus transfer payments by government to individuals.

T F 9. Imports are an injection, exports a leakage.

T F 10. Total leakages can equal total injections only when the government budget
         is in balance.

Multiple Choice

1. Which of the following is not a flow?
    a. National income.
    b. Exports.
    c. Aggregate supply
    d. All of the above are flows.

2. A firm that produced $10 million worth of shoes in a year, sold $11 million worth
    of shoes in the year, and purchased $5 million in new shoemaking equipment
    during the year would have made a total investment of
    a. $4 million.
    b. $5 million.
    c. $6 million.
    d. $17 million.

3. In an economy in which saving is the only leakage and investment the only
    injection,
    a. saving must always be equal to total investment.
    b. saving must always be equal to planned investment.
    c. saving must always be equal to fixed investment.
    d. none of the above.

4. Aggregate supply is another term for
    a. national income.
    b. national product.
    c. total expenditure.
    d. total planned expenditure.

5. Aggregate supply minus aggregate demand is equal to
    a. saving.
    b. total investment.
    c. total inventory investment.
    d. unplanned inventory investment.

6. A flow of funds from financial markets to the government indicates that
    a. the government budget is in surplus.
    b. the government budget is in deficit.
    c. total injections exceed total leakages.
    d. total leakages exceed total injections.

7. If planned investment equals saving and government purchases equal net taxes,
    then
    a. the economy must be in equilibrium.
    b. imports must equal exports.
    c. both of the above.
    d. none of the above is necessarily true.

8. If national product = 1,000, consumption = 800, planned investment = 100, government purchases = 150, exports = 50, and imports = 75, then unplanned inventory investment must be
    a. −25.
    b. 0.
    c. 25.
    d. none of the above.

9. Which of the following is not an injection?
    a. Consumption.
    b. Investment.
    c. Government purchases.
    d. Exports.

10. If exports from the United States exceed imports into the United States,
    a. foreigners must borrow from U.S. credit markets.
    b. U.S. importers must borrow from foreign credit markets.
    c. total injections cannot equal total leakages.
    d. saving must exceed investment.

11. Let C stand for consumption, I for total investment, G for government purchases, X for exports, M for imports, S for saving, and T for net taxes. Which of the following equations always holds?
    a. $C + I + G + X = C + S + T - M$.
    b. $C + I + G + X - M = C + S + T$.
    c. $G - T = I + X - S - M$.
    d. None of the above always holds.

12. If the government budget is in surplus by $100 and there is a trade deficit of $60, then
    a. saving must exceed investment by $40.
    b. saving must exceed investment by $160.
    c. investment must exceed saving by $40.
    d. investment must exceed saving by $160.

13. If planned investment exceeds saving,
    a. the economy cannot be in equilibrium.
    b. there must be either a budget surplus or a foreign trade deficit.
    c. prices and/or output must increase.
    d. none of the above.

14. National product equals
    a. consumption plus investment plus government purchases.
    b. consumption plus investment plus government purchases plus exports.
    c. consumption plus investment plus government purchases plus net exports.
    d. investment plus government purchases plus net exports.

15. If planned injections exceed total leakages,
    a. prices and/or output will tend to rise.
    b. prices and/or output will tend to fall.
    c. prices will tend to rise and output to fall.
    d. output will tend to rise and prices to fall.

ANSWERS TO CHAPTER 5 SELF TEST

True or False

1-T
2-T
3-F; they are always equal under the assumptions of this chapter.
4-F; it also includes business equipment of all kinds.
5-T
6-F; this total is known as aggregate supply.
7-T
8-T
9-F; the other way around.
10-F; only the totals need agree; individual categories of injections and leakages need not match up.

Multiple Choice

1-d
2-a; inventories of shoes fall by $1 million.
3-a
4-b
5-d
6-b
7-d
8-a
9-a
10-a
11-b
12-a
13-b
14-c
15-a

CHAPTER SIX
MEASURING NATIONAL INCOME AND PRODUCT

WHERE YOU'RE GOING

Here is what you will be able to do when you have mastered this chapter:

--Distinguish between nominal and real measurements of economic quantities.

--Define gross national product and explain how the expenditure approach is used to measure it.

--Explain how the income approach is used to measure national income, and reconcile the income and expenditure approaches.

--Calculate GNP deflators and consumer prices indexes from simple sets of data, and use price indexes to convert nominal data to real terms.

--Discuss the limitations of national income accounting, and distinguish the purposes for which national income data can properly be used from those that the data are not designed to serve.

--Explain the meaning and significance of the following additional terms and concepts:

> Final goods and services.
> Net national product.
> Personal income.
> Disposable personal income.
> Producer price index.

CHAPTER SYNOPSIS

Reading this synopsis is not a substitute for reading the chapter, but it should help you to recall the main points. If there are any you feel unsure of, refer to the full discussion in the text.

National income accounting can be divided into two parts: the measurement of nominal values and the measurement of real values. Nominal values are measurements made in terms of the actual market prices at which market transactions take place; real values are measurements that are adjusted for inflation.

The broadest nominal measure of economic activity for the U.S. economy is gross national product (GNP). GNP is the total value of all final goods and services produced by the economy. Only final goods are included in order to avoid double counting. If, for example, both the value of bread (a final good) and the value of flour (an intermediate good used to make bread) were included in GNP, the value of flour would be counted twice--once when it was sold as flour and once when it was sold baked into the loaf of bread.

Gross national product is calculated by the so-called expenditure approach. First, all consumption expenditures, investment, government purchases, and exports are added together to get total expenditures. Then imports are subtracted from the total to allow for the fact that some consumption expenditures, investment, and government purchases go to buy goods produced abroad and should not be counted as part of the U.S. gross national product.

Measured in this way, gross national product makes no allowance for the fact that some investment each year merely goes to replace capital that has worn out or become obsolete in the process of production. GNP thus overstates how much the country is really getting out of the economy. To correct for this overstatement, national income accountants subtract from GNP an estimate—called the capital consumption allowance—of the quantity of capital used up during the year in the production process. GNP minus the capital consumption allowance equals net national product.

National income, an alternate measure of aggregate economic activity, is calculated by the income approach. This involves adding together all the different types of income—wages, rent, interest, and profits—received by households. In the simplified economic world used in other chapters, GNP and national income are exactly equal. In the somewhat more complex real-world economy, however, national income equals GNP minus the capital consumption allowance, indirect business taxes, and a "statistical discrepancy" reflecting measurement errors.

National income is a measure of the total income earned by households, whereas personal income is a measure of the income that households actually receive. To arrive at personal income, social insurance contributions, corporate profits taxes, and undistributed corporate profits are first subtracted from national income. (These are forms of income eaned by households but never received by them.) Then transfer payments—income received by households but not earned by them—are added in. Subtracting personal taxes from this total gives disposable personal income.

Comparing nominal national income accounts for different years can be misleading if the price level has changed. To correct for price level changes, nominal measurements from various years are recalculated using the prices prevailing in some selected year, known as the base year. Real GNP can then be measured as current year output evaluated at base year prices, rather than at the prices at which it was actually sold.

If the price level in the current year is higher than in the base year, current year nominal GNP will exceed current year real GNP. The ratio of current year nominal GNP to current year real GNP, known as the GNP deflator, can be used as a measure of the price level in the current year.

The consumer price index (CPI), another measure of the price level, is calculated somewhat differently from the GNP deflator. The CPI is based on a selected market basket of goods typical of the purchases of an urban household. It is derived by finding the ratio of the base year market basket evaluated at current year prices to the base year market basket evaluated at base year prices and multiplying it by 100.

The national income accounts provide a reasonably good measure of the annual production and use of final goods and services. Great caution must be used, however, in interpreting national income statistics as measures of human welfare. For one thing, the price indexes used in translating nominal data to real terms are subject to significant biases. For another, statistics such as GNP and national income do not measure nonmarket activity, leisure, or such negative factors as pollution. Many things other than GNP contribute to human welfare.

WALKING TOUR

You have read the chapter at least once and have reviewed the synopsis. Now you are going to walk through the material step by step, filling in the blanks and answering the questions as you go along. After you have answered each question, check yourself by uncovering the answer given in the margin. If you do not understand why the answer given is the correct one, refer back to the proper section of the text.

Measuring Nominal National Income and Product

The questions in this section are all based on data given in Exhibit S6.1, which follows:

Exhibit S6.1

Capital consumption allowance	$180
Change in business inventories	−20
Compensation of employees	930
Contributions to social insurance	110
Corporate profit taxes	50
Dividends	30
Exports	150
Fixed investment	220
Government purchases	380
Imports	125
Indirect business taxes	140
Net interest	75
Personal consumption expenditures	975
Personal taxes	170
Proprietors' income	90
Rental income	25
Transfer payments	210
Undistributed corporate profits	10

Begin by using the expenditure approach to compute gross national product, which is _____. This is the sum of personal consumption of $975, total private investment of _____, government purchases of $380, and net exports of _____. From this total, the national income of _____ is derived by subtracting the capital consumption allowance of $180.

$1,580

$200

$25

$1,400

Next, using the income approach, compute national income which comes out to _____. This is the sum of compensation of employees of $930, rental income of $25, net interest of $75, corporate profits of _____, and proprietors' income of $90.

$1,210

$90

The difference between national income and net national product is partly accounted for by indirect business taxes of $140. The remaining _____ is accounted for by the statistical discrepancy.

$50

The next statistic to compute is personal income, which comes out to _____ on the basis of Exhibit S6.1. This is obtained by first subtracting contributions for social insurance, corporate profits taxes, and undistributed corporate profits from national income and then adding transfer payments.

$1,250

Disposable personal income is _____, which is found by $1,080
subtracting personal taxes from personal income.

Measuring Real Income and Prices

The next set of questions is based on Exhibit S6.2:

Exhibit S6.2

	1970 Quantity	1970 Price	1980 Quantity	1980 Price
Wheat (bushels)	2,000	$ 2.50	4,000	$ 4.00
Radios	200	20.00	300	40.00
Milk (gallons)	1,000	1.00	1,100	2.50

For all of the following problems, 1970 will be considered
the base year and 1980 the current year. The first task will
be to calculate real GNP in 1980. Real GNP is defined as
[current/base] year output evaluated at [current/base] year   current; base
prices. The evaluation must be made one product at a time;
the resulting figures are then summed to give total real GNP
for the current year. Beginning with wheat, multiply the
current year quantity (_____bushels) by the base year   4,000
price (_____per bushel) to get _____ as the current $2.50; $10,000
year quantity of wheat evaluated at base year prices. Proceeding in the same way, you can find the current year quantity
evaluated at the base year price to be _____ for radios $6,000
and _____ for milk. Adding these together give a 1980 $1,100
real GNP of _____. $17,100
The next task is to determine the GNP deflator for 1980.
The GNP deflator is the ratio of current year _____   nominal
GNP to current year _____ GNP, times 100. 1980 real   real
GNP has already been calculated. To get current year nominal
GNP, compute the sum of _____ year quantities valued   current
at _____ year prices. For 1980, this gives _____.   current; $30,750
The GNP deflator for 1980 is thus found to be _____.   179.8
Finally, use the data from Exhibit S6.2 to calculate a
consumer price index (CPI) for 1980. The CPI is defined as
the ratio of the _____ year market basket valued at   base
_____ prices to the _____ year market basket   current; base
valued at _____ year prices, times 100. The base year   base
market basket valued at current year prices comes out to

45

_____. The same market basket valued at the prices $18,500
at which the goods were actually sold comes out to _____. $10,000
The CPI for 1980 is thus _____.   185

SELF TEST

These sample test items will help you check how much you have learned. Answers and explanations can be found at the end of this chapter. Scoring yourself: One or two wrong -- on target. Three to five wrong -- passing, but you haven't mastered the chapter yet. Six or more wrong -- not good enough; start over and restudy the chapter.

True or False

Indicate whether each statement is true or false as it stands. If it is false, explain why in a few words.

T F   1. Nominal values are values measured in terms of the prices at which goods and services are actually sold.

T F   2. Gross national product is the total of all final and intermediate goods sold in the economy.

T F   3. National income is officially measured by the expenditure approach.

T F   4. The difference between gross national product and net national product is called the capital consumption allowance.

T F   5. National income accountants do not count purchases of bonds, stocks, and other financial instruments as investments.

T F   6. In periods of inflation, nominal GNP rises faster than real GNP.

T F   7. The GNP deflator and the consumer price index are calculated according to the same formula, but are based on different selections of goods and services.

T F   8. When the GNP deflator and consumer price index give different values for a given year, national income accountants consider the GNP deflator to be the true measure of the change in the price level.

T F   9. If adequate adjustments were made for improvements in the quality of goods and services, inflation, as measured by the consumer price index, would disappear.

T F   10. One reason that real GNP is not a good measure of human welfare is that it is not fully adjusted for the damage done by pollution.

Multiple Choice

1. Gross national product is officially measured by
   a. multiplying the quantity of each final good and service produced by the price at which it is sold and adding the totals.
   b. adding together the totals of all expenditures on newly produced final goods and services.
   c. adding together the totals of all incomes received by households from the sale of productive services.

d. multiplying the quantity of all factor services by factor prices actually paid and adding the totals.

2. Which of the following would be counted as a final good or service in calculating GNP?
   a. An automotive brake unit sold by Bendix Corporation to General Motors for use in a new Buick.
   b. A truckload of fertilizer sold to an Iowa farmer.
   c. A used typewriter purchased by a real estate agent.
   d. A haircut purchased by a retired bank teller.

3. Which of the following would not be counted as an investment for purposes of computing GNP?
   a. Construction of a new movie theater.
   b. Purchase by an appliance dealer of a newly produced refrigerator, which the dealer subsequently fails to sell to a consumer during the year in question.
   c. Construction of a new, single family house.
   d. Purchase of 1,000 shares of IBM stock by a union pension fund.

4. Which of the following would not be counted as part of government purchases of goods and services as recorded in the GNP accounts?
   a. Unemployment compensation payments.
   b. The salary of a worker in a state employment commission office.
   c. Purchase of furniture by the U.S. Department of Labor.
   d. Purchase of a new radar gun for the local sheriff's office.

5. The word "gross" in gross national product indicates that GNP includes
   a. intermediate as well as final goods.
   b. imported goods as well as domestically produced goods.
   c. investment that goes to replace worn out capital as well as investment for expansion of productive capacity.
   d. farm products consumed on the farm as well as those sold.

6. Which of the following is included in net national product but not in national income?
   a. Capital consumption allowance.
   b. Indirect business taxes.
   c. Undistributed corporate profits.
   c. Personal taxes.

7. Which of the following is included in national income but not in personal income?
   a. Capital consumption allowance.
   b. Indirect business taxes.
   c. Undistributed corporate profits.
   d. Government transfer payments.

8. Which of the following is included in personal income but not in disposable personal income?
   a. Employee contributions to social security.
   b. Undistributed corporate profits.
   c. Transfer payments.
   d. Personal taxes.

47

9. Let P_c stand for current year prices, P_b for base year prices, Q_c for the current year market basket of goods, and Q_b for the base year market basket. Then the correct formula for the consumer price index is:
   a. Q_c valued at P_c / Q_b valued at P_b.
   b. Q_c valued at P_b / Q_b valued at P_b.
   c. Q_b valued at P_c / Q_b valued at P_b.
   d. Q_c valued at P_c / Q_c valued at P_b.

10. If 1972 quantities valued at 1972 prices are 150; 1972 quantities valued at 1980 prices are 300; 1980 quantities valued at 1972 prices are 200; and 1980 quantities valued at 1980 prices are 600; the GNP deflator for 1980, using 1972 as the base year, is
    a. 200.
    b. 300.
    c. 400.
    d. impossible to calculate with the information given.

11. One way the consumer price index differs from the GNP deflator is that it
    a. uses current year quantities.
    b. includes all final goods and services.
    c. includes only goods bought by typical urban consumers.
    d. includes services as well as physical goods.

12. If there is a tendency for the consumption of goods whose prices increase relatively slowly to grow more rapidly than the consumption of goods whose prices increase relatively rapidly, then
    a. the CPI will increase more rapidly than the GNP deflator.
    b. the GNP deflator will increase more rapidly than the CPI.
    c. only the CPI will give a true measure of inflation.
    d. only the GNP deflator will give a true measure of inflation.

13. The producer price index
    a. uses base year quantities.
    b. may contain an upward bias.
    c. is thought to indicate future inflation trends for the CPI.
    d. does all of the above.

14. Suppose a typical automobile tire costs $20 in 1935 and $40 in 1980 and that the 1935 tire had a useful life of 10,000 miles whereas the 1980 tire had a useful life of 40,000 miles. If no adjustment is made for mileage,
    a. the CPI would overestimate inflation between the two years.
    b. the CPI would underestimate inflation between the two years.
    c. the CPI would accurately measure inflation between the two years.
    d. it is not possible to judge how well the CPI would measure inflation between the two years without knowing how the quantity sold changed.

15. The growth rate of real per capita GNP, as officially measured, would tend to understate the true growth rate of per capita material welfare if
    a. population growth accelerated.
    b. pollution was increasing.
    c. the underground economy was growing faster than population.
    d. the country entered a war.

ANSWERS TO CHAPTER 6 SELF TEST

True or False

1-T
2-F; final goods only
3-F; income approach.
4-T
5-T
6-T
7-F; the former uses current quantities, the latter base year quantities.
8-F; neither is a "true" measure.
9-F; but it might be less.
10-T

Multiple Choice

1-b
2-d
3-d
4-a
5-c
6-b
7-c
8-d
9-c
10-b
11-c
12-a
13-d
14-a
15-c

CHAPTER SEVEN
THE GOALS OF STABILIZATION POLICY
AND THE PERFORMANCE OF THE U.S. ECONOMY

WHERE YOU'RE GOING

Here is what you will be able to do when you have mastered this chapter:

--Identify the main provisions of the Full Employment Act of 1946 and the Humphrey-Hawkins Act.

--Define the unemployment rate and contrast the official definition of unemployment with the commonsense notions of "not working" and "can't find a job."

--Describe, in general terms, unemployment trends in the United States since 1950, and identify population groups most and least affected by unemployment.

--Describe, in general terms, inflation trends in the United States since 1950, and identify population groups most and least affected by inflation.

--Determine nominal, expected real, and realized real rates of interest, given the necessary data.

--Discuss the impact of inflation on income from various sources and on various subgroups of the population.

--Use the production possibility frontier to illustrate the concepts of economic growth and potential real output.

--Use economic analysis to evaluate arguments about the desirability and possibility of economic growth.

--Explain the meaning and significance of the following additional terms and concepts:

  Employed.
  Civilian labor force.
  Indexing.

CHAPTER SYNOPSIS

Reading this synopsis is not a substitute for reading the chapter, but it should help you to recall the main points. If there are any you feel unsure of, refer to the full discussion in the text.

   Economic stabilization policy includes all policies intended to promote the goals of full employment, price stability, and growth of real output. The legal framework for the federal government's stabilization policy is provided by the Full Employment Act of 1946. In 1978 this act was amended by the Humphrey-Hawkins Act, which for the first time established numerical goals for unemployment and inflation. The act specifies that by 1983 the unemployment rate is to be reduced to 4 percent of the labor force, with a supplementary goal of 3 percent unemployment for workers aged twenty-four and older. The rate of inflation as measured by the consumer price index is to be reduced to 3 percent per year by 1983 and to 0 percent by 1988.

The unemployment rate is officially defined as the percentage of the civilian labor force that is not employed. Unemployment statistics are based on a monthly household survey conducted by the Bureau of Labor Statistics. It is important to understand that the official definition of unemployment does not correspond exactly to the common-sense notions of "not working" or "can't find a job." In some respects, the official data are open to criticism for understating the extent of joblessness; but in other respects, they may overstate it.

The unemployment rate fluctuates from month to month and year to year; but in recent decades, it has shown a gradual upward trend. The Humphrey-Hawkins 4 percent unemployment target has not been reached since the Vietnam War years 1966-1969. The incidence of unemployment varies greatly from one group of the population to another. Teenagers, minorities, and women consistently experience higher than average unemployment rates; adult married men generally experience the lowest rates of unemployment.

The inflation rate, like the unemployment rate, has displayed an upward trend over the last decade. The impact of inflation, like the impact of unemployment, is not the same for all groups of the population. Recent evidence indicates that the relative impact of inflation is most severe for families with relatively high incomes. Inflation also tends to have a stronger than average adverse impact on the elderly.

In part, the distributional impact of inflation depends on whether inflation is expected or unexpected. Consider, for example, the impact of inflation on debtors and creditors. Accurately expected inflation is neutral between creditors and debtors because the parties will adjust the nominal rate of interest that they agree on to allow fully for the actual rate of inflation. Unexpected inflation benefits debtors at the expense of creditors, because it lowers the realized real rate of interest associated with any given nominal rate of interest. An unexpected deceleration of inflation would benefit creditors at the expense of debtors.

The process of economic growth can be represented graphically as an outward expansion of the production possibility frontier. The position of the frontier schematically represents potential real output--the output that could be produced if all resources were fully employed. If factors of production are not fully employed, actual real output may lag behind the growth of potential real output.

There is an ongoing debate about the possibility and desirability of further economic growth. Some think further economic growth is both desirable and possible; others think that growth will eventually be rendered impossible by resource depletion or that even if growth is possible, it is undesirable because it leads to a deterioration in the quality of life. This debate cannot be entirely resolved by the methods of positive economics, but the concerns of those who are skeptical about economic growth can be at least partly allayed by carefully distinguishing between changes in the quantity of output and changes in the composition of output.

WALKING TOUR

You have read the chapter at least once and have reviewed the synopsis. Now you are going to walk through the material step by step, filling in the blanks and answering the questions as you go along. After you have answered each question, check yourself by uncovering the answer given in the margin. If you do not understand why the answer given is the right one, refer back to the proper section of the text.

Full Employment

The Humphrey-Hawkins Act of 1978 sets a goal of _____   4

percent unemployment for the labor force as a whole and

_____ percent for persons twenty-four years of age and
older. These targets are based on the officially measured
unemployment rate, which in turn is based on the division of
the total population into a number of groups. The noninstitutional adult civilian population consists of all those aged _____
and older who are not in the armed forces or institutionalized.
Of these, persons who are working or actively looking for work
make up the _____. The unemployment
rate is the percentage of the civilian labor force not employed.
To be considered employed, a person must work [at least part
time/full time] for pay; people on strike, on vacation, or not
working because of bad weather are counted as [employed/
unemployed]. People with part time jobs who are looking for
full time work are officially considered [employed/unemployed].

Unemployment rates vary from one population group to
another. Generally, teenagers, minorities, and women have
[higher/lower] than average unemployment rates. Empirical
research suggests that meeting the Humphrey-Hawkins goals
for overall unemployment [would/would not] significantly reduce
unemployment among these groups.

Price Stability

Over the last century, rates of inflation rising as rapidly as
those of the 1970s have been [common/exceptional]. High rates
of inflation have brought renewed interest in the question of
who gains and who loses from inflation. As a general rule,
wage and salary income is relatively [well/poorly] protected
against inflation. Transfer income is relatively well protected
against inflation, partly because many transfers are paid in
kind and partly because social security benefits are _____
--that is, automatically adjusted for inflation.

Traditionally, inflation has been thought to injure
[creditors/debtors] and benefit [creditors/debtors]. Now it
is recognized that this is true only for inflation that is
[expected/unexpected]. For example, suppose the Albany
National Bank is willing to give you a new car loan at a 6 percent nominal rate of interest when it expects 2 percent inflation,
which will give it an expected real rate of interest of _____
percent. If instead it expected inflation to accelerate to 5
percent per year, it would have to get a _____ percent

	3
	sixteen
	civilian labor force
	at least part time
	employed
	employed
	higher
	would
	exceptional
	well
	indexed
	creditors; debtors
	unexpected
	4
	9

52

nominal rate to maintain the same expected real rate. If you too expected a 5 percent rate of inflation, you might consider 9 percent nominal rate reasonable and take out the loan. If the rate of inflation then unexpectedly accelerated to 8 percent per year, the realized real rate of interest on the loan would be _____ percent. You would thus have benefited at the bank's expense. However, if the rate of inflation over the period of the loan had unexpectedly turned out to be 3 percent, the realized real rate would turn out to be [higher/lower] than the expected real rate, and the bank would benefit at your expense.

1

higher

The tax system plays an important role in determining the distributional effects of inflation. The real burden of income and capital gains taxes [rises/falls] as the rate of inflation increases. The interaction of taxes and inflation is one reason why wealthy people are, in relation to their incomes, [more/less] adversely affected by inflation than people with low and middle-level incomes.

rises

more

Economic Growth

The real output that the economy could produce if resources were fully employed is known as _____. As officially measured, the rate of growth of potential real GNP during the 1970s was about _____ percent per year. Actual GNP is [often/rarely] below potential real GNP and [often/rarely/never] above it.

potential real GNP
  or output

3
often
rarely

According to a study by Edward F. Denison, _____ _____ has been the most important single source of growth of potential output over the past fifty years, followed by _____, _____, and _____.

advance in know-
  ledge

more work done
capital accumulation
increased education

Today not everyone considers further economic growth to be possible or desirable. In evaluating the debate over economic growth, it is important to distinguish between the size of real output and its _____. If the composition of output remains unchanged, economic growth [will/will not] result in increased environmental problems. By adjusting the composition of output in favor of environmentally "clean" goods and services, however, pollution can be controlled without growth being curtailed.

composition

will

SELF TEST

These sample test items will help you check how much you have learned. Answers and explanations can be found at the end of this chapter. Scoring yourself: One or two wrong -- on target. Three to five wrong -- passing, but you haven't mastered the chapter yet. Six or more wrong -- not good enough; start over and re-study the chapter.

True or False

Indicate whether each statement is true or false as it stands. If it is false, explain why in a few words.

T F   1.   Although the unemployment target of the Humphrey-Hawkins bill was reached the first year after the act was passed, the inflation target appears more difficult to achieve.

T F   2.   Some people are officially counted as employed even though they are not working because they have found a job that they expect to start in thirty days or less.

T F   3.   So-called discouraged workers are not counted as unemployed even though they are not working and would take a job if one came their way.

T F   4.   Women experience higher unemployment rates than teenagers.

T F   5.   Lower-income families that receive most of their personal income in the form of wages have not been harmed greatly by inflation, but those who depend mostly on transfer payments have suffered severely.

T F   6.   If the nominal rate of interest is 6 percent, the expected rate of inflation is 3 percent, and the actual rate of inflation is 2 percent, debtors are likely to benefit at the expense of creditors.

T F   7.   Traditionally, common stocks have been thought to be a good investment in times of inflation; but during the 1970s, stocks performed poorly.

T F   8.   Contrary to widespread belief, the elderly suffer no more from inflation than any other group in the population.

T F   9.   Economic growth without increased pollution is possible if the composition of output changes as growth takes place.

T F   10.   Over the past fifty years, capital accumulation has been by far the most significant source of economic growth in the United States.

Multiple Choice

1.   The Humphrey-Hawkins Act of 1978 for the first time
   a.   established economic stability as an official function of the U.S. government.
   b.   gave an official, numerical definition to the concept of unemployment.
   c.   established official numerical targets for unemployment and inflation.
   d.   established goals for inflation and unemployment equal to the average rates for the 1970s.

2. Which of the following persons would be classified as officially unemployed?
   a. A worker off the job for more than thirty days because of a strike.
   b. A person working full time, but not for pay, in a family business.
   c. A person with a part time job who is actively looking for full time work.
   d. A person who had a secure job but left it voluntarily to look for another.

3. The employment rate would rise if
   a. members of the armed forces were included in the labor force.
   b. so-called discouraged workers were counted as officially unemployed.
   c. workers on strike were counted as officially employed.
   d. part time workers seeking full time work were counted as officially unemployed.

4. Which of the following, on average, experience the highest unemployment rates?
   a. Teenagers.
   b. Women.
   c. Married men.
   d. Blacks and other minorities.

5. The 3 percent interim inflation target of the Humphrey-Hawkins Act
   a. is considered very modest, because inflation has never exceeded 3 percent for more than one year.
   b. was achieved in more than half of the years between 1950 and 1970.
   c. is technically impossible to achieve because it ignores the problem of biases in the consumer price index.
   d. is lower than the average rate of inflation in the United States between the Civil War and the 1960s.

6. Families heavily dependent on transfer payments have been protected from inflation to a considerable extent because
   a. social security payments are indexed.
   b. many transfers are made in kind.
   c. total transfer payments increased in real terms in the 1970s.
   d. all of the above are true.

7. During the 1970s, inflation had the least relative adverse impact on families whose wealth was tied up primarily in
   a. common stocks.
   b. corporate bonds.
   c. their own homes.
   d. nonindexed private pension funds.

8. If the expected real rate of interest is 4 percent and the expected rate of inflation is 6 percent, the nominal rate of interest must be
   a. 2 percent.
   b. 4 percent.
   c. 10 percent.
   d. The question cannot be answered without the actual rate of inflation being known.

9. If the actual rate of inflation exceeds the expected rate of inflation,
   a. the nominal rate of interest will be lower than the realized real rate of interest.
   b. the realized real rate of interest will be lower than the expected real rate of interest.
   c. the realized real rate of interest must be negative.
   d. creditors will gain at the expense of debtors.

10. Judging from past experience, which of the following households would experience the largest percentage reduction in real income as the result of a 2
percent acceleration in the rate of inflation?
   a. Elderly; entirely dependent on social security.
   b. Young blue collar; heavy mortgage payments on an expensive house.
   c. Poor; dependent on transfer payments.
   d. Elderly, dependent on dividends and interest from stocks and bonds.

11. Between Year 1 and Year 2 the price level rises from an index of 120 to an
index of 240. In Year 1 you buy 100 shares of stock at $5 per share, and
you sell them in Year 2 at $6 per share. You pay capital gains tax at a rate
of 25 percent. Which of the following is true?
   a. You earn a real capital gain after tax.
   b. You earn a real capital gain before tax but suffer a capital loss after tax.
   c. You earn a nominal capital gain but suffer a real capital loss both before
      and after tax.
   d. You suffer a nominal capital loss.

12. Growth of potential real GNP is
   a. represented graphically by an outward shift of the production possibility
      frontier.
   b. estimated to be about 7 percent per year at present.
   c. possible only when prices are relatively stable.
   d. possible only when resources are fully employed.

13. According to Edward F. Denison, which of the following has been most important as a source of economic growth in the postwar U.S. economy?
   a. More work done.
   b. Advances in knowledge.
   c. Capital accumulation.
   d. Increased education.

14. Which of the following statements about economic growth can be supported on
the basis of positive economic analysis?
   a. Economic growth is highly desirable, because without it, the poor tend
      to be frozen at their present rung on the ladder.
   b. Even if no change in the composition of output were to take place, the
      material gains of economic growth would continue to more than outweigh
      possible adverse environmental effects.
   c. Future growth is likely to be impossible because the discovery of new
      resources has been shown to be the most important source of growth in
      the past.
   d. Economic growth without increased pollution is possible provided that the
      composition of output changes appropriately as the quantity of output
      grows.

15. If nominal GNP grows at a rate of 10 percent per year and inflation proceeds
at a rate of 6 percent per year, real output will grow at a rate of
   a. 4 percent per year.
   b. 6 percent per year.
   c. 10 percent per year.
   d. 16 percent per year.

ANSWERS TO CHAPTER 7 SELF TEST

True or False

1-F; the unemployment target was not reached in 1979.
2-F
3-T
4-F; teenage rates are higher
5-F; neither group has suffered severely from inflation, according to the Minarik study.
6-F; if the actual rate of inflation is less than the expected rate, creditors benefit at the expense of debtors.
7-T
8-F; at every income level, the elderly suffer more.
9-T
10-F; according to the Denison study, advances in knowledge have been the most important.

Multiple Choice

1-c
2-d
3-a; their inclusion would raise the numerator and denominator of the employment rate equally, thus raising the quotient.
4-a
5-b
6-d
7-c
8-c; the expected real rate of interest is equal to the nominal rate minus the expected rate of inflation.
9-b
10-d
11-c; the nominal capital gain is figured by subtracting original cost from proceeds of the sale: $600 - $500 = $100. However, because the price level doubled, the real value of the proceeds, in Year 1 dollars, was only $300; so there was a $200 real capital loss before tax. Tax on the $100 of nominal gains was $25, so the real after-tax proceeds were only $575/2 = $287.50; the real after-tax loss was $212.50.
12-a
13-b
14-d; a and b are normative statements; c is a positive statement, but factually false.
15-a; the rate of growth of nominal GNP is equal to the rate of growth of real GNP plus the rate of inflation.

CHAPTER EIGHT
THE DETERMINANTS OF PLANNED EXPENDITURE

WHERE YOU'RE GOING

Here is what you will be able to do when you have mastered this chapter:

--Draw a consumption schedule, given values for autonomous consumption and the marginal propensity to consume.

--Draw a saving schedule, given a corresponding consumption schedule.

--Distinguish between changes in economic conditions that cause movements along the consumption schedule and those that cause shifts in the schedule.

--Discuss the determinants of planned investment in terms of the expected real rate of return and the expected real rate of interest.

--Distinguish between changes in economic conditions that cause movements along the planned investment schedule and those that cause shifts in the schedule.

--Explain the meaning and significance of the following additional terms and concepts:

Dissaving.
Marginal propensity to save.
Lump sum taxes.

In addition, after mastering the appendix to this chapter, you will be able to:

--Apply payback period analysis to a simple capital budgeting problem.

--Determine the present value of any future dollar amount, given a rate of interest at which it is to be discounted.

--Apply the net present value approach to a simple capital budgeting problem.

CHAPTER SYNOPSIS

Reading this synopsis is not a substitute for reading the chapter, but it should help you to recall the main points. If there are any you feel unsure of, refer to the full discussion in the text.

Following John Maynard Keynes, the determinants of planned expenditure can be analyzed in terms of the separate components--consumption, planned investment, government purchases, and net exports. For purposes of elementary analysis, certain details of national income accounting are ignored. For one thing, indirect business taxes, the capital consumption allowance, and the statistical discrepancy are assumed equal to zero, so that gross national product, net national product, and national income are all equal. In addition, undistributed corporate profits are assumed to be zero, so that disposable personal income is simply equal to national income minus net taxes.

Keynes's theory of consumption expenditure began from the observation that people regularly spend part, but not all, of each additional dollar of income on consumption. Similarly, when their income falls by a dollar, they reduce their consumption, but not by as much as the decline in their income. This behavior can be represented graphically in the form of an upward sloping consumption schedule. The slope of the schedule is equal to the marginal propensity to consume--the fraction of a dollar by which consumption changes for each one-dollar change in disposable income.

The short-run consumption schedule intersects the vertical axis above the origin, indicating that consumers would tend not to reduce their consumption to zero even if their income temporarily fell to zero. The amount of consumption associated with zero disposable income is known as autonomous consumption (although, of course, national income never actually is zero).

Any part of disposable personal income that does not go to consumption is, by definition, saved. It follows that the marginal propensity to save--the fraction of a dollar by which saving changes for each one-dollar change in disposable income-- is equal to 1 minus the marginal propensity to consume. At a zero level of disposable income, consumers would engage in dissaving--negative saving--equal to autonomous consumption.

The effects of changes in disposable income on consumption are represented by movements along the consumption schedule. Other changes affecting consumption expenditure are represented by shifts in the consumption schedule. Other things equal, an increase in wealth or an increase in expected future income cause an upward shift in the consumption schedule. Changes in the price level and changes in the rate of inflation have an ambiguous effect on consumption--such changes might cause the schedule to shift either up or down. For purposes of elementary analysis, it is convenient to assume that the upward and downward effects of changes in the price level or in the rate of inflation just cancel out, leaving the position of the nominal consumption schedule unchanged.

Planned investment, including both fixed investment and planned inventory investment, is a second major component of aggregate nominal expenditure. The rate of planned investment expenditure depends on the expected real rate of return on investment and the expected real rate of interest.

Anything that changes the expected real rate of interest, other things being equal, will produce a movement along the planned investment schedule. The expected real rate of interest can change either because of a change in the nominal rate of interest not accompanied by an equal change in the expected rate of inflation or because of a change in the expected rate of inflation not accompanied by an equal change in the nominal rate of interest. Changes in planned investment expenditure resulting from any cause other than a change in the expected real rate of interest are represented by a shift in the planned investment schedule. For example, an increase in the expected real rate of return on investment, other things being equal, shifts the planned investment schedule to the right.

For purposes of elementary analysis, the other two major components of planned expenditure--government purchases and net exports--can be treated as given.

WALKING TOUR

You have read the chapter at least once and have reviewed the synopsis. Now you are going to walk through the material step by step, filling in the blanks and answering the questions as you go along. After you have answered each question, check yourself by uncovering the answer given in the margin. If you do not understand why the answer given is the right one, refer back to the proper section of the text.

Consumption

As a general rule, consumers tend to devote part, but not all, of any increase in income to consumption. In numerical terms, this implies that their marginal propensity to consume is greater than _____ but less than _____. This kind of consumption behavior can be expressed in the form of a table such as the following:

Disposable Income	Consumption	Saving
1,000	1,400	-400
2,000	2,200	-200
3,000	3,000	0
4,000	3,800	200
5,000	4,600	400

zero; 1

This table incorporates a marginal propensity to consume of _____ and a marginal propensity to save of _____. Although not shown explicitly in the table, autonomous consumption can be determined to be _____. That is the level of consumption that would prevail if disposable income were to fall to _____.

0.8; 0.2

600

zero

In Exhibit S8.1, graph the consumption and saving schedules given in the table above. Begin by drawing in Exhibit S8.1a a 45° reference line--that is, a straight line passing through the origin with a slope of +1. Now draw the consumption schedule; if correctly drawn, it intersects the vertical axis at _____ and intersects the 45° reference line at a disposable income of _____. Next draw the saving schedule in Exhibit S8.1b. The saving schedule, if correctly drawn, intersects the vertical axis at a level of _____ and intersects the horizontal axis at a disposable income of _____.

$600

$3,000

-$600

$3,000

Changes in disposable income, other things being equal, can be represented graphically as [shifts in/movements along] a consumption schedule such as the one in Exhibit S8.1a. A change in consumer wealth or expectations can be represented by a [shift in/movement along] the schedule. A once and for all increase in the general price level would produce a(n) [upward/downward/uncertain] shift in the consumption schedule. For introductory purposes, the effect on the nominal consumption schedule of a once and for all change in the price level can best be assumed to be _____. A change in the rate of

movements along

shift in

uncertain

zero

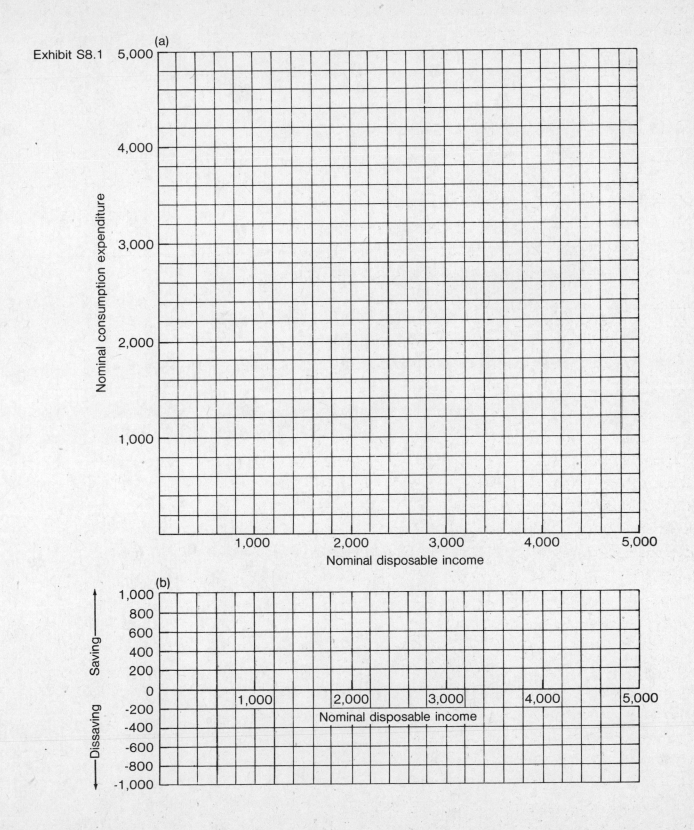

Exhibit S8.1

(a)

Nominal consumption expenditure

5,000

4,000

3,000

2,000

1,000

1,000   2,000   3,000   4,000   5,000

Nominal disposable income

(b)

Saving

1,000
800
600
400
200
0

Dissaving

-200
-400
-600
-800
-1,000

1,000   2,000   3,000   4,000   5,000

Nominal disposable income

inflation tends to produce a(n) [upward/downward/uncertain] shift in the nominal consumption schedule, although to the extent that an increase in inflation triggers anticipatory buying, the direction of the shift tends to be [upward/downward].

uncertain

upward

Investment

Planned investment expenditure is a second major component of aggregate demand. Other things being equal, planned investment is greater the greater the expected real rate of _____ and less the greater the expected real rate of _____ .

return

interest

   The relationship between planned investment and the expected real rate of interest can be represented graphically in a diagram such as Exhibit S8.2. For example, the planned investment schedule I_1 in that exhibit shows total planned investment of _____ when the expected real rate of interest is 4 percent. Beginning from that point, a 4 percentage point increase in the nominal interest rate, other things being equal, would [increase/decrease] the amount of planned investment by _____. This would be represented by a [movement along/shift in] the planned investment schedule. From that point, an increase in the expected rate of inflation, with no further change in the nominal interest rate, would [increase/decrease] planned investment expenditure and would be represented by a [movement along/shift in] the schedule I_1. Finally, suppose that the expected rate of return on investment were to increase as the result of an expected improvement

$100

decrease
$50
movement along

increase
movement along

Exhibit S8.2

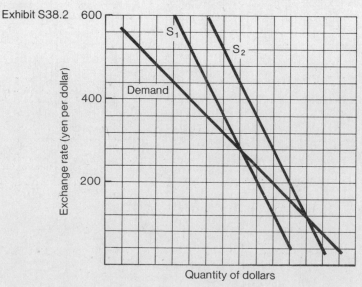

62

in general business conditions. This would produce a [movement along/shift in] the planned investment schedule. The final position of the planned investment schedule after this shift would best be represented by [I_2/I_3].

shift in

I_3

Appendix: Investment Decision Making

The formula for calculating the present value, V_p, of any sum, V_t, payable t years in the future, given an interest rate r, is:

$$V_p =$$

Apply this formula to complete the following table:

$$\frac{V_t}{(1 + r)^t}$$

V_t	r	t	V_p	
$100	0.10	1	$_____	90.90
100	0.10	2	_____	82.64
100	0.10	3	_____	75.13
100	0.10	4	_____	68.30

The information in the table you have just completed can now be used to calculate the net present value, at 10 percent interest, of the following investment project:

Year	Net Cash Flow	Discounted Net Cash Flow	
0	−$500	_____	−$500
1	50	_____	45.45
2	200	_____	165.28
3	200	_____	150.26
4	100	_____	68.30
	Net present value = _____		−70.71

The project [is/is not] worthwhile.

is not

SELF TEST

These sample test items will help you check how much you have learned. Answers and explanations can be found at the end of this chapter. Scoring yourself: One or two wrong -- on target. Three to five wrong -- passing, but you haven't mastered the chapter yet. Six or more wrong -- not good enough; start over and restudy the chapter.

True or False

Indicate whether each statement is true or false as it stands. If it is false, explain why in a few words.

T F   1. Although few economists today accept Keynes's view that consumption is an important component of aggregate nominal demand, many of his other theories are still popular.

T F   2. So long as not all of each dollar of added disposable income is devoted to consumption, the marginal propensity to consume must be less than 1.

T F   3. Autonomous consumption refers to the fact that people always save something, even when their income is near zero.

T F   4. If the marginal propensity to consume is less than 0.5, the marginal propensity to save is larger than the marginal propensity to consume.

T F   5. If consumption is $1,100 when disposable income is $1,000, the consumption schedule must lie below the 45° line at that point.

T F   6. The income level where the saving schedule crosses the horizontal axis must be the same as the income level where the consumption schedule crosses the 45° line.

T F   7. Repeated observation confirms that a once and for all increase in the price level must shift the consumption schedule downward.

T F   8. An increase in the rate of inflation may shift the consumption schedule either upward or downward, depending on circumstances.

T F   9. Other things being equal, the lower the expected real rate of interest, the greater will be planned investment spending.

T F   10. Other things being equal, an increase in the nominal rate of interest produces a movement up and to the left along the planned investment schedule.

Multiple Choice

1. According to Keynes, when disposable income increases, consumption increases
    a. but not by the full amount of the increase in disposable income.
    b. and saving decreases.
    c. by at least 90 percent of the increase in income.
    d. and saving increases by an equal amount.

2. If the marginal propensity to consume is 0.8, the marginal propensity to save
    a. is 0.2.
    b. is also 0.8.
    c. is 1/8.
    d. cannot be determined without more information.

3. If autonomous consumption were zero,
    a. the marginal propensity to consume would be 1.
    b. the marginal propensity to consume would be zero.
    c. the consumption schedule would lie entirely below the 45° reference line.
    d. saving would be less than zero for all income levels.

4. Using MPS to stand for the marginal propensity to save and MPC to stand for the marginal propensity to consume, we can write
    a. MPS = MPC.
    b. MPS = 1 - MPC.
    c. MPC = MPS - 1.
    d. MPS = 1/MPC.

5. Which of the following events would not produce a shift in the consumption schedule, other things being equal?
   a. An increase in consumer wealth.
   b. An increase in autonomous consumption.
   c. An increase in the number of consumers expecting hard times in the near future.
   d. An increase in nominal disposable income.

6. For purposes of introductory analysis, a once and for all change in the price level is assumed to have no effect on the nominal consumption schedule. Why is this true?
   a. Repeated empirical studies show no effect.
   b. The price level has no effect on any quantity defined in nominal terms.
   c. Such a change in the price level is likely to have both upward and downward effects that approximately cancel out.
   d. It is not true; some effect must always be assumed.

7. An increase in the rate of inflation, other things being equal, might
   a. trigger anticipatory buying by consumers, thus shifting the consumption schedule upward.
   b. cause consumers to worry that hard times were coming, thus shifting the consumption schedule downward.
   c. reduce the expected real rate of interest, if the nominal rate remained constant, thus stimulating planned investment.
   d. have any of the above results, but not necessarily all of them.

8. If the consumption schedule is drawn on a diagram having nominal national income on the horizontal axis, an increased lump sum tax
   a. will increase the slope of the consumption schedule.
   b. will decrease the slope of the consumption schedule.
   c. will cause an upward parallel shift in the consumption schedule.
   d. will cause a downward parallel shift in the consumption schedule.

9. Other things being equal, which of the following will cause a rightward shift in the planned investment schedule?
   a. A reduction in the nominal rate of interest.
   b. A reduction in the expected rate of inflation.
   c. An increase in the expected real rate of return.
   d. None of the above.

10. A firm calculates that installation of a computer billing system would produce an expected real rate of return of 6 percent per year. Under which of the following circumstances would it be worthwhile to undertake the investment?
    a. The nominal rate of interest is less than 6 percent and the expected rate of inflation is not less than zero.
    b. The expected rate of inflation is greater than 6 percent, regardless of the nominal rate of interest.
    c. It does not have to borrow but instead can use its own funds saved out of past profits.
    d. None of the above alternatives gives sufficient information to determine whether the project is worthwhile.

11. Government purchases are considered given for the purposes of elementary analysis because
    a. the government is immune to inflation.
    b. government purchases are usually stated in nominal terms.
    c. the government does not have to pay interest on funds it borrows from the public.
    d. even though government purchases may be indirectly affected by national income and interest rates, the effects are too complex to be easily analyzed.

12.   An increase in imports, other things being equal,
      a. adds to aggregate nominal demand.
      b. reduces aggregate nominal demand.
      c. increases the slope of the consumption schedule.
      d. does none of the above unless exports also change.

The following questions are based on the optional appendix to Chapter 8.

13.   When the payback period approach to capital budgeting is used, the projects
      that receive the highest priority are those that
      a. recapture their initial cost in the shortest period of time.
      b. have their greatest returns concentrated in early years.
      c. have their greatest returns concentrated in later years.
      d. continue to earn positive returns for the longest period.

14.   The present value of $100, payable two years in the future, discounted at
      a 10 percent rate of interest, is closest to
      a. $121.
      b. $110.
      c. $90.
      d. $81.

15.   The net present value approach to capital budgeting takes into account
      a. the time-distribution of returns within the payout period.
      b. any returns or costs that may occur beyond the end of the payout period.
      c. a, but not b.
      d. both a and b.

ANSWERS TO CHAPTER 8 SELF TEST

True or False

1-F; this view is still widely accepted.
2-T
3-F; change "save" to "spend."
4-T
5-F; it lies above.
6-T
7-F; the effect of a once and for all change in the price level could go either way and, for simplicity, can be assumed to be zero
8-T
9-T
10-T

Multiple Choice

1-a
2-a
3-c; the consumption schedule would pass through the original and have a slope less than 1.
4-b
5-d; this would produce a movement along the schedule.
6-c
7-d
8-d
9-c; a and b cause movements along the schedule
10-a; under these conditions, the expected real rate of interest must be less than 6 percent.
11-d
12-b
13-a; payback period analysis ignores the other factors.
14-d
15-d

CHAPTER NINE
THE MULTIPLIER THEORY
OF NATIONAL INCOME DETERMINATION

WHERE YOU'RE GOING

Here is what you will be able to do when you have mastered this chapter:

--Draw an aggregate nominal demand schedule for an economy given a consumption schedule and values for planned investment, government purchases, and net exports.

--Explain why the aggregate nominal supply schedule is always a 45° line passing through the origin.

--Determine the equilibrium level of nominal national income for the economy using either the Keynesian cross or the leakages-injections approach.

--Explain what is meant by the multiplier effect and calculate the value of the simple multiplier for a given aggregate nominal demand schedule.

CHAPTER SYNOPSIS

Reading this synopsis is not a substitute for reading the chapter, but it should help you to recall the main points. If there are any you feel unsure of, refer to the full discussion in the text.

The aggregate nominal demand schedule for an economy shows what the nominal level of total planned expenditure will be for each possible level of nominal national income. It is constructed by adding given values for investment, government purchases, and net exports to the consumption schedule. The aggregate nominal demand schedule thus has a slope equal to the marginal propensity to consume and a vertical intercept equal to the sum of autonomous consumption, planned investment, government purchases, and net exports.

The economy's aggregate nominal supply schedule shows the level of nominal national product associated with each level of nominal national income. Under the simplifying assumptions used in this text, nominal national product and nominal national income are equal by definition. The aggregate nominal supply schedule is thus a straight line equidistant from the horizontal and vertical axes, that is, a 45° line passing through the origin.

Drawing the aggregate nominal supply and demand schedules together on the same diagram forms a figure known as the Keynesian cross. The intersection of the two schedules that make up the Keynesian cross shows the level of nominal national income for which aggregate nominal supply and demand are equal. At that level of nominal national income, there is neither unplanned inventory accumulation nor depletion, and the circular flow is in equilibrium.

At any higher level of nominal national income, aggregate supply would exceed aggregate demand, leading to unplanned inventory accumulation and a falling level of nominal national income and product. At any lower level of nominal national income, aggregate demand would exceed aggregate supply, leading to unplanned inventory depletion and a rising level of nominal national income and product.

Alternatively, the equilibrium level of nominal national income can be determined by the intersection of the leakages and injections schedules. Whenever leakages exceed planned injections, there must be excess aggregate supply; and whenever planned injections exceed leakages, there must be excess aggregate demand.

The effects of changes in nominal national income on aggregate demand are represented by movements along the aggregate nominal demand schedule. The effects of other factors influencing aggregate nominal demand are represented by shifts in the aggregate nominal demand schedule. For example, a $100 increase in planned investment, government purchases, or net exports would be represented by a $100 upward shift in the aggregate nominal demand schedule; similarly, a $100 decrease in any of these items would be represented by a $100 downward shift.

As the aggregate nominal demand curve shifts, the equilibrium level of nominal national income changes. For example, with a marginal propensity to consume of 0.75, a $100 upward shift in the aggregate demand schedule induces a $400 increase in nominal national income. The ability of a given shift in aggregate demand to create a larger change in the equilibrium level of nominal national income is known as the multiplier effect. The ratio of the induced increase in national income to the original increase in planned expenditure is known as the simple multiplier. The formula for the value of the simple multiplier is

$$\text{Simple Multiplier} = 1/(1 - \text{MPC})$$

where MPC stands for the marginal propensity to consume.

WALKING TOUR

You have read the chapter at least once and have reviewed the synopsis. Now you are going to walk through the material step by step, filling in the blanks and answering the questions as you go along. After you have answered each question, check yourself by uncovering the answer given in the margin. If you do not understand why the answer given is the right one, refer back to the proper section of the text.

The Aggregate Demand and Supply Schedules

Exhibit S9.1 provides a space for you to construct a Keynesian cross diagram for a hypothetical economy similar but not identical to the one on which the numerical examples and diagrams

Exhibit S9.1

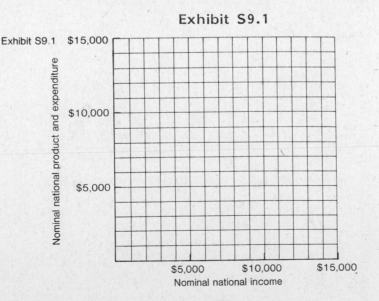

of the text are based. Begin by drawing in the aggregate nominal supply schedule. This schedule begins at _____ the origin and continues at an angle of _____.   45°

   Next construct the aggregate demand schedule. Assume a marginal propensity to consume of 0.5, autonomous consumption of $2,500 and net taxes of $1,000, planned investment of $1,000, government purchases of $1,500, and net exports of $500. The result should be a schedule that intersects the vertical axis at _____ and intersects the aggregate nom- $5,000 inal supply schedule at an equilibrium nominal national income of _____. $10,000

The Multiplier Effect

Beginning from the position now represented in Exhibit S9.1, any change in autonomous consumption, planned investment, government purchases, or net exports will produce a [shift in/ movement along] the aggregate nominal demand schedule. For   shift in example, suppose net exports were to fall from $500 to -$500. This would produce a(n) [upward/downward] shift of _____   downward; $1,000 in the aggregate nominal demand schedule. The new schedule (label it D_2) would intersect the vertical axis at _____ $4,000 and would intersect the aggregate nominal supply curve at an equilibrium nominal national income of _____. $8,000

   Comparing the new and old equilibria in Exhibit S9.1, you can see that a $1,000 decrease in aggregate nominal demand has produced a _____ decrease in equilibrium nominal $2,000 national income. It follows that the value of the multiplier for this economy is _____. This value could have been calculated   2 directly from the multiplier formula, which is:

Simple Multiplier = $1/(1 - \text{MPC})$.

Leakages-Injections Approach

Exhibit S9.2 provides a space in which to solve an income de-termination problem using the injections-leakages approach. Begin by drawing in a saving schedule, assuming autonomous consumption of $2,500 and a marginal propensity to consume of 0.5 as before. This schedule should be a straight line inter-secting the vertical axis at _____ and intersecting the   -$2,500 horizontal axis at _____. Next, adjust for net taxes $5,000 of $1,000 and imports of $1,000 to give a total leakages schedule.

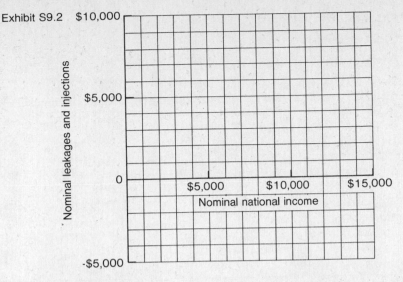

Exhibit S9.2

This schedule should intersect the vertical axis at _____ and the horizontal axis at _____.

-$1,000

$2,000

Now construct a planned injections schedule, assuming planned investment of $2,000, government purchases of $2,000, and exports of $1,000. This planned injections schedule should be a [horizontal/vertical/45°] line intersecting the vertical axis at _____.

horizontal

$5,000

The intersection of the leakages and injections schedules as drawn in Exhibit S9.2 shows the equilibrium level of nominal national income to be _____ under the assumptions used. At a nominal national income of $15,000, leakages would [exceed/fall short of] injections by _____. This would result in unplanned inventory [accumulation/depletion], which in turn would tend to cause national income to [rise/fall]. On the other hand, at a nominal national income of $10,000, leakages would [exceed/fall short of] injections, which would tend to cause nominal national income to [rise/fall] as inventories [grew/shrank].

$12,000

exceed; $1,500

accumulation

fall

fall short of

rise

shrank

SELF TEST

These sample test items will help you check how much you have learned. Answers and explanations can be found at the end of this chapter. Scoring yourself: One or two wrong -- on target. Three to five wrong -- passing, but you haven't mastered the chapter yet. Six or more wrong -- not good enough; start over and re-study the chapter.

71

True or False

Indicate whether each statement is true or false as it stands. If it is false, explain why in a few words.

T F 1. If exports are equal to imports, aggregate demand will be equal to consumption plus planned investment plus government purchases.

T F 2. The slope of the saving schedule must be equal to 1 minus the slope of the aggregate demand schedule.

T F 3. On the Keynesian cross diagram, equilibrium occurs at the intersection of the aggregate nominal supply and aggregate nominal demand schedules.

T F 4. At all points to the right of the intersection of the aggregate nominal supply and demand schedules, there will be unplanned inventory depletion.

T F 5. On the Keynesian cross diagram, there is excess aggregate demand whenever the aggregate nominal supply curve is below the aggregate nominal demand curve.

T F 6. If equilibrium nominal national income is $1,000 and the marginal propensity to consume is 0.75, there will be $25 unplanned inventory investment when nominal national income is $1,100.

T F 7. If imports exceed exports, the injections line must lie below the horizontal axis.

T F 8. If leakages equal planned injections, aggregate nominal supply must equal aggregate nominal demand.

T F 9. If the marginal propensity to consume is 0.8, the value of the simple multiplier will be 5.

T F 10. Other things being equal, a decrease in the expected real rate of interest will cause the aggregate nominal demand schedule to shift upward.

Multiple Choice

1. Which of the following would produce an upward shift in the aggregate nominal supply schedule?
   a. An increase in nominal GNP.
   b. An increase in real GNP
   c. An increase in the marginal propensity to consume.
   d. None of the above.

2. If the marginal propensity of consume of 0.75, and the aggregate nominal demand curve intersects the vertical axis at $500, where must it intersect the aggregate nominal supply curve?
   a. $500.
   b. $2,000.
   c. $2,500.
   d. Insufficient information is given for an answer to be reached.

3. When nominal national income exceeds its equilibrium value, there will be
   a. unplanned inventory depletion.
   b. unplanned inventory accumulation.
   c. a government budget deficit.
   d. a government budget surplus.

4. Whatever the actual level of nominal national income,
    a. the slope of the aggregate nominal demand curve must equal the slope of the leakages schedule.
    b. the gap between the aggregate nominal supply and demand curves must equal the gap between the injections and leakages schedules.
    c. injections must exceed leakages if aggregate nominal supply exceeds aggregate nominal demand.
    d. none of the above is true for all levels of nominal national income.

5. Other things being equal, an increase in imports will cause
    a. an increase in equilibrium nominal national income.
    b. a downward shift in the injections schedule.
    c. an upward shift in the leakages schedule.
    d. none of the above.

6. Beginning from an equilibrium position, an increase in planned investment expenditure would cause
    a. unplanned inventory depletion.
    b. an upward movement of prices, real output, or both.
    c. an upward shift in the injections schedule.
    d. all of the above.

7. If the marginal propensity to consume is 0.9, a $100 increase in planned investment expenditure, other things being equal, will cause an increase in equilibrium nominal national income of
    a. $90.
    b. $100.
    c. $900.
    d. $1,000.

8. If the marginal propensity to save is 0.4, the value of the simple multiplier will be
    a. 1.66.
    b. 2.5.
    c. 4.
    d. 6.

9. If the marginal propensity to save is equal to the marginal propensity to consume, the value of the simple multiplier must be
    a. zero.
    b. 1.
    c. 2.
    d. infinity.

10. If the simple multiplier is equal to 8 and if the aggregate nominal demand schedule intersects the vertical axis at $1,000, equilibrium nominal national income must be
    a. $800.
    b. $2,000.
    c. $8,000.
    d. none of the above.

11. If the marginal propensity to consume is 0.75, a $50 decrease in exports, other things being equal, would cause equilibrium nominal national income to
    a. increase by $50.
    b. decrease by $50.
    c. increase by $200.
    d. decrease by $200.

12.   If the equilibrium value of nominal national income is $2,000 and if unplanned inventory accumulation is $200 when nominal national income is $3,000, the value of the simple multiplier must be
a.   2.
b.   5.
c.   8.
d.   impossible to compute from the information given.

13.   Suppose that for some economy GNP = $2,000, consumption = $1,500, planned investment = $300, government purchases = $300, exports = $100, and imports = $200. It follows that
a.   the economy is in equilibrium.
b.   there must be unplanned inventory depletion.
c.   prices and/or real output will tend to rise.
d.   insufficient information is given for an answer to be reached.

14.   If an economy experiences unplanned inventory investment of $100 when nominal national income is $1,000 and if the marginal propensity to consume is 0.6, equilibrium nominal national income must be
a. $750.
b. $900
c. $1,100.
d. $1,250.

15.   If an economy is experiencing both inflation and rapid real economic growth,
a.   it must have too large a multiplier.
b.   government purchases must exceed planned investment.
c.   nominal national income must be growing.
d.   all of the above are true.

ANSWERS TO CHAPTER 9 SELF TEST

True or False

1-T
2-T
3-T
4-F; change "depletion" to "accumulation."
5-T
6-T
7-F; imports form part of the leakage, not the injection, schedule.
8-T
9-T
10-T

Multiple Choice

1-d; nothing can shift the aggregate nominal supply schedule.
2-b
3-b
4-b
5-c
6-d
7-d; the multiplier is 10 in this case.
8-b
9-c
10-c; the marginal propensity to consume would be 0.875.
11-d
12-b; the $200 excess aggregate supply represents the change in saving that occurred as income rose by $1,000. This implies a marginal propensity to save of 0.2 and a multiplier of 5.
13-a
14-a
15-c; a is a nonsense answer, b could be true but is not necessarily so.

CHAPTER TEN
FISCAL POLICY AND THE MULTIPLIER THEORY

WHERE YOU'RE GOING

Here is what you will be able to do when you have mastered this chapter:

--Use the Keynesian cross to determine the size of the contractionary or expansionary gap (if any) prevailing in the economy, given demand conditions and an income target.

--Calculate the size and direction of change in government purchases or net taxes required to fill any given contractionary or expansionary gap.

--Calculate the simple multiplier, the net tax multiplier, and the balanced budget multiplier corresponding to any given marginal propensity to consume.

--Explain the difference between discretionary fiscal policy and automatic stabilizers.

--Critically evaluate arguments concerning the burden of the national debt.

In addition, after mastering the appendix to this chapter, you will be able to:

--Express the multiplier theory of national income determination in algebraic form.

--Use the algebraic form of the theory to calculate the fiscal policy measures required to achieve given policy objectives.

CHAPTER SYNOPSIS

Reading this synopsis is not a substitute for reading the chapter, but it should help you to recall the main points. If there are any you feel unsure of, refer to the full discussion in the text.

The manipulation of aggregate nominal demand through changes in government purchases or net taxes is known as fiscal policy. By inducing changes in the equilibrium level of nominal national income--changes which may take the form of changes in real output, prices, or both--fiscal policy affects the performance of the economy in terms of employment, price stability, and economic growth.

The first step in using fiscal policy is to determine a target level of nominal national income that is judged best to serve the goals of stabilization policy. Once this income target is known, the target and equilibrium levels of nominal national income are compared. A contractionary gap is said to exist if the equilibrium level of nominal national income is below the target level; an expansionary gap is said to exist if the equilibrium level is above the target level. Graphically, the contraction-ary or expansionary gap is measured as the vertical distance between the aggregate nominal demand and supply curves at the target level of nominal national income. This gap represents the rate of unplanned inventory accumulation or depletion at the target income level under prevailing demand conditions.

A contractionary gap can be filled by means of an increase in government purchases; an expansionary gap can be eliminated by a decrease in government purchases. In either case, when government purchases are changed while taxes, planned investment, net exports, and the consumption schedule remain unchanged, equilibrium nominal national income changes--in the same direction as the change in government purchases--by an amount equal to the change in government purchases times the simple multiplier.

Alternatively, changes in the equilibrium level of nominal national income can be brought about by changes in net taxes. (The change in net taxes can take the form of either a change in taxes paid to government or a change in transfer payments made by government.) Dollar for dollar, a change in net taxes has a smaller effect on the equilibrium level of national income than a change in government purchases, because each one-dollar change in net taxes shifts the aggregate demand curve by only one dollar times the marginal propensity to consume. The formula for the net tax multiplier is -MPC/MPS, where MPC stands for the marginal propensity to consume and MPS for the marginal propensity to save. The net tax multiplier is negative because aggregate demand changes in the direction opposite to the change in net taxes; a tax increase cuts aggregate demand, and a tax reduction increases aggregate demand.

A one-dollar change in government purchases accompanied by a one-dollar change (in the same direction) in net taxes will cause equilibrium nominal national income to change in the same direction by one dollar. The balanced budget multiplier is thus said to have a value of 1.

Changes in government purchases or net taxes undertaken purposely in order to manipulate aggregate demand are known as discretionary fiscal policies. In addition, some fiscal policy actions take place automatically when the level of nominal national income changes; for example, an increase in nominal national income automatically increases the amount of income tax paid. Because these automatic changes in fiscal policy tend to have a contractionary effect when the economy is expanding and an expansionary effect when it is contracting, they are known as automatic stabilizers.

Because the federal budget is in deficit more often than it is in surplus, the total national debt has tended to grow over time. The effects of the growth of the national debt are a subject of considerable debate. Some economists minimize the possible adverse impact of the growing national debt by pointing out that it is smaller than it used to be in proportion to the economy and that it is in any event a debt that U.S. citizens owe largely to other U.S. citizens. These economists judge the national debt not to be a serious burden on future generations. Others are more concerned about the size of the debt, pointing to a reversal of the trend of its growth relative to the economy and to the fact that an increasing portion of the debt is owed to foreign countries.

WALKING TOUR

You have read the chapter at least once and have reviewed the synopsis. Now you are going to walk through the material step by step, filling in the blanks and answering the questions as you go along. After you have answered each question, check yourself by uncovering the answer given in the margin. If you do not understand why the answer given is the correct one, refer back to the proper section of the text.

Fiscal Policy in Action

Fiscal policy begins with the specification of a nominal income

target thought best to serve the policy goals of full employ-

ment, price stability, and economic growth. Suppose that

for the economy represented in Exhibit S10.1, the income

Exhibit S10.1

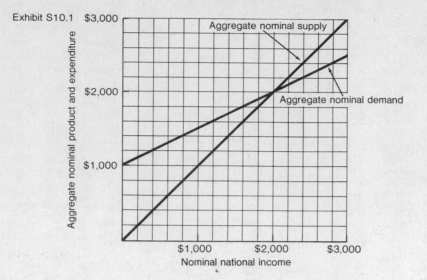

target is $1,000. This target is [above/below] the equilibrium
level of nominal national income, which is _____ as the
figure is drawn. There is thus a(n) [expansionary/contraction-
ary] gap of _____ that must be overcome. Unless some
action is taken to eliminate the expansionary gap, unplanned
inventory [buildup/rundown] will occur at the target income,
preventing equilibrium from being achieved there. This unplanned inventory rundown implies that injections would [exceed/
fall short of] leakages at the target nominal income.

     One fiscal policy action that could be used to eliminate
the expansionary gap in question would be to [increase/decrease]
government purchases by _____. Given the simple multiplier of _____ implied by the aggregate demand schedule in
Exhibit S10.1, this policy action would produce a _____
decrease in equilibrium nominal national income, moving the
equilibrium to the target level of income.

     Alternatively, the desired policy objective could be
achieved by [raising/lowering] net taxes. For the economy
shown in Exhibit S10.1, the net tax multiplier is _____,
indicating that a _____ increase in taxes would be required to move equilibrium national income to the target level.
Alternatively, the same thing could be accomplished with a
$500 increase in taxes and a _____ [increase/cut] in trans-
fer payments.

     Exhibit S10.2 presents another fiscal policy problem.
The figure shows an economy with a marginal propensity to

below
$2,000

expansionary; $500

rundown

exceed

decrease
$500
2
$1,000

raising
−1
$1,000

$500; cut

78

Exhibit S10.2

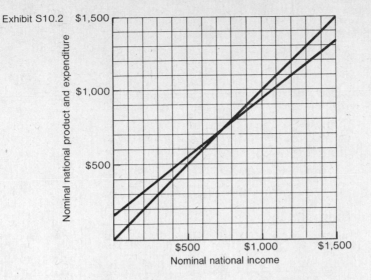

Exhibit S10.2

consume of _____, a simple multiplier of _____, and an   0.8; 5
equilibrium nominal national income of _____ under the $700
demand conditions shown.

     Suppose now that policy makers set $1,200 as their
nominal income target. Under the demand conditions shown,
there is an [expansionary/contractionary] gap of _____   contractionary; $100
at the target level of nominal national income. One fiscal
policy action that could fill the contractionary gap would be a
_____ [increase/decrease] in government purchases. Al- $100; increase
ternatively, a tax [decrease/increase] of _____ would do   decrease; $125
the job. Finally, an increase of $25 in social security pay-
ments to retired workers together with an _____ increase $80
in highway construction would put income at the target level.

     Exhibit S10.2 is drawn on the assumption of no auto-
matic stabilizers. Suppose, however, that the assumed lump
sum taxes were replaced by an income tax that took twenty
cents of each dollar of added income for all taxpayers. For
each one-dollar increase in national income, then disposable
income would increase by _____ and consumption by _____.   eighty cents;
With such an income tax in effect, the increase in government   sixty-four cents
purchases required to raise the equilibrium level of nominal
national income by any given amount would be [increased/
reduced].   increased

Appendix: Algebraic Approach to Fiscal Policy (Optional)

Problem S1: Let autonomous consumption (a) be $200, lump
sum net taxes (T) be $125, planned investment (I) be $150,

government purchases (G) be $75, net exports (X − M) be $25, and the marginal propensity to consume (b) be 0.8. What is the equilibrium level of nominal national income?

Solution: The equilibrium value of nominal national income is given by the formula

$$Y* = [1/(1-b)](a - bT + I + G + X - M).$$

Substituting the given values into this formula gives

$$Y* = \underline{\hspace{2cm}}.$$ $1,750

Problem S2: Using the solution to problem S1 as a starting point, find how large a tax cut would be required to achieve a target level of nominal national income of $2,000.

Solution: Replace Y* in the equation given above with the target value of 2,000. Then solve for T. The required value of T is _____, indicating that net taxes must be cut $62.50 in half from their initial level of $125.

SELF TEST

These sample test items will help you check how much you have learned. Answers and explanations can be found at the end of this chapter. Scoring yourself: One or two wrong -- on target. Three to five wrong -- passing, but you haven't mastered the chapter yet. Six or more wrong -- not good enough; start over and restudy the chapter.

True or False

Indicate whether each statement is true or false as it stands. If it is false, explain why in a few words.

T F   1.   Fiscal policy affects aggregate nominal demand directly but affects real output and employment only indirectly.

T F   2.   The first step in applying fiscal policy is to calculate the target level of nominal national income that corresponds to an officially measured unemployment rate of zero.

T F   3.   A contractionary gap is said to exist if the target level of nominal national income exceeds its equilibrium level.

T F   4.   An expansionary or contractionary gap is measured by the amount of unplanned inventory investment (if any) that would take place at the target level of nominal national income.

T F   5.   If injections exceed leakages at the target level of nominal national income, there is a contractionary gap.

T F   6.   If equilibrium nominal national income is $800, the income target is $1,000, and the marginal propensity to consume is 0.8, there is a $40 contractionary gap.

T F 7. A $100 increase in government purchases accompanied by a $100 tax increase would have no effect on equilibrium nominal national income.

T F 8. The net tax multiplier is always equal to the simple multiplier minus 1, regardless of the value of the marginal propensity to consume.

T F 9. A $100 increase in government purchases accompanied by a $100 increase in transfer payments would cause a $100 increase in equilibrium nominal national income, regardless of the value of the marginal propensity to consume.

T F 10. One-time worries about the burden of the national debt have eased in recent years as the proportion of the debt held by foreigners has fallen.

Multiple Choice

1. If the target level of nominal national income is $2,000, the equilibrium level of nominal national income is $2,500, and the marginal propensity to consume is 0.5, there is an expansionary gap of
    a. $500.
    b. $250.
    c. $125.
    d. none of the above.

2. If an expansionary gap were eliminated entirely through a fall in the equilibrium price level, with no change in equilibrium real output, policy makers would be
    a. delighted.
    b. disappointed.
    c. neither; the gap could not possibly be eliminated without a change in real output.
    d. neither; if real output did not change, prices would have to rise to eliminate an expansionary gap.

3. If the equilibrium level of nominal national income is $1,600, the target level of nominal national income is $2,000, and the marginal propensity to consume is 0.75, how large an increase in government purchases would be required to eliminate the contractionary gap?
    a. $75.
    b. $100.
    c. $400.
    d. None of the above; there is an expansionary gap.

4. If the target level of nominal national income exceeds the equilibrium level by $1,000 and the marginal propensity to consume is 0.8, which of the following changes in net taxes would eliminate the gap?
    a. A $200 cut.
    b. A $250 cut.
    c. A $200 increase.
    d. A $250 increase.

5. If the marginal propensity to consume is 0.9, the value of the net tax multiplier must be
    a. -1.
    b. -3.
    c. -9.
    d. -10.

6. The balanced budget multiplier has a value of 1. Why?
   a. Government purchases policy has a stronger first-round effect than net tax policy.
   b. Government purchases policy operates with a higher marginal propensity to consume than net tax policy.
   c. The U.S. constitution makes it impossible for the government to raise spending without also raising taxes.
   d. The statement is not necessarily true; the balanced budget multiplier is equal to 1 only in the special case where the marginal propensity to consume is 0.75.

7. Which of the following would act as an automatic stabilizer?
   a. A progressive income tax.
   b. A law that automatically increases unemployment benefits when the unemployment rate rises above 6 percent.
   c. A tendency for imports, but not exports, to increase when nominal national income increases.
   d. All of the above.

8. Which of the following would make it easier for the president to pursue discretionary fiscal policy?
   a. A constitutional amendment requiring a year-by-year balanced budget.
   b. A law permitting the president to order temporary tax cuts without prior approval by Congress.
   c. A law that would institute an investment tax credit in any year that the real rate of economic growth dropped below 3 percent.
   d. None of the above.

9. Which of the following best characterizes postwar U.S. federal budgetary experience?
   a. A roughly equal number of deficit and surplus years.
   b. An unbroken string of budget deficits.
   c. Deficits that have been more frequent and larger, on the average, than surpluses.
   d. Surpluses are more frequent, but on the average smaller, than deficits.

10. Which of the following characterizes the U.S. national debt at the end of the 1970s?
    a. Smaller in relation to GNP than in the 1950s.
    b. Owed increasingly to foreigners.
    c. Still a subject of debate among economists.
    d. All of the above.

11. The federal government is in a better position to pay its debts than are state and local governments. Why?
    a. Federal taxes, unlike state and local taxes, have no adverse incentive effects.
    b. The federal government, unlike state and local governments, can pay its debts with newly created money.
    c. The federal government, unlike state and local governments, does not have to pay interest on its debts.
    d. The statement is not true; the federal government has already, in some instances, been forced to default on its debts.

The remaining questions in this section can be solved either graphically or by use of the algebraic approach described in the optional appendix to Chapter 10.

12. Let autonomous consumption equal 200; net taxes, 200; planned investment, 150; government purchases, 100; net exports, 0; and the marginal propensity to consume, 0.8. The equilibrium value of nominal national income is then
   a. 290.
   b. 1,250.
   c. 1,450.
   d. none of the above.

13. Let autonomous consumption equal 400; net taxes, 200; planned investment, 500; exports, 100; imports, 200; and the marginal propensity to consume, 0.5. To achieve a target level of nominal national income of 2,000, government purchases must equal
   a. 100.
   b. 150.
   c. 300.
   d. none of the above.

14. Let autonomous consumption equal 500; planned investment, 250; government purchases, 400; net exports, 100; and the marginal propensity to consume, 0.75. In order to achieve an income target of 4,400, net taxes must be set at
   a. 150.
   b. 200.
   c. 400.
   d. 600.

15. Let autonomous consumption equal 1,000; planned investment, 500; net exports, 0; and the marginal propensity to consume, 0.8. In order to achieve a target income of 8,000 and at the same time balance the government budget, what must both net taxes and government purchases be?
   a. 100.
   b. 500.
   c. There is no unique solution to the problem.
   d. Insufficient information is given to calculate the solution.

ANSWERS TO CHAPTER 10 SELF TEST

True or False

1-T
2-F; zero measured unemployment is impossible, and the target income may also take inflation and growth into account.
3-T
4-T
5-F; there is an expansionary gap.
6-T
7-F; income would increase by $100.
8-T
9-F; change "transfer payments" to "net taxes."
10-F; the proportion held by foreigners has increased, and so have the worries.

Multiple Choice

1-b
2-a
3-b
4-b
5-c
6-a
7-d
8-b
9-c
10-d
11-b
12-c
13-c
14-b
15-b; set G = T, solve for one unknown, or calculate equilibrium = 7,500 with G = T = 0, then apply balanced budget multiplier.

CHAPTER ELEVEN
COMMERCIAL BANKS
AND OTHER FINANCIAL INTERMEDIARIES

WHERE YOU'RE GOING

Here is what you will be able to do when you have mastered this chapter:

--List the main types of financial intermediaries and explain their position in the economy in terms of the circular flow.

--Read the balance sheet of a commercial bank or other financial intermediary and explain the meaning of the major entries on the balance sheet.

--Briefly describe the structure of the Federal Reserve System.

--Discuss the nature and functions of the major types of thrift institutions.

--Explain the functions of the insurance industry as supplier of protection against risk and as financial intermediary.

--Distinguish between primary and secondary securities markets and explain the functions served by each.

--Explain the meaning and significance of the following additional terms and concepts:

> Assets.
> Liabilities.
> Net worth.
> Demand deposits.
> Savings deposits.
> Disintermediation.

CHAPTER SYNOPSIS

Reading this synopsis is not a substitute for reading the chapter, but it should help you to recall the main points. If there are any you feel unsure of, refer to the full discussion in the text.

Financial intermediaries are institutions, including commercial banks, savings and loan associations, insurance companies, securities markets, and others, that channel funds from savers to investors. As such, they serve to match the varying needs of potential lenders and potential borrowers in terms of quantity of funds, time horizons, and attitudes toward risk.

Commercial banks are the most familiar financial intermediaries. Commercial banks accept deposits from the public. These deposits appear on their balance sheets as liabilities. Demand deposits are those from which depositors can withdraw by check; they are commonly known as checking accounts. Savings deposits are interest-bearing deposits from which the depositor can make withdrawals at any time upon presentation of a passbook. Time deposits pay higher interest rates than savings deposits but can be withdrawn without penalty only after a fixed period of time ranging from ninety days to ten years. Commercial banks use the funds received on deposit to acquire income-earning assets by extending loans and buying securities.

Banking regulations also require banks to hold a certain portion of their assets in the form of non-interest-bearing reserves.

The central banking system of the United States is the Federal Reserve System (Fed, for short), established in 1913. The Fed provides banking services to the federal government and member commercial banks. It also regulates activities of commercial banks in a number of respects. The Fed's regulatory authority gives it the important power of controlling the total quantity of money in circulation. That part of the Fed's functions forms the subject of Chapter 12.

Thrift institutions include savings and loan associations, mutual savings banks, and credit unions. Like commercial banks, they accept savings and time deposits from the public, but they do not accept demand deposits. (In 1979 legislation was introduced in Congress which would lessen the gap between commercial banks and thrift institutions in this respect, however.) The assets of savings and loan associations and mutual savings banks consist almost entirely of mortgage loans. (Credit unions make small consumer loans to their members.) Thrift institutions are a very important source of mortgage funds for home construction. If, as sometimes happens, large numbers of depositors withdraw their funds from thrift institutions in search of higher interest yields elsewhere--a phenomenon known as disintermediation--the construction industry can be hurt severely.

The insurance industry fills a dual economic role, selling protection against risk and at the same time acting as a major financial intermediary. They offer risk protection by spreading risk among a large number of policy holders. The lag from the time that premiums are collected until the time benefits are paid--especially long in the case of life insurance--provides insurance companies with a pool of funds that can be used to purchase income-earning assets such as corporate stocks and bonds and real estate.

The markets in which stocks, bonds, and other securities are bought and sold also function as financial intermediaries. Primary securities markets are those in which newly issued securities are sold; secondary markets are those in which previously issued securities are handled.

WALKING TOUR

You have read the chapter at least once and have reviewed the synopsis. Now you are going to walk through the material step by step, filling in the blanks and answering the questions as you go along. After you have answered each question, check yourself by uncovering the answer given in the margin. If you do not understand why the answer given is the right one, refer back to the proper section of the text.

Commercial Banks

A good way to understand the functions of a commercial bank

(or any other financial intermediary) is to look at its balance

sheet. The balance sheet of the Acme National Bank consists

of the following items, listed here in alphabetical order:

Demand deposits	$500
Loans	500
Miscellaneous assets	50
Reserves	150
Securities	300
Savings deposits	200
Time deposits	200

In the space that follows, put these entries in balance sheet form.

_____

_____

First divide the space into two columns. The left-hand column will contain all of the things to which the bank holds legal claim, that is, its _____. Label it accordingly. The right-hand column will contain financial claims against the bank, or _____, and also the difference between assets and liabilities, or _____.

      Now begin by filling in the assets column. The two items from which the bank earns the majority of its income are _____ and _____. Funds kept on deposit with the Federal Reserve and vault cash are included here under _____. Tangible assets such as the bank's buildings and office equipment are listed as _____. Total assets of the Acme bank thus come to _____.

      Moving to the right-hand side of the balance sheet, begin by listing checking accounts, more exactly known as _____ deposits. Next come those deposits on which checks cannot be written but from which funds can be withdrawn at any time upon presentation of a passbook, that is, _____ deposits. These are followed by deposits that can be withdrawn without penalty only at the expiration of a predetermined period, that is, _____ deposits. Draw a line under this list of deposits and add them up, labeling the sum as <u>total liabilities</u>. On a line below this enter the bank's net worth, which in this case is _____. Note that assets equal liabilities plus net worth; this is the fundamental equality underlying your balance sheet, which is now complete.

The Federal Reserve System

The Federal Reserve System functions as the central bank of the United States. It consists of _____ district banks;

assets

liabilities
net worth

loans; securities

reserves
miscellaneous assets
$1,000

demand

savings

time

$100

twelve

87

the system as a whole is run by a board of governors located
in Washington, D.C. Approximately [40/75/98] percent of   40
all banks are members of the Federal Reserve System. These
member banks together account for about [40/75/98] percent of   75
total commercial bank assets. In addition, approximately
[40/75/98] percent of all banks are members of the Federal   98
Desposit Insurance Corporation, which insures depositors' funds
against bank failure.

Nonbank Financial Intermediaries

Savings and loan associations, mutual savings banks, and
credit unions, collectively known as _____ institutions,   thrift
also serve as financial intermediaries. Their balance sheets
differ from those of commercial banks in terms of both assets
and liabilities. Unlike commercial banks, thrift institutions
do not accept _____ deposits, although this restriction   demand
was under review by Congress as of 1979. The assets of
savings and loans and mutual savings banks consists mainly of
_____. Those of credit unions consist   home mortgages
largely of _____ to their own members.   consumer loans

     Insurance companies act as financial intermediaries and
also sell _____. The lag between the time   risk protection
premiums are paid in and the time claims are paid out gives
the companies a large pool of funds, which they use to acquire
such assets as _____, _____, and _____.   stocks; bonds;
                                                                 commercial mortgages

     The markets in which stocks and bonds are sold also
play a key role in channeling funds from savers to investors.
Sales of newly issued securities from firms to households and
other financial and nonfinancial firms through brokers and
underwriters take place in _____ securities markets.   primary
Markets like the New York Stock Exchange, where previously
issued securities are traded among asset holders, are known
as _____ securities markets.   secondary

SELF TEST

These sample test items will help you check how much you have learned. Answers
and explanations can be found at the end of this chapter. Scoring yourself: One
or two wrong -- on target. Three to five wrong -- passing, but you haven't mastered the chapter yet. Six or more wrong -- not good enough; start over and
restudy the chapter.

True or False

Indicate whether each statement is true or false as it stands. If it is false, explain why in a few words.

T F 1. A majority of commercial banks in the United States are members of the Fed, and the number is increasing.

T F 2. Demand deposits are a major asset of commercial banks.

T F 3. The Federal Reserve System was created by act of Congress in 1931 in an effort to end a wave of bank failures brought on by the Great Depression.

T F 4. Although the chairman of its board of governors is appointed by the president, the Fed is legally entitled to conduct its economic policy with considerable independence from the administrative branch.

T F 5. Reserves of member banks appear on the Fed's balance sheet as liabilities.

T F 6. Home mortgages are a major asset of thrift institutions.

T F 7. The term _disintermediation_ refers to the withdrawal of funds from thrift institutions in periods of unusually high nominal interest rates.

T F 8. Life insurance companies are the largest single source of funds for home mortgages in the United States today.

T F 9. Life insurance is not true insurance, because death is not a risk; it is a certainty.

T F 10. Secondary security markets make it easier to match the requirements of lenders and borrowers in terms of time horizons and attitude toward risk.

Multiple Choice

1. Government participates in financial markets
   a. always as a net borrower.
   b. always as a net lender.
   c. as a net lender only if there is a budget surplus.
   d. as a net lender only if there is a budget deficit.

2. If a bank has assets of $100 and liabilities of $80, its net worth is
   a. $20.
   b. -$20.
   c. $180.
   d. none of the above; by definition, assets must equal liabilities.

3. The most important protection that depositors have against loss because of bank failure is
   a. the requirement that banks hold cash reserves in their vaults at all times.
   b. that offered by the Federal Deposit Insurance Corporation.
   c. the fact that paper currency is a liability of the Federal Reserve.
   d. the fact that when a major bank fails, Congress usually passes emergency legislation reimbursing depositors.

4. Which of the following is not an important asset of commercial banks?
   a. Reserves.
   b. Loans.
   c. Securities.
   d. Demand deposits.

5. The type of bank account from which the depositor may withdraw funds at any time, without penalty, upon presentation of a passbook is known as a
   a. demand deposit.
   b. savings deposit.
   c. time deposit.
   d. certificate of deposit.

6. In its day-to-day operations, the Federal Reserve is legally subject to the authority of
   a. Congress.
   b. the president's Council of Economic Advisers.
   c. the Treasury Department.
   d. none of the above.

7. Membership in the Federal Reserve is held by
   a. all national banks.
   b. only national banks.
   c. all commercial banks.
   d. all commercial banks and thrift institutions.

8. Which of the following reforms would be most likely to attract greater membership in the Federal Reserve System?
   a. Permit member banks to use the Fed's teletype wires to transfer funds.
   b. Pay interest on reserve deposits held with the Fed.
   c. Permit large member banks to sell correspondent services to smaller member banks.
   d. Tighten Federal Reserve regulations regarding capital, mergers, and branches of member banks.

9. Which of the following declined during the 1970s?
   a. The percentage of banks holding membership in the Federal Reserve System.
   b. The percentage of all banking assets held by banks that were members of the Federal Reserve System.
   c. a, but not b.
   d. Both a and b.

10. In practice, the right of depositors to participate in management is not often important except in the case of
    a. commercial banks.
    b. savings and loan associations.
    c. credit unions.
    d. insurance companies.

11. Which of the following items would you not expect to find on the balance sheet of a savings and loan association?
    a. Demand deposits.
    b. Time deposits.
    c. Mortgage loans.
    d. Assets.

12. Which of the following reforms would be most likely to help prevent disinter-mediation?
    a. Lower ceilings on mortgage interest rates.
    b. Higher ceilings on mortgage interest rates.
    c. Lower ceilings on deposit interest rates.
    d. Higher ceilings on deposit interest rates.

13. If car owners had one chance in a hundred of having an accident in any given year and the average damage per accident was $5,000, a premium of $50 per car owner per year
    a. would not bring in enough money to pay claims.
    b. would not allow a margin for administrative costs.
    c. would, over time, generate a large pool of funds that could be used by the company to purchase commercial real estate, securities, and so on.
    d. would be too high to attract car owners to buy insurance from this company.

14. Insurance companies earn income in part by
    a. selling risk protection.
    b. buying corporate securities and commercial mortgages.
    c. selling annuities.
    d. all of the above.

15. Newly issued securities are sold for the first time through
    a. primary securities markets.
    b. secondary securities markets.
    c. either of the above.
    d. neither of the above.

ANSWERS TO CHAPTER 11 SELF TEST

True or False

1-F; a minority, and decreasing.
2-F; liability.
3-F; created in 1913.
4-T
5-T
6-T
7-T
8-F; thrift institutions are the largest.
9-F; it insures against premature death.
10-T

Multiple Choice

1-c
2-a
3-b
4-d
5-b
6-d
7-a
8-b
9-d
10-c
11-a
12-d
13-b
14-d
15-a

CHAPTER TWELVE
THE SUPPLY OF MONEY

WHERE YOU'RE GOING

Here is what you will be able to do when you have mastered this chapter:

--Define money in terms of the functions it performs and explain why money is the most liquid asset.

--Explain how M_1 and M_2 are traditionally measured and discuss the problems with these definitions that have led some economists to recommend new ways of measuring the quantity of money.

--Explain the relationship between credit cards and money.

--Trace the process of expansion or contraction of the money supply in response to a change in commercial bank reserves, using balance sheets for a simplified banking system.

--Calculate the money multiplier for a simplified banking system and explain why the money multiplier for the actual U.S. economy is subject to variation over time.

--List the three major instruments of Federal Reserve monetary policy and explain the operation of each in terms of a simplified banking system.

--Explain how the Fed can use the interest rate prevailing in the federal funds market as a day-to-day policy target.

--Describe the nature of the money growth targets set by the Fed and explain why the Fed does not always maintain actual money growth within the prescribed target ranges.

--Explain the meaning and significance of the following additional terms and concepts:

> Near money.
> Repurchase agreements.
> Required reserve ratio.
> Excess reserves.
> Open market operations.
> Discount rate.

CHAPTER SYNOPSIS

Reading this synopsis is not a substitute for reading the chapter, but it should help you to recall the main points. If there are any you feel unsure of, refer to the full discussion in the text.

Money is an asset that serves as a means of payment, a store of purchasing power, and a unit of account. Because money can be used directly as a means of payment without first having to be exchanged for anything else and because it never experiences a gain or loss in nominal value, it is said to be perfectly liquid. No other asset is as liquid as money.

Traditionally, just two kinds of assets have been viewed as sufficiently liquid to be counted as money: <u>currency</u> (coins and paper money) and <u>demand deposits</u> (checking account balances). The sum of these two forms of money is known as M_1. A commonly used broader measure of the quantity of money is M_2, which adds savings and time deposits to M_1. During the 1970s, however, a number of innovations in banking and finance began to call into question the continued usefulness of these long-established measures of the money supply. NOW accounts and other hybrid savings-checking accounts made savings accounts more liquid than they had been. Highly liquid <u>near monies</u> such as repurchase agreements and money market mutual funds increased in popularity. At the same time, time deposits, traditionally included in M_2, became less liquid as penalties for early withdrawal were strengthened. As a result of these developments, the Fed began to consider replacing the traditional M_1 and M_2 with new measures of the money stock, but no final decision on the new definitions had been reached by the end of 1979.

However money is defined, demand deposits at commercial banks will continue to be of central importance. Much can be learned about the way the real-world banking system operates by examining a simplified banking system in which demand deposits are the only form of money. In such a system, the quantity of money in existence is equal to the total quantity of commercial bank reserves divided by the <u>required reserves ratio</u>. New reserves injected into the banking system by the Fed become the basis for a multiple expansion of deposits as banks employ their excess reserves to make loans or purchase securities. If the Fed withdraws reserves from the banking system, demand deposits undergo a corresponding multiple contraction. The ratio of demand deposits to total reserves (equal in the simplified banking system to 1 over the required reserve ratio) is known as the <u>money multiplier</u>.

In the actual U.S. economy, the Federal Reserve has three major instruments of policy available for controlling the money supply. <u>Open market operations</u>--sales and purchases of government securities by the Fed--are the most frequently used. Changes in the <u>discount rate</u>--the rate charged by the Fed for reserves borrowed by member banks--are the second instrument. Changes in required reserve ratios are the third. However, these three policy instruments do not, in practice, give the Fed perfect control over the money supply. This is partly because the money multiplier for the U.S. economy is subject to significant variations over time. Until late 1970, the Fed's ability to control the money supply was also complicated by its use of the federal funds rate as a day-to-day guide for the conduct of open market operations. In late 1979, in an effort to gain better control over the growth of monetary aggregates, the Fed changed its operating procedures in such a way as to de-emphasize day-to-day control of the federal funds rate and to emphasize instead the growth of member bank reserves.

WALKING TOUR

<u>You have read the chapter at least once and have reviewed the synopsis. Now you are going to walk through the material step by step, filling in the blanks and answering the questions as you go along. After you have answered each question, check yourself by uncovering the answer given in the margin. If you do not understand why the answer given is the correct one, refer back to the proper section of the text.</u>

Money and Its Functions

Any asset that can be used directly as a means of payment

(or easily converted into a means of payment) and which runs

little or no risk of change in nominal value is termed <u>liquid</u>.

Using this definition, rank the following assets in order of
their liquidity (1 = most liquid):

Corporate stocks	5
Ninety-day certificate of deposit	4
Coins	1
Passbook savings deposit.	3
NOW account	2
Real Estate	6

Traditionally, the most widely used measure of the money
supply, consisting of currency plus demand deposits, is the
quantity known as _____. Adding savings and time deposits M_1
at commercial banks gives a broader measure of the money
supply known as _____. Many economists, however, think M_2
that changes in banking institutions and regulations may make
it necessary to change these definitions--for example, by including checking-type deposits at thrift institutions in _____ M_1
and excluding time deposits from _____. M_2

Creation of Money by the Banking System

One way to understand better how the banking system works
and how the Fed controls the supply of money is to look at a
simplified banking system in which demand deposits are the
only form of money and the only commercial bank liability.
Suppose that demand deposits are subject to a uniform 20
percent required reserve ratio and that initially all banks in
the system have balance sheets that look like this:

	Assets		Liabilities
Reserves	$20,000	Demand deposits	$100,000
Required	$20,000		
Excess	0		
Loans	50,000		
Securities	30,000		
Total assets	$100,000	Total liabilities	$100,000

Suppose now that the Fed makes an open market purchase of
$1,000 in government securities for the purpose of [increasing/
decreasing] reserves available to the banking system. The   increasing
seller of the securities is paid with a check drawn on the Fed;
when this check is deposited in the Littletown National Bank,

the effect will be to make its balance sheet, which initially looked like the one above, look like this:

	Assets		Liabilities	
Reserves	[1]_____	Demand deposits	[2]_____	
Required [3]_____				
Excess [4]_____				
Loans	50,000			
Securities	30,000			
Total assets	[5]_____	Total liabilities	[6]_____	

Answers: [1] $21,000; [2] $101,000; [3] $20,200; [4] $800; [5] $101,000; [6] $101,000

The Littletown National Bank could now increase its earnings by using its excess reserves to finance _____ in new loans or buy the equivalent in additional securities. Suppose that it chooses to make the loan and that the borrower writes a check for the amount of the proceeds, which is subsequently deposited in the Norrisville National Bank. After all of these transactions have taken place, total reserves at the Littletown National Bank will be _____, _____ of which will be required reserves, given the _____ in demand deposits. Assuming that the Norristown bank starts with the same initial balance sheet, its deposits will now be _____. Its total reserves will be _____, of which _____ will be required and _____ excess. That means that it can add earning assets of _____ in the form of loans or securities. As the process continues, more and more of the initial $1,000 in reserves injected into the banking system by the Fed will be converted into required reserves. When the money expansion process is complete, total demand deposits of all banks (and hence the total money supply) will have increased by _____. The value of the money multiplier for this simplified economy is thus seen to be _____.

$800

$20,200; all
$101,000

$100,800
$20,800; $20,160
$640
$640

$5,000

5

Instruments and Problems of Monetary Policy

In the example given above, the Fed was able to set in motion an expansion of the money supply by making an open market [purchase/sale]. Alternatively, it could have accomplished the same objective by [raising/lowering] the required reserve

purchase
lowering

96

ratio or by [raising/lowering] the discount rate.   lowering

Despite the variety of policy instruments available, the
Fed is not able to exercise perfect control over the money
supply. One reason is that as funds are shifted from one type
of account to another, from member to nonmember banks, or
from bank accounts to currency, the _____   money multiplier
varies. In addition, under operating procedures used until
1979, the Fed did not attempt to use the money supply or
total reserves as a day-to-day operating target but instead
focused on the _____. Use of the federal   federal funds rate
funds rate target permitted the Fed to offset variations in
reserves arising from forces beyond its control. For example,
a sudden drain in reserves from the system would make the
federal funds rate [rise/fall] as banks caught with deficient   rise
reserves tried to borrow from other banks. The Fed could
offset this with an open market [sale/purchase] that would   purchase
inject new reserves into the system, causing the federal funds
rate to return to its previous level.

However, according to some critics of the Fed, the federal
funds rate target worked less well when unexpected changes
in loan demand took place. An increase in the demand for
loans would cause member banks to try to borrow reserves to
finance those loans, thus [raising/lowering] the federal funds   raising
rate. If the Fed reacted by injecting new reserves in an
attempt to stabilize the rate, it could unintentionally allow the
money supply to increase faster than the target rate. In some
years, the growth rate of the money supply [exceeded/fell
short of] official Fed targets for several quarters in a row.   exceeded
The federal funds rate target may have been partly to blame.
In late 1979, the Fed moved to de-emphasize the federal funds
rate target.

SELF TEST

These sample test items will help you check how much you have learned. Answers
and explanations can be found at the end of this chapter. Scoring yourself: One
or two wrong -- on target. Three to five wrong -- passing, but you haven't mastered the chapter yet. Six or more wrong -- not good enough; start over and
restudy the chapter.

True or False

Indicate whether each statement is true or false as it stands. If it is false, explain why in a few words.

T F   1.   Money is said to be liquid because of its unique ability to serve as a store of purchasing power.

T F   2.   Inflation erodes the liquidity of currency as a form of money.

T F   3.   Serious consideration has been given to including NOW accounts as part of M_1 because they are a very close substitute for conventional demand deposits.

T F   4.   In a simplified system where all banks have uniform reserve requirements and demand deposits are the only form of money, the money multiplier is equal to 1 over the required reserve ratio.

T F   5.   In a simplified banking system, a bank receiving a $10,000 deposit will immediately find itself with $10,000 in additional excess reserves.

T F   6.   In a simplified banking system, the money multiplier tends to be smaller if banks use excess reserves to purchase securities rather than to extend new loans.

T F   7.   In the real world banking system, shifts of deposits from member to nonmember banks can cause the money multiplier to vary over time.

T F   8.   During the 1970s, the primary policy instrument used by the Fed in its day-to-day operations was control of the discount rate.

T F   9.   Although the Fed has consistently managed to keep the major monetary aggregates within their target growth rate ranges, critics complain that the ranges themselves are too broad.

T F   10.   In a major change of operating procedures, the Fed moved in 1979 to de-emphasize day-to-day control of the federal funds rate.

Multiple Choice

1.   Which of the following assets is least liquid?
   a. Coins
   b. Demand deposits.
   c. Time deposits.
   d. NOW accounts.

2.   If M_1 were redefined to include NOW accounts, ATS accounts, and money market mutual fund shares, the rate of growth of this monetary aggregate during the late 1970s would appear
   a. higher than under the old definition.
   b. lower than under the old definition.
   c. the same as under the old definition.
   d. to be zero.

3. In a simplified system where all banks are subject to a uniform 20 percent reserve requirement and where demand deposits are the only form of money, a $2,000 open market purchase by the Fed would cause the money supply to
    a. increase by $2,000.
    b. decrease by $2,000.
    c. increase by $10,000.
    d. decrease by $10,000.

4. In a simplified banking system where all banks are subject to uniform reserve requirements, where demand deposits are the only form of money, and where the initial quantity of money is $100 million, an increase in the required reserve ratio from 10 percent to 20 percent would cause the money supply to
    a. fall to $50 million.
    b. fall to $20 million.
    c. rise to $200 million.
    d. rise to $500 million.

5. In a simplified banking system where all banks are subject to a uniform reserve requirement of 20 percent and where demand deposits are the only form of money, a bank receiving a new deposit of $10,000 would be able to extend a maximum of what amount in new loans?
    a. $2,000.
    b. $8,000.
    c. $9,000.
    d. $10,000.

6. If a bank subject to a 10 percent required reserve ratio has $20,000 in excess reserves, it can purchase, at a maximum, which amount of new securities?
    a. $2,000.
    b. $18,000.
    c. $20,000.
    d. $200,000.

7. If Bank A is subject to a 10 percent required reserve ratio on demand deposits and Bank B is subject to a 20 percent required reserve ratio, a shift of funds from Bank A to Bank B would
    a. tend to cause the money supply to fall.
    b. tend to cause the money supply to rise.
    c. have no effect on the money supply.
    d. tend to cause a in the simplified system, b in the real world.

8. In the real world, the money multiplier (M_1 to total reserves multiplier)
    a. is pegged at a constant value by Federal Reserve policy.
    b. is influenced by Federal Reserve policy but is subject to significant variations because of factors beyond the Fed's control.
    c. must be accepted as given by the Fed.
    d. is highly predictable and has shown a steady upward trend over time.

9. The rate of interest charged by the Federal Reserve to member banks for reserves borrowed from the Fed is known as
    a. the federal funds rate.
    b. the discount rate.
    c. the repurchase rate.
    d. the Q-ceiling rate.

10. The Humphrey-Hawkins Act of 1978
   a. caused the Fed to reveal its money growth targets for the first time.
   b. made the Fed's money growth targets legally binding for the first time.
   c. prescribed specific penalties if the Fed undershot or overshot its announced money growth targets.
   d. did none of the above.

11. In the real-world banking system, a decision by depositors to withdraw funds from demand deposits and hold them in the form of currency would
   a. tend to cause M_1 to contract.
   b. tend to cause M_1 to expand.
   c. have no effect on M_1 because both demand deposits and currency are part of M_1.
   d. affect only M_2, not M_1.

12. Which of the following best describes the Fed's performance in relationship to its own money growth targets during the late 1970s?
   a. Occasionally missed growth target for a single quarter but never over a sustained period.
   b. Sometimes exceeded growth targets for M_1 or M_2 for as long as a year at a stretch.
   c. Never succeeded in meeting stated money growth targets.
   d. Never fell short of stated money growth targets.

13. In its October 6, 1979 reform the Fed
   a. pledged to control the federal funds rate more closely.
   b. de-emphasized the federal funds rate as a day-to-day guide to policy.
   c. pledged for the first time to adopt money growth targets consistent with the policy goals set forth in the annual report of the president's Council of Economic Advisers.
   d. did none of the above.

14. The events leading up to the Fed's October 1979 policy change included
   a. large quarter-to-quarter variations in money growth rates.
   b. criticism by economists outside the Fed.
   c. concern over the rate of inflation.
   d. all of the above.

15. Which of the following statements can be made about M_1 in recent years?
   a. It has generally grown faster than M_2.
   b. It has generally grown more slowly than M_2.
   c. It has generally decreased when M_2 has grown, and vice versa.
   d. None of the above is a valid generalization.

ANSWERS TO CHAPTER 12 SELF TEST

True or False

1-F; because of its use as a medium of exchange and because of its fixed nominal value.
2-F; erode purchasing power but not liquidity.
3-T
4-T
5-F; there will be some new required reserves.
6-F; no difference.
7-T
8-F; open market operations.
9-F; has not kept the aggregates within the ranges.
10-T

Multiple Choice

1-c
2-a
3-c
4-a
5-b
6-c
7-a
8-b
9-b
10-d; it changed only the manner of reporting the targets.
11-a
12-b
13-b
14-d
15-b

CHAPTER THIRTEEN
THE DEMAND FOR MONEY
AND THE MONEY MARKET

WHERE YOU'RE GOING

Here is what you will be able to do when you have mastered this chapter:

--Explain what is meant by portfolio balance using as examples both your own portfolio of financial assets, durable goods, and so on and the portfolio of a typical individual in a simplified economy where the only assets are money and bonds.

--Explain why the nominal rate of interest is the proper measure of the opportunity cost of holding money.

--Explain why a rise in the nominal interest rate is associated with a fall in the price of bonds, and a fall in the interest rate with a rise in the price of bonds.

--Explain a typical money demand schedule in tabular form, and explain--with reference to the transactions, precautionary, and speculative motives for holding money--why the demand for money varies directly with nominal income and inversely with the nominal interest rate.

--Explain why the income velocity of money tends to increase as the nominal rate of interest increases.

--Using money supply and money demand curves, trace the reactions to an excess supply or demand for money, and explain why only one nominal rate of interest is consistent with equilibrium in the money market.

--Using money supply and money demand curves, trace the effects of an increase or decrease in the quantity of money, assuming that nominal national income does not change.

--Using money supply and money demand curves, trace the effects of an increase or decrease in nominal national income, assuming that the money supply does not change.

CHAPTER SYNOPSIS

Reading this synopsis is not a substitute for reading the chapter, but it should help you to recall the main points. If there are any you feel unsure of, refer to the full discussion in the text.

The concept of portfolio balance refers to the process of making adjustments in the collection of assets one owns. Suppose, for example, that you suddenly won $10,000 in a lottery. You might first deposit the funds in your checking account, but you would probably not want to keep your portfolio so heavily biased in favor of money. Instead, you would probably buy some consumer goods, you might use all or part of the money as a downpayment on a house, and you might transfer some of your funds to an interest-bearing account of some kind. When you had made all of these adjustments to your satisfaction, you could consider your portfolio of assets to be balanced.

In the example just given, you would not necessarily use all of the $10,000 to acquire nonmonetary assets. There are a number of reasons why you might want to keep at least some of your new-found wealth in the form of money (that is, in your checking account or in cash). One reason for holding money--known as the transaction motive--is that money is useful as a means of payment. Another--known as the precautionary motive--is that money provides a reserve of purchasing power quickly available in unanticipated situations. A third--known as the speculative motive--is that holding money provides protection against possible capital loss if the nominal value of alternative assets is expected to fall.

The discussion of the demand for money can be simplified by imagining an economy in which there are just two assets--money and bonds. In such a world, the opportunity cost of holding money is measured by the nominal rate of interest that could be earned by holding bonds. The nominal rate of interest, it will be recalled, is equal to the expected real rate of interest (normally positive) plus the expected rate of inflation. In holding money rather than bonds, then, one foregoes both an expected real return and an expected protection from inflation.

Changes in the nominal rate of interest are associated with changes in the price of bonds. This is easily understood if one imagines a bond that pays interest of $100 per year over a long period. If the bond is priced at $1,000, this annual payment represents a 10 percent rate of interest; if the bond is priced at $2,000, the $100 annual payment represents only a 5 percent rate of interest, and so on. Looking at the matter another way, a person who wanted to earn at least a 10 percent rate of interest would pay up to, but not more than, $1,000 for a bond paying $100 per year; but if willing to settle for a 5 percent nominal rate of interest (perhaps because of a lower expected rate of inflation), the buyer would be willing to pay $2,000 for the same bond. However the matter is viewed, an increase in the nominal interest rate is associated with a decline in the price of bonds, and a decrease in the nominal interest rate with an increase in the price of bonds.

The quantity of money demanded in the simple two-asset economy depends on the level of nominal national income and on the nominal rate of interest. An increase in nominal national income increases the quantity of money demanded at any given interest rate because more money is wanted to carry out the increased volume of transactions. A higher nominal interest rate reduces the quantity of money demanded, for a given nominal income, partly because it raises the opportunity cost of holding money for transactions and precautionary purposes and partly because it depresses the price of bonds, thus making it less attractive to hold money in speculation of a further fall in the price of bonds. The money demand schedule can be represented graphically as a downward-sloping curve on a diagram with the nominal rate of interest on the vertical axis and the quantity of money on the horizontal axis. Such a money demand curve is shifted to the right by an increase in nominal national income and to the left by a decrease in nominal national income.

If the Fed is assumed to exercise control over the supply of money and not to allow the quantity of money to vary as the nominal interest rate varies, a money supply curve can be drawn as a vertical line. This money supply curve, together with the money demand curve, can be used to show that only one nominal rate of interest is compatible with money market equilibrium, given a value for nominal national income.

If the interest rate is above the equilibrium level, there will be an excess supply of money. People will attempt to exchange the excess money in their portfolios for bonds, in the process driving up the price of bonds and driving the rate of interest down to the equilibrium level. Similarly, if the nominal interest rate is below equilibrium, there will be an excess demand for money. Attempting to acquire more money for their portfolios, people will sell bonds, thus driving down the price of bonds and driving the interest rate up to the equilibrium level.

103

The money supply and demand curves can be used to determine the effects on the money market of a change in the supply of money, given a level of nominal national income. An increase in the money supply initially creates an excess supply of money, which in turn causes the nominal interest rate to fall to a new, lower equilibrium level, as described above. A decrease in the money supply results in a new, higher equilibrium nominal interest rate. The same supply and demand curves can be used to show the effects of a change in nominal national income for a given money supply. A higher nominal national income shifts the money demand curve to the right, raising the equilibrium nominal interest rate. A lower nominal national income shifts the money demand curve to the left, lowering the equilibrium nominal interest rate.

WALKING TOUR

You have read the chapter at least once and have reviewed the synopsis. Now you are going to walk through the material step by step, filling in the blanks and answering the questions as you go along. After you have answered each question, check yourself by uncovering the answer given in the margin. If you do not understand why the answer given is the correct one, refer back to the proper section of the text.

Portfolio Balance

The collection of assets of all kinds that a person owns is known as that person's _____. The demand for money can be usefully analyzed in terms of the attempts people make to keep their portfolios balanced among various assets.

portfolio

One reason people want to hold money in their portfolios is for use as a means of payment; this is known as the _____ motive for holding money. Another reason people want to hold money is to maintain liquidity in case unforeseen situations arise; this is known as the _____ motive. Finally, people sometimes want to hold money to avoid capital losses if they think the nominal value of other assets may fall; this is known as the _____ motive.

transactions

precautionary

speculative

Offsetting the advantages of holding money is the disadvantage that money, at least in the traditional forms of currency and demand deposits, pays no interest. The opportunity cost of holding money is thus the _____ rate of interest that could be earned on other assets.

nominal

Some aspects of the demand for money can be understood more clearly in an economy where there are only two assets, money and bonds. Because bondholders receive periodic payments that are fixed in _____ terms, an increase in the price of bonds is equivalent to a/an [increase/decrease]

nominal

decrease

in the nominal rate of interest, and vice versa.

In this simplified economy, other things being equal, an increase in nominal national income causes people to [increase/decrease] the quantity of money they want to hold in their portfolios, because of the _____ motive. Given the level of nominal income, an increase in the nominal rate of interest tends to [increase/decrease] the amount of money they want to hold, because it raises the opportunity cost of holding money. Thus, if a money demand schedule is drawn on a set of axes with the quantity of money on the horizontal axis and the nominal interest rate of the vertical axis, it has a [positive/negative] slope. Other things being equal, an increase in the nominal rate of interest causes a [shift in/movement along] such a money demand schedule. An increase in nominal income causes the schedule to shift to the [right/left], and a decrease in nominal income causes it to shift to the [right/left].

The relationship between money and income can also be expressed in terms of the concept of velocity. The income velocity of money is the ratio of _____ to _____. When nominal interest rates rise, velocity [rises/falls]; people economize on the use of money because its opportunity cost has risen.

The Money Market

The money market can be represented diagramatically by drawing a money supply and a money demand curve on the same diagram, as in Exhibit S13.1. The curves drawn there indicate an equilibrium nominal interest rate of _____ percent. At a lower nominal rate of interest, say 8 percent, the quantity of money people wanted to hold would _____ the quantity supplied by about _____. At this low interest rate, people would try to get the additional money they wanted by [buying/selling] bonds; this activity would drive the price of bonds [down/up] and drive the nominal interest rate [down/up]. Equilibrium would be restored. In the process, the total quantity of money [would/would not] change.

A diagram such as Exhibit S13.1 can be used to illustrate the effects of a change in monetary policy, assuming that

increase
transactions

decrease

negative

movement along

right
left

nominal income
quantity of money
rises

10

exceed
$40 million

selling
down
up
would not

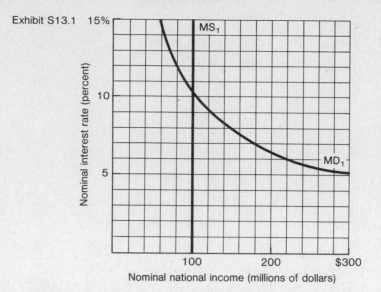

Exhibit S13.1

nominal national income remains constant. Draw in a new money
supply curve MS_2 representing a doubling of the money supply
to $200 million. The immediate effect of this policy action is to
cause an excess [supply/demand] of money. People will react   supply
by [buying/selling] bonds, thus causing the price of bonds to   buying
[rise/fall] and the nominal interest rate to [rise/fall]. Through-   rise; fall
out this process, the quantity of money will [rise/fall/not change]   not change
from its new level of $200 million. Equilibrium will be restored
when the interest rate has fallen to _____ percent, which   6
is low enough to make people willing to hold $200 million worth
of money in their portfolios.

  The same diagram can be used to trace the effects of a
change in nominal national income, assuming the quantity of
money remains unchanged. Draw a new money demand curve
MD_2 in Exhibit S13.1 corresponding to an increased level of
nominal national income. This new demand curve should lie to
the [right/left] of the old one. Assume that the money supply   right
remains at its new value of $200 million. The initial effect of
the increase in income will be to [increase/decrease] the trans-   increase
actions demand for money, thus causing an excess [supply/
demand]. People will react to this excess demand by [buying/   demand
selling] bonds in an attempt to get the money they want. This   selling
[will/will not] increase the total quantity of money available.   will not
It will, however, [increase/decrease] the price of bonds and   decrease
cause the nominal interest rate to [rise/fall]. The new equil-   rise
ibrium interest rate will thus be [above/below] 6 percent.   above

106

SELF TEST

These sample test items will help you check how much you have learned. Answers and explanations can be found at the end of this chapter. Scoring yourself: One or two wrong -- on target. Three to five wrong -- passing, but you haven't mastered the chapter yet. Six or more wrong -- not good enough; start over and restudy the chapter.

True or False

Indicate whether each statement is true or false as it stands. If it is false, explain why in a few words.

T F   1. Everyone can be thought of as holding a portfolio of assets even if they do not own any stocks, bonds, or other kinds of securities.

T F   2. Using the nominal rate of interest to measure the opportunity cost of holding money fails to take into account the effect of inflation on the real purchasing power of currency and demand deposits.

T F   3. Doubling the nominal interest rate will cut the price of a long-term bond approximately in half.

T F   4. As the money demand curve is usually drawn, an increase in the nominal interest rate, other things being equal, tends to shift the curve to the left.

T F   5. The income velocity of money tends to rise as the nominal interest rate rises.

T F   6. In a simple two-asset economy, people will react to an excess supply of money by buying bonds.

T F   7. When individuals sell bonds to try to increase the quantity of money in their own portfolios, the result is an increase in the quantity of money in the economy as a whole.

T F   8. An increase in the supply of money, other things being equal, tends to raise the equilibrium nominal interest rate.

T F   9. An increase in nominal national income, other things being equal, tends to lower the equilibrium interest rate.

T F   10. Other things being equal, a fall in nominal national income would tend to cause the price of bonds to fall.

Multiple Choice

1. People who deposit their monthly paychecks in their checking accounts and spend all or most of the money during the course of the month illustrate
    a. the transactions motive for holding money.
    b. the precautionary motive for holding money.
    c. the speculative motive for holding money.
    d. the unit-of-account motive for holding money.

2.   The speculative motive for holding money is likely to be at its strongest when
        a. bond prices are at historically low levels.
        b. bond prices are low but are expected to recover soon.
        c. the nominal interest rate is low but is expected to rise.
        d. the nominal interest rate is judged equally likely to rise or fall in the
            near future.

3.   The opportunity cost of holding money is best measured by
        a. the nominal rate of interest.
        b. the expected real rate of interest.
        c. the realized real rate of interest.
        d. the expected rate of inflation.

4.   If a currently issued long-term bond with an annual payment of $100 can be
        purchased now for $1,000, a bond issued last year having a $50 annual
        payment will have a current price closest to which of the following?
        a. $50.
        b. $500.
        c. $950.
        d. $2,000.

5.   The quantity of money that people want to hold in their portfolios can be
        expected
        a. to increase as the nominal interest rate increases and decrease as nominal
            national income increases.
        b. to decrease as the nominal interest rate increases and increase as nominal
            national income increases.
        c. to increase both as the nominal interest rate increases and as nominal
            national income increases.
        d. to decrease both as the nominal interest rate increases and as nominal
            national income increases.

6.   A graph illustrating the relationship between the quantity of money demanded
        and nominal national income, given a fixed nominal interest rate,
        a. would have a positive slope.
        b. would have a negative slope.
        c. would be perfectly horizontal.
        d. could not be drawn from the information given.

7.   If the money demand schedule is drawn in the usual way, with the nominal
        rate of interest on the vertical axis and the quantity of money on the horizon-
        tal axis, an increase in nominal national income will be represented graphically
        by
        a. a movement up along the money demand curve.
        b. a movement down along the money demand curve.
        c. a rightward shift in the money demand curve.
        d. a leftward shift in the money demand curve.

8.   Historical data indicate
        a. that the income velocity of money has risen over time.
        b. that the income velocity of money tends to increase as the nominal rate
            of interest increases, other things being equal.
        c. that the quantity of money demanded per dollar of nominal GNP has
            tended to fall over time.
        d. all of the above.

9. If velocity is measured as the ratio of nominal GNP to M_1, which of the following might explain, in part, the changes in velocity during the late 1970s?
   a. Increased use of currency for illegal transactions.
   b. Transfers of funds from demand deposits to NOW accounts.
   c. Transfers of funds from savings deposits to time deposits.
   d. A trend toward paying people monthly rather than weekly.

10. If the money multiplier tended to increase as the nominal interest rate increased (for example, because of a tendency of banks to reduce their excess reserves as the nominal interest rate increased), and if the Fed did not take action to offset this tendency, then the money supply curve
    a. would have to be drawn with a negative slope.
    b. would have to be drawn with a positive slope.
    c. would have to be drawn as a horizontal line.
    d. would be none of the above; it would still be a vertical line.

11. People tend to react to an excess demand for money by
    a. selling bonds, thus driving up the nominal interest rate.
    b. selling bonds, thus driving down the nominal interest rate.
    c. buying bonds, thus driving up the nominal interest rate.
    d. buying bonds, thus driving down the nominal interest rate.

12. If nominal national income increases, other things being equal, which of the following is not expected to be a consequence?
    a. A decline in bond prices.
    b. An increase in the nominal interest rate.
    c. An increase in the equilibrium quantity of money supplied.
    d. All of the above are normal consequences of an increase in the level of nominal national income.

13. Other things being equal, an open market sale of securities is likely to have which of the following consequences?
    a. A lower equilibrium price for bonds.
    b. A higher equilibrium nominal interest rate.
    c. Both of the above.
    d. None of the above.

14. If the Fed wanted to stabilize the nominal interest rate as nominal national income rose, it could
    a. expand the supply of money.
    b. contract the supply of money.
    c. raise the price of bonds.
    d. raise the velocity of money.

15. If nominal national income declined and the Fed took no offsetting monetary action,
    a. the nominal interest rate would tend to rise.
    b. the nominal interest rate would tend to fall.
    c. the money demand curve would shift to the right.
    d. none of the above would occur.

ANSWERS TO CHAPTER 13 SELF TEST

True or False

1-T
2-F; it takes inflation into account because expected inflation affects the nominal interest rate.
3-T
4-F; causes a movement to the left along the curve.
5-T
6-T
7-F; the supply of money does not change.
8-F; lower the nominal rate.
9-F; raise the nominal rate.
10-F; to rise.

Multiple Choice

1-a
2-c
3-a
4-b
5-b
6-a
7-c
8-d
9-b
10-b
11-a
12-c
13-c
14-a
15-b

CHAPTER FOURTEEN
THE INTERACTION OF MONEY AND THE MULTIPLIER

WHERE YOU'RE GOING

Here is what you will be able to do when you have mastered this chapter:

--Distinguish between partial equilibrium analysis and general equilibrium analysis.

--Identify the major channels of interaction between the money market and the circular flow of income and product (as represented by the Keynesian cross).

--Explain why there is one unique pair of equilibrium values for nominal national income and the nominal interest rate, under given conditions, in a general equilibrium framework.

--Explain the origin of the crowding out effect, and understand how this effect modifies the simple multiplier analysis of Chapters 9 and 10.

--Trace the effects of various types of monetary policy (including accommodating monetary policy) in a general equilibrium framework.

--List the main areas of disagreement between monetarist and Keynesian economists.

--Show in general terms, how the general equilibrium framework used in the early part of this chapter can be modified to take inflationary expectations into account.

--Explain the difference between the adaptive expectations and rational expectations hypotheses, as applied to financial markets.

In addition, after mastering the appendix to this chapter, you will be able to:

--State the general equilibrium model of nominal income determination in algebraic form.

--Use the algebraic form of the general equilibrium model to solve problems in monetary and fiscal policy.

CHAPTER SYNOPSIS

Reading this synopsis is not a substitute for reading the chapter, but it should help you to recall the main points. If there are any you feel unsure of, refer to the full discussion in the text.

A more complete analysis of national income determination than that given in earlier chapters requires making a transition from partial equilibrium analysis to general equilibrium analysis. The difference between the two lies in the role played by the "other things being equal" assumption. For example, Chapters 9 and 10 traced the effects on nominal national income of a change in fiscal policy, assuming that interest rates and planned investment did not change. That was an example of partial equilibrium analysis. The present chapter will use general equilibrium analysis to trace the effects of fiscal policy taking into account possible changes in interest rates and planned investment that result indirectly from the policy. That is an example of general equilibrium analysis.

There are two main channels of interaction between the circular flow of nominal income and product, as represented by the Keynesian cross, and the money market. One channel runs from the nominal interest rate, via the effect of the interest rate on planned investment, to the investment component of aggregate nominal demand. The other runs from the level of nominal national income, as determined by aggregate supply and demand, to the position of the money demand curve. In tracing these interactions, it is convenient to assume initially that no inflation is expected, so that the nominal interest rate and the expected real interest rate are equal.

The money market and the circular flow can be in equilibrium simultaneously only if a certain unique pair of values for the interest rate and nominal national income prevail. Let r represent the interest rate and Y the level of nominal national income. Then the level of r must be just right to induce the amount of planned investment needed to sustain Y, and Y must be just right to put the money demand curve in a position intersecting the money supply curve at r.

The general equilibrium framework just described can be used to trace the effects of fiscal policy as follows: Assume, for example, that government purchases are increased by $100. This initially shifts the aggregate nominal demand curve up by that amount. The excess aggregate demand causes inventories to be depleted, and in reaction, firms raise prices and/or output, setting off an expansion of nominal national income. As nominal national income begins to rise, the money demand curve starts to shift to the right, creating an excess demand for money. People try to obtain more money for their portfolios by selling bonds, thus driving up the rate of interest. As the interest rate rises, the quantity of planned investment falls in accordance with the planned investment schedule. The drop in planned investment partially offsets the initial increase in government purchases, so that the eventual upward shift in the aggregate nominal demand schedule is less than $100. Because of this crowding out effect of the increased government purchases, national income rises by less than the simple multiplier times the change in government purchases. Instead the increase in equilibrium nominal national income is equal to the simple multiplier times the change in total aggregate demand, taking both the change in government purchases and the reduction in planned investment into account. In the new equilibrium, both nominal national income and the nominal interest rate are higher than they were initially.

Sometimes fiscal and monetary policy are used in tandem to stimulate the growth of nominal national income. For example, when the government increases its purchases without raising taxes, the Treasury must sell bonds to finance the resulting deficit. The Fed can reduce the rate of interest the Treasury must pay on the bonds it sells by simultaneously conducting open market purchases, thus expanding the money supply. This type of coordination between the Fed and the Treasury is known as accommodating monetary policy.

There are a number of ongoing controversies among economists over the role of monetary and fiscal policy in determining nominal national income. One set of controversies matches the so-called monetarist economists against the Keynesians. Monetarists tend to consider the crowding out effect quite important and to consider monetary policy more powerful than fiscal policy as a determinant of nominal national income. Monetarists and Keynesians also disagree over the way the effects of monetary policy are transmitted from financial markets to the rest of the economy. Further aspects of the Keynesian-monetarist debate will be examined in later chapters.

Other controversies concern the effects of monetary policy in a world where, contrary to the earlier assumption of this chapter, inflation is not expected to be zero. The previous analysis can be altered to take expectations of inflation into account by inserting a wedge equal to the expected rate of inflation between the nominal rate of interest, shown on the vertical axis of the money market diagram, and the expected real rate of interest, shown on the vertical axis of the planned investment diagram.

But how is the expected rate of inflation itself determined? One hypothesis-- the adaptive expectations hypothesis--emphasizes the influence of the inflationary experience of the immediate past on the formation of inflationary expectations. Alternatively, the rational expectations hypothesis emphasizes the rational weighing of all available evidence about future inflation, including evidence about the probable effects of present and future economic policy. Whichever hypothesis is held, sustained and rapid monetary expansion, if sufficient to raise the rate of inflation in the economy, can have the eventual effect of raising, rather than lowering, the nominal rate of interest.

WALKING TOUR

You have read the chapter at least once and have reviewed the synopsis. Now you are going to walk through the material step by step, filling in the blanks and answering the questions as you go along. After you have answered each question, check yourself by uncovering the answer given in the margin. If you do not understand why the answer given is the right one, refer back to the proper section of the text.

The Interaction of Money and National Income

Exhibit S14.1 shows money supply and demand curves, a planned investment schedule, and aggregate nominal supply and demand curves for a hypothetical economy. As the figure is drawn, the economy is in equilibrium; the interest rate is

_____ percent, planned investment is _____, and nom-   8; $200
inal national income is _____. It can be shown that this $2,000
pair of equilibrium values is unique, given the assumptions
underlying the exhibit. Consider the possibility, for example,
that there might be another equilibrium with a lower level of
nominal national income. Sketch in a new aggregate nominal
demand curve that would give a lower equilibrium nominal
national income, and label it AND_2. AND_2 lies [above/below]   below
AND_1. The new level of nominal national income, in turn,
affects the money market; to be specific, it shifts the money
[demand/supply] curve to the [right/left]. Sketch in the   demand; left
approximate location of the new money demand curve, and
label it MD_2. The equilibrium interest rate implied by MD_2
is [higher/lower] than before. This new lower interest rate,   lower
in turn will cause planned investment to [increase/decrease].   increase
The effect on aggregate demand of this increased investment
will be to cause an [upward/downward] shift of the aggregate   upward

Exhibit S14.1

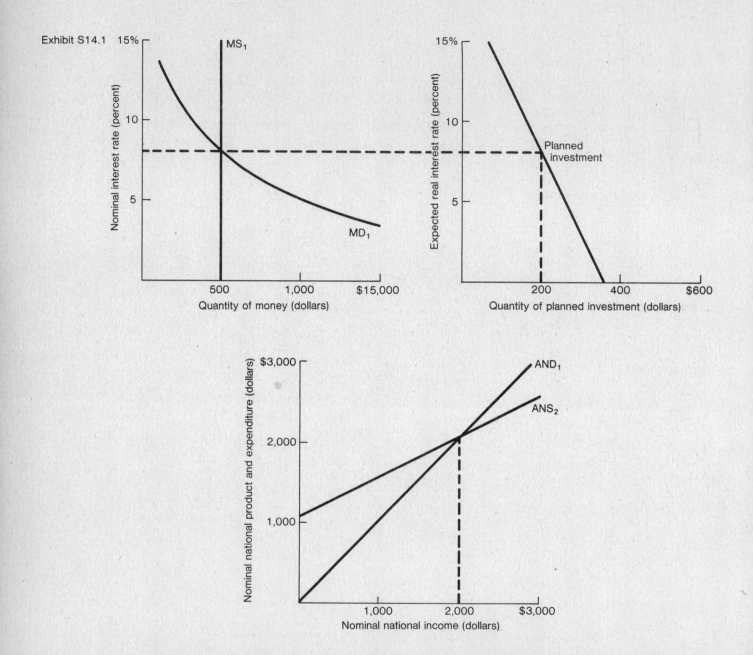

nominal demand curve from its initial position, AND_1. But this is not consistent with the initial assumption that the aggregate nominal demand curve shifted downward; the assumption of a pair of equilibrium values for national income and the interest rate other than $2,000 and 8 percent has thus led to a contradiction.

The general equilibrium framework developed in this chapter makes it necessary to revise the analysis of the effects of fiscal and monetary policy given in Chapter 10. (In tracing through the following examples, you may find it helpful to refer to Exhibit S14.1, sketching in new curves as appropriate. However, this type of diagram is not well suited to calculating exact numerical solutions to policy problems--if you want to be able to do that, study the algebraic version of the general equilibrium model given in the appendix to this chapter).

Problem 1: In the economy shown in Exhibit S14.1, the marginal propensity to consume is _____, making the net tax multiplier _____. According to the partial equilibrium analysis of Chapter 10, then, a $400 tax increase would [raise/lower] the equilibrium level of nominal national income by _____. Trace the effects of this policy action in a general equilibrium framework to determine whether the change would be larger or smaller than the partial equilibrium analysis predicts.

0.5

−1

lower
$400

Solution: The tax increase, other things being equal, would shift the aggregate nominal demand curve [upward/downward] by _____. This would cause nominal national income to begin to [expand/contract]. As this change in national income took place, the money [supply/demand] curve would shift to the [right/left], thus pushing the nominal interest rate [upward/downward]. Assuming no inflation is expected, this change in the nominal interest rate would induce a [shift in/ movement along] the planned investment schedule, and planned investment would [increase/decrease]. The change in planned investment would thus [limit/add to] the downward shift in the aggregate demand schedule that resulted from the tax increase. As a result, the eventual decrease in equilibrium nominal national income resulting from the tax increase would be [less/greater] than the $400 predicted by partial equilibrium analysis.

downward
$200
contract
demand
left
downward

movement along
increase
limit

less

Problem 2: The Federal Reserve makes an open market sale, thereby [increasing/decreasing] the money supply. What will be the effects of this policy on the nominal interest rate and on the equilibrium level of nominal national income?

decreasing

Solution: The decrease in the money supply shifts the money supply curve to the left, causing an excess [supply/demand] for money. In order to restore their portfolios to balance, people will begin [buying/selling] bonds. This will tend to [raise/depress] the price of bonds, and the nominal interest rate will [rise/fall]. Assuming zero expected inflation, this change in the nominal interest rate will cause planned investment to [increase/decrease]; this in turn will produce an [upward/downward] shift in the aggregate nominal demand schedule. Firms will react to the resulting unplanned inventory [accumulation/depletion] by [raising/lowering] output and/or prices. Nominal national income will thus fall. This in turn will cause a leftward [shift in/movement along] the money demand curve, cutting short the rise in the nominal interest rate. In the final equilibrium, the nominal interest rate will thus be somewhat [higher/lower] than before the change in the money supply, and nominal national income will be somewhat [higher/lower].

demand

selling
depress
rise

decrease
downward

accumulation;
lowering

shift in

higher

lower

Appendix: The Elementary Algebra of Money and Income

Problem 3: Let a = 100, b = 0.75, c = 200, d = -500, e = 80, f = 0.2, g = -400, G = 200, T = 100, MS = 400, and X = M. Calculate the equilibrium values of nominal national income and the interest rate given the initial data.

Solution: Begin by substituting the given values into Equations 14A.1 and 14A.5 from the text (page 249). This gives

$$MD = 80 + 0.2Y - 400r$$

for the money demand equation, and

$$AND = 425 + 0.75Y - 500r$$

for the aggregate nominal demand equation.

In equilibrium, money demand must equal money supply and aggregate nominal demand must equal nominal income. Substituting these equilibrium conditions (MD = MS and AND = Y) into the equations given above and setting them equal to zero gives these two equations:

$$320 - 0.2Y + 400r = 0.$$
$$-1,700 + Y + 2,000r = 0.$$

To solve for r, multiply the first equation by 5 and add

the two equations. This gives the single equation in one
unknown

$$-100 + 4{,}000r = 0,$$

which gives as its solution r = _____ .   0.025

   Using this result to solve one of the original equations
for Y gives the result Y = _____ .   1,650

SELF TEST

These sample test items will help you check how much you have learned. Answers
and explanations can be found at the end of this chapter. Scoring yourself: One
or two wrong -- on target. Three to five wrong -- passing, but you haven't mastered the chapter yet. Six or more wrong -- not good enough; start over and
restudy the chapter.

True or False

Indicate whether each statement is true or false as it stands. If it is false, explain
why in a few words.

T F   1.   General equilibrium analysis assumes that when one market adjusts to a
            new equilibrium, other markets also adjust to new equilibriums.

T F   2.   According to general equilibrium analysis, changes in government pur-
            chases cannot affect the equilibrium level of nominal national income, but
            only the equilibrium interest rate.

T F   3.   According to general equilibrium analysis, one result of a tax cut will
            be a new equilibrium level of planned investment somewhat lower than the
            initial level.

T F   4.   The crowding out effect refers to the tendency for saving to fall as
            nominal national income falls, thus partially eliminating one important
            source of funds for private investment.

T F   5.   General equilibrium analysis shows that a given change in the money
            supply will have a larger effect on the equilibrium nominal rate of interest
            than the effect predicted by a partial equilibrium analysis that assumed
            no change in nominal national income.

T F   6.   If government purchases are increased and the Fed pursues an accommo-
            dating monetary policy, nominal national income will change by more than
            if the Fed had held the money supply constant.

T F   7.   Monetarists criticize Keynesians for putting too much of the blame for the
            Great Depression on the Fed and the banking system.

T F   8.   Other things being equal, the steeper the money demand curve, the
            greater the impact on equilibrium nominal national income of any given
            change in the money supply.

T F   9.   Empirical resolution of the Keynesian-monetarist controversy has been ham-
            pered by the fact that fiscal and monetary authorities rarely coordinate
            their activities.

117

T F 10. The adaptive expectations hypothesis is based, in part, on the common-sense notion that people learn from experience.

Multiple Choice

1. A full understanding of the effects of monetary and fiscal policy requires general equilibrium analysis because
   a. the demand for money depends on the level of nominal national income.
   b. the level of planned investment depends, other things being equal, on the nominal interest rate.
   c. the level of aggregate nominal demand depends on the level of planned investment.
   d. all of the above are true.

2. In a general equilibrium framework, an increase in the money supply is likely to
   a. lower both the interest rate and nominal GNP.
   b. raise both the interest rate and nominal GNP.
   c. raise the interest rate and lower nominal GNP.
   d. lower the interest rate and raise nominal GNP.

3. If the marginal propensity to consume is 0.8 and the crowding out effect is taken into account, a $100 increase in government purchases would be most likely to have which of the following effects on equilibrium nominal GNP?
   a. An increase of more than $500.
   b. A $500 increase.
   c. An increase, but of less than $500.
   d. No change.

4. In a general equilibrium framework, which of the following would not be expected to increase planned investment expenditure?
   a. An increase in the money supply.
   b. An increase in net taxes.
   c. An increase in net exports.
   d. A cut in transfer payments.

5. If expected inflation is assumed to be zero, a government that wants to stimulate aggregate demand and at the same time keep interest rates low would be best advised to rely on
   a. monetary policy.
   b. government purchases policy.
   c. tax policy.
   d. any of the above; there is no difference in the effects of these policies.

6. In a general equilibrium framework, a $100 increase in government purchases financed by a $100 increase in taxes would have which of the following effects on nominal national income?
   a. A $100 increase.
   b. An increase, but of less than $100.
   c. An increase only with accommodating monetary policy.
   d. No effect.

7. According to general equilibrium analysis, an open market purchase by the Fed will cause a new equilibrium in which
   a. both the money supply and money demand curves shift to the left.
   b. the money supply, but not the money demand, curve shifts to the left.
   c. the money supply curve shifts to the left and the money demand curve shifts to the right.
   d. both the money supply curve and the money demand curve shift to the right.

8. An accommodating monetary policy could best be represented graphically by
   a. a horizontal money demand curve.
   b. a horizontal money supply curve.
   c. a horizontal planned investment schedule.
   d. a vertical planned investment schedule.

9. Monetarists tend to think
   a. that Federal Reserve policy played a substantial role in causing the Great Depression.
   b. that the effects of monetary policy are transmitted to the economy solely through the bond market.
   c. that planned investment is insensitive to changes in interest rates.
   d. that the crowding out effect can, in practice, be ignored.

10. Which of the following would be sufficient to eliminate the crowding out effect?
    a. A vertical planned investment schedule.
    b. A horizontal money demand curve.
    c. A horizontal money supply curve.
    d. Any one of the above would be sufficient.

11. According to the monetarists, which of the following might be part of the mechanism that transmits changes in monetary policy to the rest of the economy?
    a. Effects on bond prices.
    b. Effects on stock prices.
    c. Effects on purchases of consumer durables.
    d. All of the above.

12. If the nominal rate of interest is 10 percent and the expected rate of inflation is 6 percent, the rate of planned investment expenditure will be the same as if the expected rate of inflation were zero and the nominal rate of interest were
    a. 4 percent.
    b. 6 percent.
    c. 10 percent.
    d. 16 percent.

13. According to the rational expectations hypothesis, in forming their expectations about inflation, people will tend to look at
    a. the inflation rate in the previous year.
    b. the money growth targets announced by the Fed.
    c. the likely outcome of the next presidential election.
    d. all of the above.

14. In a general equilibrium framework in which expected inflation is taken into account, which of the following conclusions about monetary policy may not hold?
    a. Open market purchases will cause the money supply to grow.
    b. The long-run effect of a sustained increase in the rate of money growth will be a reduction in the nominal rate of interest.
    c. Sustained growth of the money supply will result in growth of nominal GNP.
    d. Part of any increase in nominal GNP that takes place in the long run may take the form of inflation rather than increase in real output.

15. If perfect inflation forecasting were possible, changes in the money supply might have no effect on
    a. the nominal rate of interest.
    b. the expected real rate of interest.
    c. the rate of growth of nominal GNP.
    d. the position of the money demand curve.

ANSWERS TO CHAPTER 14 SELF TEST

True or False

1-T
2-F; both are affected.
3-T
4-F; it refers to the tendency for rising nominal income to push up the interest rate, thus cutting investment demand.
5-F; the effect is smaller under general equilibrium analysis
6-T
7-F; monetarists blame the Fed more than Keynesians do
8-T
9-F; it has been hampered by the fact that they rarely work at cross purposes.
10-F; it says they do learn from experience.

Multiple Choice

1-d
2-d
3-c; not enough information is given to calculate the effect exactly, but it has to be greater than zero and less than the $500 predicted by the simple multiplier analysis.
4-c; an increase in exports would push up the AND curve, leading to a rise in interest rates.
5-a
6-b; the balanced budget multiplier would predict $100, but there will be some crowding out.
7-d
8-b; the Fed adjusts the money supply to whatever level is needed to keep interest rates constant
9-a
10-d
11-d
12-a
13-d
14-b
15-b

CHAPTER FIFTEEN
UNEMPLOYMENT AND INFLATION:
SOME TRADITIONAL ANSWERS

WHERE YOU'RE GOING

Here is what you will be able to do when you have mastered this chapter:

--Explain the quantity theory of prices and the assumptions on which the theory is based.

--Explain the crude Keynesian theory of inflation, using the Keynesian cross diagram.

--Sketch a Phillips curve, and explain why it is not possible to treat the Phillips curve as a fixed policy menu.

--Distinguish between cost-push and demand-pull inflation and between cost-push inflation and the cost-push illusion.

--Explain the meaning and significance of the following additional terms and concepts:

Hyperinflation.
Profit-push inflation.
Wage-push inflation.
Commodity inflation.

CHAPTER SYNOPSIS

Reading this synopsis is not a substitute for reading the chapter but it should help you to recall the main points. If there are any you feel unsure of, refer to the full discussion in the text.

This chapter begins a four-chapter section devoted to the question of how a given rate of growth of nominal national income is split up into effects on the price level, on the one hand, and effects on real output and employment, on the other. The chapter takes the form of a discussion of four traditional views of unemployment and inflation: the quantity theory, the crude Keynesian theory, the Phillips curve theory, and the cost-push theory.

The quantity theory begins with the concept of the income velocity of money-- the ratio of nominal GNP to the money supply. Using P to represent the price level, y to represent real income, M_1 to represent the money supply, and V to represent velocity, we can say that the following relationship must, by definition, always hold in the economy:

$$P = M_1 V / y.$$

If it is further assumed that velocity is at least approximately constant and that real income is determined entirely by nonmonetary factors such as population, technology, and resources, then the above equation can be interpreted as implying that the price level is proportional to the quantity of money. Any change in the quantity of money would, other things equal, thus lead to a proportional change in the price level.

The quantity theory of prices does appear to hold at least approximately for the case of hyperinflation--very rapid inflation. As a short-run forecasting tool, however, the quantity theory does not work so well. The reason is that neither velocity nor real income is independent of changes in the money supply, undermining the simplifying assumptions on which the theory is based.

A second theory of inflation, which can be called the crude Keynesian theory of inflation, is based on the idea that the price level remains stable as long as nominal income remains below some specified "full employment" level. Only after nominal income exceeds the full employment threshold does inflation begin. A major problem with the crude Keynesian theory is that it does not explain how high rates of inflation and unemployment can prevail simultaneously, as they have in several recent years.

A third theory of inflation--the Phillips curve theory--holds that there is a tradeoff between inflation and unemployment; as unemployment falls, inflation gradually accelerates, and as unemployment rises, inflation slows down. This theory received its inspiration from empirical studies carried out by A. W. H. Phillips, who showed such an unemployment-inflation tradeoff for Great Britain over a long period of time. Recent experience suggests, however, that the tradeoff is not a stable one in the long run; the Phillips curve is subject to shifts, and the shifts may, in part, be caused by policies designed to move the economy along the Phillips curve.

All of the three theories mentioned so far are called demand-pull theories of inflation, because they identify increases in aggregate nominal demand as the ultimate cause of increases in the price level. A fourth theory is the cost-push theory of inflation, which holds that price increases may sometimes be touched off by cost increases that are unrelated to increases in demand. There are several variants of the cost-push theory. The wage-push variant singles out increases in wages (usually the wages paid to members of powerful labor unions) as the spark that ignites inflation. Profit-push inflation is inflation touched off by an increase in profit margins unrelated to an increase in demand for the products in question. And commodity inflation begins with increases in the prices of basic commodities such as oil or wheat.

There is clearly some truth to the cost-push theory, just as there is to each of the other three. However, it is important, in practice, to distinguish between genuine cost-push inflation and the cost-push illusion, the latter referring to demand-pull inflation that masquerades as cost-push inflation because of the cushioning effect of inventories along the chain of distribution from producers to consumers.

WALKING TOUR

You have read the chapter at least once and have reviewed the synopsis. Now you are going to walk through the material step by step, filling in the blanks and answering the questions as you go along. After you have answered each question, check yourself by uncovering the answer given in the margin. If you do not understand why the answer given is the correct one, refer back to the proper section in the text.

The Quantity Theory

The quantity theory of prices assumes that _____   real income

and _____ are fixed; the price level thus   velocity

becomes proportional to the _____.   quantity of money

The theory has been observed to hold at least approximately

for episodes of very rapid inflation, exceeding, say, 100

percent per year. Such episodes, known as _____   hyperinflation are always accompanied by very large increases in the money supply.

In its simplest form, the quantity theory is not a very good tool for short-run inflation forecasting, because both velocity and real income are subject to significant variations. For example, in Chapter 13 it was shown that velocity tends to rise as _____ rises. Also, short-run changes in monetary and fiscal policy may affect real income as well as nominal income. Modern theories of inflation must take these variations into account.

nominal interest

The Crude Keynesian Theory

An early theory of inflation associated with Keynesian economics held that inflation is a problem only when the level of nominal national income is [above/below] the full employment level. Below that level, any change in nominal GNP will take the form of a change in [prices/real output]. The major shortcoming of the crude Keynesian theory is that it does not explain how high rates of inflation and unemployment can occur simultaneously.

above

real output

The Phillips Curve

In 1958, A. W. H. Phillips published the results of an empirical study that showed that the rate of increase of wages tended to [rise/fall] as the unemployment rate fell. The tradeoff appeared to have been stable over a long time period in Great Britain. At first, the Phillips curve appeared to offer a policy menu from which various combinations of inflation and unemployment could be chosen. However, if inflation-unemployment combinations for the 1970s are plotted on a graph along with a Phillips curve from the 1960s, the more recent points lie [above/below] the curve, rather than on it. This suggests that a more complete theory of inflation must explain why the position of the Phillips curve changes over time.

rise

above

The Cost-Push Theory

The cost-push theory of inflation attempts to explain why the price level sometimes rises when there is no apparent pressure from _____. Instead, the rise in the price level is touched off by some spontaneous

aggregate demand

increase in wage costs, profits, or prices of basic commodities.

Some inflationary episodes do appear to fit the cost-push theory. However, care must be taken in distinguishing cost-push inflation from the cost-push _____   illusion that occurs when inventory adjustments transmit demand-pull inflation along the chain of distribution from producer to consumer.

Some versions of the cost-push theory also appear to be based on a misapprehension of the effects of monopoly power. Microeconomic analysis suggests that, other things being equal, producers with monopoly power may charge relatively _____ prices, but gives no reason to   high believe they will charge steadily rising prices.

SELF TEST

These sample test items will help you check how much you have learned. Answers and explanations can be found at the end of this chapter. Scoring yourself: One or two wrong -- on target. Three to five wrong -- passing, but you haven't mastered the chapter yet. Six or more wrong -- not good enough; start over and restudy the chapter.

True or False

Indicate whether each statement is true or false as it stands. If it is false, explain why in a few words.

T F 1. The major goals of economic stabilization policy are price stability, full employment, and growth of nominal income.

T F 2. The percentage rate of change in nominal national income must always be equal to the percentage rate of change in real GNP plus the percentage rate of inflation.

T F 3. According to the quantity theory of prices, the price level tends to double each time the quantity of money is cut in half.

T F 4. During periods of hyperinflation, the rate of inflation would be even more rapid than the rate of increase in the money supply if real output declined or if velocity increased.

T F 5. According to the crude Keynesian theory of inflation, it is not possible to have high rates of inflation and unemployment at the same time.

T F 6. According to the crude Keynesian theory of inflation and assuming that the full employment and target levels of national income are equal, the price level would be most likely to rise when there was an expansionary gap in the economy.

T F 7. A. W. H. Phillips's original study concerned the relationship between unemployment and the rate of increase in the consumer price index in Great Britain.

T F 8. The cost-push theory of inflation is the only theory that can explain why, over time, unit labor costs and the price level tend to move together.

T F 9. The cost-push illusion refers to the fact that many unions appear to have more monopoly power than they actually have.

T F 10. Microeconomic theory establishes that monopolies are likely to charge prices that are not only high, but steadily rising.

Multiple Choice

1. If nominal national income is growing at a rate of 10 percent and the rate of inflation is 7 percent, the rate of growth of real output must be
   a. -3 percent.
   b. 3 percent.
   c. 10 percent.
   d. 13 percent.

2. If V stands for velocity, M_1 for money, and Y for nominal income, the correct formula for velocity is
   a. $V = Y/M_1$.
   b. $V = M_1/Y$.
   c. $V = M_1 Y$.
   d. none of the above.

3. According to the quantity theory of prices, if the number of cowrie shells in circulation in West Africa doubles, other things being equal,
   a. the price of oxen will double relative to the price of cowrie shells.
   b. the general price level, measured by a cowrie-shell index, will double.
   c. the purchasing power of the cowrie shell will double.
   d. all of the above will happen.

4. The relationship between the price level and the quantity of money is likely to hold most closely for
   a. relatively short periods, because velocity is stable in the short run.
   b. periods when there are large up and down swings in the money supply over a relatively short time span.
   c. long periods when money growth is slow but steady.
   d. sustained periods of steady and rapid increase in the money supply.

5. According to the crude Keynesian theory of inflation, expansion of aggregate nominal demand will be inflationary only if
   a. the economy is already at full employment.
   b. productivity grows more slowly than its long-term trend.
   c. the expansion of demand arises from monetary policy.
   d. the expansion of demand arises from deficit-financed fiscal policy.

6. Assuming that the target level of national income and the full employment level are the same, the crude Keynesian theory predicts which of the following?
   a. Policies undertaken to fill a contractionary gap will cause only real output to change.
   b. Policies undertaken to fill a contractionary gap will cause only the price level to change.
   c. Policies undertaken to fill a contractionary gap will have results divided about equally between changes in real output and changes in the price level.
   d. The crude Keynesian theory says nothing about these matters.

7. Which of the following is not an implication of the crude Keynesian theory of inflation?
   a. Inflation is caused primarily by fiscal policy.
   b. A contractionary gap is likely to cause the price level to fall.
   c. As the economy approaches full employment, the rate of inflation will gradually begin to rise.
   d. None of the above is a conclusion of the theory.

8. The crude Keynesian theory implies
   a. an L-shaped Phillips curve with a sharp corner at full employment.
   b. a vertical Phillips curve.
   c. a horizontal Phillips curve.
   d. different Phillips curves for monetary and fiscal policies.

9. The Phillips curve is no longer thought to represent a stable policy menu because
   a. the degree of monopoly power held by business and labor is much higher than it was in the 1950s and 1960s.
   b. A. W. H. Phillips's original work has been shown to suffer from serious methodological errors.
   c. points representing years in the 1970s lie below a Phillips curve drawn for the period 1950-1965.
   d. points representing years in the 1970s lie above a Phillips curve drawn for the period 1950-1965.

10. If the Phillips curve were a vertical line drawn through a point on the horizontal axis corresponding to full employment,
    a. it would be futile to try to lower the unemployment rate by cutting taxes.
    b. monetary policy could be focused on the job of fighting unemployment without inflation being a problem.
    c. inflation could not be controlled by conventional monetary or fiscal policies.
    d. none of the above would be true.

11. When people blame part of the inflation of the late 1970s on the increase in OPEC oil prices, they are talking about
    a. demand-pull inflation.
    b. commodity inflation.
    c. wage-push inflation.
    d. the Phillips curve.

12. According to microeconomic theory, possession of monopoly power by unions or firms is most likely to cause
    a. prices in the industry in question to be higher than those in more competitive industries.
    b. prices in the industry in question to rise more rapidly than those in more competitive industries.
    c. both a and b.
    d. neither a nor b.

13. The cost-push illusion arises because
    a. housewives buying products like meat are usually poorly informed about economic trends and conditions.
    b. retailers and wholesalers are likely, at first, to respond to unexpected decreases in inventories by increasing the quantities ordered from suppliers rather than by raising prices.
    c. the extent of monopoly power in agricultural markets is hard to recognize, being far removed from the ultimate consumer along the chain of distribution.
    d. people fail to distinguish carefully between the real and nominal rates of inflation.

14. Over time, prices and unit labor costs move closely together. This observed pattern
    a. is conclusive evidence in favor of wage-push inflation.
    b. is conclusive evidence in favor of the Phillips curve.
    c. could mean either that wages are pushing up prices or that prices are pushing up wages.
    d. began to disappear during the 1970s.

15. Which of the following is now thought to contain no valid insights into the inflationary process?
    a. The crude quantity theory.
    b. The crude Keynesian theory.
    c. The cost-push theory.
    d. All of the above have something to contribute, but none is a complete explanation of inflation.

ANSWERS TO CHAPTER 15 SELF TEST

True or False

1-F; growth of real income.
2-T
3-F; each time the quantity of money doubles.
4-T
5-T
6-T
7-F; his original study used an index of wages to measure inflation.
8-F; prices could be pulling up wages.
9-F; it refers to demand-pull inflation looking like cost-push inflation.
10-F; high, but not steadily rising.

Multiple Choice

1-b
2-a
3-b
4-d
5-a
6-a
7-d
8-a
9-d
10-d
11-b
12-a
13-b
14-c
15-d

CHAPTER SIXTEEN
A CLOSER LOOK AT UNEMPLOYMENT

WHERE YOU'RE GOING

Here is what you will be able to do when you have mastered this chapter:

   --Explain the sources of changes in the unemployment rate in terms of flows of workers among various population groups.

   --Define the employment rate, and explain the circumstances under which the employment rate can give a better picture of labor market trends than the unemployment rate.

   --State the relationship between unemployment and the growth of real output embodied in Okun's law.

   --Explain the relationship between the duration of unemployment and the unemployment rate.

   --Discuss the relationship between unemployment and inflation in terms of the theory of job search, and explain how this relationship offers a possible explanation of the Phillips curve.

   --Explain the meaning of the natural rate of unemployment, and discuss a variety of policies through which changes might be made in the natural rate.

   --Explain the meaning and significance of the following additional terms and concepts:

      Frictional unemployment.
      Dual labor market.
      Reservation wage.

CHAPTER SYNOPSIS

Reading this synopsis is not a substitute for reading the chapter, but it should help you to recall the main points. If there are any you feel unsure of, refer to the full discussion in the text.

   As shown in Chapter 7, the noninstitutional adult civilian population can be divided into three groups: those not in the labor force, those in the labor force and employed, and those in the labor force and unemployed. The unemployment rate, on which so much discussion of economic policy is focused, is the percentage of the labor force that is unemployed. Changes in the unemployment rate over time depend on the relationship between the number of people entering the unemployed group and the number leaving it. People may become unemployed either when they leave a job and begin to look for another or when they enter the labor force and do not immediately find a job. They may leave the ranks of the unemployed either by finding a job or by leaving the labor force without having found a job. In the latter case, they may become discouraged workers.

   Because of the way the unemployment rate is measured, an increase in the number of jobs supplied by the economy does not necessarily result in a reduction in the unemployment rate. In times of economic expansion, many jobs are filled by people newly drawn into the labor force rather than by those previously unemployed. If new entrants flowing into the labor force are distributed between the employed and unemployed groups in the same proportion as those already in the labor force, the unemployment rate may, for a time, not fall even when employment and real output expand. For this reason, many economists favor the employment rate--as a measure of labor market conditions.

Despite the possible occurrence of the circumstances just described, there is a tendency, although not an absolute one, toward an association between changes in real output and changes in the unemployment rate. This relationship is often expressed in the form of a rule of thumb known as Okun's law. According to this rule, for each three percentage points by which real economic growth exceeds (or falls short of) the growth rate of potential real GNP in any year, the unemployment rate will tend to fall (or rise) by one percentage point.

The unemployment rate depends not only on the number of people who experience a spell of unemployment during a year, but on how long, on the average, they remain unemployed. For this reason, much recent work in unemployment theory has focused on what determines the length of time that a worker will spend in the process of job search (remember that by definition all unemployed workers are searching for jobs) before finding one. On the average, the longer people search, the better the job offers they will turn up; this tendency can be represented graphically in the form of an upward-sloping wage offer curve. At the same time, the longer people search, the lower the minimum offer they will settle for; that is, the lower the reservation wage. This can be represented graphically as a downward-sloping reservation wage curve. The process of job search ends when the rising wage offer curve intersects the falling reservation wage curve.

Such an analysis of the process of job search can be put to work to demonstrate a relationship between inflation and unemployment. As inflation actually takes place, it shifts the wage offer curve upward, because wages and prices tend to rise together. At the same time, expected inflation shifts the reservation wage curve upward. If the actual and expected rates of inflation are equal, the unemployment rate remains at a benchmark level known as the natural rate of unemployment. If the expected rate of inflation exceeds the actual rate of inflation, the average duration of job search is shortened and unemployment drops below the natural rate. If actual inflation proceeds more slowly than expected, the average duration of job search is drawn out, and unemployment rises above the natural rate.

The behavior just described gives rise to a negatively sloped Phillips curve, at least in the short run. However, the position of the Phillips curve is dependent on the expected rate of inflation. As the expected rate of inflation increases, the curve shifts upward. In the long run, it can be presumed that expectations will adapt to any given rate of inflation if that rate prevails long enough. Once the actual and expected rates of inflation are equal, unemployment returns to the natural rate. A long-run Phillips curve can thus be drawn as a vertical line intersecting the horizontal axis at the natural rate of unemployment.

The exact numerical value of the natural rate of unemployment depends on a number of demographic and institutional factors. Economists have devoted much research in recent years to discovering why the natural rate of unemployment has increased from its level of two decades ago. Among the possible explanations that appear to have some empirical support are the following:

1. Shifts in the composition of the labor force, with more women and teenagers participating than formerly.
2. Minimum wage laws, which tend to create a shortage of jobs for low-skill workers.

3. Unemployment compensation, which tends to lower the opportunity cost of job search and thus lengthen its average duration.
4. Work registration requirements, which tend to draw into the labor force certain classes of welfare recipients who otherwise would not have sought work.

The natural rate of unemployment now appears to be above 5 percent, perhaps even above 6 percent. This means that the 4 percent unemployment goal of the Humphrey-Hawkins Act cannot be reached in a noninflationary way unless steps are taken to reduce the natural rate. One approach is to modify minimum wage laws, unemployment compensation rules, or work registration requirements in such a way as to mitigate their effects on unemployment. Another approach is to take direct steps to fit unemployed workers into jobs through job placement, manpower training, or public employment programs.

WALKING TOUR

You have read the chapter at least once and have reviewed the synopsis. Now you are going to walk through the material step by step, filling in the blanks and answering the questions as you go along. After you have answered each question, check yourself by uncovering the answer given in the margin. If you do not understand why the answer given is the right one, refer back to the proper section of the text.

Unemployment, Job Search, and Inflation

Let N_p stand for the number of people in the noninstitutional adult civilian population, N_l for the number in the civilian labor force, N_e for the number of employed workers, and N_u for the number of unemployed workers. The unemployment rate can then be stated as _____ and the | N_u/N_l

employment rate as _____. From these definitions | N_e/N_p

alone, it [follows/does not follow] that as the total number | does not follow

of employed workers grows, the unemployment rate will fall. Nonetheless, although expansion of the economy need not always result in a reduction in unemployment, usually it does. According to a widely used rule of thumb, for each

_____ percentage points by which the rate of growth | three

of real output exceeds (or falls short of) the trend rate of growth of real output in a given year, the unemployment

rate will fall (or rise) by _____ percentage point. This | one

rule of thumb is known as _____. | Okun's law

For example, suppose the long-term growth trend of potential real GNP is 3 percent. Let real GNP at the beginning of Year 1 be $1,000 billion and the unemployment rate 6 percent. If real GNP reaches $1,060 billion by the end of Year 1, then according to Okun's law, the unemploy-

ment rate will [rise/fall] to _____ percent. If, by | fall; 5

the end of the next year, real GNP were to fall back to
$1,000 billion, the unemployment rate would [rise/fall/return]   rise
to _____ percent.   8

    It has been observed that when the unemployment rate
rises, the average duration of unemployment [rises/falls].   rises
For this reason, much recent work in employment theory has
focused on what determines the average duration of the
unemployed worker's process of job search. Exhibit S16.1
can be used to illustrate some of the findings of this
research. This exhibit contains two wage offer curves,
labeled W_1 and W_2, and two reservation wage curves,
labeled R_1 and R_2. Assume that if there is no inflation
and none is expected, the curves W_1 and R_1 apply. In
that case, the average duration of unemployment would be
_____ weeks, and the unemployment rate would be at   ten
the _____ rate. Assume now that in Year 1, the   natural
actual rate of inflation accelerates to 5 percent per year.
Of the curves given in Exhibit S16.1, the pair that would
best represent the situation in Year 1 would be _____. R_1 and W_2
The average duration of unemployment in Year 1 would thus
[rise/fall] to _____ weeks, and the unemployment rate   fall; six
would [rise above/fall below] the natural rate. Assume   fall below
next that in Year 2 inflation continues at 5 percent per
year and that workers come to expect this rate of inflation
to continue indefinitely. Of the curves drawn in the exhibit,
the pair best representing the situation in Year 2 would be
_____. The average duration of unemployment R_2 and W_2

Exhibit S16.1

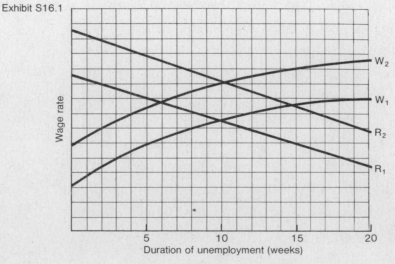

Exhibit S16.1

Exhibit S16.2

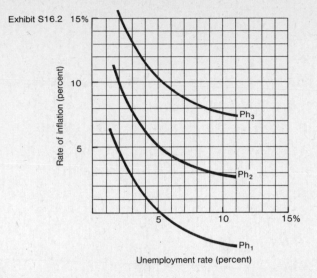

in Year 2 would [rise/fall/return] to _____ weeks, and   return; ten
the unemployment rate would [rise above/fall below/return to]   return to
the natural rate. Finally, assume that in Year 1, the actual
rate of inflation had been zero but that workers had expected
the price level to rise at a 5 percent rate. Of the curves
shown, those best representing that situation would be
_____. The average duration of unemployment R_2 and W_1
would [rise/fall] to _____ weeks, and the unemployment   rise; fifteen
rate would [rise above/fall below] the natural rate.   rise above

The theory of job search gives some important insights
into the Phillips curve. Consider, for example, the Phillips
curve Ph_1 shown in Exhibit S16.2. Assuming the natural
rate of unemployment to be 5 percent per year, this Phillips
curve reflects zero expected inflation. If the actual rate of
inflation were also zero, the unemployment rate would be
_____ percent. Label this Point A on the exhibit.   5
Beginning from this point, if the rate of inflation in Year 1
accelerates to 5 percent while workers continue to expect
no inflation, there will be a [shift in/movement along] the   movement along
Phillips curve to an unemployment rate of _____ percent.   2
Label this Point B. In Year 2, assume that the actual rate
of inflation continues at 5 percent but that actual rate of
inflation catches up with the actual rate. This will produce
a [shift in/movement along] the Phillips curve. Of the   shift in
curves shown in Exhibit S16.2, the one appropriate for
Year 2 would be _____. The unemployment rate in Ph_2

133

Year 2 will be _____ percent; label this Point C. Finally,   5
assume that in Year 4 the actual rate of inflation falls to
4 percent while the expected rate of inflation remains at
5 percent. This will produce a [shift in/movement along]   movement along
the Phillips curve. The unemployment rate in Year 4 will
reach _____ percent. Label this Point D. Notice that   about 6
Points A, B, C, and D trace out a clockwise loop; you will
learn more about how loops of this kind can occur in the
real-world economy.

SELF TEST

These sample test items will help you check how much you have learned. Answers
and explanations can be found at the end of this chapter. Scoring yourself: One
or two wrong -- on target. Three to five wrong -- passing, but you haven't mastered the chapter yet. Six or more wrong -- not good enough; start over and
restudy the chapter.

True or False

Indicate whether each statement is true or false as it stands. If it is false, explain
why in a few words.

T F   1.   The employment rate is the ratio of the number of people employed to the
         number of people in the labor force.

T F   2.   It is impossible that the unemployment rate and the employment rate could
         both rise at the same time.

T F   3.   According to Okun's law, for each three percentage points by which real
         economic growth exceeds (or falls short of) the growth rate of potential
         real GNP in any year, the unemployment rate will tend to fall (or rise)
         by one percentage point.

T F   4.   Statistical evidence indicates that the unemployment rate and the average
         duration of unemployment move closely together from year to year.

T F   5.   According to the dual labor market theory, secondary sector workers typ-
         ically spend short periods between jobs but have frequent spells of unem-
         ployment.

T F   6.   According to job search theory, the high cost and imperfect distribution of
         information in the labor market is a major cause of unemployment.

T F   7.   According to job search theory, an increase in the expected inflation rate,
         other things being equal, will tend to cause the unemployment rate to rise.

T F   8.   The natural rate of unemployment receives its name from the fact that the
         rate has changed very little over the past half-century.

T F   9.   In terms of the job search theory, it can be said that unemployment insur-
         ance tends to increase the unemployment rate because it lowers the oppor-
         tunity cost of unemployment.

T F 10. Econometric studies that indicate that work registration requirements tend to raise the unemployment rate indicate that these programs have failed in their primary objective of getting welfare recipients into the labor market.

Multiple Choice

1. The employment rate is the ratio of the number of employed workers to
   a. the total population.
   b. the noninstitutional adult civilian population.
   c. the civilian labor force.
   d. the number of unemployed workers.

2. Some economists think the employment rate gives a better picture of labor market conditions than the unemployment rate because
   a. the employment rate is not distorted by the failure to include armed forces personnel in the labor force.
   b. the unemployment rate may not change, and it may even rise, when employment and real output are expanding.
   c. the employment rate is not affected by changes in the minimum wage.
   d. the employment rate is not subject to seasonal variations.

3. The term frictional unemployment refers to
   a. workers in the secondary sector of the labor force.
   b. workers whose skills are obsolete because technology has changed before they have reached retirement age.
   c. the same thing as the natural rate of unemployment.
   d. workers spending relatively short periods between jobs.

4. According to the job search theory of unemployment, an increase in the expected rate of inflation, other things being equal, will shift
   a. the reservation wage curve.
   b. the wage offer curve.
   c. both of the above.
   d. neither of the above.

5. The natural rate of unemployment is
   a. the rate of unemployment that would prevail if teenagers and secondary sector workers were not counted in the labor force.
   b. the rate of unemployment that would prevail if the actual and expected rates of inflation were equal.
   c. simply a name for the long-term average unemployment rate.
   d. about 4 percent of the labor force as of 1979.

6. According to the job search theory of unemployment, an increase in the actual rate of inflation, other things being equal, will
   a. increase the average period of job search and decrease the unemployment rate.
   b. decrease the average period of job search and increase the unemployment rate.
   c. increase both the average period of job search and the unemployment rate.
   d. decrease both the average period of job search and the unemployment rate.

7. According to the job search theory of unemployment
   a. unemployment will fall below the natural rate only if workers have imperfect information about wages and prices.
   b. the short-run Phillips curve has a negative slope.
   c. the longer people look for jobs, the lower the wage they may be willing to accept.
   d. all of the above are true.

8. Assuming both the adaptive expectations hypothesis and the job search theory of unemployment to be valid,
   a. the long-run Phillips curve is vertical.
   b. the short-run Phillips curve is vertical.
   c. both a and b are true.
   d. neither a nor b is true.

9. If the natural rate of unemployment is 5 percent, the rate of unemployment in Year 1 is 3 percent, the actual rate of inflation in Year 1 is 7 percent, and the actual rate of inflation is Year 2 remains 7 percent, the unemployment rate in Year 2 is likely to be
   a. 3 percent.
   b. greater than 3 percent.
   c. less than 3 percent.
   d. impossible to determine from the information given.

10. The short-run Phillips curve for any year intersects the long-run Phillips curve
    a. at the actual rate of inflation.
    b. at the expected rate of inflation.
    c. at the previous year's expected rate of inflation.
    d. at zero inflation.

11. According to the job search theory of unemployment, which of the following is likely to be associated with the highest rate of unemployment?
    a. Unexpected inflation.
    b. Accurately expected inflation.
    c. Falsely expected inflation.
    d. Zero expected inflation.

12. Exempting teenagers from the minimum wage law would be likely to
    a. lower the natural rate of unemployment.
    b. make it difficult for teenagers to receive on-the-job training.
    c. lower the number of teenagers employed.
    d. have all of the effects mentioned above.

13. Which of the following would be most likely to lower the natural rate of unemployment without imposing undue hardship on those who really depend on unemployment compensation to make ends meet?
    a. Reduce the number of weeks for which unemployment compensation can be paid.
    b. Reduce the level of unemployment benefits as a percentage of pay while employed.
    c. Subject unemployment compensation payments to the income tax.
    d. Limit unemployment compensation to adult males.

14. Empirical research indicates that work registration requirements
    a. raise the natural rate of unemployment.
    b. raise the employment rate.
    c. raise both a and b.
    d. raise neither a nor b.

15. Which of the following statements most accurately characterizes the prospects for meeting the economic stabilization goals of the Humphrey-Hawkins Act?
    a. The goals are clearly impossible.
    b. The unemployment goal cannot be reached without the inflation goal being sacrificed.
    c. The unemployment and inflation goals cannot both be reached without the natural rate of unemployment being lowered.
    d. The unemployment goal cannot be reached without the public sector acting as the employer of last resort.

ANSWERS TO CHAPTER 16 SELF TEST

True or False

1-F; to the number in the noninstitutional adult civilian population.
2-F; new entrants could increase the number of unemployed more rapidly than they increase the number of employed.
3-T
4-T
5-F; the duration of unemployment is long for such workers too.
6-T
7-T
8-F; the rate has risen.
9-T
10-F; they have raised the unemployment rate at the same time they may have raised the employment rate.

Multiple Choice

1-b
2-b
3-d
4-a
5-b
6-d; among the other things equal is, of course, the expected rate of inflation.
7-d
8-a
9-b; because the Phillips curve will be shifting upward as expectations catch up to the actual 7 percent inflation rate.
10-b
11-c; meaning an expected rate of inflation higher than the actual rate.
12-a
13-c
14-c
15-c

CHAPTER SEVENTEEN
THE DYNAMICS OF INFLATION

WHERE YOU'RE GOING

Here is what you will be able to do when you have mastered this chapter:

--List and explain the four major building blocks of a theory of inflation.

--Explain how the effects of an initial dose of expansionary fiscal or monetary policy are split up between a change in inflation and a change in unemployment, assuming a standing start.

--Explain how a policy of continued acceleration of inflation can be used to keep unemployment below the natural rate for a prolonged period.

--Explain the conditions under which an inflationary recession can occur.

--Explain how, during a period of reflation, fiscal and monetary policy can be used to lower the unemployment rate with little or no penalty in terms of rising inflation.

--Explain the economic and political causes of the stop-go policy cycle.

--Use the simple theory of the dynamics of inflation to interpret recent U.S. macroeconomic experience, including events that will have taken place since the publication of this text.

CHAPTER SYNOPSIS

Reading this synopsis is not a substitute for reading the chapter, but it should help you to recall the main points. If there are any you feel unsure of, refer to the full discussion in the text.

The theory of inflation was a central subject of economic research throughout the 1970s. Not all controversies have yet been resolved, but most of the major competing theories share a common core of ideas on which this chapter is based. This central core of ideas rests on four important building blocks:

1. Through the use of monetary and fiscal policy, the government can, as demonstrated in Chapters 8 through 14, control the rate of growth of nominal GNP, at least within reasonable limits.
2. At all times the rate of growth of nominal national product must be equal to the rate of growth of real output plus the rate of inflation.
3. According to Okun's law, for each three percentage points by which real economic growth exceeds (or falls short of) the long-term trend of potential real output in a given year, the unemployment rate will tend to fall (or rise) by one percentage point.
4. According to the job search theory of unemployment, a change in the actual rate of inflation, with the expected rate of inflation constant, moves the economy along a short-run Phillips curve, and a change in the expected rate of inflation causes the short-run Phillips curve to shift.

To see how these building blocks can be used to construct a theory of the dynamics of inflation, begin by assuming that the economy is in a "standing start" position:

unemployment is at the natural rate and has not changed during the current year, the actual and expected rates of inflation are both zero, and the rate of growth of nominal GNP is equal to the long-term trend of potential real output growth (here assumed to be 3 percent per year).

From this initial position, suppose that the government applies expansionary monetary or fiscal policy to accelerate the rate of growth of aggregate nominal demand. In the familiar sequence of events, firms respond to the stimulus by raising output and/or prices, and the economy begins to move up and to the left along the Phillips curve. A question now arises: How far along the Phillips curve will it move? The answer is that it will move along the curve until the entire growth rate of nominal GNP has been accounted for by the sum of three items: (1) the 3 percent annual rate of growth of potential real GNP; (2) the additional growth of real GNP associated, according to Okun's law, withe the decline in the unemployment rate; and (3) the rate of inflation. Given the shape and position of the Phillips curve, the initial rate of unemployment, and the rate of growth of nominal GNP, with the rate of inflation and the unemployment rate can be determined exactly.

In the example just given, an initial burst of expansionary fiscal or monetary policy moved the economy up and to the left along a given short-run Phillips curve. If such expansionary policy is repeated in subsequent years, expectations will begin to adapt to the resulting inflation and the Phillips curve will begin to shift upward. A constant rate of inflation will not serve to keep unemployment below the natural rate indefinitely; instead, a constant acceleration of inflation will be required.

If contractionary monetary and fiscal policy is applied after a prolonged period of acceleration, the economy will not move smoothly down along the Phillips curve with the rate of inflation dropping as the unemployment rate rises. Instead, as the policy change initially takes place, the Phillips curve will still be shifting upward as expectations continue to adjust to recent experience. This continued shift in the Phillips curve combined with contractionary aggregate demand policy will cause an inflationary recession--inflation will remain high or even continue to accelerate somewhat as the unemployment rate rises.

Continued deceleration of the rate of growth of aggregate demand will eventually result in a reduction in the rate of inflation, with the unemployment rate remaining above the natural rate during the process. The Phillips curve will begin to shift downward as people adapt to the slowing rate of inflation. In principle, the economy can eventually be maneuvered to a soft landing with inflation stabilized at a low rate and unemployment returning to the natural rate.

However, at any time during the period of deceleration, policy makers can, rather than choosing a soft landing, choose to reflate. This means once again accelerating the growth rate of aggregate demand through expansionary fiscal or monetary policy. If this occurs while the Phillips curve is still shifting downward, the economy will temporarily enjoy the best of both worlds--inflation will remain low, or possibly even slow further, while unemployment will drop sharply. But reflation works only temporarily--as soon as expectations begin to adapt to what is happening, inflation will begin to accelerate again.

If the government pursues a stop-go policy of alternating acceleration, inflationary recession, deceleration, and reflation, the economy will trace out a series of clockwise loops on an inflation-unemployment diagram. If political pressure to do something about unemployment is on the average stronger than political pressure to do something about inflation, the stop-go cycle will be given an inflationary bias. The postwar macroeconomic experience of the U.S. economy can plausibly be interpreted as the result of a stop-go policy cycle with an inflationary bias, although the height of the last two loops of the 1970s was distorted by commodity inflation caused by the rise in international oil prices.

WALKING TOUR

You have read the chapter at least once and have reviewed the synopsis. Now you are going to walk through the material step by step, filling in the blanks and answering the questions as you go along. After you have answered each question, check yourself by uncovering the answer given in the margin. If you do not understand why the answer given is the right one, refer back to the proper section of the text.

Effects of Accelerating Inflation

Point A in Exhibit S17.1 shows the economy in a standing start position: the actual and expected rates of inflation are zero, and the current and previous year's unemployment rates are 5 percent, which we assume to be the natural rate. The Phillips curve Ph_1 has been drawn as a straight line rather than as a curve to simplify calculations. The long-term trend growth rate of potential real GNP is assumed to be 3 percent per year, and the growth rate of nominal GNP in the initial position is also assumed to be 3 percent per year.

Exhibit S17.1

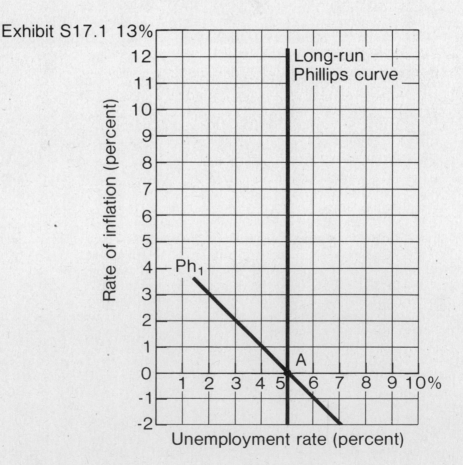

Exhibit S17.1

140

Assume now that in Year 1, the government applies
sufficient fiscal and monetary stimulus to accelerate the
rate of growth of nominal GNP to 11 percent per year.
This stimulus will cause the economy to move up and to
the left along the Phillips curve Ph₁ to a point where the
inflation rate is _____ percent and the unemployment   2
rate is _____ percent. Label this Point B. At Point B,   3
the 11 percent rate of growth of nominal GNP is divided
as follows: _____ percent for the growth of potential   3
real GNP; an additional _____ percent of real GNP   6
growth associated with the _____ percentage point decline   2
in the unemployment rate, as specified by Okun's law; and
_____ percent inflation.   2

   If the government had wanted to limit the rate of
inflation to 1 percent, it could have restrained the growth
of aggregate nominal demand to no more than _____ percent.   7
If it had been willing to tolerate 3 percent inflation, it could
have expanded aggregate nominal demand by _____ percent,   15
in which case unemployment would have fallen all the way
to _____ percent   2

   Return now to the assumption that it is Point B that
is actually reached in Year 1. If we assume a simple adaptive expectations rule under which each year's expected
rate of inflation is equal to the previous year's actual rate
of inflation, the Phillips curve for Year 2 will shift [upward/
downward] until it intersects the long-run Phillips curve   upward
at _____ percent inflation. Sketch in this new Phillips   2
curve, parallel to the old one and label it Ph₂. The new
Phillips curve can now be used to find what will happen if
the growth rate of nominal GNP is kept at 11 percent during
Year 2. You can do this simply by trial and error, moving
out along Ph₂ until you reach a point where all the 11
percent nominal growth is accounted for.

   Regardless of the point reached on the Phillips curve,
3 percent of the 11 percent total will be accounted for by
the growth of potential GNP; that leaves 8 percent to be
accounted for. Assume, as a first trial, that the unemployment rate does not fall further in Year 2 but remains at
3 percent. Label this Point C on Ph₂. At C, in addition
to the 3 percent potential GNP growth, there is 4 percent

inflation, for a total of 7 percent. However, since there has been no <u>change</u> in unemployment from Year 1, Okun's law contributes nothing, leaving 4 percent unaccounted for. Try going a little farther along Ph_2, letting the unemployment rate drop another percentage point to 2 percent. This drop in unemployment will add _____ percentage   three
point(s) to the growth of real output, according to Okun's law, giving 6 percent real growth in all including the potential GNP trend. At this point on Ph_2, inflation is _____   5
percent. $3 + 3 + 5 = 11$, so all the 11 percent nominal growth is now accounted for. Label this Point C', and draw an arrow to it from Point B.

In Year 3, the Phillips curve will again shift up until it intersects the long-run Phillips curve at _____ percent   5
inflation. Sketch in this curve, labeling it Ph_3. If nominal growth is allowed to grow at 11 percent for a third year, the inflation rate will reach _____ percent and   8
the unemployment rate will [rise to/drop to/remain at]   remain at
_____ percent. Label the point for Year 3 Point D.   2
If policy makers want to keep the unemployment rate at 2 percent for a fourth year, the rate of growth of nominal GNP must be [kept at/raised to/lowered to] _____ percent.   raised to; 14
Label the point for Year 4 Point E.

Inflationary Recession

Begin now with the clean diagram given in Exhibit S17.2. The Phillips curve Ph_4 and Point E in this exhibit are where the fourth year of the previous example concluded. In Year 5, the expected rate of inflation will rise to _____ percent,   11
and the Phillips curve will shift up until it intersects the long-run Phillips curve at that rate of inflation. Sketch this Phillips curve, labeling it Ph_5. In order to keep the unemployment rate at 2 percent in Year 5, the government would have to expand nominal GNP at a rate of _____   17
percent, allowing the rate of inflation to rise to 14 percent. Suppose, though, that political pressure builds up for the government to do something about the high rate of inflation and that the government responds by cutting the rate of growth of nominal GNP to 9 percent. Again, use a trial and error approach to find the unemployment and inflation

142

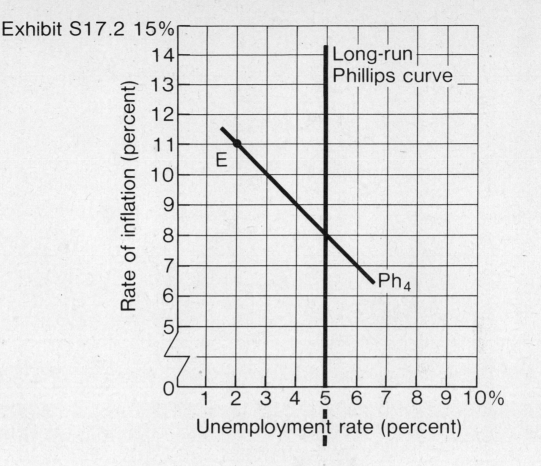

Exhibit S17.2

rates for Year 5. As a first trial, assume that the inflation
rate remains at 11 percent. That would put the economy
just at the point where Ph5 intersects the long-run Phillips
curve. Label this Point F. To reach F, the unemployment
rate would have to rise three percentage points. According
to Okun's law, this would require a growth rate of real
output _____ percentage points [above/below] the 3   nine; below
percent long-term trend of potential real GNP, for a net
real growth of _____ percent. Inflation at Point F is   −6
11 percent. 11 − 6 = 5 does not fully account for the
assumed 9 percent growth in nominal GNP, so evidently F
is too far to the [right/left] along Ph5. For a second   right
trial, assume that the unemployment rate rises just two
points, to 4 percent, allowing the inflation rate to rise
to 12 percent. Label this Point F' on Ph5. At F', the net
growth rate of real output is _____ percent, taking both   −3
the 3 percent rise in potential output and the _____   two

percentage point [rise/drop] in the unemployment rate   rise
into account. 12 percent inflation minus 3 percent change
in real GNP gives 9 percent growth of nominal GNP, just
as required. F' is thus the correct point for Year 5;
connect it to E with an arrow. The events of Year 5 would
be termed an _____.   inflationary recession

Appendix: A More Detailed Model of Inflationary Dynamics
In the previous example, a certain amount of trial and error
work was necessary to determine the exact inflation and
unemployment rates for any given year. The appendix to
this chapter presents two more precise ways to make this
determination, one graphical and one algebraic.

The graphical method relies on a line known as the
demand pressure curve, a graphical representation of Okun's
law adapted to fit on the same set of axes as the Phillips
curve. The demand pressure curve has a slope of -3, which
reflects the fact that, other things equal, each percentage
point increase in unemployment cuts three percentage points
from the rate of real growth and hence adds three percentage points to inflation. The demand pressure curve for
each year passes through a point corresponding to the
previous year's unemployment rate, and the current year's
rate of growth of nominal output, minus 3. (All this is
explained in detail in the text.)

Exhibit S17.3 will give you some practice in drawing
the demand pressure curves appropriate to various assumed
conditions. First locate the demand pressure curve corresponding to the standing start condition: unemployment in
the previous year is 5 percent (the natural rate), and
the current year rate of growth is 3 percent, equal to the
long-term trend of potential real GNP. These conditions
are represented by the demand pressure curve _____. DP_2
Suppose that in Year 1, the rate of growth of nominal GNP
is increased to 9 percent. The demand pressure curve for
Year 1 thus becomes _____. Suppose that during DP_4
Year 1 the unemployment rate drops to 4 percent and that
in Year 2 the rate of growth of nominal GNP continues at
9 percent. The demand pressure curve for Year 2 is now
found on the basis of the Year 1 unemployment rate and

144

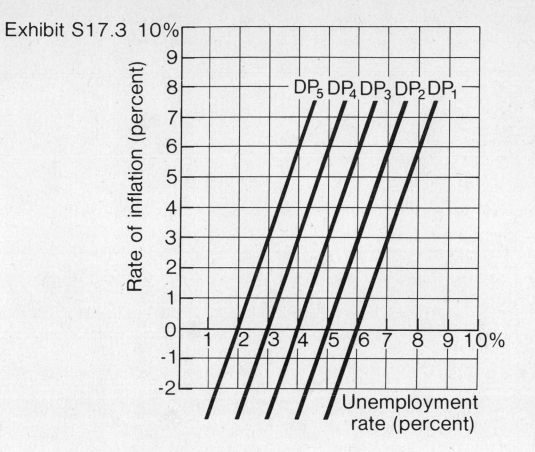

Exhibit S17.3

the Year 2 nominal growth rate; this is the curve _____. DP_5
Finally, suppose that in Year 2 the unemployment rate drops
to 3 percent and that in Year 3 the rate of growth of nominal GNP is cut to 3 percent. The Year 3 demand pressure
curve will then be _____. DP_4

Now that you are familiar with the use of the demand
pressure curve, go back to the examples in Exhibits S17.1,
and S17.2 and draw in the demand pressure curve for each
year. Note that this eliminates trial and error work in
reaching the solution to each part of the problem.

An algebraic method can also be used to solve problems
like those given above. It is based on the equations

$$\dot{P}_t = \dot{P}_{t-1} - (U_t - 5)$$

for the Phillips curve and

$$\dot{P}_t = \dot{Y}_t - 3 + 3(U_t - U_{t-1})$$

for the demand pressure curve. (See pages 299 and 301 of

the text.) These equations can be used to solve all of the examples given in connection with Exhibits S17.1 and S17.2. For example, consider the situation in Year 1, for which $U_{t-1} = 5$, $\dot{P}_{t-1} = 0$, and $\dot{Y}_t = 11$. This gives the pair of equations

$$\dot{P}_t + U_t - 5 = 0 \qquad \text{(the Phillips curve).}$$
$$\dot{P}_t - 3U_t + 7 = 0 \qquad \text{(the demand pressure curve).}$$

Solving these for the two unknowns gives $\dot{P}_t = 2$ and $U_t = 3$, which are the same values obtained by the other methods. As an exercise, go through the rest of the examples given above, solving them by the algebraic method just outlined.

SELF TEST

These sample test items will help you check how much you have learned. Answers and explanations can be found at the end of this chapter. Scoring yourself: One or two wrong -- on target. Three to five wrong -- passing, but you haven't mastered the chapter yet. Six or more wrong -- not good enough; start over and restudy the chapter.

True or False

Indicate whether each statement is true or false as it stands. If it is false, explain why in a few words.

T F 1. If the economy begins from a standing start position, the unemployment rate can initially be lowered without any increase in inflation.

T F 2. The theory of inflationary dynamics given in this chapter implies that the unemployment rate is sensitive not so much to the rate of inflation as to changes in the rate of inflation.

T F 3. During a period of accelerating inflation, workers tend to be unduly pessimistic about job market conditions and to prolong their normal period of job search accordingly.

T F 4. In each year, the economy will move to a point on the Phillips curve where the sum of the rate of inflation, the unemployment rate, and the trend rate of growth of potential real GNP is equal to the growth rate of nominal GNP.

T F 5. According to the theory of inflationary dynamics given in this chapter, it is sometimes possible for both the rate of inflation and the unemployment rate to rise in the same year.

T F 6. According to the theory of inflationary dynamics given in this chapter, an inflationary recession can occur only if the growth rate of nominal GNP is brought below zero.

T F 7. According to the theory of inflationary dynamics given in this chapter, the inflation rate will slow only if unemployment is permitted to rise above the natural rate.

T F   8.   According to the theory of inflationary dynamics given in this chapter, the inflation rate can continue unchanged from one year to the next if unemployment remains at the natural rate.

T F   9.   An examination of postwar U.S. macroeconomic experience shows no evidence of cost-push inflation, once the internal dynamics of inflation and unemployment are taken into account.

T F 10.   The stop-go policy cycle may have political as well as purely economic origins.

Multiple Choice

1.   If, beginning from a standing start position, nominal national income were to fall below its previous level, the likely result would be
   a.   an inflationary recession.
   b.   accelerating inflation and falling unemployment.
   c.   a decline in the price level and a rise in unemployment.
   d.   a decline in the price level and a drop in unemployment.

2.   According to the theory of inflationary dynamics given in this chapter, unemployment can be kept below the natural rate for a sustained period under which of the following conditions?
   a.   Only at the cost of a constantly high rate of inflation.
   b.   Only at the cost of continuously accelerating inflation.
   c.   Only at the cost of declining growth of potential GNP.
   d.   None of the above; unemployment can fall below the natural rate only temporarily.

3.   The ability of accelerating inflation to draw the unemployment rate below the natural rate depends, in part, on
   a.   an assumption of rational expectations on the part of workers.
   b.   an assumption that inflationary expectations do not instantly adjust to the current rate of inflation.
   c.   an assumption that workers' reservation wages rise at the same pace as actual wage offers.
   d.   none of the above.

4.   The accelerating inflation scenario given in this chapter is best characterized as
   a.   an important theoretical possibility, but one not yet experienced in the U.S. economy.
   b.   a pattern that prevailed throughout most of the 1950s.
   c.   a pattern that prevailed throughout most of the 1960s.
   d.   a pattern that prevailed throughout most of the 1970s.

5.   Beginning from a standing start position, suppose the rate of growth of nominal GNP accelerates to 7 percent in the next year. Assuming the trend growth rate of potential real GNP to be 3 percent and the natural rate of unemployment to be 5 percent, which of the following is a possible inflation-unemployment combination for that year?
   a.   4 percent unemployment and 1 percent inflation.
   b.   3 percent unemployment and 1 percent inflation.
   c.   4 percent unemployment and 3 percent inflation.
   d.   Insufficient information is given for an answer to be reached.

6. According to the theory of inflationary dynamics given in this chapter, an inflationary recession is most likely to occur
   a. after a prolonged period of accelerating inflation.
   b. beginning from a standing start.
   c. when fiscal or monetary policy gets too restrictive after a period of deceleration has already begun.
   d. when the rate of growth of nominal GNP is increased while the unemployment rate is already above the natural rate.

7. If the expected rate of inflation in each year is equal to the actual rate of inflation in the previous year, can the rate of inflation be the same two years in a row?
   a. Only if unemployment is at the natural rate in the first year.
   b. Only if unemployment is at the natural rate in the second year.
   c. Only if unemployment is at the natural rate in both years.
   d. None of the above.

8. According to the theory of inflationary dynamics given in this chapter, unemployment higher than the natural rate is associated with
   a. accelerating inflation.
   b. decelerating inflation.
   c. a constant rate of inflation.
   d. a zero rate of inflation.

9. If the current rate of inflation is 9 percent, the growth rate of potential GNP is 3 percent, last year's unemployment rate was 4 percent, and this year's unemployment rate is 5 percent, this year's rate of growth of nominal GNP must be
   a. 3 percent.
   b. 4 percent.
   c. 5 percent.
   d. 9 percent.

10. If, during an inflationary recession, the unemployment rate rises from 4 percent in one year to 6 percent in the next, and if the growth rate of potential real GNP is assumed to be 3 percent, what will be the growth rate of actual real GNP?
    a. -6 percent.
    b. -3 percent.
    c. 0 percent.
    d. 3 percent.

11. During accelerating inflation,
    a. workers have lower reservation wages than they would have if their inflationary expectations were accurate.
    b. workers have higher reservation wages than they would have if their inflationary expectations were accurate.
    c. workers' inflationary expectations are accurate.
    d. unemployment exceeds the natural rate.

12. Cost-push inflation is likely to be a factor in
    a. inflationary recession.
    b. deceleration.
    c. reflation.
    d. the approach to a soft landing.

13. U.S. macroeconomic experience in the postwar period is best characterized as
    a. continuous acceleration of inflation.
    b. a stable stop-go cycle.
    c. a stop-go cycle with an inflationary bias.
    d. prolonged economic stagnation.

14. Inflation accelerated steadily from 1976 through 1979, and the unemployment rate was below its 1975 level throughout the period. From the perspective of late 1979, the least likely occurrence for 1980 would have been
    a. for the unemployment rate to rise and the rate of inflation to fall.
    b. for the unemployment rate to fall and the rate of inflation to rise.
    c. for both the unemployment rate and the rate of inflation to rise.
    d. for both the unemployment rate and the rate of inflation to fall.

15. If the rational expectations hypothesis were combined with the theory of inflationary dynamics given in this chapter,
    a. monetary and fiscal policy would have less effect on inflation.
    b. monetary and fiscal policy would have less effect on unemployment.
    c. monetary and fiscal policy would have less effect on nominal GNP.
    d. the short-run Phillips curve would be flatter.

ANSWERS TO CHAPTER 17 SELF TEST

True or False

1-F; inflation must increase at least a little.
2-T
3-F; they are unduly optimistic and shorten job search
4-F; make it three times the change in the unemployment rate.
5-T
6-F; the growth rate of nominal GNP need only slow down.
7-T
8-T
9-F; some peak periods of inflation were aggravated by commodity inflation.
10-T

Multiple Choice

1-c
2-b
3-b
4-c
5-a
6-a
7-b
8-b
9-d
10-b
11-a
12-a
13-c
14-d
15-b

CHAPTER EIGHTEEN
FURTHER TOPICS IN STABILIZATION POLICY

WHERE YOU'RE GOING

Here is what you will be able to do when you have mastered this chapter:

--Give a brief recap of the tools and effects of economic stabilization policy.

--Summarize the case for and against fine tuning.

--Explain the implications of rational expectations theory for the conduct of stabilization policy.

--Suggest fiscal and monetary policy rules that might be used as alternatives to fine tuning in guiding stabilization policy.

--Identify the circumstances under which an incomes policy is most and least likely to work.

--Explain how indexing might, under certain circumstances, help reduce inflation as well as make it easier for some people to live with inflation.

--Explain the meaning and significance of the following additional terms and concepts:

Inside lag.
Outside lag.
Full employment balanced budget.
Tax-based incomes policy (TIP).

CHAPTER SYNOPSIS

Reading this synopsis is not a substitute for reading the chapter, but it should help you to recall the main points. If there are any you feel unsure of, refer to the full discussion in the text.

Through the use of fiscal and monetary policy, the government is able to control aggregate nominal demand, and hence nominal national income, within at least general limits. Nonetheless, demand management as actually practiced during recent decades has not been fully successful in achieving the primary goals of stabilization policy-- namely, full employment, price stability, and real economic growth. This failure has led to a general reappraisal of past demand management policy. The current debate centers on the two general issues of fine tuning versus policy rules and the possible need for policies going beyond traditional demand management.

Fine tuning means frequent use of expansionary or contractionary policy in an attempt to keep the economy moving closely along a chosen growth path for nominal GNP. The case for fine tuning is based on three beliefs: that, left to itself, the private economy is seriously unstable; that the tools of fiscal and monetary policy work quickly and predictably; and that these tools will be used judiciously with the long-run public interest in mind.

The case against fine tuning questions each of these three propositions but emphasizes in particular that policy does not always work quickly and predictably.

Instead, monetary and fiscal policies operate only with lags--inside lags, which are delays between the need for a policy change and the implementation of the change, and outside lags, which are delays between the implementation of a policy and the occurrence of its effects. When policy lags are long and unpredictable, fine tuning not only may fail to achieve its objectives, but may actually be destabilizing.

Economists of the rational expectations school cite another reason for skepticism about fine tuning. Part of the claimed effectiveness of demand management policy rests on the assumption that expected rates of inflation (and other expectations) will adjust only slowly to what is actually happening in the economy. If expectations adjust more rapidly than the fine-tuners assume, demand mangement policy will be less effective than it otherwise would be.

As an alternative to fine tuning, many economists have advocated steady-as-you-go policy rules. For monetary policy, the most frequently suggested rule calls for a steady rate of monetary growth. For fiscal policy, the most commonly suggested rule envisions a full employment balanced budget--that is, a budget that would be balanced assuming expenditures and tax collections were at a level corresponding to full employment.

Given the less than complete success of past demand management policy, it is not surprising that some economists think demand management is not enough. One policy alternative is to try to control inflation directly through incomes policies--policies that try to influence wages and prices directly through mandatory controls or voluntary guidelines. The United States has experimented with incomes policies of various kinds during several periods. The various experiments suggest that incomes policy may sometimes be useful as a supplement to efforts to fight inflation with contractionary demand management policy but that, except in the very short run, incomes policy is not a workable substitute for monetary and fiscal restraint.

Indexing has also been advanced as a possible supplement to contractionary demand management policy in the fight against inflation. The hope is that indexing, by offering to protect people against the effects of future inflation, would lessen the cost-push pressures arising from soaring inflationary expectations that are a major factor in inflationary recession. However, some economists are concerned that indexing could make things worse, rather than better, during episodes of pure commodity inflation.

WALKING TOUR

You have read the chapter at least once and have reviewed the synopsis. Now you are going to walk through the material step by step, filling in the blanks and answering the questions as you go along. After you have answered each question, check yourself by uncovering the answer given in the margin. If you do not understand why the answer given is the correct one, refer back to the proper section of the text.

Recap of Inflation and Unemployment Theory

According to previous chapters of this book, the govern-

ment can, within limits, control the level of [real/nominal]   nominal

national income but is able to control employment, inflation

and real growth only indirectly. Expansion of aggregate

demand can reduce unemployment if it causes the actual

rate of inflation to [exceed/fall short of] the expected rate   exceed

inflation. However, unemployment can be kept below the

natural rate for a sustained period only if inflation steadily

_____ . When inflation unexpectedly slows

accelerates

after a period of acceleration, [inflation/unemployment/both

inflation and unemployment] are likely to increase; this is

both inflation and
unemployment

called a/an_____.

inflationary recession

Continued contractionary policy can eventually end inflation,

but only slowly. As long as inflation continues to fall, with

the actual rate of inflation less than the expected rate, un-

employment will remain [above/below] the natural rate.

above

Fine Tuning versus Policy Rules

Fine tuning means frequent, active use of demand manage-

ment policy to keep nominal national income on a planned

growth path. One thing that makes fine tuning difficult is

the presence of lags in the economy. There is the lag

between the time a policy is needed and the time it is taken,

known as the _____ lag, and also the lag between

inside

the time a policy is taken and the time its effects are felt,

known as the _____ lag. The longer and less

outside

predictable these lags, the more difficult successful fine

tuning will be. Steady-as-you-go policy rules are an al-

ternative to fine tuning.

Beyond Demand Management

Because past demand management policies have not resulted

in achievement of all the goals of economic stabilization,

economists have looked for additional policy alternatives.

One is to try to control prices and wages directly by use of

_____ policy.

incomes

If the attempt is made to control inflation by means of

an incomes policy without limiting the growth of nominal in-

come, the policy will either fail to restrain inflation or will

lead to shortages and general economic disruption. However,

as illustrated in Exhibit S18.1, incomes policy can, in theory,

help control inflation through its effects on inflationary ex-

pectations if used in conjunction with contractionary demand

management policy.

In Year 1, at Point A in the figure, suppose inflation

is running at 8 percent with unemployment at the natural

rate. Normally, in Year 2, the Phillips curve _____ will

Ph_1

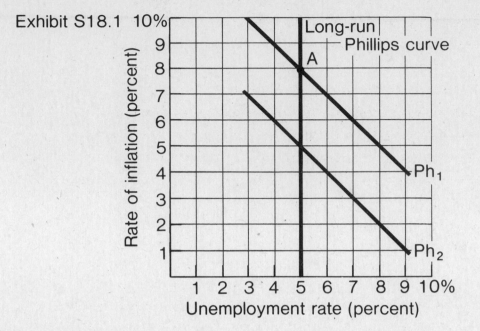

Exhibit S18.1 10%

Rate of inflation (percent)

Long-run Phillips curve

A

Ph₁

Ph₂

Unemployment rate (percent)

apply, assuming the Year 2 expected rate of inflation is
equal to the Year 1 actual rate. To slow inflation to 5
percent in Year 2 would thus require unemployment to rise
to _____ percent. To reach this point (allowing for 3   8
percent growth in potential real income) nominal income
would have to grow by _____ percent and real income   -1
by _____ percent.   -6

     Suppose, however, that the government announces an
incomes policy aimed at preventing prices and wages from
rising by more than 5 percent per year, and suppose that
everyone believes this policy will be successful. Convinced
by the policy change, everyone lowers their inflationary
expectations in Year 2 to 5 percent. This would be represented by a [shift in/movement along] the short-run   shift in
Phillips curve to the position _____. Given this position   Ph₂
of the Phillips curve, inflation could be cut to 5 percent if
nominal income growth were held to _____ percent; unem-   8
ployment would not change, and real income would grow by
3 percent, its trend rate.

     Suppose, however, that after announcing the 5 percent
incomes policy, the government allowed nominal income to
grow by, say, 12 percent. In that case, still assuming the
Phillips curve Ph₂ to apply, unemployment in Year 2 would

be _____ percent and inflation _____ percent. Not   4; 6
only would the inflation target be missed, but the credibility
of the incomes policy would be called into question. Both
inflationary expectations and the Phillips curve would begin
to shift upward again, and the effort would have failed.

A final idea for restraining inflation is indexing.
Indexing would be intended to control the cost-push element
in inflation by making it unnecessary for workers to demand
higher wages to cover anticipated inflation. In an ideally
indexed world, all workers, firms, and investors would make
exactly the decisions they would make if inflation were zero,
and unemployment would remain at or close to the _____   natural
rate even while the rate of inflation was falling.

SELF TEST

True or False

Indicate whether each statement is true or false as it stands. If it is false, explain
why in a few words.

T F   1. Unemployment can be kept below the natural rate for a number of years
           if the rate of inflation is not permitted to accelerate.

T F   2. Fine tuning has been associated more with Keynesian than with monetarist
           economics.

T F   3. The shorter and less variable the policy lags, the more successful fine
           tuning is likely to be.

T F   4. The delay between the time a policy is needed and the time its effects are
           felt is known as the inside lag.

T F   5. Monetarists emphasize that the problem of lags is serious for fiscal but
           not for monetary policy.

T F   6. Rational expectations theorists think demand management may not be an
           effective way of manipulating employment and real output.

T F   7. One suggested policy rule is to let the money supply grow at the same
           rate as potential real GNP.

T F   8. A full employment balanced budget would eliminate many automatic stabil-
           izers that now operate in the economy.

T F   9.   An incomes policy cannot control inflation without creating shortages.

T F   10.   Indexing would be particularly effective in controlling commodity inflation.

Multiple Choice

1.   Which of the following is not an implication of the theories covered in previous chapters?
     a.   Unemployment tends to be relatively low when inflation is accelerating.
     b.   Unemployment tends to be relatively high when inflation is slowing down.
     c.   Inflation can never be cured by demand management alone.
     d.   All of the above are implications of the theories.

2.   Which of the following would not make the fine tuning type of demand management policy more effective?
     a.   If the length of outside lags were more predictable.
     b.   If the lag between the change in the actual rate of inflation and the change in the expected rate of inflation were shorter.
     c.   If the lag between the effects of a policy and the availability of data on those effects were shorter.
     d.   If the private economy were inherently more stable.

3.   Which of the following is an element of the case against fine tuning?
     a.   Policy makers sometimes look no farther ahead than the next election.
     b.   Policy lags are long and variable.
     c.   The private economy is fairly stable if economic policy pursues a steady course.
     d.   All of the above are elements in the case against fine tuning.

4.   Although both the inside and outside lags are variable to some extent, it appears likely that
     a.   the inside lag is shorter for fiscal than for monetary policy.
     b.   the inside lag is shorter for monetary than for fiscal policy.
     c.   both the inside and outside lags are shorter for fiscal policy.
     d.   both the inside and outside lags are shorter for monetary policy.

5.   The destabilizing effects of policy lags would tend to be worst if
     a.   the lags were very long, no matter how predictable they were.
     b.   the lags were of such a length that a contractionary policy aimed at fighting inflation took effect in the bottom of the next recession.
     c.   fear of lags prevented policy makers from changing basic policies when short-run economic conditions changed.
     d.   the inside and outside lags were of exactly the same length.

6.   According to rational expectations theory, demand management policy is not likely to have much effect on employment and real output
     a.   if such policies are changed frequently and unpredictably.
     b.   if the effects of such policies cannot rationally be predicted.
     c.   if the direction and timing of policy changes are widely known in advance.
     d.   if expectations adjust only slowly to actual events.

7.   Under a full employment balanced budget rule,
     a.   there could never be a budget surplus or deficit.
     b.   there would tend to be deficits when unemployment was high.
     c.   there would tend to be surpluses when unemployment was high and deficits when unemployment was low.
     d.   there would be no automatic stabilizers.

8. A law requiring an actual balanced budget every year
   a. would make discretionary fiscal policy more difficult to conduct.
   b. would seriously limit the effectiveness of automatic stabilizers.
   c. would probably not have as much of a stabilizing effect as a full employ-
      ment balanced budget rule.
   d. would do all of the above.

9. Which of the following best characterizes U.S. experience with incomes policy
   during the Nixon administration?
   a. Some initial slowing of inflation accompanied by serious shortages throughout
      the economy.
   b. No measurable impact on inflation during any of the phases.
   c. Some favorable impact initially without shortages, but less effect on inflation
      later on.
   d. Proved that effective incomes policy is possible without danger of shortages.

10. According to the theory of inflation presented in this book, an incomes policy
    would be most likely to be effective against which type of inflation?
    a. Demand-pull inflation.
    b. Accelerating inflation.
    c. Commodity inflation.
    d. Inflation already beginning to slow.

11. According to the theory of inflation presented in this book, the mechanism
    through which incomes policies operate most effectively is
    a. slowing the growth of aggregate nominal demand.
    b. slowing the growth of real GNP.
    c. raising the unemployment rate.
    d. reducing inflationary expectations.

12. A tax-based incomes policy (TIP) might
    a. be based on tax penalties for violators.
    b. be based on tax incentives for those in compliance.
    c. be more effective than a purely voluntary program.
    d. be all of the above.

13. Indexing is advocated because it is hoped it would
    a. make inflation easier to live with until it could be controlled.
    b. help control inflation.
    c. do both of the above.
    d. do none of the above.

14. Indexing would probably work least well against which of the following types
    of inflation?
    a. Commodity inflation.
    b. Wage-push inflation in the unionized sector.
    c. Inflation caused by excessive inflationary expectations.
    d. Inflation caused by high nominal interest rates.

15. Which of the following best characterizes indexing as a policy to fight inflation?
    a. Accepted by virtually all economists, but untried in practice.
    b. Tried in some countries, but not accepted by all economists as effective
       against all types of inflation.
    c. Tried and proved effective during the Nixon administration.
    d. Tried and then abandoned by the Carter administration during 1978-1979.

ANSWERS TO CHAPTER 18 SELF TEST

True or False

1-F; strike "not."
2-T
3-T
4-F; between the need and the implementation.
5-F; serious for both types of policy.
6-T
7-T
8-F; automatic stabilizers would remain.
9-F; it can if used in conjunction with the right demand policies.
10-F; particularly ineffective.

Multiple Choice

1-c
2-b
3-d
4-b
5-b
6-c
7-b
8-d
9-c
10-d
11-d
12-d
13-c
14-a
15-b

CHAPTER NINETEEN
SUPPLY AND DEMAND: BUILDING ON THE BASICS

WHERE YOU'RE GOING

Here is what you will be able to do when you have mastered this chapter:

--Use supply and demand curves to show how changes in economic conditions affect equilibrium price and quantity in the market in question.

--Define price elasticity of demand, and explain why knowing elasticity of demand is important in economic decision making.

--Calculate price elasticity of demand for any specified range of price along a demand curve.

--Define price elasticity of supply, and calculate price elasticity of supply for any specified range of price along a supply curve.

--Define income elasticity of demand, and calculate income elasticity of demand given data on income and quantity changes.

--Explain the meaning and significance of the following additional terms and concepts:

Elastic demand.
Inelastic demand.
Unit elastic demand.
Perfectly inelastic demand.

CHAPTER SYNOPSIS

Reading this synopsis is not a substitute for reading the chapter, but it should help you to recall the main points. If there are any you feel unsure of, refer to the full discussion in the text.

Both supply and demand curves illustrate how changes in the quantity of a good supplied or demanded change in response to changes in the price of the good, other things being equal. Changes in quantities supplied or demanded are thus illustrated by movement along the curves. If any of the items covered by the "other things being equal" clause change, the supply or demand curve will shift to a new position. Such changes are described as changes in supply or demand.

On a diagram with an upward sloping supply curve and a downward sloping demand curve, the equilibrium price and quantity are determined by the intersection of the two curves. At any price above the equilibrium, there will be an excess supply of the good; unsold inventories will tend to accumulate, putting downward pressure on the price until equilibrium is restored. At any price below the equilibrium, there will be an excess demand for the good. Depletion of inventories will put upward pressure on the price of the good until equilibrium is restored.

The ratio of the percentage change in the quantity of a good demanded to the percentage change in the price of the good is known as the price elasticity of demand. If the quantity changes by a larger percentage than the price, demand is said to be elastic. If quantity changes by a smaller percentage than the price, it is said to be inelastic. A demand curve along which price and quantity change in the same proportion is said to be unit elastic. A vertical demand curve is said to be perfectly inelastic, and a horizontal demand curve is said to be perfectly elastic.

Elasticity of demand is important to economic decision making because of the relationship between elasticity and changes in revenue. Along an elastic demand curve, total revenue increases as the price decreases. Along an inelastic demand curve, total revenue falls as the price decreases. Along a unit elastic demand curve, revenue does not change as the prices changes.

Price elasticity of demand can be calculated according to the following formula:

$$\frac{(Q_1 - Q_2) \ / \ (Q_1 + Q_2)}{(P_1 - P_2) \ / \ (P_1 + P_2)}$$

For demand curves along which elasticity varies, this formula should be used only for relatively small changes in price and quantity.

The concept of elasticity can also be applied to situations other than changes in quantity demanded resulting from changes in price. For example, the price elasticity of supply is defined as the ratio of the percentage change in the quantity of a good supplied to the percentage change in its price. Similarly, the income elasticity of demand is defined as the ratio of the percentage change in the demand for a good to the percentage change in the per capita income of buyers.

WALKING TOUR

You have read the chapter at least once and have reviewed the synopsis. Now you are going to walk through the material step by step, filling in the blanks and answering the questions as you go along. After you have answered each question, check yourself by uncovering the answer given in the margin. If you do not understand why the answer given is the right one, refer back to the proper section of the text.

Review of the Basics

Exhibit S19.1 shows hypothetical supply and demand curves for soybeans. As the graph is drawn, the equilibrium

price for soybeans is _____ per bushel, and the equil- $7

ibrium quantity produced is _____ million bushels   1,600

per year.

Given demand curve D_1 and supply curve S_1, no other equilibrium price or quantity is possible. For example, if the price were $9 per bushel, there would be an excess

quantity [supplied/demanded] of _____ million bushels   supplied; 600

per year. Such an excess quantity supplied would result

in [accumulation/depletion] of inventories, which in turn   accumulation

would cause [upward/downward] pressure on the price   downward

until equilibrium was restored. Similarly, if the price were $3 per bushel, there would be an excess quantity [supplied/

demanded] of _____ million bushels per year. This   demanded; 1,200

160

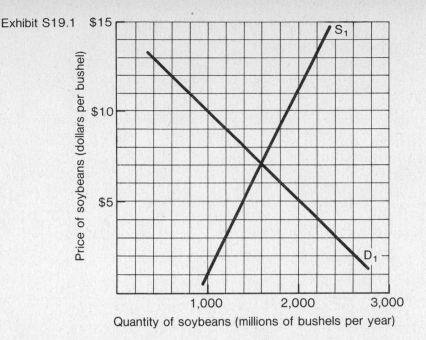

Exhibit S19.1

Price of soybeans (dollars per bushel)

$15

$10

$5

S_1

D_1

1,000   2,000   3,000

Quantity of soybeans (millions of bushels per year)

situation would cause [accumulation/depletion] of inven-   depletion
tories and [upward/downward] pressure on price until   upward
equilibrium was restored.

    Exhibit S19.1 can also be used to illustrate the effects
of changes in economic conditions on the market for soybeans. Suppose, for example, that an improvement in farm
technology cut the cost of producing soybeans by $3 per
bushel below what it formerly was for any given quantity.
This change would be represented by a [shift in/movement
along] the supply curve for soybeans. Sketch in the new   shift in
supply curve, labeling it S_2. It should be parallel to S_1
and have a height of _____ at 2,000 million bushels per $8
year. The initial effect of this shift in the supply curve
would be to create an excess [supply/demand] of _____   supply; 300
million bushels per year, causing [upward/downward]   downward
pressure on price and a [shift in/movement along] the   movement along
demand curve. The new equilibrium price would be _____ $6
per bushel.

    With the new supply curve S_2 in place, suppose next
that a failure of the Brazilian soybean crop caused an increase in demand for U.S. soybeans; at any given price,
buyers are now willing to purchase an additional 600 million
bushels per year. Sketch in the new demand curve,
labeling it D_2. It should be parallel to D_1 and indicate a

161

purchase of _____ million bushels at a price of $7 per   2,200
bushel. The initial effect of this shift in the demand
curve would be an excess [supply/demand] of _____   demand; 600
million bushels per year. This will cause [upward/downward]   upward
pressure on the price, a [shift in/movement along] the   movement along
supply curve, and a new equilibrium with a price of _____ $8
per bushel and a quantity of _____ million bushels per   2,000
year.

Elasticity

The price elasticity of demand is the ratio of the percentage
change in [price/quantity demanded] of a good to the per-   quantity demanded
centage change in its [price/quantity demanded]. Elasticity   price
is closely related to what happens to total revenue as price
changes. If total revenue increases as the price decreases,
demand is said to be _____. If total revenue   elastic
does not change as the price falls, demand is said to be
_____. If total revenue falls as the price   unit elastic
falls, demand is said to be _____. A ver-   inelastic
tical demand curve is said to be _____   perfectly inelastic
and a horizontal demand curve _____.   perfectly elastic

   Numerical values for price elasticity of demand can be
calculated with the formula given in the text and in the
chapter synopsis above. Suppose, for example, that a
grocer found that sales of pork chops increased from 100
pounds per day to 200 pounds per day when the price
was reduced from $1.20 per pound to 80 cents per pound.
This would indicate an elasticity of demand of _____.   1.66

SELF TEST

These sample test items will help you check how much you have learned. Answers
and explanations can be found at the end of this chapter. Scoring yourself: One
or two wrong -- on target. Three to five wrong -- passing but you haven't mastered the chaper yet. Six or more wrong -- not good enough; start over and
restudy the chapter.

True or False

Indicate whether each statement is true or false as it stands. If it is false, explain
why in a few words.

T F 1. A change in the supply of wheat is represented graphically as a movement
         along the wheat supply curve.

T F   2.   A change in the supply of pork, other things being equal, will be followed by a change in the demand for pork as part of the process of establishing a new equilibrium.

T F   3.   Beginning from a position of equilibrium, a leftward shift in the demand curve for oak flooring will initially cause an excess demand for oak flooring.

T F   4.   An excess demand for candles, other things being equal, will tend to put upward pressure on the price of candles.

T F   5.   An excess demand for a service such as housepainting, which cannot be stored in inventory, will not effectively put upward pressure on the price.

T F   6.   A vertical supply curve indicates perfect elasticity of supply.

T F   7.   If the manager of the Washington, D.C., Metro (subway) system found that revenues increased when fares were raised, they would conclude that demand for subway services was inelastic.

T F   8.   A demand curve having the form of a straight line with a slope of –1 would have unit elasticity throughout its length.

T F   9.   If demand for a good is price elastic, it must also be income elastic.

Multiple Choice

1.   An increase in consumer income, other things being equal, would be likely to have which of the following effects on the market for cars?
     a.   First a shift in the demand curve, then a shift in the supply curve.
     b.   First a shift in the supply curve, then a shift in the demand curve.
     c.   First a shift in the demand curve, then a movement along the supply curve.
     d.   First a movement along the demand curve, then a shift in the supply curve.

2.   If Good x is an inferior good, an increase in consumer income will
     a.   shift the demand curve to the left.
     b.   shift the demand curve to the right.
     c.   cause an upward movement along the demand curve without shifting it.
     d.   cause a downward movement along the demand curve without shifting it.

3.   Which of the following would cause a movement along the supply curve for lawnmowers, without shifting the curve?
     a.   A change in the wage rate of lawnmower workers.
     b.   A change in the technology of lawnmower production.
     c.   A change in the price of hired lawn care services.
     d.   None of the above.

4.   Assuming beef to be a normal good, which of the following would not happen on the way to a new equilibrium if, other things being equal, consumer income increased?
     a.   Depletion of inventories.
     b.   A shortage.
     c.   An upward movement of prices.
     d.   An upward shift of the supply curve.

5.   In July 1979, Moore's grocery sold thirty-two jars of pickles, earning a total
      revenue of $31.36. In July 1980, the same store sold thirty-two jars of pickles,
      earning a total revenue of $38.08. From this data, it can be concluded that
      a.   the supply of pickles is perfectly inelastic.
      b.   the demand for pickles is elastic.
      c.   the supply curve for pickles shifted upward.
      d.   none of the above is necessarily true.

6.   If the excess quantity of wheat supplied is 300 million bushels per year when
      the price is $3 per bushel and 600 million bushels per year when the price
      is $3.20 per bushel, which of the following can be concluded?
      a.   The demand for wheat is elastic.
      b.   The supply of wheat is elastic.
      c.   At least one of the above is true.
      d.   None of the above can be concluded from the information given.

7.   A horizontal demand curve is described as
      a.   perfectly inelastic.
      b.   perfectly elastic.
      c.   unit elastic.
      d.   negatively elastic.

8.   If the number of movie tickets sold increases by 10 percent when the price is
      cut by 20 percent, other things being equal, it can be concluded that
      a.   demand is price elastic.
      b.   demand is price inelastic.
      c.   demand is income elastic.
      d.   demand is income inelastic.

9.   If deregulation of airline fares, other things being equal, led to lower prices
      and higher revenues, it could be concluded that
      a.   demand was elastic.
      b.   demand was inelastic.
      c.   supply was elastic.
      d.   supply was inelastic.

10.   If raising the cigarette tax from 10 cents per pack to 20 cents per pack left
      cigarette tax revenues unchanged, it could be concluded that the price elas-
      ticity of demand for cigarettes was
      a.   elastic.
      b.   inelastic.
      c.   unit elastic.
      d.   impossible to calculate from the information given.

11.   Which of the following statements can be made about a downward sloping,
      straight-line demand curve?
      a.   It is more elastic at the top than at the bottom.
      b.   It is more elastic at the bottom than at the top.
      c.   It has a constant elasticity throughout its length.
      d.   Insufficient information is given for an answer to be reached.

12.   A supply curve that is a straight line passing through the origin
      a.   must be unit elastic.
      b.   has a constant elasticity, but need not be unit elastic.
      c.   is more elastic at the top than at the bottom.
      d.   is more elastic at the bottom than at the top.

13. If the quantity of apples sold at a certain fruit stand increases from 20 pounds per day to 30 pounds per day when the price is lowered from 40 cents per pound to 30 cents per pound, the elasticity of demand is closest to which of the following?
   a. 0.2.
   b. 0.7.
   c. 1.4.
   d. 4.1.

14. Other things being equal, we expect that a given change in price will have a greater effect on quantity demanded
   a. in the short run than in the long run.
   b. in the long run than in the short run.
   c. the less income elastic the demand.
   d. the less price elastic the demand.

15. If the income elasticity of demand for intercity bus travel is -0.5, we would expect, other things equal,
   a. that bus company revenues will rise when incomes fall.
   b. that bus company revenues will fall when incomes fall.
   c. that a is true, but only if demand is also price elastic.
   d. that a is true, but only if demand is also price inelastic.

ANSWERS TO CHAPTER 19 SELF TEST

True or False

1-F; shift in the curve.
2-F; movement along the pork demand curve.
3-F; excess supply.
4-T
5-F; will be effective.
6-F; perfect inelasticity.
7-T
8-F; elasticity would vary.
9-F; no relation between the two.
10-F; greater than zero.

Multiple Choice

1-c
2-a
3-d
4-d
5-d; any of the above might be true, but none need be true.
6-d; not enough information given to determine elasticity.
7-b
8-b
9-a
10-a; doubling the tax less than doubles the total price.
11-a
12-a
13-c
14-b
15-a

CHAPTER TWENTY
THE LOGIC OF CONSUMER CHOICE

WHERE YOU'RE GOING

Here is what you will be able to do when you have mastered this chapter:

--Explain what economists mean by utility and why economists approach the question of satisfying human needs from a different point of view than do psychologists.

--Define marginal utility, and explain what is meant by the principle of diminishing marginal utility.

--Explain the state of consumer equilibrium as the solution to a problem of pure economizing.

--Discuss the law of demand in terms of income and substitution effects.

In addition, when you have mastered the appendix to this chapter, you will be able to:

--Analyze patterns of consumer preference in terms of indifference curves.

--Use indifference curves to solve problems in consumer equilibrium.

--Use indifference curves to derive demand curves.

--Discuss the meaning and significance of the following additional terms and concepts:

> Indifference set.
> Marginal rate of substitution.
> Indifference map.
> Transitivity.
> Budget line.

CHAPTER SYNOPSIS

Reading this synopsis is not a substitute for reading the chapter, but it should help you to recall the main points. If there are any you feel unsure of, refer to the full discussion in the text.

Economists refer to the pleasure and satisfaction that people get from the consumption of material goods and services as utility. Unlike psychologists, economists are not particularly interested in the reasons why people get utility from some goods and services rather than others. Instead, they are primarily interested in the concept of utility because of the insights the concept gives into the operation of the law of demand and other aspects of consumer choice.

As soon as economists in the nineteenth century began thinking of consumer behavior in terms of utility, they noticed an important regularity: the principle of diminishing marginal utility. According to this principle, the greater the rate of consumption of any good or service, the smaller the increase in utility from a unit increase in consumption--the smaller, that is, the marginal utility of the good or service in question.

The principle of diminishing marginal utility is helpful in understanding how consumers solve the problems in pure economizing that they face every day--problems requiring a choice among many alternative desirable goods, each available at a known price, with the ability to realize the objective of maximum utility limited by the constraint of a fixed budget. In their attempts to maximize utility given their limited budgets, consumers must choose carefully. If they consume too much of one good, the utility they get from the last few units of dollars spent on it will turn out to be less than the utility they could have gotten from spending the same money on other goods having higher marginal utilities per dollar's worth consumed. The solution is to consume each good just to the point where the marginal utility derived from a dollar's worth of any one good consumed is just equal to the marginal utility derived from a dollar's worth of each other good consumed. When expenditures have been adjusted according to this rule, consumers are said to be in a state of consumer equilibrium.

The concepts of marginal utility and consumer equilibrium can be used to give an intuitively appealing, if not altogether precise, explanation of the law of demand. Assume that you are in consumer equilibrium with respect to the two goods food and clothing. The quantities you consume are such as to equalize the marginal utilities per dollar's worth of the two goods. Then suppose the price of clothing goes down while the price of food does not change. That will increase the marginal utility you get from a dollar's worth of clothing, because a "dollar's worth" now represents a bigger physical bundle of clothing than before. One way you can get back into equilibrium is by consuming more clothing, thus driving down the marginal utility of the last dollar's worth purchased. That action conforms to the law of demand-- the price of clothing went down, so you bought more clothing.

The concepts of income and substitution effects can be used to give an alternative explanation of the law of demand that does not rely on the somewhat slippery concept of marginal utility. The substitution effect is defined as the part of the increase in quantity demanded of a good whose price has fallen that is attributable to the tendency of consumers to substitute relatively cheap goods for relatively expensive goods. The substitution effect taken alone thus always leads to an increase in consumption of a good when the price of that good goes down. The income effect is the part of the change in quantity demanded of a good whose price has fallen that is attributable to the change in real income resulting from the price change. When the price of a good goes down, other prices and income remaining the same, a consumer is able to consume the same quantities as before and still have funds left over (that is, the consumer experiences an increase in real income). If the good is a normal one, some of this additional real income will go to purchase more of the good in question; for normal goods, then, the income and substitution effect both work to increase consumption when the price falls, confirming the law of demand. If the good is an inferior one, then the income effect, taken alone, will lead to a decrease in the quantity consumed of the good whose price has fallen. However, with few if any exceptions, the substitution effect is stronger than the income effect even for inferior goods; so the net result is that the law of demand holds for inferior goods, too.

WALKING TOUR

You have read the chapter at least once and have reviewed the synopsis. Now you are going to walk through the material step by step, filling in the blanks and answering the questions as you go along. After you have answered each question, check yourself by uncovering the answer given in the margin. If you do not understand why the answer given is the right one, refer back to the proper section of the text.

Consumption and Utility

Economists refer to the pleasure and satisfaction that people get from the consumption of goods and services as _____. The utility one gets from the consumption of one additional unit of a good is known as the _____ of that good. The important principle of diminishing marginal utility says that as consumption increases the additional satisfaction received from a one-unit increase in consumption [rises/falls]. In practice, utility cannot be directly measured, but if there were such a thing as a utility meter, it might give a set of readings like those shown in the table below. Use the data given in the total utility column to fill in the marginal utility column.

utility

marginal utility

falls

Number of Units of Goods Consumed	Total Utility	Marginal Utility	
1	100		
		_____	20
2	120		
		_____	15
3	135		
		_____	10
4	145		
		_____	8
5	153		

The concept of diminishing marginal utility is useful in analyzing the problem in pure economizing that all consumers face. In this problem, the various goods and services available represent _____. The prices of the goods, together with the consumer's budget, provide the _____ of the problem. Maximizing utility is the _____. The problem is solved by choosing a selection of goods that makes the [marginal/total] utility per dollar's worth of each good just equal to the marginal utility per dollar's worth of each other good. An equivalent way to express this rule is to say that in consumer equilibrium, the ratio of the marginal utility of each good to its _____ must be the same for all goods consumed.

alternative activities

constraints

objective

marginal

price

169

Substitution and Income Effects

The change in quantity consumed of a good whose price has fallen can be divided into two parts. The part of the increase in consumption resulting from substituting more of the relatively cheap good is known as the _____ effect. The part resulting from the effective increase in real income is known as the _____ effect. The substitution effect leads to an increase in quantity demanded when price falls for [normal/inferior/all] goods. The income effect leads to an increase in quantity demanded when price falls for [normal/inferior/all] goods and to a decrease in quantity demanded when price falls for [normal/inferior/all] goods. Even for inferior goods, the [income/substitution] effect is normally the stronger of the two, so that in all or virtually all cases, quantity demanded increases when the price [falls/rises].

substitution

income

all

normal

inferior
substitution

falls

Appendix: Indifference Curves

An indifference curve is the graphical representation of a set of baskets of goods, none of which is preferred to any other basket in the set. Such curves have certain standard properties, including the following: They all have [positive/negative] slopes. The slope of an indifference curve at any point is equal to the ratio of the marginal utility of the good on the [horizontal/vertical] axis to the marginal utility of the good on the [horizontal/vertical] axis. The slope of an indifference curve [increases/decreases] as one moves down and to the right along the curve. An indifference curve can be drawn through any point between the axes. Indifference curves do not cross because of the property of _____ of preferences.

negative

horizontal
vertical
decreases

transitivity

Exhibit S20.1 will give you some practice in using indifference curves. The indifference map drawn there represents (hypothetically) my preferences for books versus movies. You have to figure out how many books and how many movies I will consume under various price conditions. Assume throughout the exercise that the price of movies is $3 per movie and that my entertainment budget (spent entirely on these two items) is $120 per year.

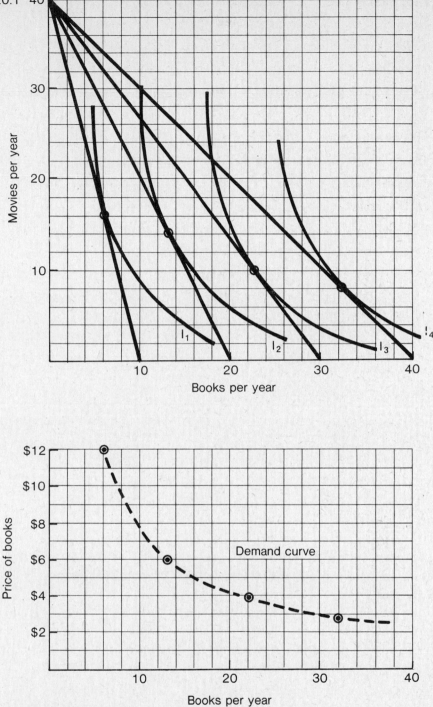

Begin by assuming that the price of books is $3. Given
this book price, together with the movie price and my budget,
construct my budget line as follows: If I spend all my money
on movies, I will be able to see _____ movies per year.   forty
So mark a point at 40 on the vertical axis. If I spend all

171

my money on books, I will be able to buy _____ books   forty
per year. So mark a point at 40 on the horizontal axis.
Connecting these two points gives you my budget line
under the assumed prices. The point I will choose given
this budget line is the point where the indifference curve
_____ is _____ to the budget line. This will I_4; tangent
mean consuming approximately _____ books and _____   thirty-two; eight
movies per year.

     Assume now that the price of books rises to $4. If
I spend all my money on movies, I can still see forty movies,
but if I spend it all on books, I can buy only _____   thirty
books. So the new budget line runs from _____ on the   40
vertical axis to _____ on the horizontal axis. The point   30
I will choose on this new budget line will be at the tangency
of indifference curve _____. This will mean consuming I_3
approximately _____ movies and _____ books. (Note   ten; twenty-two
that consuming ten movies and twenty-two books would
leave $2 unspent.)

     Proceed in a similar fashion to discover what I will
consume if the price of books rises to $6 while my budget
and the price of movies remains the same. You will discover that at $6 per book I would buy approximately _____   thirteen
books and see _____ movies. Finally, perform the   fourteen
same exercise for a book price of $12. At that price, I
would consume approximately _____ books and _____   six; sixteen
movies. Now use the data from your figure to fill in the
following table:

Price of books	Quantity of books	
$12	_____	6
6	_____	13
4	_____	22
3	_____	32

Finally, use the table you have just constructed to fill in
my demand curve for books in the lower part of Exhibit
S20.1. Your completed diagram should look like the one
shown in the answers section at the end of this chapter.

172

SELF TEST

These sample test items will help you check how much you have learned. Answers and explanations can be found at the end of this chapter. Scoring yourself: One or two wrong -- on target. Three to five wrong -- passing, but you haven't mastered the chapter yet. Six or more wrong -- not good enough; start over and restudy the chapter.

True or False

Indicate whether each statement is true or false as it stands. If it is false, explain why in a few words.

T F 1. Economists are interested not so much in why people want goods as in how much they are willing to pay for them.

T F 2. According to the principle of diminishing marginal utility, the marginal utility per added dollar's worth of a good declines as the price of the good decreases, other things being equal.

T F 3. One of the major advances of economics in the late nineteenth century was the development of practical ways to make actual measurements of utility.

T F 4. Consumers tend to shift their pattern of consumption from one good to another as long as by doing so they can increase their utility without increasing their total expenditures.

T F 5. In consumer equilibrium, the ratio of the marginal utility of a good to its price must be the same for all goods consumed.

T F 6. The substitution effect always tends to cause the quantity demanded of a good to increase as its price decreases.

T F 7. For inferior goods, the income effect, in almost all cases, outweighs the substitution effect.

T F 8. According to the theory of income and substitution effects, if there are any genuine exceptions to the law of demand, they must be sought among inferior goods.

T F 9. Transitivity means that if A is preferred to B and B is preferred to C, then A will be preferred to C.

T F 10. The slope of an indifference curve increases as one moves up and to the left along it.

Multiple Choice

1. The theory of marginal utility is studied today chiefly because
    a. it demonstrates that there is a hierarchy among various categories of human needs.
    b. of the recent invention of workable methods of measuring utility.
    c. it is the only basis for derivation of the law of demand.
    d. it provides insights into the problem of consumer choice.

2. According to the principle of diminishing marginal utility, if consumption of a third slice of bread with a meal yields 10 utils, consumption of a sixth slice of bread must give
    a. more than 10 utils.
    b. less than 10 utils.
    c. between 5 and 10 utils.
    d. between 0 and 5 utils.

3. If the consumer choice problem is thought of as a problem in pure economizing, the role of constraint is best represented by
    a. the range of alternative goods available.
    b. the consumer's budget.
    c. the consumer's total capacity for enjoyment.
    d. the consumer's previous patterns of consumption.

4. Assume for a moment that utility is measurable. Then if a loaf of bread at 20 cents per loaf gives 10 utils, a quart of milk costing 50 cents must give how many utils in consumer equilibrium?
    a. 5 utils.
    b. 12.5 utils.
    c. 25 utils.
    d. 50 utils.

5. Let MU_a represent the marginal utility of Good a, MU_b the marginal utility of Good b, P_a the price of Good a, and P_b the price of Good b. Then in consumer equilibrium, which of the following must hold?
    a. $MU_a = MU_b$.
    b. $P_a = P_b$.
    c. $MU_a/MU_b = P_a/P_b$.
    d. $MU_a/MU_b = P_b/P_a$.

6. In equilibrium, a certain person consumes two units of Good x, which costs 30 cents per unit, and four units of Good y, which costs 50 cents per unit. It can be concluded that for that person, in equilibrium, the ratio of the marginal utility of Good x to the marginal utility of Good y is
    a. 2/4.
    b. 4/2.
    c. 3/5.
    d. 5/3.

7. The change in consumption of a good that occurs when its price falls is the result of
    a. the substitution effect.
    b. the income effect.
    c. both of the above effects in combination.
    d. the complementarity of normal and inferior goods.

8. A good with an upward sloping demand curve
    a. must be an inferior good.
    b. must be a normal good.
    c. must have no substitution effect.
    d. must have no income effect.

9. Martha Smith is observed to consume ten quarts of milk per week at 50 cents per quart. One week the price of milk drops to 40 cents per quart; but in the same week, a thief steals $1 from her purse, reducing her weekly budget by that amount. On the basis of the theory of consumer behavior, which of the following quantities of milk would she be most likely to consume that week?
    a. Less than ten quarts.
    b. 10 quarts.
    c. More than ten quarts.
    d. More than ten quarts, but only if milk is assumed to be a normal good.

10. In July 1979, Ed Schwartz ate six ice cream cones at a price of 50 cents per cone. In July 1980, he ate seven ice cream cones at a price of 60 cents per cone. Which of the following is the most likely explanation of his behavior?
    a. His demand curve for ice cream cones slopes upward.
    b. Ice cream is an inferior good for him; he prefers cake if he can afford it.
    c. The marginal utility of ice cream increases, rather than decreases, as his consumption goes up, other things being equal.
    d. His income and the prices of other goods went up from 1979 to 1980.

Note: The remaining questions are based on the appendix to Chapter 20.

11. Which of the following baskets of goods cannot be a member of an indifference set to which the other three belong?
    a. Four pounds of meat, four pounds of cheese.
    b. Three pounds of meat, ten pounds of cheese.
    c. Five pounds of meat, three pounds of cheese.
    d. Four pounds of meat, three pounds of cheese.

12. In 1979, during a series of baseball games, the Reds beat the Astros, the Astros beat the Giants, and the Giants beat the Reds. We conclude that the relationship denoted by the word "beats" is
    a. subject to transitivity.
    b. not subject to transitivity.
    c. inherently meaningless.
    d. none of the above.

13. An upward sloping indifference curve might be possible in which of the following cases?
    a. If the rule of transitivity were violated.
    b. If the principle of diminishing marginal utility were violated.
    c. If the marginal utility of one of the goods diminished so far that it actually became negative.
    d. None of the above.

14. If a consumer has a budget of $10 per week, if eggs cost $1 per dozen, and if milk costs 50 cents per quart, then the consumer's budget line will have what slope (assuming eggs to be represented on the vertical axis)?
    a. 1/2.
    b. -1/2.
    c. 2.
    d. -2.

15. Given an indifference map, a fixed budget, and a fixed price for the good represented on the vertical axis, an increase in the price of the good represented on the horizontal axis is likely to move the consumption point
    a. up and to the right.
    b. up and to the left along the same indifference curve.
    c. to the left, although either upward or downward, so long as the good is a normal good.
    d. to the left and downward so long as the two goods are substitutes.

ANSWERS TO CHAPTER 20 SELF TEST

True or False

1-T
2-F; as the quantity consumed increases.
3-F; utility cannot be measured.
4-T
5-T
6-T
7-F; it is opposite in direction, but virtually always less in magnitude.
8-T
9-T
10-T

Multiple Choice

1-d
2-b
3-b
4-c
5-c
6-c; the marginal utility ratio must equal the price ratio in equilibrium.
7-c
8-a
9-c; the theft eliminates the income effect, but the price effect acting alone is enough to cause her to consume more milk.
10-d; the first three are only remotely possible explanations.
11-d; d is clearly inferior both to a and to d; thus it cannot be a member of an indifference set containing either a or c.
12-b
13-c
14-b
15-c; if substitutes, to the left and up; if complements, to the left and down.

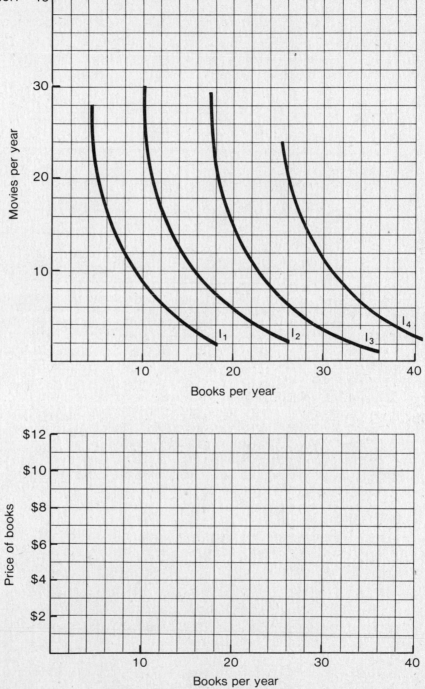

Exhibit S20.1

CHAPTER TWENTY-ONE
THE NATURE OF THE FIRM

WHERE YOU'RE GOING

Here is what you will be able to do when you have mastered this chapter:

--Distinguish between market coordination and managerial coordination as methods of organizing economic activity.

--Explain why firms exist and what limits the size of the firm in a market economy, in terms of the two principles of coordination.

--Define sole proprietorship, partnership, and corporation, and explain the advantages and disadvantages of each type of business organization.

--Explain why the interests of corporate managers and stockholders may sometimes diverge, and discuss the mechanisms that constrain the ability of managers to act independently of the interests of the stockholders.

CHAPTER SYNOPSIS

Reading this synopsis is not a substitute for reading the chapter, but it should help you to recall the main points. If there are any you feel unsure of, refer to the full discussion in the text.

In a modern economy, economic activity can be coordinated by one of two methods: market coordination, which utilizes the price system to transmit information and provide incentives, or managerial coordination, which relies on directives issued by managers to subordinates. In a famous essay on the nature of the firm, Ronald Coase noted that firms use managerial coordination internally, while at the same time their relations with other firms are coordinated by the market mechanism.

Why, Coase asked, is the whole economy not organized as one big firm, with managerial coordination used throughout? Or why, for that matter, is every individual worker or resource owner not a separate firm, coordinating his or her economic activity with that of all others via the market? The answer he gave was that, in a market economy, each task tends to be organized according to that principle found by trial and error to be more efficient. Small-scale coordination, such as that within a firm, appears to be done more efficiently by the managerial principle; but beyond a point, the market mechanism becomes more efficient. So firms tend to grow until they find that the cost of organizing one more task internally by the managerial method becomes more expensive than organizing the additional task via the market.

All firms make use of managerial coordination in their internal affairs, but they differ in many other respects. In the U.S. economy, there are three major forms of business organization: the sole proprietorship, the partnership, and the corporation.

A sole proprietorship is owned and managed by a single person, who receives all of the profits of the firm and bears all of the risks. Independence for the owner and ease of organization and dissolution are major advantages of the sole proprietorship; unlimited liability and difficulty in raising large sums of capital are disadvantages.

A partnership is a firm owned jointly by two or more persons, who share the profits and risks. Compared with a sole proprietorship, a partnership has the advantage of attracting additional talent and capital. However, it retains the disadvantages of unlimited liability of each partner for all obligations of the partnership.

A corporation is a firm in which the ownership is divided into equal shares, with each owner's liability limited to the amount invested in the firm. The corporation is the organizational form most suited to large-scale business, as large sums of capital can be raised from many individuals, each of whom contributes only a small amount and each of whom bears only limited liability. However, corporations have the disadvantage of being more heavily taxed and regulated than are other forms of business organization.

In practice, each form of business organization finds its own place in the U.S. economy. More than three-quarters of all firms are sole proprietorships, but most of them are small; the 15 percent of firms that are corporations account for more than 85 percent of all business receipts. Partnerships occupy an intermediate position in terms of size.

One widely debated issue concerning corporations is the possible separation of corporate ownership and control. Although individual shareholders have the right to elect corporate boards of directors, which determine the general policies of the firm and appoint day-to-day managers, many shareholders do not actively exercise these rights. That gives managers the opportunity, in some instances, to pursue their own interests rather than those of the stockholders if the two diverge. For example, corporate managers are sometimes said to favor growth over profitability, to favor corporate image over efficiency, and to be more cautious in risk taking than stockholders would want them to be. However, the ability of corporate managers to act independently is, in practice, limited. For one thing, some corporations have incentive plans, such as paying managers partly in stock options, that give managers a direct interest in profits. More importantly, if a management is not profit motivated, stockholders in the firm may sell their shares, driving the market price of the shares down. That opens an opportunity for some other firm or some group of individuals to take over the corporation, oust the management, and replace them with a more profit-minded group.

WALKING TOUR

You have read the chapter at least once and have reviewed the synopsis. Now you are going to walk through the material step by step, filling in the blanks and answering the questions as you go along. After you have answered each question, check yourself by uncovering the answer given in the margin. If you do not understand why the answer given is the correct one, refer back to the proper section of the text.

Coordinating Economic Activity

Two major forms of coordinating economic activity are

used in the U.S. economy. Market coordination relies on

the market to transmit _____ and to pro-   information

vide the necessary _____. Managerial coor-   incentives

dination relies on _____ for communication   directives

and relies for incentives on the fact that subordinates have

pledged obedience, at least within certain limits, as a

condition of employment. For each of the following tasks,

which form of organization would be more appropriate?

--Deciding which worker sweeps the floors and which

washes the windows: _____.   managerial

--Deciding whether a clothing firm should specialize

in coats or dresses: _____.   market

--Deciding how investment funds should be divided be-

tween farming and industry: _____.   market

--Deciding which plant of a multiplant auto firm should

specialize in trucks: _____.   managerial

As a general principle, the size of a firm is limited by the
number of tasks it can efficiently coordinate by use of the
managerial principle.

Forms of Business Organization

Firms differ not only in size and complexity, but also in
terms of legal form of organization. A firm owned and
managed by one person is known as a _____.   sole proprietorship
The owner of such a firm is subject to [limited/unlimited]   unlimited
liability. A firm owned jointly by two or more people,
each of whom retains unlimited liability, is known as a
_____. A firm having ownership   partnership
divided into many _____, with each share-   shares
holder having [limited/unlimited] liability, is known as a   limited
_____. Corporations are the most   corporation
suitable form of organization for [large/small] business   large
and account for about 85 percent of the receipts of all
business firms in the U.S. economy.

SELF TEST

These sample test items will help you check how much you have learned. Answers
and explanations can be found at the end of this chapter. Scoring yourself: One
or two wrong -- on target. Three to five wrong -- passing, but you haven't mastered the chapter yet. Six or more wrong -- not good enough; start over and restudy the chapter.

True or False

Indicate whether each statement is true or false as it stands. If it is false, indicate
why in a few words.

T F 1. Managerial coordination relies on complex negotiations between managers
and subordinates to coordinate economic activity.

T F 2. The managerial form of coordination is commonly used within individual
firms.

T F 3. Most coordination decisions within the firm could probably be handled by market coordination, but it would presumably be less efficient for them to be so handled.

T F 4. If managerial coordination were costless, the economy would very likely be organized as a single gigantic firm.

T F 5. According to Coase's theory, small firms must be proprietorships and larger firms corporations in order to minimize costs of coordination.

T F 6. Proprietorships suffer from the disadvantage that the legal life of the firm ends when the owner dies.

T F 7. Partnerships are particularly common in the law and medical professions because they offer partners limited liability, which is important in case of malpractice suits.

T F 8. Service industries have a higher than average percentage of partnerships.

T F 9. In recent years, corporations have for the first time come to outnumber proprietorships in the agricultural sector of the economy.

T F 10. One purpose of corporate stock option plans is to encourage corporate managers to pay attention to shareholder interests.

Multiple Choice

1. Which of the following coordination decisions is not commonly made by means of the managerial mechanism in the U.S. economy?
   a. Who should do the hubcaps and who should do the steering wheels in a Ford assembly plant.
   b. Which Ford plant should build Pintos and which should build LTDs.
   c. How many Fords and how many Toyotas should be sold each year.
   d. How much of a Ford plant expansion should be financed by stocks and how much by bonds.

2. If market coordination were costless and managerial coordination costly, then
   a. the economy would probably be all one big firm.
   b. the economy would probably be fragmented into tens of millions of tiny firms.
   c. corporations would have a bigger advantage over proprietorships than they currently do.
   d. corporate management would be more isolated from corporate ownership than it currently is.

3. Which of the following is not an advantage of the sole proprietorship?
   a. Unity of ownership and control.
   b. Limited liability.
   c. Ease of set-up and dissolution.
   d. Independence for the owner.

4. Which of the following is clearly an advantage of the partnership in comparison with the sole proprietorship?
   a. Unlimited liability.
   b. Ease of raising capital.
   c. Ease of set-up and dissolution.
   d. Minimization of internal management disputes.

5. Which of the following is not an advantage of the corporate form of organization?
   a. Low taxes.
   b. Limited liability.
   c. Unlimited life of the firm.
   d. Flexibility in changing managers.

6. Which of the following forms of business has the disadvantage that an individual owner may find it difficult to withdraw capital contributions to invest elsewhere?
   a. Sole proprietorship.
   b. Partnership.
   c. Corporation.
   d. All of the above are about equal in this respect.

7. Which of the following forms of business has the advantage when it comes to raising large amounts of capital from many small investors?
   a. Sole proprietorship.
   b. Partnership.
   c. Corporation.
   d. All of the above are about equal in this respect.

8. Which of the following forms of business has the advantage of unlimited life of the firm?
   a. Sole proprietorship.
   b. Partnership.
   c. Corporation.
   d. All of the above are about equal in this respect.

9. Which of the following forms of business has the disadvantage of having higher taxes than the others?
   a. Sole proprietorship.
   b. Partnership.
   c. Corporation.
   d. All of the above are about equal in this respect.

10. Which of the following forms of business organization accounts for the largest share of total business receipts in the U.S. economy?
    a. Sole proprietorship.
    b. Partnership.
    c. Corporation.
    d. Receipts are about equally divided among all of the above.

11. Which of the following sectors of the economy contains the highest percentage of individual proprietorships?
    a. Agriculture.
    b. Mining.
    c. Services.
    d. Manufacturing.

12. Which of the following sectors of the economy contains the largest percentage of partnerships?
    a. Wholesale and retail trade.
    b. Services.
    c. Construction.
    d. Agriculture.

13. Which of the following sectors of the economy contains the highest percentage of corporations?
   a. Agriculture.
   b. Construction.
   c. Manufacturing.
   d. Services.

14. In which of the following respects is it believed that corporate management may have different interests than corporate shareholders?
   a. How many risks to take.
   b. How fast to grow.
   c. How deep a carpet to put on the floor of the president's office.
   d. All of the above.

15. Which of the following is probably the least effective as a means of persuading managers to keep shareholder interests in mind?
   a. Stock option plans.
   b. Takeover threats.
   c. Votes by small shareholders in the annual meeting.
   d. All of the above are equally ineffective.

ANSWERS TO CHAPTER 21 SELF TEST

True or False

1-F; it relies on simple directives.
2-T
3-T
4-T
5-F; the proposition may conceivably be true, but that isn't what Coase's theory is about.
6-T
7-F; they have unlimited liability.
8-T
9-F; proprietorships still predominate.
10-T

Multiple Choice

1-c
2-b
3-b
4-b
5-a
6-b
7-c
8-c
9-c
10-c
11-a
12-b
13-c
14-d
15-c

CHAPTER TWENTY-TWO
THE THEORY OF COST

WHERE YOU'RE GOING

Here is what you will be able to do when you have mastered this chapter:

--Explain what economists mean by cost, distinguishing between <u>explicit</u> and <u>implicit</u> costs.

--Explain what economists mean by profit, distinguishing between <u>pure economic profit</u> and <u>accounting profit</u>.

--Define <u>total</u> and <u>normal</u> rates of return to capital, explaining the relationship between the two in terms of pure economic profit.

--State the <u>law of diminishing returns</u>, and give examples of its operation.

--Explain what is meant by the <u>short run</u> and the <u>long run</u> in economic analysis.

--Draw an illustrative set of short-run and long-run cost curves for a hypothetical typical firm.

--Explain why, according to the <u>marginal average rule</u>, the marginal cost curve must always intersect the average total and variable cost curves at their lowest points.

--Use representative long-run average total cost curves to define and illustrate the concepts of <u>economies of scale</u>, <u>diseconomies of scale</u>, and <u>constant returns to scale</u>.

--Discuss the sources of economies of scale at the plant level and in multiplant firms.

--Explain the meaning and significance of the following additional terms and concepts:

> <u>Fixed inputs.</u>
> <u>Variable inputs.</u>
> <u>Marginal physical product</u> (of an input).
> <u>Marginal cost.</u>
> <u>Minimum efficient scale.</u>

CHAPTER SYNOPSIS

<u>Reading this synopsis is not a substitute for reading the chapter, but it should help you to recall the main points. If there are any you feel unsure of, refer to the full discussion in the text.</u>

A firm's costs are the payments it must make to suppliers and the incomes it must provide to resource owners in order to attract labor, capital, and natural resources away from their alternative uses. Economists refer to costs taking the form of explicit payments to outsiders as <u>explicit costs</u>. The opportunity costs to the firm of using resources owned by the firm itself or contributed without explicit payment by owners of the firm are known as <u>implicit costs</u>. When economists talk about a firm's costs without specifying implicit or explicit costs, they mean the sum of the two.

A proper understanding of the distinction between explicit and implicit costs is necessary for understanding what economists mean by profit. Pure economic profit means total revenue minus both implicit and explicit costs   This differs from the everyday notion of accounting profit, which means revenue minus explicit costs only.

The opportunity cost of capital to a firm, expressed in terms of the percentage payment per year necessary to attract capital away from other potential uses, is known as the normal rate of return to capital for the firm. The total rate of return to capital for the firm is the opportunity costs of capital plus pure economic profit (or less pure economic loss), expressed as a percentage of total capital invested in the firm.

In discussing how a firm's costs vary as its level of output varies, it is useful to distinguish between two time horizons and two kinds of inputs. In the short run, it is assumed that the quantities used of some inputs (known as variable inputs) can be altered while the quantities of other inputs (known as fixed inputs) cannot. In the long run, it is assumed that all inputs can be varied.

According to the well-known law of diminishing returns, as the quantity of one variable input used in a production process is increased (with the quantities of all other inputs remaining fixed), a point will eventually be reached beyond which the quantity of output added per unit of added variable input (that is, the marginal physical product of the variable input) begins to decrease. An implication of the law of diminishing returns is that as the output of a firm is increased in the short run, the added cost needed to produce each added unit of output (called the marginal cost) begins to increase beyond some point.

Marginal cost is only one of a whole family of cost concepts important to under-standing the relationship of costs to output in the short run. You should refer to the detailed exhibits and examples given in the text to learn the relationship among the various short-run cost concepts. One important relationship, known as the marginal average rule, deserves mention here. According to this rule, marginal cost must be equal to average cost when average cost is at its minimum. In geometric terms, this means the marginal cost curve must cut the average total and variable cost curves at their lowest points.

In the short run, the quantity of fixed inputs that a firm has available defines the size of its plant. In the long run, the plant can be expanded in order to pro-duce larger quantities of output at the lowest possible average cost. If, as a firm expands, its average cost of production decreases, it is said to experience economies of scale. If its average cost increases as output is expanded in the long run, it is said to experience diseconomies of scale. If long-run average cost does not change as output expands, the firm is said to experience constant returns to scale. Empirical studies have indicated that, in practice, firms often have roughly L-shaped long-run cost curves. Along such a cost curve, the point where economies of scale are ex-hausted and constant returns to scale begin is known as the firm's minimum efficient scale.

Much effort has gone into investigating the sources of economies of scale. At the plant level, many economies of scale arise because increases in the rate of output permit a more efficient division of labor within the plant or the use of larger, more efficient equipment. Other economies of scale arise not from the rate of output in a single plant, but from the total number of units of output produced over time. Multiplant firms are often able to realize additional cost advantages in research, man-agement, financial, and marketing functions.

WALKING TOUR

You have read the chapter at least once and have reviewed the synopsis. Now you are going to walk through the material step by step, filling in the blanks and answering the questions as you go along. After you have answered each question, check yourself by uncovering the answer given in the margin. If you do not understand why the answer given is the right one, refer back to the full discussion in the text.

The Nature of Costs

The Acme Photo Company is a small firm that sells darkroom supplies to professional photographers. You have the following information about the firm's operations during 1980:

Fuel bills	$ 15,000
Foregone salary of owner/manager	35,000
Materials purchased	10,000
Capital invested by owner	100,000
Total revenue	100,000
Wages paid	30,000
Opportunity cost of capital	15 percent per year

From this information, you conclude that the firm had explicit costs of _____ during 1980, leaving it with $55,000
an accounting profit of _____. In addition, $45,000
the firm had certain implicit costs, including the owner's
foregone salary plus _____ representing the 15 $15,000
percent return the owner could have realized on the
$100,000 of capital had it been invested elsewhere. Total
implicit costs thus come to _____ for the year, $50,000
leaving a pure economic profit of _____--that is,   -$5,000
a pure economic loss. The total return to capital for the
firm can thus be calculated as the opportunity cost of
capital (_____) plus pure economic profit $15,000
(_____) expressed as a percentage of total capital   -$5,000
which comes to _____ percent per year. As always   10
when a firm experiences a pure economic loss, this percentage is [above/below] the normal rate of return on   below
capital for the economy.

Production and Costs in the Short Run

The following table gives you some production data for
another firm, the Bravo Company. Use the data given

to fill in the marginal product column of the table.

Labor Hours Input	Total Physical Product	Marginal Physical Product	
0	0		
1	2	_____	2
2	7	_____	5
3	17	_____	10
4	30	_____	13
5	38	_____	8
6	42	_____	4
7	45	_____	3

Now that you have completed the table, draw a graph of
the marginal product curve in Exhibit S22.1.   First put
in points for each entry in the marginal physical product
column of the table.   (Plot them between the points shown
on the labor hours axis--for example, at $\frac{1}{2}$, $1\frac{1}{2}$, $2\frac{1}{2}$, and
so on.)   Your completed graph should look like the one
shown in the answers and solutions section at the end of
this chapter.   It shows diminishing returns beginning with
the _____ unit of labor input.   fifth

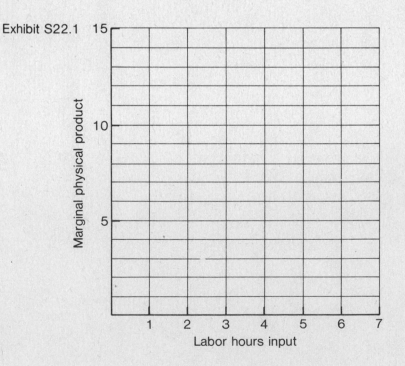

Exhibit S22.1

The next exercise will help you understand the relationships among the various members of the family of short-run cost curves for a typical firm. Exhibit S22.2a gives a total cost curve for the Campbell Company. This total cost curve provides all the information needed to sketch the complete family of cost curves in Exhibits S22.2a and S22.2b. Get a pencil, an eraser and a ruler, and proceed as follows:

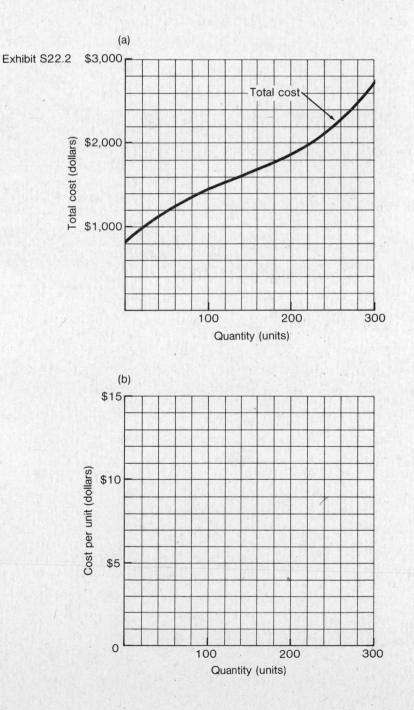

Exhibit S22.2

First, sketch in the total variable cost curve in Part
a of the exhibit. Because total variable cost is equal to
total cost minus fixed cost, the total variable cost curve
will be parallel to the total cost curve and below it by a
distance equal to total fixed cost, which in this case is
_____. (The value of total fixed cost can be found $800
by looking at the vertical intercept of the total cost
curve.) Measure carefully at several points to keep the
two curves parallel.

Next, sketch in the marginal cost curve in Part b of
the exhibit. The height of the marginal cost curve at
any point is equal to the slope of the total cost curve for
that level of output. You can start by finding the minimum of the marginal cost curve. Do this by sliding a ruler
along the total cost curve and tangent to it until you find
the "inflection point"--the point where it stops getting
flatter and starts getting steeper. That happens at about
_____ units of output. The slope of the curve at   130
that point indicates about a _____ increase in cost $3
for each unit of output. so put in a point at 130 units
and $3 on the lower graph, labeling it "Min MC."

According to the marginal average rule, the marginal
cost curve must pass through the minimum points on the
average cost curves, so find these points next. The
average total cost at any quantity of output can be found
in Part a as the slope of a straight line from the origin
to the total cost curve. The slope of such a line (and
hence average total cost) is at a minimum where the line
is just tangent to the total cost curve from below. This
happens at about _____ units of output. The slope   260
of the tangent line at that point indicates about a _____ $9
increase in total cost for each unit increase in output.
So plot a point in Part b of the figure at 260 units and
$9, labeling it "Min ATC." Proceed to find the minimum
point of the average variable cost curve in the same way.
If you have drawn the total variable cost curve carefully,
"Min AVC" should come out at about _____ units of   200
output and _____ in the lower diagram. $5

190

Once you have these three important reference points, you can sketch in the three curves freehand. Draw a U-shaped marginal cost curve with its minimum point at Min MC and passing through Min AVC and Min ATC. Draw somewhat more shallow U's for the two average cost curves, using their minimum points as reference. Your completed figure should look like the one given in the answers and solutions section at the end of the chapter.

Long-Run Costs and Economies of Scale

Exhibit S22.3 gives you one more exercise--an easier one-- this time concerning long-run costs and economies of scale. The exhibit shows a number of possible short-run average total cost curves, each corresponding to a different plant size for the Davidson Corporation. If Davidson planned to produce 1,600 units of output per day in the long run, it would choose the plant represented by Curve _____; if it planned to produce 3,000 units per day, it would choose the larger plant represented by _____; and so on.

C_3

C_6

Use these curves now to sketch in the long-run average total cost curve for the Davidson Corporation.

Exhibit S22.3

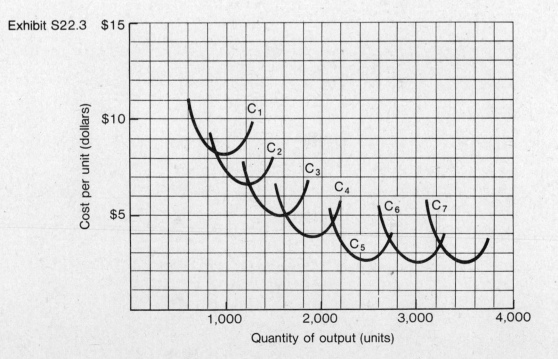

It should be drawn as the "envelope" of the short-run curves--that is, it should just be tangent to each of them in turn.

Looking now at your new long-run average total cost curve, you can see that Davidson experiences economies of scale up to _____ units of output and _____   2,400
_____ scale beyond that point. The   constant returns to
minimum efficient scale for the firm is thus _____ units   2,400
of output.

SELF TEST

These sample test items will help you check how much you have learned. Answers and explanations can be found at the end of this chapter. Scoring yourself: One or two wrong -- on target. Three to five wrong -- passing, but you haven't mastered the chapter yet. Six or more wrong -- not good enough; start over and restudy the chapter.

True or False

Indicate whether each statement is true or false as it stands. If it is false, explain why in a few words.

T F   1.   If a firm's accounting profits are greater than zero, its pure economic profits must also be greater than zero.

T F   2.   If the total rate of return to capital for a firm is greater than the normal rate of return, the firm must be earning a pure economic profit.

T F   3.   The inputs determining the size of a firm's plant in the short run are called fixed inputs.

T F   4.   There are no fixed inputs in the long run.

T F   5.   If the total cost of producing 4,500 bushels of grain on a certain farm is $10,000 and the cost of producing 4,501 bushels is $10,003, then the marginal cost of grain for that range of output is $3 per bushel.

T F   6.   According to the law of diminishing returns, marginal physical product cannot increase as output increases over any range of output.

T F   7.   The marginal cost curve passes through the average fixed cost curve at the minimum point of the latter.

T F   8.   Firms are said to operate in the short run and plan in the long run.

T F   9.   The long-run average total cost curve for a firm passes through the minimum points of all the firm's various possible short-run average total cost curves.

T F 10.   The minimum efficient scale for a firm is the scale at which economies of scale begin to be realized.

Multiple Choice

1. If a firm has revenues of $100 million, explicit costs of $90 million, and implicit costs of $20 million, its pure economic profit is
   a. $80 million.
   b. $70 million.
   c. $10 million.
   d. –$10 million.

2. Let A stand for accounting profit, P for pure economic profit, E for explicit costs, and I for implicit costs. Then
   a. $P = A - E$.
   b. $P = A - I$.
   c. $A = P - I$.
   d. $A = P - E$.

3. A firm has total capital of $500 million. The opportunity cost of capital is 12 percent per year. The firm earns a pure economic profit of $15 million. Its total rate of return on capital is thus
   a. 3 percent.
   b. 9 percent.
   c. 12 percent.
   d. 15 percent.

4. If a firm decided it could save on total cost by unplugging itself from the local electric utility and buying its own generating equipment, we could assume that
   a. both its fixed and variable costs would fall.
   b. both its fixed and variable costs would rise.
   c. its fixed costs would rise and its variable costs would fall.
   d. its fixed costs would fall and its variable costs would rise.

5. The costs defining the size of a firm's plant are
   a. fixed in the short run and variable in the long run.
   b. fixed in the long run and variable in the short run.
   c. fixed in both the long and the short run.
   d. variable in both the long and the short run.

6. The law of diminishing returns implies that the marginal physical product curve
   a. must be U-shaped.
   b. must be shaped like an upside-down U.
   c. must have a negative slope throughout its length.
   d. must have a negative slope for at least part of its length.

7. If a marginal physical product curve and an average physical product curve were both drawn on a single diagram,
   a. the marginal curve would cut the average curve at the minimum point of the latter.
   b. the marginal curve would cut the average curve at the minimum point of the former.
   c. the marginal curve would cut the average curve at the maximum point of the latter.
   d. the marginal curve would cut the average curve at the maximum point of the former.

8. Where the marginal cost curve is below the average variable cost curve,
   a. the average variable cost curve must have a negative slope.
   b. the marginal cost curve must have a negative slope.
   c. the average variable cost curve must have a positive slope.
   d. the marginal cost curve must have a positive slope.

9. The quantity of output where the total variable cost curve stops getting flatter and starts getting steeper must be the quantity corresponding to the minimum of which of the following?
   a. Average total cost.
   b. Average variable cost.
   c. Average fixed cost.
   d. Marginal cost.

10. Suppose that for a certain firm, average variable cost is $10 per unit at twenty units of output and $11 per unit at twenty-one units of output. It follows that marginal cost for that range of output must be
    a. about $1.
    b. about $11.
    c. about $31.
    d. impossible to calculate from the information given.

11. Short-run average total cost is equal to long-run average cost
    a. for all levels of output with a plant of given size.
    b. whenever short-run average total cost is at its minimum.
    c. where long-run average cost is at its minimum.
    d. none of the above.

12. The long-run average cost curve
    a. passes through the minimum points of all short-run average total cost curves.
    b. passes through the minimum points of all short-run average variable cost curves.
    c. is the envelope of all short-run average total cost curves.
    d. is the envelope of all short-run average variable cost curves.

13. A firm is said to experience economies of scale over the range of output for which long-run average cost
    a. is constant.
    b. is falling.
    c. is rising.
    d. economies of scale are not related to long-run average cost.

14. The minimum efficient scale for a firm is the level of output at which
    a. economies of scale cease.
    b. diseconomies of scale begin.
    c. short-run average variable cost first exceeds long-run average cost.
    d. none of the above.

15. Empirical evidence indicates that the minimum efficient scale for a plant in most U.S. industries
    a. is less than 10 percent of U.S. consumption.
    b. is greater than 50 percent of U.S. consumption.
    c. is greater than 100 percent of U.S. consumption.
    d. cannot be measured empirically.

ANSWERS TO CHAPTER 22 SELF TEST

True or False

1-F; implicit cost could exceed accounting profit.
2-T
3-T
4-T
5-T
6-F; beyond some point it must decrease.
7-F; true only for average variable and average total costs.
8-T
9-F; it is the envelope of the short-run curves.
10-F; at which they are exhausted.

Multiple Choice

1-d
2-b
3-d
4-c
5-a
6-d
7-c; this is a variant on the average marginal rule.
8-a
9-d
10-c
11-c
12-c
13-b
14-a
15-a

Solution to Exhibit S22.1

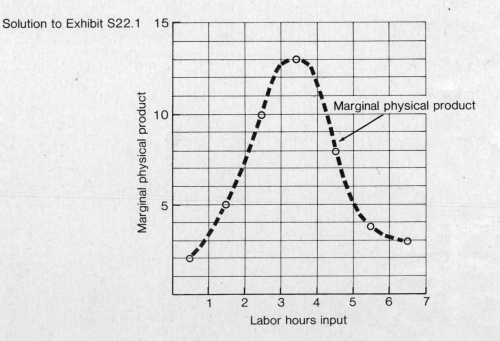

Solution to Exhibit S22.1

Solution to Exhibit S22.2

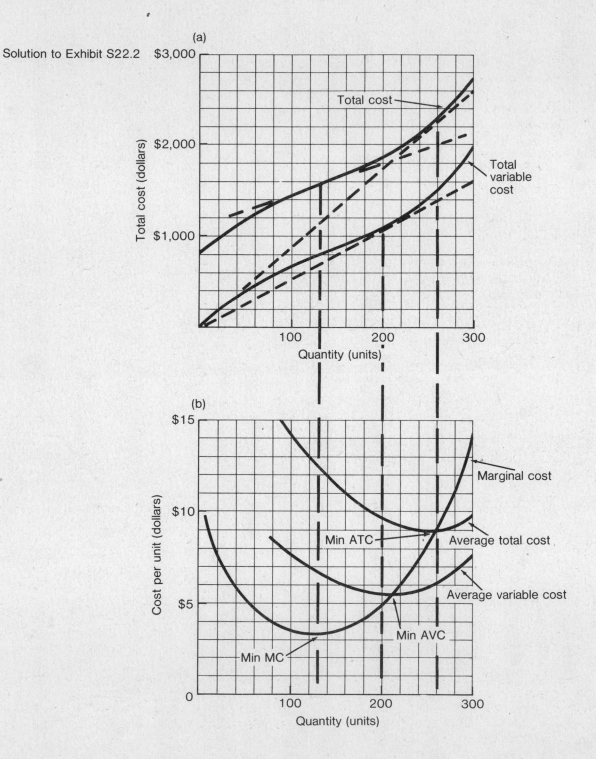

CHAPTER TWENTY-THREE
SUPPLY UNDER PERFECT COMPETITION

WHERE YOU'RE GOING

Here is what you will be able to do when you have mastered this chapter:

--Give the defining characteristics of the market structure known as perfect competition.

--Explain what is meant when it is said that a firm in a perfectly competitive market is a price taker.

--Show how a perfectly competitive firm maximizes short-run profits (or min- imizes short-run losses) by producing the quantity of output for which marginal cost is equal to marginal revenue.

--Show how a supply curve for a perfectly competitive firm can be derived from its cost curves.

--Show how a short-run supply curve for an industry can be derived from the short-run supply curves of the individual firms in that industry.

--List the characteristics of long-run equilibrium in a perfectly competitive industry, and show how such an industry adjusts in the long run to an increase or a decrease in demand.

--Explain what is "perfect" about perfect competition.

CHAPTER SYNOPSIS

Reading this synopsis is not a substitute for reading the chapter, but it should help you to recall the main points. If there are any you feel unsure of, refer to the full discussion in the text.

Economists use the term market structure to refer to such characteristics as the number of firms operating in a market, the extent to which the products of various firms resemble one another, and the difficulty or ease of entry and exit. One of the most important market structures is that known as perfect competition. This describes a market in which: (1) there are many buyers and sellers, each of whom sells or buys only a small fraction of all that is bought and sold; (2) the product traded is entirely homogeneous; (3) all participants are well informed; and (4) entry and exit are very easy. An individual firm in such a market will be a price taker, which is to say that it will sell its product at a price determined entirely by forces outside its own control. Such a firm faces a horizontal demand curve for its product.

The perfectly competitive firm must solve a problem in pure economizing having as its objective the maximum profit subject to prevailing constraints. Profit is max- imized at that level of output for which total revenue exceeds total cost by the greatest possible amount. This point can be identified by total cost and total revenue curves for the firm.

Alternatively, the process of profit maximization for the competitive firm can be demonstrated by a marginal approach. This approach requires a new concept, margin- al revenue, which is the amount by which total revenue increases as a result of a one-unit increase in the firm's output. If marginal revenue exceeds marginal cost, then producing an extra unit of output brings more into the firm than it pays out in costs. The firm thus maximizes its profit by increasing output up to, but not beyond, the point where marginal cost begins to exceed marginal revenue.

A complete analysis of the short-run behavior of the competitive firm must take into account the possibility that there might be no level of output at which a positive pure economic profit can be earned. In that case, the best the firm can do is to minimize loss. This is done by producing the quantity that makes marginal cost and marginal revenue equal, so long as price exceeds average variable cost at that point. If average variable cost is greater than price where marginal cost and revenue are equal, the firm minimizes losses in the short run by shutting down.

It follows from the analysis of short-run profit maximization and loss minimization that the short-run supply curve for a perfectly competitive firm is that portion of the firm's marginal cost curve lying above its intersection with the average variable cost curve.

The short-run supply curve for a perfectly competitive industry can be obtained by horizontal summation of the individual firms' supply curves, provided that input prices do not vary as industry output varies. If input prices increase as industry output increases, the short-run industry supply curve will be somewhat steeper than the sum of the firms' supply curves. If input prices decrease, the industry supply curve will be somewhat flatter.

In the long run, perfectly competitive firms can adjust the quantities of fixed as well as variable inputs that they use. In addition, firms can enter or leave the industry in the long run. When a perfectly competitive industry is in long-run equilibrium, three conditions must hold: First, marginal cost must be equal to price for each firm. Second, each firm must operate with a plant of just the size necessary to minimize long-run average cost; at that point, long-run and short-run average costs are equal. Third, long-run average cost must be equal to price, so that firms in the industry earn exactly a normal rate of return on capital (zero pure economic profit). If this third condition is not satisfied, firms will have an incentive either to enter or to leave the industry.

If demand conditions change in a perfectly competitive industry, the industry must adjust to a new long-run equilibrium having these same properties. This process of adjustment requires exit or entry of firms. If demand increases, the product price will be bid up, enabling firms already in the industry to temporarily earn a higher than normal rate of return. New firms will be attracted into the industry until the price is driven back down to the level of long-run average cost. Similarly, if demand decreases, prices will fall, leading temporarily to a lower than normal rate of return for firms in the industry. Some firms will exit from the industry, and the price will rise back to the level of long-run average cost.

The discussion of perfect competition can be concluded by explaining what is "perfect" about it. A market is fundamentally a mechanism through which people carry out mutually beneficial transactions. A perfect market, then, can be said to be one in which all possible mutually beneficial transactions are completed. A perfectly competitive market is perfect in this sense, because it carries production all the way to the point where marginal cost (representing the minimum payment resource owners will accept to supply the good) is equal to price (representing the maximum amount consumers are willing to pay for the good).

WALKING TOUR

You have read the chapter at least once and have reviewed the synopsis. Now you are going to walk through the material step by step, filling in the blanks and answer-

ing the questions as you go along. After you have answered each question, check
yourself by uncovering the answer given in the margin. If you do not understand
why the answer given is the right one, refer back to the proper section of the text.

The Structure of Perfect Competition

The market structure known as <u>perfect competition</u> has
four defining characteristics, which are, in brief, as
follows:

1. _____   many small sellers

2. _____   homogeneous product

3. _____   good information

4. _____   free entry and exit

A firm operating in such a market has no control over the
price at which it sells its product; that is to say, the firm
is a _____. Another way to put it is   price taker
to say that the perfectly competitive firm faces a
_____ demand curve for its product.   perfectly elastic

Short-run Supply under Perfect Competition

A perfectly competitive firm maximizes profit by choosing
the output for which total revenue exceeds total cost by
the greatest amount. The profit maximizing output can
also be found by using a diagram like that in Exhibit S23.1,
which is based on a marginal approach. For example,
suppose the product of the firm in question sells at a
market price of $150 per unit. To find the profit maxim-
izing level of output, first draw in the appropriate marginal

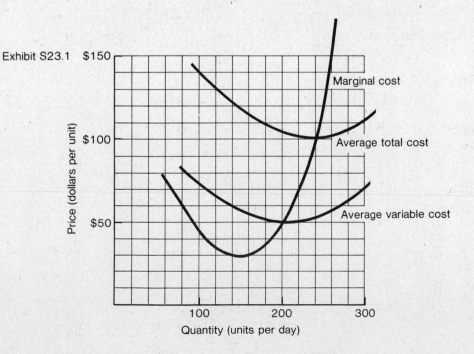

Exhibit S23.1

199

revenue curve, which will have the form of a

_____ line at a height of _____.   horizontal; $150

Given this marginal revenue curve, the firm will find it

profitable to expand production as long as the _____   marginal

cost is less than _____; that is, up to an output of $150

_____ units. Mark this as Point A on the exhibit.   260

Profit per unit at this point on the marginal cost curve is

equal to the price of $150 minus [marginal/average total/

average variable] cost, which at 260 units of output is   average total

about _____. Profit per unit is thus _____, $102; $48

giving the firm a total profit of _____. $12,480

    If the product's price falls, the firm will adjust by

moving down along its _____ cost curve,   marginal

keeping marginal cost equal to marginal revenue. For

example, at a price of $100, the firm would produce

_____ units of output. Mark this as Point B. Pure   240

economic profit at Point B is _____. That means $0

that the firm is earning [nothing/ a normal return] on its   a normal return

invested capital.

    Suppose now that the price drops still further, say

to $70. At this price, the firm would produce _____   220

units. Mark this as Point C. The firm's average total

cost at this point is about _____ per unit, giving $101

it a total cost of _____ in all. Average variable $22,220

cost is about _____ per unit at Point C, or _____ $51; $11,220

in all. That leaves a total fixed cost of _____. $11,000

It can be seen that the firm's total revenue of _____ $15,440

is enough to cover all of the firm's variable cost, plus

_____ of the fixed cost. The firm is left with a $4,400

loss of _____, but this is less than the loss of $6,820

_____ that it would sustain if it shut down. $11,000

In the short run, then, the firm stays in production even

at a loss.

    Now suppose that the price falls all the way to $50.

If the firm continues to operate at the point where mar-

ginal cost and marginal revenue are equal, it will produce

_____ units per day. Mark this as Point D. At   200

Point D it would have total revenues of _____, $10,000

total costs of _____, and it would run a total loss $21,000

of _____, just equal to total fixed cost. Alter- $11,000 natively, the firm could shut down. Mark the shutdown point ($50 and zero units) as Point D'. At D' the firm would have total revenues of _____, total costs of _____, and a loss of _____. This is the same as the loss at D. It follows that at a price of $50, the firm will be indifferent between shutting down and staying in production.

$0

$11,000; $11,000

Finally, suppose the price drops all the way to $40. In that case, setting marginal cost equal to marginal revenue would give an output of _____ units. Mark this as Point E. At Point E, average variable cost would be _____ per unit, for a total variable cost of _____. The total revenue of _____ would not even be enough to cover variable cost, let alone the _____ total cost. The firm would run a loss of _____. In comparison, by shutting down it would run a loss of just _____, equal to total fixed cost. Clearly, then, at a price of $40 the firm is better off shutting down. Mark this shutdown point ($40, 0 units) as Point E'. Now connect points A, B, C, D, D', and E', and you have traced out the firm's entire short-run supply curve.

180

$51

$9,180; $7,200

$20,380

$13,180

$11,200

Perfect Competition in the Long Run

In the long run, the free entry and exit property of perfect competition becomes important. The conditions for long-run competitive equilibrium can be characterized in terms of three equalities. In order that each individual firm have no incentive to increase or decrease output, _____ must be equal to _____ for each firm. In order that each firm have no incentive to change the size of plant in which it operates, _____ cost must equal the _____ cost. And in order that firms have no incentive either to enter or leave the industry, _____ cost for each firm must be equal to _____. Only when these conditions hold; that is, when the marginal cost curve, marginal revenue (price) curve, short-run average total cost curve, and long-run average cost curve all pass

price; marginal cost

short-run average total

long-run average

long-run average

price

through a single point, can the competitive market be in
long-run equilibrium.

SELF TEST

These sample test items will help you check how much you have learned. Answers and explanations can be found at the end of this chapter. Scoring yourself: One or two wrong -- on target. Three to five wrong -- passing, but you haven't mastered the chapter yet. Six or more wrong -- not good enough; start over and restudy the chapter.

True or False

Indicate whether each statement is true or false as it stands. If it is false, explain why in a few words.

T F   1.   In a perfectly competitive market, there should be an almost infinite number of styles and varieties of the product.

T F   2.   As long as marginal revenue exceeds marginal cost for a firm, total revenue must exceed total cost.

T F   3.   If a perfectly competitive firm's marginal cost is increasing and exceeds its marginal revenue, it should reduce output.

T F   4.   As long as price exceeds minimum marginal cost, a firm should not shut down in the short run.

T F   5.   A firm can have a pure economic loss but still be earning a normal rate of return on capital, so long as price exceeds average variable cost.

T F   6.   The downward sloping part of a perfectly competitive firm's marginal cost curve cannot be part of its short-run supply curve.

T F   7.   Short-run average total cost, long-run average cost, and short-run marginal cost can all be equal for a firm only when it is operating at the minimum point on its long-run average cost curve.

T F   8.   If the price of a specialized input used by an industry rises in the long run as industry output expands, the industry's long-run supply curve will tend to have a positive slope.

T F   9.   Firms will tend to enter a perfectly competitive industry as long as the total rate of return to capital in that industry is greater than zero.

T F 10.   A perfectly competitive market is perfect in the sense that it permits all potentially mutually beneficial transactions to be carried out.

Multiple Choice

1.   Which of the following is not a characteristic of perfect competition?
     a. Many firms, each of which is small.
     b. A homogeneous product.
     c. An intense climate of secrecy and business rivalry.
     d. Free entry and exit.

2. Which of the following is most satisfactory as an example of perfect competition in action?
   a. Production of soybeans by U.S. farmers.
   b. The U.S. auto industry.
   c. Rival department stores in a medium-sized city.
   d. Electric versus gas utilities.

3. A perfectly competitive firm sells its output for $50 a unit. At 1,000 units of output, marginal cost is $40 and is increasing, average variable cost is $35, and average total cost is $60. To maximize short-run profit, what should the firm do?
   a. Increase output.
   b. Decrease output but not shut down.
   c. Maintain its current rate of output.
   d. Shut down.

4. A perfectly competitive firm sells its output for $50 a unit. At 500 units of output its marginal cost is $50 and is decreasing, average variable cost is $55 per unit, and average total cost is $65 per unit. To maximize profit, what should the firm do?
   a. Increase output.
   b. Decrease output or shut down temporarily.
   c. Retain its present rate of output.
   d. Insufficient information given for an answer to be reached.

5. A perfectly competitive firm sells its output at $40 per unit. At 100 units of output it has an average total cost of $40. Marginal cost is below average total cost at that point. To maximize profit, what should the firm do?
   a. Increase output.
   b. Decrease output.
   c. Retain its present rate of output.
   d. Insufficient information given for an answer to be reached.

6. A perfectly competitive firm's short-run supply curve is best described as
   a. its marginal cost curve.
   b. the upward sloping portion of its marginal cost curve.
   c. the upward sloping part of its marginal cost curve lying above average variable cost.
   d. the upward sloping portion of its marginal cost curve lying above average total cost.

7. If a perfectly competitive firm is operating at a point where marginal cost and product price are between average variable cost and average total cost, its accounting profit must be
   a. positive.
   b. zero.
   c. negative.
   d. impossible to determine from the information given.

8. If, in the short run, input prices rise as the output of a perfectly competitive industry expands, then the short-run industry supply curve will
   a. be somewhat steeper than the sum of the individual firms' supply curves
   b. be somewhat flatter than the sum of the individual firms' supply curve.
   c. be the same as the sum of the individual firms' supply curves.
   d. have a negative slope.

9. Which of the following is not equal to the others for a perfectly competitive firm in long-run equilibrium?
   a. Average variable cost.
   b. Long-run average cost.
   c. Short-run marginal cost.
   d. Marginal revenue.

10. A firm will have no incentive to change the size of its plant in the long run if
    a. price is equal to marginal cost.
    b. short-run average total cost equals long-run average cost.
    c. price is equal to long-run average total cost.
    d. marginal revenue is equal to marginal cost.

11. In long-run equilibrium for a perfectly competitive firm, which of the following is not at its minimum?
    a. Short-run average total cost.
    b. Short-run average variable cost.
    c. Long-run average cost.
    d. All of the above are at their minimum points.

12. If there is an increase in demand for the product of a perfectly competitive industry,
    a. firms already in the industry will for a time earn pure economic profits.
    b. new firms will be attracted to the industry.
    c. price will rise more in the short run than in the long run, assuming the change in demand to be permanent.
    d. all of the above will occur.

13. If there is a permanent increase in demand for the product of a perfectly competitive industry known to have a perfectly elastic long-run supply curve,
    a. each individual firm in the industry will, in the long run, increase its rate of output.
    b. industry output will expand via the entry of new firms.
    c. both of the above will occur.
    d. none of the above will occur.

14. If input prices for a perfectly competitive industry decline as the output of the industry expands in the long run, the long-run industry supply curve
    a. will have a positive slope.
    b. will have a negative slope.
    c. will be perfectly elastic.
    d. will be vertical.

15. The demand curve for a product can be interpreted as indicating
    a. the minimum price buyers are willing to pay for an extra unit of the product.
    b. the maximum price that buyers are willing to pay for an extra unit of the product.
    c. the minimum price resource owners are willing to accept for the inputs needed to produce an extra unit of the product.
    d. the maximum price resource owners are willing to accept for the inputs needed to produce an extra unit of the product.

ANSWERS TO CHAPTER 23 SELF TEST

True or False

1-F; the product should be homogeneous.
2-F; profit could be either positive or negative.
3-T
4-F; minimum average variable cost.
5-F; a pure economic loss implies lower than normal rate of return.
6-T
7-T
8-T
9-F; so long as pure economic profits are greater than zero.
10-T

Multiple Choice

1-c
2-a
3-a
4-d; although average variable cost is above price at 500 units, it may (or may not) drop below price at some higher rate of output.
5-a
6-c
7-d; accounting profit is a matter of implicit versus explicit costs, about which nothing has been said.
8-a
9-a
10-b
11-b
12-d
13-b
14-b
15-b

CHAPTER TWENTY-FOUR
THE THEORY OF MONOPOLY

WHERE YOU'RE GOING

Here is what you will be able to do when you have mastered this chapter:

--Define pure monopoly and distinguish between natural monopolies and franchised monopolies.

--Demonstrate the relationship between output and revenue for a pure monopolist.

--Compare the short-run profit maximization decision of a pure monopolist with that of a perfectly competitive firm.

--Explain the sense in which pure monopoly is an imperfect market structure, and discuss the limitations on the policy conclusions that can be drawn from this imperfection.

--Discuss the significance of indirect competition in monopolistic markets, and define monopolistic competition.

--Define and illustrate price discrimination, and discuss the pros and cons of price discrimination.

--Explain what a cartel is, and compare profit maximization for a cartel with profit maximization for a pure monopolist and a perfectly competitive industry.

--Discuss the stability problem encountered by all cartels.

CHAPTER SYNOPSIS

Reading this synopsis is not a substitute for reading the chapter, but it should help you to recall the main points. If there are any you feel unsure of, refer to the full discussion in the text.

A pure monopoly is a firm that accounts for 100 percent of sales in the industry it represents. A pure monopolist is assumed not only to have no current competitors, but also to be protected from the potential competition of new entrants. Protection may arise from the technology of the industry or be based on ownership of a unique natural resource, in which case the firm can be described as a natural monopoly, or it may arise from a patent, license, or other exclusive government grant of monopoly privilege, in which case the firm is known as a franchised monopoly.

A pure monopolist, unlike a perfectly competitive firm, is not a price taker. The pure monopolist faces a downward sloping demand curve for its product; so as its output increases, the maximum price for which it can sell that output decreases. As a result, marginal revenue for the pure monopolist is always less than average revenue (price).

A pure monopolist, like a perfectly competitive firm, maximizes short-run profits at the point where marginal cost and marginal revenue are equal. However, for the pure monopolist, price exceeds marginal revenue at that point. If price also exceeds average total cost, the monopolist will earn a pure economic profit; and because the pure monopolist faces no direct threat of competition by new entrants, this pure economic profit may persist in the long run. However, a pure monopolist need not always earn a pure economic profit. A decrease in demand for the product or the pressure of indirect competition may leave it in a position where the best it can do is break even, or perhaps even where the best it can do is minimize loss. A firm facing a great many indirect competitors offering products that are fairly close substitutes has so little monopoly power that it is likely just to break even. A market structure in which this pattern of behavior takes place is known as monopolistic competition.

Pure monopoly is not a perfect market structure in the sense that perfect competition is. When a monopolist reaches a profit maximizing equilibrium position, some opportunities for mutually beneficial transactions between buyers and resource owners go unrealized. That is because the monopolist's equilibrium price, representing what buyers would be willing to pay for an extra unit, exceeds its equilibrium marginal cost, representing what resource owners would be willing to accept for the inputs needed to produce an extra unit. However, buyers do not deal directly with resource owners; and the profits of the monopolist, which acts as an intermediary between the two, would decrease if the extra unit of output were produced.

Under certain conditions, monopolists may find it profitable to practice price discrimination, that is, to charge different prices to different users or classes of users, when those price differences are not based on differences in costs of serving the various users. In order to practice price discrimination, resale of the product must be impossible or at least inconvenient, and the monopolist must have some way of classifying users into groups with relatively elastic and relatively inelastic demand. To the extent that price discrimination permits some users to be served who would be priced out of the market were a uniform profit maximizing price to be charged, the practice may somewhat mitigate the imperfection of pure monopoly.

A cartel is an agreement among a number of independent suppliers of a product to coordinate their activities in order to earn monopoly profits. A cartel formed of previously competing firms would restrict total industry output in order to raise the price of the product and would assign output quotas to each of its members. If the agreement to restrict output is honored, all members of the cartel can earn higher profits than if they acted competitively. However, cartels are often unstable; they are vulnerable to disruption by outsiders who will be attracted into the industry by a greater than normal rate of return and are vulnerable to disruption by members who will be tempted to cheat on their output quotas. Relatively few attempts to form cartels achieve long-term success.

WALKING TOUR

You have read the chapter at least once and have reviewed the synopsis. Now you are going to walk through the material step by step, filling in the blanks and answering the questions as you go along. After you have answered each question, check yourself by uncovering the answer given in the margin. If you do not understand why the answer given is the right one, refer back to the proper section of the text.

Profit Maximization for the Pure Monopolist

The first step in understanding the pure monopolist's

profit maximization problem is understanding the relation-

ship between output and revenue for such a firm. The first

two columns of the following table give part of the demand

curve for a hypothetical pure monopolist. Use that data

to complete the total revenue and marginal revenue columns

of the table.

Quantity	Price	Total Revenue	Marginal Revenue		
17	$46	_____		$782	
18	44	_____	_____	$792	$10
19	42	_____	_____	$798	$6
20	40	_____	_____	$800	$2
21	38	_____	_____	$798	−$2
22	36	_____	_____	$792	−$6

Next use the information in the table to sketch the demand and marginal revenue curves for the firm in Exhibit S24.1. Extend the demand curve all the way to the vertical and horizontal axes. The vertical intercept is _____ and the horizontal intercept is _____ units. Extend the marginal revenue curve to 25 units of output. Note that the marginal revenue curve lies halfway between the demand curve and the vertical axis at all points.

$80

40

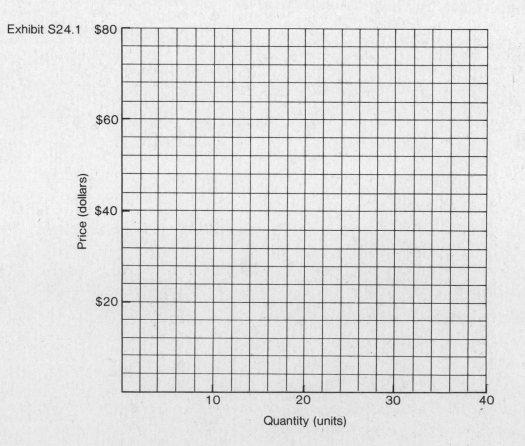

Exhibit S24.1

208

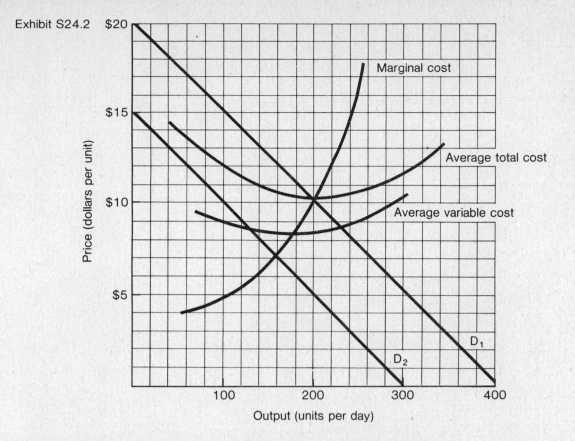

Exhibit S24.2

Now turn your attention to Exhibit S24.2, which shows
a set of cost curves and two demand curves for a hypothetical pure monopolist. Begin by sketching in the marginal revenue curve corresponding to demand curve D_1.
(Pay no attention to D_2 for the moment.) Label this curve
MR_1; it should intersect the vertical axis at _____ and $20
the horizontal axis at _____ units of output. If demand   200
conditions are represented by D_1, then the firm will maximize profits by producing at the point where the marginal
cost curve intersects the _____   marginal revenue
curve; this happens at _____ units of output per day.   140
The price at which this output will be sold is determined
by the height of the _____ curve _____   demand; D_1
at this quantity; this price is _____ per unit. Average $13
total cost at 140 units of output is _____ per unit, so $11
the firm makes a total [profit/loss] of _____ under   profit; $280
the demand conditions indicated by D_1.

Suppose now that because, say, of a recession in the
economy at large or because of indirect competition from
other firms, this monopolist's demand curve shifts to the

209

position D_2. Sketch in the marginal revenue curve corresponding to D_2, labeling it MR_2. MR_2 should intersect
the vertical axis at _____ and the horizontal axis $15
at _____ units of output per day. Profit is maxim-   150
ized at _____ units of output given the new demand   100
conditions. This 100 units of output will be sold at a
price of _____ per unit. This is [above/below] the $10; below
average total cost of _____ per unit, so the firm has $12
a [profit/loss] of _____ under the demand conditions   loss; $200
given by D_2. However, note that at 100 units of output,
average total cost exceeds average variable cost by
_____ per unit, indicating a total fixed cost of $3
_____. This means that if the firm were to shut $300
down in the short run, it would suffer a _____ loss $300
per day, which is more than it suffers at 100 units of
output. The firm thus should not shut down unless
demand conditions deteriorate still further.

Monopoly and Consumer Welfare

Go back now for a moment to the situation in Exhibit S24.2
where the demand curve D_1 called for producing 140 units
of output and selling them at a price of $13 per unit.
Starting from that point, consumers would be willing to
pay a [minimum/maximum] of about _____ for a   maximum; $12.95
141st unit of the product. (This is indicated by the height
of the _____ curve at 141 units.) At the   demand
same time, the _____ curve in-   marginal cost
dicates that suppliers of labor, capital, and natural
resources would be willing to supply the inputs needed
to produce the 141st unit for a [minimum/maximum] of   minimum
about _____. It can be seen, then, that a poten- $6.05
tially mutually beneficial transaction between consumers
and resource owners is being passed up; any price between
$6.05 and $12.95 could satisfy both.

However, if we continue to assume that the monopolist
must charge the same price for all units sold, the 141st
unit of output would not be produced. Total revenue from
selling 140 units at $13 per unit is _____; total $1,820
revenue from selling 141 units at $12.95 would be _____ $1,825.95

so, the 141st unit would bring in _____ in new $5.95

revenue. As the marginal cost curve indicates, however,

the 141st unit would add _____ to total cost. $6.05

The monopolist's profit would thus [rise/fall] by _____   fall; 10 cents

if the 141st unit were produced and sold.

    Note, though, that if the monopolist could maintain

the price of $13 for the first 140 units while selling the

141st unit for any price between _____ and _____ $12.95; $6.05

all three parties--consumers, resource owners, and the

monopolist--could be made better off. In principle,

_____ of this kind could   price discrimination

result in production of as many as _____ units of   200

output per day, with the last unit sold at a price of

_____. $10

SELF TEST

These sample test items will help you check how much you have learned. Answers and explanations can be found at the end of this chapter. Scoring yourself: One or two wrong -- on target. Three to five wrong -- passing, but you haven't mastered the chapter yet. Six or more wrong -- not good enough; start over and restudy the chapter.

True or False

Indicate whether each statement is true or false as it stands. If it is false, explain why in a few words.

T F   1. If a pure monopolist is to earn a greater than normal rate of return on capital, in the long run it must not only have 100 percent of sales in its own industry but must also be protected from the potential competition of new entrants.

T F   2. A monopolist's marginal revenue curve must intersect the horizontal axis at the same output for which its total revenue curve reaches a maximum.

T F   3. A pure monopolist maximizes profit in the short run by setting a price equal to the height of the intersection of the marginal cost and marginal revenue curves.

T F   4. A monopolist's total cost and total revenue curves intersect at the point of profit maximization.

T F   5. Whenever a pure monopolist cannot earn a pure economic profit in the short run, it should temporarily shut down until demand conditions improve.

T F   6. Indirect competition can force a monopolist to a break-even level of profit in the long run.

T F   7. In a world where transactions costs were zero, consumers and resource owners could both benefit from negotiating directly with one another rather than working through a monopolistic firm acting as an intermediary.

T F 8. Price discrimination is likely to be most damaging to the poorest customers of a monopolist.

T F 9. To be successful, a cartel must either be able to restrict entry into the industry or be able to impose output quotas on its members.

T F 10. According to the theory of pure monopoly, breaking up a monopolist into a number of competing firms will improve consumer welfare.

Multiple Choice

1. A taxi company having an exclusive license to carry passengers for hire in a certain city would be an example of
   a. natural monopoly.
   b. franchised monopoly.
   c. monopolistic competition.
   d. a cartel.

2. Which of the following is true of a perfect competitor but not of a pure monopolist?
   a. The firm is a price taker.
   b. The firm maximizes profit by setting marginal cost equal to marginal revenue.
   c. The firm may have to shut down in the short run if price does not cover average variable cost.
   d. The firm can earn a pure economic profit in the short run if demand conditions are favorable.

3. If a pure monopolist can sell 100 units of output at $50 per unit and 101 units of output at $49.90 per unit, marginal revenue in that range of output is approximately
   a. -10 cents per unit.
   b. -$10 per unit.
   c. $39.90 per unit.
   d. $49.90 per unit.

4. At the point where the marginal revenue curve intersects the horizontal axis, a monopolist's demand curve must be
   a. elastic.
   b. inelastic.
   c. unit elastic.
   d. perfectly elastic.

5. If a monopolist is operating at a point where its marginal revenue curve intersects its marginal cost curve, and if marginal cost is below average variable cost at that point, then to maximize profit, the firm should do which of the following?
   a. Increase output.
   b. Shut down.
   c. Maintain that rate of output.
   d. Insufficient information given for an answer to be reached.

6. At an output of 100 units, a monopolist's marginal cost is $33, its marginal revenue is $33, its average variable cost is $30, and its average total cost is $38. To maximize profit or minimize loss in the short run, what should the firm do?
   a. Produce more than 100 units of output.
   b. Produce exactly 100 units of output.
   c. Shut down.
   d. Insufficient information given for an answer to be reached.

7. Monopolistic competition resembles perfect competition
   a. in that the product of all firms is homogeneous.
   b. in that firms are likely to earn zero pure economic profit in the long run.
   c. in that all firms are price takers.
   d. in none of the above respects.

8. Other things being equal, we would expect a price discriminating monopolist to produce which of the following?
   a. More output than a nondiscriminating monopolist.
   b. Less output than a nondiscriminating monopolist.
   c. The same output as a nondiscriminating monopolist.
   d. No reason to expect one rather than another of the above.

9. Which of the following markets would appear to offer the best opportunity for price discrimination?
   a. Groceries.
   b. Gasoline.
   c. Psychiatric services.
   d. Wheat.

10. Other things being equal, we would expect a price discriminating monopolist to charge the highest prices to the group with
   a. the least elastic demand.
   b. the most elastic demand.
   c. perfectly elastic demand.
   d. the least per capita income.

11. An agreement among a number of independent producers of the same good to restrict output and raise prices is known as
   a. pure monopoly.
   b. franchised monopoly.
   c. monopolistic competition.
   d. a cartel.

12. A cartel maximizes total profits for its membership by setting output at the point where the industry's marginal cost curve intersects
   a. the horizontal axis.
   b. the industry's demand curve.
   c. the industry's marginal revenue curve.
   d. none of the above.

13. If an individual member of a cartel could be certain of escaping detection, it would be tempted to cheat by
   a. increasing price.
   b. increasing output.
   c. doing both of the above.
   d. doing neither of the above.

14. An attempt by U.S. auto makers to form a cartel would be aided if
   a. members agreed to exchange information about the number of cars sold each month.
   b. strict import controls were imposed on foreign autos.
   c. the bylaws of the cartel were written up in the form oa a legally enforce-able contract.
   d. all of the above were done.

15. Which of the following is an implication of the theory of pure monopoly?
   a. It always pays to increase the number of firms in a market.
   b. Consumers benefit when price discrimination is prohibited.
   c. Monopoly hurts consumers by raising per unit costs.
   d. None of the above is an implication of the theory.

ANSWERS TO CHAPTER 24 SELF TEST

True or False

1-T
2-T
3-F; at a level given by the demand curve above the intersection of marginal cost and revenue.
4-F; they are parallel at that point.
5-F; it will shut down only if price is below average variable cost.
6-T
7-T
8-F; they are most likely to be priced out of the market if discrimination is prohibited.
9-F; it must do both.
10-F; nothing is said about what happens to cost.

Multiple Choice

1-b
2-a
3-c
4-c
5-d; location of the demand curve must be known to establish price.
6-b; exact location of demand curve is not known, but it must be above the marginal revenue curve.
7-b
8-a
9-c
10-a
11-d
12-c
13-b
14-d
15-d

CHAPTER TWENTY-FIVE
COMPETITION AND PUBLIC POLICY IN AGRICULTURE

WHERE YOU'RE GOING

Here is what you will be able to do when you have mastered this chapter:

--Explain why perfect competition, where present in agricultural markets, has sometimes been felt to be a mixed blessing.

--Describe agricultural marketing orders, and explain how they permit farmers to realize some of the benefits of membership in a cartel.

--Compare the effects of price supports, acreage controls, and target prices as alternative methods of securing higher and more stable farm prices than would result from perfect competition.

--Explain the meaning and significance of the following additional terms and concepts:

Very short run.
Parity price ratio.

CHAPTER SYNOPSIS

Reading this synopsis is not a substitute for reading the chapter, but it should help you to recall the main points. If there are any you feel unsure of, refer to the full discussion in the text.

Many agricultural markets fit the four characteristics of perfect competition rather closely: there are many small firms, none of which supplies an appreciable share of total production; the products are broadly homogeneous; information networks are well developed; and entry and exit are free. However, farmers have not always liked the results--in the short run, competition has often led to unstable prices, and in the long run, to lengthy periods of depressed farm incomes.

One reason for the short-run instability of prices is the relative inelasticity of demand for many farm products. This is seen most clearly in the very short run-- a period of time so short, as between one harvest and the next of a perishable crop, that output cannot be increased at all. With an inelastic demand, prices vary sharply according to the quantity supplied, and total revenue is relatively low when output is comparatively large.

Over a longer period, increasing productivity and income-inelastic demand for farm products have made it necessary to reduce the farm population. In competitive farm markets, the necessary exit of farmers has been accomplished through low farm incomes and a high incidence of rural poverty. (However, the historical gap between farm and nonfarm incomes has closed somewhat in recent years.)

Not surprisingly, farmers have often wished that farm prices were higher and more stable than they are under competition. In response to these wishes, the government has, since the 1930s, instituted a number of farm policies that restrict competition in agricultural markets in various ways.

The Agricultural Marketing Act of 1937 is one example of such restrictive policy. This act permits growers of certain crops to establish <u>agricultural marketing orders</u> as a means of coordinating their supply decisions. The details vary from crop to crop, but all marketing orders have some degree of power to control the supply of produce to particular markets, thereby raising prices above competitive levels. Many marketing orders practice price discrimination—for example, by supplying lemons to be sold fresh at a higher price than lemons to be sold for processing. Marketing orders are not always perfect cartels, however, and the potential monopoly profits of members are often eroded by new entrants into the group.

Wheat, feed grains, cotton, rice, peanuts, and a number of other farm products are subject to a different set of policies. For these crops, prices are raised and, in principle, stabilized by <u>price supports</u>, <u>acreage controls</u>, and <u>target prices</u>. Under price supports, the government guarantees a minimum price and becomes the buyer of last resort, purchasing and storing the surpluses that often result. Acreage controls attempt to raise prices without generating surpluses. However, acreage controls encourage farmers to farm their remaining acreage more intensely than they would under competitive market conditions, thereby raising the cost of producing a crop of any given size. Under a system of target prices, crops are sold for what they will bring on the market, and the government then makes deficiency payments to farmers equal to the difference between the market price and the target price. From the consumer point of view, target prices have the advantage of keeping market prices low while providing the same benefits to farmers as do price supports. Current agricultural policy relies to some extent on each of these three devices to control farm prices and output.

WALKING TOUR

<u>You have read the chapter at least once and have reviewed the synopsis. Now you are going to walk through the material step by step, filling the blanks and answering the questions as you go along. After you have answered each question, check yourself by uncovering the answer given in the margin. If you do not understand why the answer given is the right one, refer back to the proper section of the text.</u>

Origins of the Farm Problem

The farm problem in the United States has traditionally been seen as one of unstable prices and low farm incomes. The short-run problem of unstable prices is in part caused by the relatively [low/high] [price/income] elasticity of   low; price

demand for farm output. The inelastic demand means that in a year of good crops, farm incomes tend to be [higher/lower] than in a year of poor crops. One measure   lower

of price instability is year-to-year change in the <u>parity price ratio</u>, which is the ratio of prices [paid/received]   received

by farmers to prices they [pay/receive]. This ratio has   pay

often fluctuated substantially from year to year.

The long-term problem of low farm incomes and rural poverty is caused in part by [high/low] [price/income]   low; income

elasticity of demand for farm products and in part by increasing farm _____. In combination,   productivity

217

these factors have reduced the number of farmers needed to produce the national farm output. In a competitive market, the normal way to encourage exit from an industry is through a prolonged period of [high/low] earnings. As recently as 1960, farm earnings were only 50 percent of nonfarm earnings, although the gap is now much smaller.

low

Farm Policy

A number of policies have been devised for shielding farmers to some extent from the effects of competition in agricultural markets. One device, used for many types of fresh produce, is to permit farmers to form a sort of cartel known as a _____. These agreements permit farmers to coordinate their supply decisions in order to earn higher revenues for sale of their crops.

marketing order

Marketing orders sometimes practice price discrimination. For example, if it were discovered that the demand for milk to be sold fresh in retail stores was less price elastic than the demand for milk sold for processing into butter, ice cream, and so forth, then a group of farmers making up a marketing order could profit by selling to the fresh milk market at a [higher/lower] price than to the processing market.

higher

Wheat, feed grains, and several other crops are subject to a different set of policies: price supports, acreage controls, and target prices. Exhibit S25.1 provides an exercise in comparing the effects of these three policies.

The diagram shows hypothetical supply and demand curves for soybeans, a crop that, as of this writing, is produced and sold in a relatively uncontrolled market. Under competitive conditions, the price of soybeans would be _____ per bushel, and _____ million bushels per year would be produced. If farmers were not satisfied with the $7 price and instead wanted to receive $10 per bushel, one of the three policies mentioned above, or a combination of them, could be employed.

$7; 1,600

First, consider price supports. On the diagram, draw in a dotted line to indicate a $10 support price. At that price, the quantity supplied would be _____ million bushels per year, and the quantity demanded would be

2,000

218

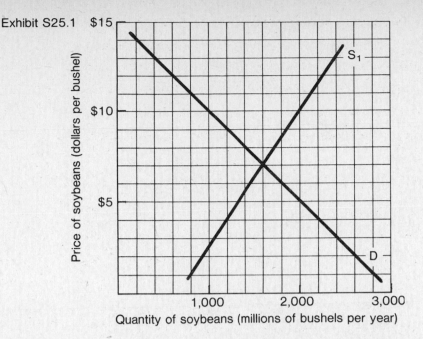

Exhibit S25.1

just _____ million bushels per year. This would   1,000
result in a [surplus/shortage] of _____ million   surplus; 1,000
bushels per year, which the government would have to buy
and store or somehow dispose of without depressing the
market price. Under this price control scheme, consumers
would spend _____ billion for _____ million $10; 1,000
bushels; the total revenue of soybean growers would be
_____ billion, and the total cost to the government $20
(exclusive of administrative costs) would be _____ $10
billion.

Alternatively, the price of $10 per bushel could be
achieved through acreage controls. Show how this policy
would work by sketching in a new supply curve, S_2,
parallel to S_1 and intersecting the demand curve at a price
of $10. Under this program, there would be [a shortage/   neither a shortage
a surplus/neither a shortage nor a surplus]. Total farm   nor a surplus
revenue would be _____ billion and consumer expen- $10
ditures would be _____ billion. Note that the mar- $10
ginal cost of producing the 1,000 millionth bushel of
soybeans (indicated by the height of the supply curve at
that quantity) would be _____ per bushel under $10
acreage controls, compared with about _____ without $2.50
them.

Finally, the government could establish a target price

of $10 and agree to make up the difference between that
and the market price through deficiency payments. Total
production at the $10 target price would be _____   2,000
million bushels per year, and total revenue would be
_____ billion. The market price would fall to $20
_____ per bushel; consumers would pay a total of $5
_____ billion and get _____ million bushels $10; 2,000
for their money. The government would have to make a
deficiency payment of _____ per bushel on all soybeans $5
sold, for a total budgetary cost of _____ billion. $10

SELF TEST

These sample test items will help you check how much you have learned. Answers
and explanations can be found at the end of this chapter. Scoring yourself: One
or two wrong -- on target. Three to five wrong -- passing, but you haven't mastered the chapter yet. Six or more wrong -- not good enough; start over and
restudy the chapter.

True or False

Indicate whether each statement is true or false as it stands. If it is false, explain
why in a few words.

T F 1. In the absence of restrictive government policies, the market structure of
         most agricultural markets would closely resemble that of monopolistic
         competition.

T F 2. If the parity price ratio is used as a guide, farmers have rarely since
         been as prosperous as they were just before World War I.

T F 3. Abundant crops are associated with high farm incomes for most crops.

T F 4. Although price elasticity of demand for most farm crops is low, income
         elasticity is rather high.

T F 5. Farmers have consistently demanded policies to increase competition in
         agricultural markets.

T F 6. During the Great Depression, the economic problems of the United States
         were often blamed on excessive competition.

T F 7. Under the Agricultural Marketing Act, a unanimous vote of farmers in a
         region is required before a marketing order can be established.

T F 8. Agricultural marketing orders are common in markets for wheat, feed
         grains, cotton, and rice.

T F 9. An advantage of acreage controls, compared with price supports and target
         prices, is that they require relatively low government expenditures.

T F 10. Although price supports are harmful to consumers, they are at least a
         fairly efficient way of transferring income to poor farmers.

220

Multiple Choice

1. The structure of the market for wheat, in the absence of restrictive policies, would best be described as
   a. perfect competition.
   b. pure monopoly.
   c. monopolistic competition.
   d. a cartel.

2. Sharp year-to-year fluctuations in farm prices are a likely result of
   a. high income elasticity of demand.
   b. low income elasticity of demand.
   c. high price elasticity of demand.
   d. low price elasticity of demand.

3. The parity price ratio is a ratio of
   a. prices received by farmers to prices paid by farmers.
   b. prices paid by farmers to prices received by farmers.
   c. an index of farm prices to the GNP deflator.
   d. none of the above.

4. During the 1970s, the historical gap between farm and nonfarm incomes
   a. widened.
   b. remained constant.
   c. narrowed.
   d. was reversed.

5. A purely private, voluntary effort to establish a cartel for a crop like citrus fruits would probably fail even if it were legal because
   a. it would be too hard to restrict entry by new producers.
   b. it would be too hard to agree upon and enforce output quotas.
   c. it would be too hard to detect cheating by cartel members.
   d. of all the above reasons in combination.

6. Agricultural marketing orders date from
   a. the period 1910–1914.
   b. the Great Depression.
   c. World War II.
   d. the 1950s.

7. A marketing order practicing price discrimination will tend to charge the highest prices in the market having
   a. the highest price elasticity of demand.
   b. the lowest price elasticity of demand.
   c. the highest income elasticity of demand.
   d. the lowest income elasticity of demand.

8. A marketing order for lemons is likely to be most detrimental to the interests of which of the following groups?
   a. Consumers of fresh lemons.
   b. Consumers of processed lemon products.
   c. Manufacturers of processed lemon products.
   d. Lemon growers.

9. In a price discriminating marketing order without entry control,
   a. the original members would eventually lose all the advantages that the marketing order originally gave them.
   b. consumers in the low-price market segment would be harmed more than if entry control could be enforced.
   c. a part of the crop might be sold at price below its marginal cost of production.
   d. none of the above would be true.

10. Which of the following policies is likely to be most detrimental to productive efficiency in the farm economy?
    a. Price supports.
    b. Acreage controls.
    c. Target prices.
    d. All of the above are about equal with regard to efficiency.

11. Which of the following farm policies would require the least budgetary expenditure by the government, beyond administrative costs?
    a. Price supports.
    b. Acreage controls.
    c. Target prices.
    d. The three would be about equal with regard to expenditures.

12. Which of the following farm policies would result in the largest farm surpluses?
    a. Price supports.
    b. Acreage controls.
    c. Target prices.
    d. All of the above would be about equal with regard to surpluses.

13. Which of the following farm policies would result in the lowest prices paid by consumers?
    a. Price supports.
    b. Acreage controls.
    c. Target prices.
    d. All of the above would be about equal from the consumers' point of view.

14. The Food and Agricultural Act of 1977 relied on which of the following farm policies?
    a. Price supports.
    b. Acreage controls.
    c. Target prices.
    d. All of the above.

15. U.S. farm policies have been notably effective in
    a. relieving rural poverty.
    b. stabilizing farm prices.
    c. improving consumer welfare.
    d. none of the above ways.

ANSWERS TO CHAPTER 25 SELF TEST

True or False

1-F; perfect competition.
2-T
3-F; with low incomes because of inelastic demand.
4-F; both are low for most crops.
5-F; to restrict competition.
6-T
7-F; a two-thirds vote.
8-F; for fresh produce and milk.
9-T
10-F; they are a very leaky bucket.

Multiple Choice

1-a
2-d
3-a
4-c
5-d
6-b
7-b
8-a
9-c
10-b
11-b
12-a
13-c
14-d
15-d

CHAPTER TWENTY-SIX
OLIGOPOLY: COMPETITION AMONG THE FEW

WHERE YOU'RE GOING

Here is what you will be able to do when you have mastered this chapter:

--Explain what is meant by oligopoly, and compare business rivalry under oligopoly with competition of the kind that takes place in perfectly competitive markets.

--Discuss the relative importance of various determinants of market concentration.

--Explain what is meant by oligopolistic interdependence and why such interdependence makes it difficult to develop formal theories of oligopoly.

--Discuss in an informal way various factors on which the performance of oligopolistic markets may depend.

--Discuss the conclusions reached by various attempts at empirical measurement of market performance under oligopoly.

--Explain the meaning and significance of the following additional terms and concepts:

Concentration ratio.
Price leadership.

CHAPTER SYNOPSIS

Reading this synopsis is not a substitute for reading the chapter, but it should help you to recall the main points. If there are any you feel unsure of, refer to the full discussion in the text.

The "competition" to which the term "perfect competition" refers is a matter of market structure. In everyday usage, however, the verb "to compete" refers to a form of conduct--a process of business rivalry that is largely absent under perfect competition because each firm is too small to have much influence on its fellow competitors. As the number of firms in a market decreases, however, rivalry becomes a more and more important part of business life. In markets where there are only a few firms--oligopolies--rivalry becomes a matter of central importance. In particular, attention becomes focused on the question of whether the market structure of perfect competition is necessary for satisfactory market performance or whether rivalry among a few large firms is enough.

Markets dominated by just a few firms are quite common in the U.S. economy. Concentration ratios provide one way of measuring the extent of oligopoly in the economy. In many industries, such as those making cigarettes, automobiles, and tires, the largest eight firms account for more than 90 percent of industry output-- that is, the eight-firm concentration ratio is 90 percent or more. Eight-firm concentration ratios of 50 percent or more are quite common.

A number of factors contribute to determining the number of firms in an industry and the way output is distributed among those firms. Economies of scale are one important factor. Economies of scale at the plant level alone are not sufficient to explain the prevailing degree of market concentration entirely, however. Other kinds of economies of scale also contribute to market concentration, as do random differences in growth rates of firms and barriers to entry. (A barrier to entry, in this context, is something that prevents new entrants from duplicating the performance of existing firms in terms of cost or quality of product.)

In a market with only a few firms, it matters very much to each firm what its rivals do in terms of price, output, product characteristics, and marketing strategies. Economists refer to this situation as <u>oligopolistic interdependence</u>. Oligopolistic interdependence makes it very difficult to construct formal theories of oligopolistic behavior like those used to analyze perfect competition and pure monopoly. Economic decision making under oligopoly is less a matter of pure economizing and more a complex game in which rival entrepreneurs try to guess their rivals' reactions to each move they make and plan countermoves to make in turn. Most attempts to construct formal theories of oligopoly make some simplifying assumption about how each firm expects its rivals to react. For example, one can explore what would happen in an oligopolistic market if each firm assumed its rivals would tacitly coordinate price and output decisions to the joint interest of all firms. Alternatively, one could assume that each firm would expect that its rivals would always react in the most disadvantageous possible way. Unfortunately, reliance on such simplifying assumptions may make the formal theories too unrealistic to be very useful.

Although economists have not developed a widely accepted formal theory of oligopoly, they tend to agree informally on a list of market characteristics that are likely to affect market performance under oligopoly. For example, other things equal, the number and size of firms is likely to make a difference--an industry with very few firms is more likely to permit tacit cartel-like coordination than is an industry with a relatively greater number of firms. Also, the presence of one very strong firm that may act as a <u>price leader</u> is widely thought to contribute to tacit coordination. The nature of the product, the quality of information in the market, and the pace of growth and innovation are also likely to affect market performance.

Lacking a strong theoretical basis for predicting market performance under oligopoly, a number of economists have attempted to measure market performance empirically. Early empirical work seemed to detect a positive relationship between market concentration and profit, which in turn was interpreted to indicate that concentrated industries had cartel-like performance characteristics. More recent research has challenged this concentration-profits relationship and its interpretation, however, so the matter must now be regarded as an open question.

<u>WALKING TOUR</u>

<u>You have read the chapter at least once and have reviewed the synopsis. Now you are going to walk through the material step by step, filling in the blanks and answering the questions as you go along. After you have answered each question, check yourself by uncovering the answer given in the margin. If you do not understand why the answer given is the right one, refer back to the proper section of the text.</u>

<u>Market Concentration and Its Determinants</u>

Concentration ratios are the most commonly used measure of

market concentration. Consider, for example, the following

hypothetical sales data for the U.S. auto industry in a

certain year:

225

Firm	Units Sold
GM	9.0 million
Ford	2.5 million
Chrysler	1.0 million
VW of America	1.0 million
American Motors	0.5 million

On the basis of this data, you would calculate the four-firm concentration ratio for the U.S. auto industry to be _____ percent and the eight-firm concentration ratio   96.4
to be _____ percent. Because these figures do not   100
take foreign sales in the United States into account, however,
they represent an [understatement/overstatement] of the   understatement
actual degree of competition in the U.S. auto market.

In looking for explanations of the degree of concentration in this industry, your first thought would be of the cost advantages of making large numbers of cars--that is, of _____. In the auto   economies of scale
industry, these would include [plant level/multiplant/both plant level and multiplant] economies. You would also want   both plant level and
to know if there were any factors that prevented potential   multiplant
new auto firms from duplicating the performance of firms already in the industry--that is, if there were any
_____. _____ influ-   entry barriers; Random
ences might explain much of the remaining extent of concentration.

Coordination and Interdependence

Imagine now that the auto industry consists of just two firms, Ford and GM, and that these firms are of equal size. At the beginning of 1980, each is faced with the decision of whether to spend large sums making the traditional annual model change or whether to continue producing 1979 models for another year. Each calculates that if both change, they will split the market and earn $1 billion profit apiece. If neither changes, they will again split the market, but cost savings will be so great that each will earn $2 billion. But if one changes and the other doesn't, the firm with the new model will steal so many of the other's sales that it will earn $2.5 billion, while the firm with the old models will earn just $0.5 billion.

Under these conditions, if the firms explicitly coordinated their activities to maximize joint industry profits, _____ would change models and total industry earnings would be _____ billion. Without a formal agreement, a tacit assumption by each that the other will do what is best for everyone would bring the same result. However, suppose Ford decides that whatever GM does, it will take the course that gives highest Ford profits given the GM decision. That means [making/not making] the model change if GM makes it and [making/not making] the change if GM does not. If GM follows the same strategy, [both/neither] will make the model change, and total industry profits will be _____ billion.

neither
$4

making
making

both
$2

It is hard to say which of the above outcomes would result in any given industry, but certain rules of thumb have been suggested. Other things being equal, tacit coordination is thought to be more likely the [more/less] concentrated the industry and the [more/less] rapid the pace of growth and innovation.

more
less

SELF TEST

These sample test items will help you check how much you have learned. Answers and explanations can be found at the end of this chapter. Scoring yourself: One or two wrong -- on target. Three to five wrong -- passing, but you haven't mastered the chapter yet. Six or more wrong -- not good enough; start over and restudy the chapter.

True or False

Indicate whether each statement is true or false as it stands. If it is false, explain why in a few words.

T F 1. All markets having fewer than the "large number" of firms required for perfect competition are known as oligopolies.

T F 2. Some degree of oligopoly is present in many markets, although markets with eight-firm concentration ratios of 50 percent or more are almost unknown in the U.S. economy.

T F 3. Most market concentration in the U.S. economy can be explained by economies of scale at the plant level.

T F 4. Not every effort, risk, or expense that an entrepreneur must undertake in order to enter a market is a barrier to entry in the sense in which the term is used in this book.

T F 5. Oligopolistic firms are interdependent in the sense that what each one does depends crucially on what each of its rivals does.

T F 6. In a market characterized by price leadership, only the leader can be sure that other firms will follow both its upward and downward price moves.

T F 7. Oligopoly theory implies that market performance is improved by poor information.

T F 8. Early empirical studies by Joe Bain of the University of California suggested that firms in highly concentrated industries earned higher profits than those in less concentrated industries.

T F 9. Oligopoly theory can produce realistic results only so long as it concentrates on pure economizing.

T F 10. Despite many differences of approach, economists are broadly agreed that rivalry among a few large firms is not enough to guarantee satisfactory market performance.

Multiple Choice

1. The steel industry in the United States would best be described as
   a. pure monopoly.
   b. perfect competition.
   c. oligopoly.
   d. monopolistic competition.

2. An industry with an eight-firm concentration ratio of 95 percent and a formal agreement on prices and output among the top eight firms would best be described as
   a. pure monopoly.
   b. monopolistic competition.
   c. oligopoly.
   d. a cartel.

3. About what share of all manufacturing output comes from industries having a four-firm concentration ratio of 50 percent or more?
   a. 0-30 percent.
   b. 30-50 percent.
   c. 50-90 percent.
   d. 90-100 percent.

4. An international comparisons study by F. M. Scherer and others indicated that plant level economies of scale
   a. were sufficient to explain the existing degree of concentration in the United States for most industries investigated.
   b. explained most, but not all, of the existing degree of concentration in the United States for most industries investigated.
   c. explained only a small part of the existing degree of concentration in the United States for many industries investigated.
   d. were of no help in explaining concentration for any of the industries investigated.

5. Which of the following could be considered a barrier to entry into the inter-state trucking industry?
   a. The necessity of raising capital to buy trucks.
   b. The necessity of advertising the newly offered service.
   c. The right of existing firms to protest, and often quash, applications from new firms for government trucking permits.
   d. The tendency of shippers to prefer doing business with familiar carriers.

6. An industry has two identical firms, A and B. If both firms do X, each will earn $1. If A does X and B does Y, A will earn $2 and Y will earn 10 cents. If both do Y, each will earn $1.50. It can be concluded that
   a. both firms will do X.
   b. both firms will do Y.
   c. A will do X and B will do Y, or vice versa.
   d. not enough information is given for an answer to be reached.

7. If firms in an oligopoly follow the "golden rule" of doing unto others as they would have others do unto them, all firms are likely to earn
   a. higher than normal returns.
   b. normal returns.
   c. lower than normal returns.
   d. zero returns.

8. Which of the following is likely to make tacit coordination easier in an oligopolis-tic market?
   a. A small number of firms.
   b. An agreement among firms to exchange information on sales and prices.
   c. The presence of one clearly dominant firm.
   d. All of the above.

9. Which of the following is likely to make tacit coordination more difficult in an oligopolistic market?
   a. A small number of firms.
   b. Presence of single dominant firms.
   c. Rapid growth and innovation.
   d. All of the above.

10. Which of the following statements best characterizes the relationship between information and market performance?
    a. Secrecy makes tacit coordination difficult, so the less information, the better market performance.
    b. Certain types of information exchange can facilitate tacit coordination and thereby be detrimental to good market performance.
    c. Improved communication can always be counted upon to improve market performance.
    d. Information is irrelevant to market performance.

11. Economists who have made empirical studies of the relationship between concen-tration and market performance have generally looked at data comparing
    a. quantities of output actually produced by firms in concentrated markets with quantities produced in less concentrated markets.
    b. prices charged by firms in concentrated markets with prices charged in less concentrated markets.
    c. rates of return in concentrated markets with rates of return in less con-centrated markets.
    d. the gap between price and marginal cost in concentrated markets with the gap in less concentrated markets.

12. An early study by Joe Bain concluded
    a. that profits were always higher in more concentrated than in less concentrated industries.
    b. that there was a moderate but persistent tendency for firms in concentrated industries to earn relatively high profits.
    c. that there was no difference in terms of profits between more concentrated and less concentrated industries.
    d. that concentrated industries had satisfactory market performance.

13. Which of the following might cause firms in more concentrated industries to earn higher rates of return, on the average, than firms in less concentrated industries?
    a. Oligopolies operate much like formal cartels.
    b. Concentrated industries happen, on the average, to grow faster than less concentrated industries.
    c. Data on rates of return are distorted by failure to account properly for advertising expenditures.
    d. Any of the above might cause such a relationship.

14. It is universally agreed among economists that
    a. rivalry among a few firms is just as good as perfect competition.
    b. oligopolies perform less well than perfectly competitive markets.
    c. oligopolies closely resemble formal cartels in terms of price and output decisions.
    d. all of the above conclusions are still being actively debated.

15. Which of the following aspects of decision making under oligopoly is a matter of pure economizing?
    a. Determining an optimal advertising strategy.
    b. Determining how to react to a rival's price changes.
    c. Determining how and when to enter a new market.
    d. None of the above.

ANSWERS TO CHAPTER 26 SELF TEST

True or False

1-F; such markets also include pure monopolies and cartels.
2-F; 50 percent concentration ratios are fairly common.
3-F; only a small amount can be so explained.
4-T
5-T
6-T
7-F; although exchange of certain types of information may make coordination easier.
8-T
9-F; such a narrow focus works against realism.
10-F; there is no such broad agreement.

Multiple Choice

1-c
2-d
3-b
4-c
5-c
6-d; one must also know how each firm expects its rival to act.
7-a
8-d
9-c
10-b
11-c
12-b
13-d
14-d
15-d

CHAPTER TWENTY-SEVEN
ADVERTISING AND NONPRICE COMPETITION

WHERE YOU'RE GOING

Here is what you will be able to do when you have mastered this chapter:

--Distinguish the entrepreneurial element in consumer decision making from the element of pure economizing.

--Discuss a variety of mechanisms through which advertising affects consumer behavior.

--Summarize the normative economic cases for and against advertising.

--Discuss the evidence for and against the proposition that advertising is a barrier to entry into concentrated markets.

--Demonstrate the conditions for short-run and long-run equilibrium under monopolistic competition, and outline the controversy over market performance under monopolistic competition.

--Distinguish between static and dynamic efficiency, and discuss the debate over the Schumpeter hypothesis in terms of these two types of efficiency.

CHAPTER SYNOPSIS

Reading this synopsis is not a substitute for reading the chapter, but it should help you to recall the main points. If there are any you feel unsure of, refer to the full discussion in the text.

This chapter concentrates on several important entrepreneurial elements in economic decision making--advertising, product innovation, and other forms of nonprice competition. These have remained in the background in earlier chapters, which concentrated on price and output decisions (pure economizing).

The discussion of advertising begins with an analysis of its effects on consumers. In Chapter 20, consumers were represented as pure economizers, searching for the best way to spend their money from among a set of alternatives about which they have complete information. In practice, however, consumer choice also requires searching for new alternatives and experimenting with new ways of fulfilling the objective of maximum utility. It is in this entrepreneurial phase of consumer decision making that advertising is important. For one thing, advertising helps dispel consumer ignorance about available alternatives and their relative costs. Equally important, advertising affects consumer tastes and preferences, thereby altering the satisfaction that consumers get from any given combination of goods and services.

Advertising has been attacked by some on the grounds that it creates false wants and needs in the minds of consumers in place of the true wants and needs they ought to seek to satisfy. Others, however, dispute the notion that there are any true or innate human needs beyond such basic needs as food, shelter, affection, self esteem, and so on. They contend that advertising, rather than replacing these basic needs with others, simply determines the particular brands and styles of goods used to fulfill them.

In addition to the normative issue of advertising and consumer sovereignty, there are a number of positive economic issues concerning advertising. There is, for example, the issue of whether advertising acts as a barrier to entry in concentrated industries. The mechanism by which advertising is said to act as a barrier to entry is the creation of brand loyalties. This view gained support from an empirical study by Comanor and Wilson that appeared to show a positive association between advertising expenditures and rates of return in a number of industries. Other economists have challenged the Comanor and Wilson conclusions, however. They suggest that their statistical results were distorted by improper accounting methods. Instead of being a barrier to entry, these economists say, advertising is an important tool enabling new firms to break down old brand loyalties and enter new markets.

A third area of controversy centers on the role of advertising in monopolistic competition. In monopolistic competition, there are many firms and no barriers to entry, but the product differs from firm to firm, with advertising frequently used to emphasize or increase product differentiation. As a result, the demand curve facing each monopolistically competitive firm is less than perfectly elastic, and a gap remains between price and marginal cost in equilibrium. This gap has been interpreted as evidence of less than perfect market performance under monopolistic competition. This conclusion too has been challenged, however. Some economists see the apparently different "products" offered by, say, French and Italian restaurants as just different production technologies for a more broadly defined, homogeneous product "dining pleasure." Others argue that product diversity is desirable in itself and that attempts to force monopolistically competitive industries into the perfectly competitive mold by suppressing advertising and product differentiation would reduce, not increase, consumer welfare.

Still another area of economic controversy revolves around the notions of <u>static</u> and <u>dynamic efficiency</u>. Static efficiency means the ability of an economy to get the most out of existing resources and technology, while dynamic efficiency means the ability to increase consumer welfare through growth and innovation. In previous chapters, such market structures as pure monopoly, oligopoly, and monopolistic competition have been analyzed and criticized primarily in terms of static efficiency. According to a hypothesis advanced by Joseph Schumpeter, however, these same market forms may be superior to perfect competition in terms of dynamic efficiency. A number of attempts have been made to subject the Schumpeter hypothesis to empirical tests; but to date, these attempts remain inconclusive.

In summary, it can only be said that the economics profession remains deeply divided on two of the most important questions concerning industrial organization and market structure: whether perfect competition, or something close to it, is the natural state of the economy and whether perfect competition is necessary to guarantee satisfactory market performance.

WALKING TOUR

You have read the chapter at least once and have reviewed the synopsis. Now you are going to walk through the material step by step, filling in the blanks and answering the questions as you go along. After you have answered each question, check yourself by uncovering the answer given in the margin. If you do not understand why the answer given is the right one, refer back to the proper section of the text.

Advertising and the Consumer

To the extent that consumers seek to maximize utility by

choosing among known alternatives with given constraints,

they are acting as _____. Adver-   pure economizers

233

tising plays relatively little role in this aspect of consumer choice; it is important because consumers also engage in

_____ decision making, seeking out new   entrepreneurial
ways to satisfy old needs and new needs to satisfy. Advertising affects entrepreneurial consumer decisions by giving
consumers _____ about new alternatives and   information
sources of supply, by changing _____ and   tastes
_____, and by building or destroying   perceptions
_____.   brand loyalties

    Harvard professor John Kenneth Galbraith has attacked
advertising on the grounds that it violates _____
_____. This idea that advertising deflects   consumer sovereignty
consumers from "true" needs to "false" needs is also sometimes referred to by the term consumer _____.   alienation
Many economists are skeptical about the concept of "true"
needs, however, suggesting that it may simply reflect the
preferences of a self-appointed elite.

Advertising and Market Performance

Advertising has also been attacked on the grounds that it
is a barrier to entry. In a 1967 study, Comanor and Wilson
found evidence that industries with high advertising out-
lays earn, on the average [higher/lower] rates of return   higher
than those doing less advertising. However, University
of Chicago economist Yale Brozen has challenged the statistical methodology of the Comanor and Wilson study and
has also argued that advertising is most important to firms
[entering/already in] a market.   entering

    Advertising also plays an important role in monopo-
listically competitive markets; that is, in markets where
there are [few/many] firms, [high/low] barriers to entry,   many; low
and a [homogeneous/differentiated] product. Exhibit S27.1   differentiated
will help you understand how equilibrium is achieved under
monopolistic competition.

    The exhibit contains demand, marginal cost, and aver-
age total cost curves for a typical monopolistically competitive firm. Begin by adding the marginal revenue curve
for the firm. It lies _____ between the   halfway
demand curve and the [vertical/horizontal] axis; it thus   vertical
intersects the vertical axis at _____ and the horizon- $14

234

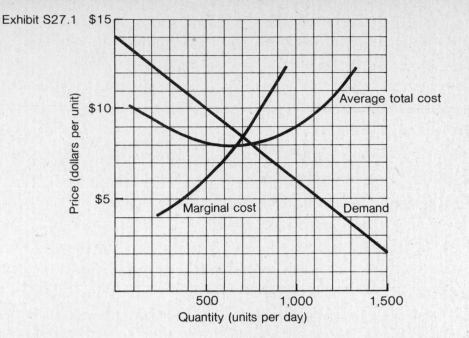

Exhibit S27.1

Price (dollars per unit)

$15

$10

$5

Average total cost

Marginal cost

Demand

500   1,000   1,500

Quantity (units per day)

tal axis at _____ units of output. Next determine the   850
quantity of output that will maximize profit for the firm in
the short run. This quantity is found where the marginal
cost curve intersects the _____ curve,   marginal revenue
which happens at _____ units of output as the diagram   500
is drawn. At that output, the product can be sold for
_____ per unit, and average total cost per unit is $10
_____. The firm's total profit is thus _____ per $8; $1,000
day.

    Under monopolistic competition, this state of affairs
[can/cannot] persist in the long run. Because this firm   cannot
and others like it are earning higher than normal rates of
return, [entry into/exit from] the market will be expected.   entry into
As new firms enter with competing products, the demand
curve shown in Exhibit S27.1 will [rise/fall]. If the firm   fall
tries to defend its market share by advertising or product
innovations, its average total cost curve will [rise/fall].   rise
Eventually, the firm (and others like it) will end up in a
position where the average total cost curve is _____   tangent to
the demand curve at the quantity of output for which marginal cost is equal to _____. When   marginal revenue
this position is reached (sketch it in the diagram), pure
economic profit for the firm will be _____ and entry   zero
will cease. The industry will then be in long-run equilibrium.

235

Market Dynamics and Entrepreneurial Competition

A distinction can be made between a type of economic
efficiency that consists in getting the most out of available resources, called _____ efficiency,   static
and a type that consists in successfully expanding output
through growth and innovation, called _____   dynamic
efficiency.   In earlier chapters, it was noted that many
economists think perfect competition to be superior to
monopoly, oligopoly, and monopolistic competition in terms
of _____ efficiency.   However, according to the   static
Schumpeter hypothesis, perfect competition may be inferior
in terms of _____ efficiency.   Attempts have   dynamic
been made to test this hypothesis empirically; these tests
have for the most part been [conclusive/inconclusive],   inconclusive
largely because of the difficulty of measuring the rate of
_____ in an industry.   innovation

SELF TEST

These sample test items will help you check how much you have learned.   Answers
and explanations can be found at the end of this chapter.   Scoring yourself: One
or two wrong -- on target.   Three to five wrong -- passing, but you haven't mastered the chapter yet.   Six or more wrong -- not good enough; start over and
restudy the chapter.

True or False

Indicate whether each statement is true or false as it stands.   If it is false, explain
why in a few words.

T F   1.   Advertising acts on consumers primarily in their roles as pure economizers.

T F   2.   Empirical studies have shown that advertising can change tastes, but not
perceptions.

T F   3.   Empirical studies have indicated that brand loyalty cannot develop in the
absence of advertising.

T F   4.   Empirical studies have proved successful in distinguishing true from false
consumer needs.

T F   5.   If advertising were a barrier to entry, industries with higher advertising
expenditures would be expected to show higher profits than industries with
low advertising expenditures, other things being equal.

T F   6.   Pure economic profit must be zero in long-run equilibrium for a monopolistically competitive industry.

T F 7. Other things being equal, consumers are better off the more homogeneous an industry's product.

T F 8. New products tend to be advertised more intensely than old products.

T F 9. Attempts to test the Schumpeter hypothesis have been hampered by the difficulty of measuring rates of innovation.

T F 10. Empirical studies indicate that a policy of breaking up the largest firms into separate competing firms would improve dynamic efficiency in virtually all industries.

Multiple Choice

1. Which of the following consumer decision making situations would involve an element of entrepreneurship?
    a. Getting competing bids from several contractors on a plumbing job.
    b. Trying a new brand of low-calorie beer.
    c. Looking at fall fashion ads in a popular magazine.
    d. All of the above.

2. On the basis of studies presented in this book, advertising is least likely to be able to do which of the following?
    a. Cause consumers to perceive an advertised brand of food as tasting better than a physically identical unadvertised brand.
    b. Try an unknown, newly advertised brand.
    c. Induce repeat purchases of a product that consumers perceive as inferior to an unadvertised brand.
    d. Strengthen existing brand loyalties.

3. According to John Kenneth Galbraith, advertising
    a. is a method by which firms that fill wants at the same time create wants.
    b. is an essential source of information for consumers to use in entrepreneurial decisions.
    c. is a major protection against consumer alienation.
    d. should be treated as an investment, not a current business expense.

4. Which of the following pieces of evidence would not tend to confirm the hypothesis that advertising is a barrier to entry?
    a. Firms in industries that advertise heavily earn higher than average profits.
    b. Firms in concentrated industries advertise more than firms in less concentrated industries.
    c. Brand loyalty is highest in markets where advertising expenditures are highest.
    d. New brands tend to be advertised more heavily than old brands.

5. To say that advertising is a barrier to entry implies, among other things,
    a. that advertising is not available to newly entering firms on the same terms as it is available to existing firms.
    b. that advertising represents a large share of total cost.
    c. that advertising conveys little useful information to consumers.
    d. all of the above.

6. Concern over advertising as a potential barrier to entry is highest for which of the following market structures?
    a. Natural monopoly.
    b. Oligopoly.
    c. Monopolistic competition.
    d. Perfect competition.

7. Which of the following is true in long-run equilibrium for both perfect competition and monopolistic competition?
   a. Long-run average cost equals price.
   b. Marginal cost equals price.
   c. Long-run average cost is at its minimum.
   d. All of the above.

8. Which of the following industries best fits the definition of monopolistic competition?
   a. Soybean production.
   b. Basic steel production.
   c. Electric utilities.
   d. Auto repair shops.

9. Which of the following best characterizes the effect of introducing advertising into the legal profession?
   a. Lower prices and an increased variety of services.
   b. Lower prices and a decreased variety of services.
   c. Higher prices and an increased variety of services.
   d. Higher prices and a decreased variety of services.

10. A study showing that, other things equal, eyeglasses cost less in states where advertising was permitted than in states where it was prohibited would be evidence that
   a. advertising is an important barrier to entry.
   b. eyeglasses production is not monopolistically competitive.
   c. advertising is not detrimental to market performance.
   d. the eyeglasses market is perfectly competitive where no legal restrictions on advertising exist.

11. Which of the following indicates that the economy is enjoying good static efficiency?
   a. The economy is operating on its production possibility frontier.
   b. The economy is operating inside its production possibility frontier.
   c. The production possibility frontier is shifting outward rapidly.
   d. The production possibility frontier is becoming less curved.

12. According to the Schumpeter hypothesis, which of the following market structures would be most likely to exhibit good dynamic efficiency?
   a. Perfect competition.
   b. Monopolistic competition.
   c. Oligopoly.
   d. Natural monopoly.

13. The Schumpeter hypothesis implies that which of the following policies would do the most, in the long run, to improve consumer welfare?
   a. Break up large firms into small ones.
   b. Permit firms introducing major innovations to earn temporary monopoly profits.
   c. Reward firms making major innovations by protecting them from foreign competition.
   d. Increase government subsidies to research and development.

14. Attempts to subject the Schumpeter hypothesis to empirical tests appear to indicate which of the following?
   a. Large firms provide a more than proportional share of innovations in all industries.
   b. Small firms provide a more than proportional share of innovations in all industries.
   c. Supergiant firms are more innovative in proportion to their size than merely giant firms.
   d. Firms of all sizes manage to make important contributions to innovation.

15. Policies designed to break up large firms into small ones would tend to be supported by which of the following?
   a. A finding that the existing degree of concentration in most markets is the result of artificial barriers to entry.
   b. Confirmation of the Schumpeter hypothesis.
   c. A finding that larger firms spend a higher portion of their revenues on R&D than smaller firms.
   d. A finding that monopolistic competition is just as efficient as perfect competition.

ANSWERS TO CHAPTER 27 SELF TEST

True or False

1-F; as entrepreneurs.
2-F; can change both.
3-F; can develop.
4-F; these are purely subjective concepts.
5-T
6-T
7-F; other things being equal, variety is good.
8-T
9-T
10-F; the results are mixed and, if anything, lean the other way.

Multiple Choice

1-d
2-c
3-a
4-d
5-a
6-b
7-a
8-d
9-a
10-c
11-a
12-c
13-b
14-d
15-a

CHAPTER TWENTY-EIGHT
GOVERNMENT AND BUSINESS: ANTITRUST POLICY

WHERE YOU'RE GOING

Here is what you will be able to do when you have mastered this chapter:

--List the major antitrust laws and their main provisions.

--Explain actual antitrust policies in the areas of price fixing, mergers, vertical restraints, and price discrimination.

--Present a brief critique of the antitrust laws as currently enforced.

--Draw alternative sketches of the possible future of antitrust policy.

--Explain the meaning and significance of the following additional terms and concepts:

> Horizontal mergers.
> Vertical mergers.
> Conglomerate mergers.

CHAPTER SYNOPSIS

Reading this synopsis is not a substitute for reading the chapter, but it should help you to recall the main points. If there are any you feel unsure of, refer to the full discussion in the text.

Public policy toward market structure and competitive behavior is embodied in a set of laws known as the antitrust laws. Antitrust laws are not economic theory translated into legislation. Instead, these laws rest as much on broad social concerns for fairness, decentralization of power, and protection of small business as on purely economic concerns about static and dynamic efficiency.

The first major federal antitrust law was the Sherman Act of 1890. In sweeping terms, it outlaws conspiracies in restraint of trade and attempts to monopolize, leaving many actual policy decisions to the interpretation of the courts.

The Clayton Act and the Federal Trade Commission Act, both passed in 1914, attempted to strengthen antitrust law in two respects. The Clayton Act listed several specific business practices considered to be anticompetitive, including price discrimination, tying contracts, certain kinds of mergers, and interlocking directorates. The Federal Trade Commission Act created the FTC as an independent agency with the power to initiate antitrust cases.

More recent additions to the antitrust laws have been the Robinson-Patman Act of 1936, which strengthened the law against price discrimination, and the Celler-Kefauver Act of 1950, which strengthened the law against mergers.

The actual development of antitrust policy has depended as much on interpretation as on the law itself. Major areas of antitrust policy at present include price fixing, mergers, vertical restraints, and price discrimination.

Open price fixing, meaning explicit agreements among firms as to prices charged, is treated as a per se violation of the Sherman Act. That means that only the fact of price fixing need be established to secure a conviction--it need not be proved that the prices established were unreasonable or even that the attempt to fix prices was successful. The law against price fixing is also interpreted as prohibiting other cartel-like practices such as restrictions of output or divisions of markets.

The original antimerger provisions of the Clayton Act were not very effective until amended in 1950 by the Celler-Kefauver Act. Since that time, policy has become very restrictive with regard to horizontal mergers (mergers among firms in the same line of business) and vertical mergers (mergers among firms in a supplier-customer relationship). Conglomerate mergers (mergers among firms in unrelated lines of business) are also often opposed by the government, but the law is not as strong here as in other areas of mergers.

Antitrust law also opposes many kinds of so-called vertical restraints, that is, agreements on business practices among suppliers and their customers. Among the types of vertical restraint outlawed are resale price maintenance (agreements by retailers not to sell below a price set by wholesalers), territorial restrictions imposed by manufacturers on retailers, tying agreements (contracts requiring buyers of one product to buy another product from the same company), and exclusive dealing agreements (agreements by a retailer not to deal in the products of a manufacturer's competitor).

The original price discrimination provisions of the Clayton Act were strengthened by the Robinson-Patman Act of 1936, sometimes called the "Chain Store Act" because small retailers thought it would give them protection against competition by chain stores. In recent years, enforcement of the Robinson-Patman Act has become less vigorous.

Many economists are critical of one or more aspects of antitrust policy. Some criticize the size, length, and complexity of modern antitrust cases. Others complain that the antitrust laws, as currently enforced, give too little attention to efficiency and too much attention to noneconomic considerations. Merger policy is criticized especially for ignoring the possible economic advantages of mergers. Finally, antitrust policy is criticized for doing too much to protect the interests of specific competitors and not enough to protect the integrity of the competitive process as a whole.

The future of antitrust policy is currently subject to conflicting pressures. Within the government, many antitrust officials are hoping to strengthen the law's ability to operate in such areas as "shared monopoly" (oligopoly) and conglomerate mergers. Within the academic community, however, many critics would prefer to see an antitrust policy concentrating more narrowly on economic concerns rather than pursuing broader social purposes.

WALKING TOUR

You have read the chapter at least once and have reviewed the synopsis. Now you are going to walk through the material step by step, filling in the blanks and answering the questions as you go along. After you have answered each question, check yourself by uncovering the answer given in the margin. If you do not understand why the answer given is the right one, refer back to the proper section of the text.

Antitrust Laws and Policies

The first federal antitrust act in the United States was

the _____ of _____. This act   Sherman Act; 1890

outlaws conspiracies to restrict commerce and attempts to

monopolize. The act was strengthened in 1974, when

violation was made a _____. A practical result | felony
of that has been more frequent _____ | jail sentences
for violators.

In 1914, two more antitrust acts were passed. One
lists specific anticompetitive practices and is known as
the _____ Act. The other established an in- | Clayton
dependent agency to initiate antitrust cases, the _____. | FTC
The antitrust laws were further strengthened by the
Robinson-Patman Act of 1936, which deals with _____
_____, and the Celler-Kefauver Act of 1950, | price discrimination
which deals with _____. | mergers

The antitrust laws, as currently enforced, prevent the
formation of cartels by outlawing _____ | price fixing
and related practices such as _____ | output restrictions
and _____. Attempts to form | market division
single-firm monopolies through _____ | horizontal
mergers are also effectively prohibited. In addition, the
government also opposes mergers among firms in a seller-
customer relationship (_____ mergers) and | vertical
mergers among firms in unrelated lines of business
(_____ mergers). Many kinds of agree- | conglomerate
ments among suppliers and customers, known as _____
_____, are outlawed too. Sometimes, but | vertical restraints
not as often as formerly, the government also prosecutes
_____ under the Robinson-Patman | price discrimination
Act.

Critical Perspectives on Antitrust Policy
Many economists are critical of antitrust laws. They cite
such cases as the IBM case, begun in 1969, as evidence
that big antitrust cases are too _____and _____. | long; complex
The antitrust laws, they say, are more effective against
_____ and _____ than | monopolies; cartels
against _____. Also, economic critics | oligopolies
complain that the law pays too little attention to _____ | efficiency
and too much attention to ill-defined social concerns.

Within federal antitrust agencies, however, many officials would like to broaden, rather than narrow, the scope
of antitrust activity--for example, by the passage of new
laws permitting more effective action against so-called

"_____" and against   shared monopolies

_____ mergers.   conglomerate

SELF TEST

These sample test items will help you check how much you have learned. Answers and explanations can be found at the end of this chapter. Scoring yourself: One or two wrong -- on target. Three to five wrong -- passing, but you haven't mastered the chapter yet. Six or more wrong -- not good enough; start over and restudy the chapter.

True or False

Indicate whether each statement is true or false as it stands. If it is false, explain why in a few words.

T F   1. Antitrust law is an invention of the twentieth century.

T F   2. The Supreme Court has sometimes considered protection of the interests of "small dealers and worthy men" more important than economic efficiency.

T F   3. Tying contracts are so called because they tie the sale of one product to the sale of another.

T F   4. The Clayton Act outlaws interlocking directorates.

T F   5. One problem with antitrust policy is that the courts have narrowly followed the specific language of the antitrust laws rather than interpreting them broadly.

T F   6. Price fixing is considered a per se violation of the Sherman Act.

T F   7. Conglomerate mergers are those that are both vertical and horizontal at the same time.

T F   8. Enforcement of the Robinson-Patman Act has become more vigorous in recent years.

T F   9. Protecting competitors amounts to the same thing as protecting the process of competition.

T F 10. The term "shared monopoly" is used to refer to oligopolies that are believed not to display satisfactory market performance.

Multiple Choice

1. In the nineteenth century, people were hostile to the "trusts" primarily because
   a. they were economically inefficient.
   b. they were dominated by foreign stockholders.
   c. they were big and powerful.
   d. they were blamed for the Civil War.

2. Which of the following penalties is available to the government in Sherman Act cases?
   a. Fines
   b. Jail sentences.
   c. Injunctions.
   d. All of the above.

3. Which of the following laws prohibits tying agreements?
   a. The Sherman Act.
   b. The Clayton Act.
   c. The Celler-Kefauver Act.
   d. The Robinson-Patman Act.

4. The Federal Trade Commission Act was passed in
   a. 1890.
   b. 1914.
   c. 1936.
   d. 1950.

5. The original antimerger section of the Clayton Act was aimed specifically at which of the following types of mergers?
   a. Vertical mergers.
   b. Conglomerate mergers.
   c. Mergers via acquisition of stocks.
   d. Mergers via acquisition of assets.

6. Except where special antitrust exemptions exist, it is not possible for firms in the United States to form cartels, because it is illegal to
   a. fix prices.
   b. divide markets.
   c. restrict output.
   d. do any of the above.

7. Current merger law (as of 1979) is least effective against which type of merger?
   a. Vertical .
   b. Horizontal.
   c. Conglomerate.
   d. Equally effective against all of the above.

8. Which of the following practices would be subject to challenge under current (1979) antitrust law?
   a. A contract requiring buyers of Kodak cameras to use only Kodak film.
   b. An agreement that Kodak dealers would not sell the cameras below the manufacturer's suggested retail price.
   c. An agreement that Kodak dealers would not sell Polaroid cameras.
   d. All of the above would probably be subject to challenge under the antitrust laws.

9. Which of the following antitrust laws is currently less vigorously enforced than it was formerly?
   a. The Sherman Act.
   b. The Clayton Act.
   c. The Robinson-Patman Act.
   d. The Celler-Kefauver Act.

10. Which of the following cases demonstrates the problem of excessive length and complexity?
    a. The IBM case.
    b. The Trans-Missouri Freight case.
    c. The Von's Grocery case.
    d. The Utah Pie case.

11. Against which market structure is antitrust law least effective?
    a. Pure monopoly.
    b. Oligopoly.
    c. Cartels.
    d. About equally effective against all of the above.

12. In the Utah Pie case, the defendants were convicted, in part,
    a. because they cut prices.
    b. because they competed vigorously against a local monopoly.
    c. because they refused to bow out of the market when a new competitor entered.
    d. because of all of the above.

13. Vertical restrictions
    a. are an example of a trade practice that even antitrust critics condemn.
    b. are defended as actually improving efficiency in some cases.
    c. are not currently illegal under antitrust laws.
    d. are none of the above.

14. The Von's Grocery case is an example of antitrust action in an industry having which of the following structures?
    a. Pure monopoly.
    b. Oligopoly.
    c. Monopolistic competition.
    d. Cartel.

15. Many advocates of a stronger antitrust policy want new laws against conglomerate mergers that would
    a. allow evidence of their adverse economic effects to be introduced in court.
    b. require merging firms of a certain size or larger to show beneficial effects if the merger is to be permitted.
    c. prevent even the smallest conglomerate mergers.
    d. do none of the above.

ANSWERS TO CHAPTER 28 SELF TEST

True or False

1-F; the Sherman Act was passed in 1890.
2-T
3-T
4-T
5-F; the acts have been interpreted quite broadly.
6-T
7-F; that are neither.
8-F; less vigorous.
9-F; it is often the opposite.
10-T

Multiple Choice

1-c
2-d
3-b
4-b
5-c
6-d
7-c
8-d
9-c
10-a
11-b
12-d
13-b
14-c
15-b

CHAPTER TWENTY-NINE
GOVERNMENT AND BUSINESS: REGULATION

WHERE YOU'RE GOING

Here is what you will be able to do when you have mastered this chapter:

--Explain the regulatory solution to the problem of natural monopoly, and discuss its limitations.

--Give examples of regulation of inherently competitive industries.

--Explain the cartel and distributional theories of regulation as applied to inherently competitive industries.

--Discuss the positive and normative controversies surrounding health and safety regulation as currently practiced.

--List the major general reasons that economists are increasingly critical of regulation.

CHAPTER SYNOPSIS

Reading this synopsis is not a substitute for reading the chapter, but it should help you to recall the main points. If there are any you feel unsure of, refer to the full discussion in the text.

All industries are regulated in one respect or another, but this chapter concentrates on two particular types of regulation not discussed elsewhere: first, that practiced in the traditional "regulated industries," especially utilities and transportation, and second, health and safety regulation, the effects of which are felt throughout the economy.

In a natural monopoly, total costs are minimized by having just one producer serve the entire market--residential gas, electric, water, and telephone services are frequently cited examples. Firms providing these services are usually subject to regulation in the rates they charge and in other aspects of their operation. The traditional rationale is that an unregulated private firm would take advantage of its monopoly position to raise its price above marginal cost and restrict output below the optimal level. It is hoped that regulation will force the firm to produce at a point where marginal cost and price are equal, or nearly so, as they would be for a competitive firm.

The problem of regulating a natural monopoly is easy to solve on paper by drawing hypothetical demand and cost curves; but in practice, regulators do not have such curves to work with. At most, they have observations of costs and revenues that correspond to single historical points on the cost and demand curves. Given this limited information, utility regulation focuses on the firm's rate of return. It is reasoned that a higher than normal rate of return indicates too high a price and too little output, while a lower than normal rate of return indicates a need to charge more and produce less.

Lack of information is just one of the limits on the effectiveness of utility regulation. In addition, regulations distort incentives in ways that may raise the cost of producing any given quantity of output. Even where regulation does successfully control rates of return, then, the result in terms of overall market performance may fall short of the ideal.

Regulation of rates and outputs is not limited to natural monopolies--many inherently competitive industries are also regulated. Regulation of air and surface transportation is a case in point. Regulation was introduced in these industries during the 1930s to curb what was then seen as the danger of excessive competition, believed to be a cause of the Great Depression. Traditionally, airline, railroad, and trucking regulators set minimum as well as maximum prices for services offered and strictly limited entry into new markets by new or existing firms.

Regulation of inherently competitive industries has been almost unanimously condemned by economists. Some have seen such regulation as a device by which the regulators act in the interests of the regulated firms as virtual cartel managers. Others see such regulation as a means by which the product of the industry is distributed among firms, users, unions, suppliers, and other groups in a way different from the way it would be distributed under competition, at the expense of efficiency. Partly in response to these criticisms, traditional regulatory practices in the transportation industry began to undergo significant reform toward the end of the 1970s, with the result that more competition is now permitted.

While regulation was on the retreat in industries such as transportation, other kinds of regulation, notably health and safety regulation, were spreading. Despite general agreement that health and safety are good in themselves, this kind of regulation too has proved a source of controversy among economists. Some of the controversies are of a normative nature--is it morally defensible to place a dollar value on human life and health, and if a value is placed, whose standard of values should be used? Other controversies lie in the realm of positive economics, notably, the controversy over performance standards versus engineering controls as the least-cost method of achieving regulatory objectives.

In the future, it appears that economists will continue to be critical of many types of regulation on two grounds: first, on the ground that efforts to use regulation to redistribute income inevitably harm economic efficiency, and second, on the ground that regulation is often, if not always, inferior to the market as a mechanism for utilizing information and allocating resources.

WALKING TOUR

You have read the chapter at least once and have reviewed the synopsis. Now you are going to walk through the material step by step, filling in the blanks and answering the questions as you go along. After you have answered each question, check yourself by uncovering the answer given in the margin. If you do not understand why the answer given is the right one, refer back to the proper section of the text.

Regulating Natural Monopoly

Under natural monopoly, costs are minimized by having just one firm serve the entire market. This implies that the minimum efficient scale in the industry is at least _____   50 percent of industry output, and perhaps greater. In order to realize all potentially mutually beneficial transactions in such a market, as in any market, output should be expanded up to the point where _____   marginal cost is equal to _____. However, an unregulated,   price profit maximizing monopolist would product at the point where marginal cost is equal to _____,   marginal revenue

at which point output is [lower/higher] and price [lower/
higher] than the optimum.

      If a regulator could determine the optimal price and
output for the firm, a price [ceiling/floor] could be set
at that level, causing the regulated firm to act as a
_____ and to produce the desired
output. In order to keep the firm in business without
subsidy in the long run, the price charged would have to
be at least equal to _____ cost so
that the firm could earn a _____ rate of
return.

      If the regulators were not able to directly determine
the quantity of output making marginal cost and price equal,
they could work backward along the line of reasoning described above. First they would determine the firm's rate
of return; then, if it was higher than normal, they would
[raise/lower] the price, and if it was lower than normal,
[raise/lower] the price. This would work if there were just
one level of cost and output for which a normal rate of
return were possible. However, when the regulators set a
price, the firm may respond by adjusting its costs upward
to bring its rate of return down to the normal level rather
than by adjusting its output. Even worse, if by error the
regulators set a target rate of return that is higher than
the true _____ cost of capital to the firm, it
may be tempted to invest without limit in questionable facil-
ities, forcing the regulators to continuously raise the price
to keep the rate of return at the target level.

Regulating Inherently Competitive Industries
Some industries are regulated despite the fact that they are
not natural monopolies--_____ and
_____ are traditional examples. In these
industries, regulators have set [minimum/maximum] prices
and restricted [entry/exit]. The original rationale for such
regulation was to prevent _____.
Today, many economists think the effect was to permit these
industries to operate as _____. However, not
all of the high prices charged by these presumed cartels
have gone into higher profits. Some also have gone to

Answer column (right margin):

lower
higher

ceiling

price taker

average total
normal

lower
raise

opportunity

trucking companies
airlines
minimum
entry
excessive competition

cartels

_____ and _____. The result   workers; suppliers
has been [increased/reduced] efficiency.   reduced

Health and Safety Regulation

Health and safety regulation is the most rapidly growing
area of regulation at present. Controversies over health
and safety regulation arise from both positive and normative
economics. The controversy over how health and safety
benefits should be translated into dollar terms, if they
should be at all, is an example of a _____   normative
economic dispute. The controversy over engineering controls versus _____ is an ex-   performance standards
ample of an issue in _____ economics.   positive

SELF TEST

These sample test items will help you check how much you have learned. Answers
and explanations can be found at the end of this chapter. Scoring yourself: One
or two wrong -- on target. Three to five wrong -- passing, but you haven't mastered the chapter yet. Six or more wrong -- not good enough; start over and
restudy the chapter.

True or False

Indicate whether each statement is true or false as it stands. If it is false, explain
why in a few words.

T F 1. In the U.S. economy, no sharp dividing line separates regulated from unregulated industries.

T F 2. In a natural monopoly, the minimum efficient scale for an individual firm is
large in relation to total industry output.

T F 3. An unregulated natural monopoly would maximize profits at the point where
price equals long-run average cost.

T F 4. The process of rate regulation begins with statistical reconstruction of the
regulated firm's cost and demand curves.

T F 5. The trucking industry, although regulated, can be considered inherently
competitive in part because it has a very large number of firms.

T F 6. According to the cartel theory of regulation, firms in regulated industries
will tend to earn higher rates of return than firms in unregulated industries.

T F 7. During the 1970s, regulation of the private sector was reduced in all areas.

T F 8. The issue of health and safety warnings versus restrictions on sales of
certain products is one that can, in principle, be settled by empirical
investigation.

T F 9. In debates with regulators, economists usually argue that engineering controls are more efficient than performance standards.

251

T F 10.   Economists are critical of regulation in part because distributional rather than allocational considerations tend to dominate regulatory decisions.

Multiple Choice

1.   Which of the following industries is subject to government regulation?
     a.   Trucking.
     b.   Steel.
     c.   Banking.
     d.   All of the above.

2.   Which of the following industries is regulated because it is a natural monopoly?
     a.   Airlines.
     b.   Electric utilities.
     c.   Cotton mills.
     d.   All of the above.

3.   In a pioneering study of utility regulation, Stigler and Friedland concluded that
     a.   regulation raised both costs and prices.
     b.   regulation raised neither costs nor prices.
     c.   regulation raised costs but not prices.
     d.   regulation raised prices but not costs.

4.   Regulation of inherently competitive industries differs from regulation of natural monopolies in that the regulators pay greater attention to
     a.   maximum prices.
     b.   service obligations.
     c.   entry control.
     d.   rates of return.

5.   A major rationale for introducing regulation of airlines and trucking during the 1930s was
     a.   the fear of excessive competition.
     b.   the fear that many firms would fail, leaving a monopoly.
     c.   the fear that without regulation, the firms would form private cartels.
     d.   the desire to lower excessive rates of return in the industries.

6.   A study of trucking regulation by Thomas Gale Moore concluded that the benefits of regulation
     a.   were divided among trucking firms, labor, and perhaps certain shippers.
     b.   were captured entirely by a cartel of trucking firms.
     c.   went largely to consumers.
     d.   were nonexistent--that is, no one benefitted from the regulations.

7.   Which of the following theories implies that deregulation of airlines would bring lower prices and higher output of service?
     a.   The Stigler-Friedland theory.
     b.   The cartel theory.
     c.   The theory that airlines are natural monopolies.
     d.   None of the above.

8.   Which of the following groups favors the continuation of regulation in trucking?
     a.   The trucking firms.
     b.   Labor.
     c.   Shippers.
     d.   All of the above.

9. Assume the cartel theory of regulation to be correct. Then if entry restrictions were dropped while the current level of rates remained in force, we would expect
   a. the number of firms to rise and profits to fall.
   b. the number of firms to fall and profits to rise.
   c. both the number for firms and profits to rise.
   d. both the number of firms and profits to fall.

10. Which of the following theories of regulation predicts the highest rate of return for firms in the industry?
    a. The Stigler-Friedland theory.
    b. The cartel theory.
    c. The distributional theory.
    d. The theory that regulation is needed primarily for stability.

11. Which of the following regulatory agencies grew most rapidly during the 1970s?
    a. The CAB.
    b. OSHA.
    c. The ICC.
    d. None of the above grew during the 1970s.

12. Economists who think that regulatory agencies should take into account tradeoffs between health and safety, on the one hand, and dollar costs, on the other, do so in part because
    a. they think people make such tradeoffs every day in the normal course of living.
    b. they are confident that modern empirical methods can measure the dollar value of health and safety accurately.
    c. they think that normative considerations should play no role in policy formation.
    d. they think health and safety unimportant relative to economic efficiency.

13. To deal with the hazards of cigarette smoking by using warning labels and publicity campaigns rather than by outlawing tobacco implies that tradeoffs between health and other consumer goals should be made according to the values of
    a. the consumers themselves.
    b. government-appointed experts.
    c. econometricians.
    d. the tobacco industry.

14. In the 1978 policy debate over cotton dust regulations, President Carter's Council of Economic Advisers took the position that
    a. the health hazards involved were negligible.
    b. strong engineering controls should be adopted.
    c. engineering controls would sap incentives to develop more cost effective pollution control methods in the future.
    d. economists should stay out of this type of issue.

15. Economists often criticize the use of regulation to accomplish distributional goals because
    a. they are generally happy with income distribution as it is.
    b. they think regulation tends to favor the poor over the rich.
    c. they think regulation tends to favor the rich over the poor.
    d. they think there are more efficient ways of redistributing income.

ANSWERS TO CHAPTER 29 SELF TEST

True or False

1-T
2-T
3-F; where marginal revenue equals marginal cost.
4-F; these curves usually cannot be reconstructed.
5-T
6-T
7-F; health and safety regulation grew stronger.
8-F; it is primarily a normative issue.
9-F; that performance standards are more efficient.
10-T

Multiple Choice

1-d
2-b
3-b
4-c
5-a
6-a
7-b
8-d
9-a
10-b
11-b
12-a
13-a
14-c
15-d

CHAPTER THIRTY

FACTOR MARKETS AND MARGINAL PRODUCTIVITY THEORY

WHERE YOU'RE GOING

Here is what you will be able to do when you have mastered this chapter:

--Explain the role played by factor markets in the functional and personal distribution of income.

--Derive a firm's marginal revenue product curve from data on marginal physical product and marginal revenue, and explain why the marginal revenue product curve is the factor demand curve for a firm that is a price taker in the market where it purchases the factor.

--Derive marginal factor cost curves from factor supply curves for both competitive and monopsonistic firms.

--Explain the origin and shape of an individual's factor supply curve in terms of the income and substitution effects.

--Compare factor market equilibrium under competition and monopsony.

--Discuss the marginal productivity theory of distribution in both positive and normative terms.

CHAPTER SYNOPSIS

Reading this synopsis is not a substitute for reading the chapter, but it should help you to recall the main points. If there are any you feel unsure of, refer to the full discussion in the text.

Factor markets--the markets in which labor, capital, and natural resources are bought and sold--perform important functions in determining how goods and services are produced and for whom they are produced. They perform the function of determining how things are produced because the relative prices of factors determine the proportions in which they are used in the production process. These same relative factor prices determine the functional distribution of income--that is, the distribution of income among factor owners. The functional distribution, together with the distribution of factor ownership among individuals, in turn determines the personal distribution of income--that is, the distribution of income among individuals.

In factor markets, firms are the buyers and households the sellers. The quantity of a factor of production purchased in equilibrium by a profit maximizing firm is determined by three considerations: the quantity of output produced by a unit of the factor, the revenue from sale of what is produced, and the cost of obtaining the factor.

The quantity of output produced by an added unit of a factor, the quantities of other factors being constant, is governed by the law of diminishing returns. According to this law, as the quantity used of a variable factor increases with the quantities of the fixed factors held constant, a point will eventually be reached beyond which the marginal physical product of the variable factor decreases.

The revenue generated from sale of the output produced by an added unit of a variable factor is equal to the marginal physical product of the factor times the marginal revenue per unit of output. This quantity is known as the <u>marginal revenue product</u> of the factor. For a firm that is a price taker in its output market, the marginal revenue product is equal to marginal physical product times the output price. For a firm possessing monopoly power in its output market, marginal revenue is less than price, and marginal revenue product is equal to marginal revenue times marginal physical product.

The cost to the firm of obtaining an extra unit of a factor of production is known as <u>marginal factor cost</u>. For a firm that is a price taker in the factor market—that is, a firm for which the factor price does not change as the quantity of the factor it purchases changes—factor price and marginal factor cost are equal.

Once the necessary information is known, the firm maximizes profit by purchasing each factor just up to the point where marginal revenue product is equal to marginal factor cost. The firm's marginal revenue product curve for a factor is thus also its demand curve for the factor.

Because households are the sellers of factor services, individual factor supply curves can be derived by applying the theory of consumer choice developed in Chapter 20. The case of your own supply of labor to the market can serve as an illustration. As a worker or potential worker, you face a tradeoff between work and leisure. As the wage available to you increases, your work-versus-leisure decision is affected in two ways. First, there is a substitution effect: the increased wage encourages you to work more, because you get more income for each hour of leisure foregone. But second, there is an income effect: the higher wage increases your real income, and you will want to "spend" part of that increased income on increased leisure. The net effect of an increase in your wage, then, can be to cause you either to increase or to decrease the number of hours per year that you work. At low wage levels, the substitution effect is likely to predominate, giving your labor supply curve a positive slope. At higher income levels, the income effect is likely to predominate, giving your labor supply curve a negative slope.

Even though individual labor supply curves may often have negative slopes, the market supply curve for any particular type of labor—typing, engineering, steelworking, or whatever—will be positively sloped. That is because as the wage in one labor market rises, other wage rates remaining the same, additional workers will be drawn into that particular occupation regardless of whether those already working at that occupation increase or decrease the hours of work supplied per workers per year.

A competitive labor market, then, will be characterized by a downward sloping labor demand curve and an upward sloping labor supply curve. The equilibrium wage and quantity are determined by the intersection of the two curves. The equilibrium wage rate is equal to the factor's marginal revenue product.

A factor market in which there is only one buyer is called a <u>monopsony</u>. A monopsonist is not a price taker—as the quantity of the factor such a firm purchases increases, the factor price also increases, in accordance with the supply schedule. For such a firm, marginal factor cost exceeds factor price. In equilibrium, a monopsonist, like a competitive firm, buys that quantity of labor that makes marginal revenue product equal to marginal factor cost; but for a monopsonist, such an equilibrium means a wage rate that is lower than marginal revenue product.

In a competitive factor market, each factor is rewarded in proportion to its contribution to production. This is known as the <u>marginal productivity theory of distribution</u>. The resulting distribution of income is considered by some to be both fair and efficient. However, others add the qualification that distribution to marginal product is fair only if the underlying pattern of factor ownership is also accepted as fair.

WALKING TOUR

You have read the chapter at least once and have reviewed the synopsis. Now you are going to walk through the material step by step, filling in the blanks and answering the questions as you go along. After you have answered each question, check yourself by uncovering the answer given in the margin. If you do not understand why the answer given is the right one, refer back to the proper section of the text.

The Demand for Factors of Production

The factor demand curve for a firm that is a price taker in the market where it buys its inputs is that firm's marginal _____ curve for the factor. Marginal revenue product is equal to marginal _____ times marginal _____. Complete the following table, which shows the derivation of the marginal revenue product curve:

Quantity of Factor	Total Physical Product	Marginal Physical Product	Marginal Revenue	Marginal Revenue Product
120	2000			
		_____	$100	$_____
121	2010			
		_____	98	_____
122	2019			
		_____	96	_____
123	2027			
		_____	94	_____
124	2034			
		_____	92	_____
125	2040			

(margin answers)

revenue product

physical product; revenue

10; $1000
9;   882
8;   768
7;   658
6;   552

A firm maximizes profit by hiring each factor up to the point where marginal revenue product is equal to marginal _____. If the firm is a price taker in the market where it buys the factors, marginal factor cost is equal to factor _____.

(margin answers)

factor cost

price

The Labor Supply Curve

[Note: The following exercise is based on material covered in the appendix to Chapter 20. If you did not work through that appendix, do so now, or skip ahead to the next exercise in this section.]

Because households are the sellers in the labor market, a theory of the labor supply curve is an outgrowth of the theory of consumer choice. Exhibit S30.1 shows how the indifference curve version of this theory can be used to

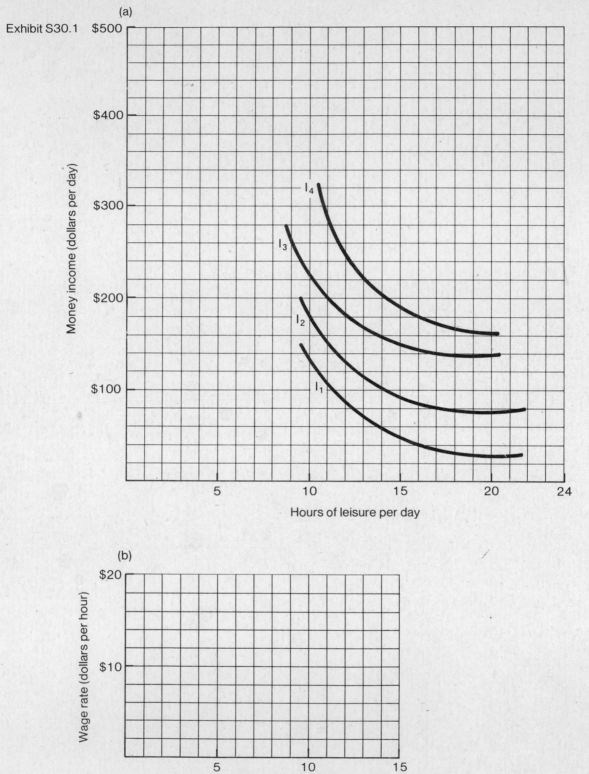

Exhibit S30.1

(a)

Money income (dollars per day)

$500

$400

$300

$200

$100

I_4

I_3

I_2

I_1

5   10   15   20   24

Hours of leisure per day

(b)

Wage rate (dollars per hour)

$20

$10

5   10   15

Hours of work per day

derive a labor supply curve for an individual worker. Suppose that the indifference map drawn in Part a of that exhibit represents your preferences regarding money income (represented on the vertical axis) versus leisure time (represented on the horizontal axis). Suppose initially that you can get a job paying $5 per hour and that you can work any number of hours from zero to twenty-four per day at this job. Draw a budget line in the exhibit that shows the various combinations of money income and leisure time available to you under these circumstances, and label it "W = $5." This budget line should intersect the horizontal axis at _____ hours, indicating all leisure and no income. It should intersect the vertical axis at _____, indicating your hypothetical maximum income if you worked around the clock.

twenty-four

$120

According to the indifference map shown in the exhibit, you would choose to work about _____ hours per day at $5 per hour, earning a total income of _____. This preferred position corresponds to the point where the indifference curve _____ is _____ to the budget line you just drew. Label this Point A.

eight

$40

I_1; tangent

Suppose now that the wage available to you rises to $10 an hour. Draw a new budget line, labeling it "W = $10." This budget line intersects the horizontal axis at _____ hours as before. It intersects the vertical axis at _____. With this new budget line, you will work about _____ hours per day and earn a total income of _____. This corresponds to the tangency of the $10 per hour budget line with the indifference curve _____. Label this Point B.

twenty-four

$240

ten

$100

I_2

Repeat the same steps for wages of $15 per hour and $20 per hour. The $15 per hour wage gives a Point C with _____ hours of work per day and a total income of _____. The $20 per hour wage gives a Point D with _____ hours of work per day and _____ total income.

twelve

$180

eleven; $220

Now use Points A, B, C, and D from Exhibit S30.1a to plot your labor supply curve in Exhibit S30.1b. Notice that the axes in Part b are different--the horizontal axis now has hours of work rather than hours of leisure, and the vertical axis has the wage in dollars per hour rather than total

income in dollars per day. At Point A in Exhibit S30.1a,
you worked _____ hours per day at _____ per   eight; $5
hour, so plot this point in Exhibit S30.1b, labeling it Point
A. At B, you worked _____ hours at _____ per   ten; $10
hour, so this becomes Point b in S30.1b, and so forth.
Your completed diagram should look like the one shown in
the solutions section at the end of this chapter. Note
the backward bending individual labor supply curve.

Equilibrium in the Labor Market

Turn your attention now to Exhibit S30.2, which you can
use to compare labor market equilibrium under conditions
of competition and monopsony in the labor market. As
drawn, the exhibit shows a downward sloping labor demand
(marginal revenue product) curve and an upward sloping
labor supply curve. If employers behave as price takers
in hiring labor, the equilibrium wage rate will be _____ $7.50
per hour and the quantity of labor hired will be _____   750
labor hours per day. Label this equilibrium E_c in the exhibit.

Suppose now that the marginal revenue product curve
shown is that of a single monopsonistic employer. To determine equilibrium under monopsony, first construct the marginal factor cost curve corresponding to the supply curve
shown. Do this by plotting two sample points and drawing
a straight line through them. For example, consider first
the range from 400 to 401 labor hours. As the supply curve

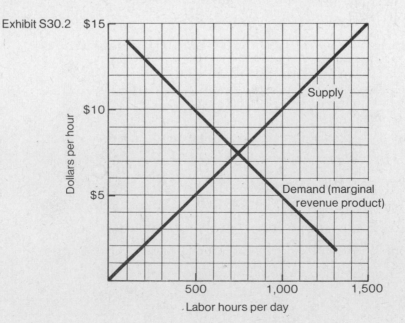

Exhibit S30.2

is drawn, you can see that to attract one extra labor hour
at any point, the wage rate must be raised by _____.   1 cent
Thus, to hire 400 labor hours per day, the firm must pay
_____ per hour, and to hire 401 labor hours, it must $4
pay _____ per hour. The total wage bill for 400 $4.01
labor hours comes to _____, and the total wage bill $1,600
for 401 labor hours comes to _____. Marginal labor $1,608.01
cost in the range 400 to 401 labor hours is thus _____ $8.01
per hour. Plot a point at 400.5 hours and $8.01; label it
Point A. Proceeding in the same manner, calculate marginal labor cost in the range 500 to 501 labor hours per day.
To get 500 labor hours, the wage must be _____ per $5
hour, and the total wage bill will thus be _____. To $2,500
get 501 labor hours, the wage must be _____ per hour $5.01
for a total wage bill of _____. Marginal labor cost $2,510.01
in the range 500 to 501 labor hours is thus _____ per $10.01
hour. Plot Point B at 500.5 labor hours and a wage of
$10.01. Draw a straight line through Points A and B, and
label it "marginal labor cost."

Now that you have the monopsonist's marginal labor
cost curve, it is a simple matter to discover the equilibrium
wage rate and quantity of labor. The monopsonist will hire
workers up to the point where marginal _____   labor cost
is equal to marginal _____. In Exhibit   revenue product
S30.2, this happens at _____ labor hours. To hire   500
this many labor hours, the firm must, according to the supply
curve, pay a wage of _____ per hour. So the point $5
corresponding to 500 labor hours and $5 per hour is the
monopsony equilibrium; lable it E_m.

In comparing the competitive equilibrium E_c with the
monopsony equilibrium E_m, note the following points: under
monopsony, the number of labor hours hired per day is
[higher/lower] than under competition, and the wage rate   lower
is [higher/lower]. Under competition, the wage rate is   lower
[greater than/less than/equal to] marginal revenue product;   equal to
under monopsony, the wage rate is [greater than/less than/
equal to] marginal revenue product. These results will be   less than
of interest in the discussion of labor unions in the next
chapter.

SELF TEST

These sample test items will help you check how much you have learned. Answers and explanations can be found at the end of this chapter. Scoring yourself: One or two wrong -- on target. Three to five wrong -- passing, but you haven't mastered the chapter yet. Six or more wrong -- not good enough; start over and restudy the chapter.

True or False

Indicate whether each statement is true or false as it stands. If it is false, explain why in a few words.

T F 1. The personal distribution of income depends partly on the functional distribution of income and partly on the distribution of factor ownership among individuals.

T F 2. In factor markets, as in product markets, firms are the sellers and households the buyers.

T F 3. Marginal revenue product is equal to marginal physical product times marginal revenue both for competitive firms and for firms that are monopolists in their output markets.

T F 4. The law of diminishing returns together with the law of demand guarantees that beyond some point the marginal revenue product curve must slope downward.

T F 5. For a firm that is a price taker in the market where it buys its inputs, marginal factor cost is equal to factor price.

T F 6. Individual labor supply curves must be positively sloped.

T F 7. Under competitive equilibrium, the wage rate must be equal to marginal revenue product.

T F 8. In order to become a monopsonist, a firm must first be a monopolist.

T F 9. If the labor supply curve in a market is positively sloped, then the marginal factor cost curve for that market will also be positively sloped.

T F 10. Distribution according to marginal productivity can be considered fair only if the distribution of factor ownership is also considered to be fair.

Multiple Choice

1.   Factor markets help determine
     a. how output is produced.
     b. for whom output is produced.
     c. both of the above.
     d. none of the above.

2.   The increase in quantity of output resulting from a one unit increase in a variable factor, with the quantities of fixed factors held constant, is known as
     a. the marginal physical product of that factor.
     b. the marginal revenue product of that factor.
     c. the marginal factor cost of that factor.
     d. the diminishing marginal product of that factor.

3. If by increasing the quantity of labor employed by one unit, other things being equal, a monopolist can increase its total revenue by $50, then the marginal revenue product of labor for the firm is
   a. $50.
   b. less than $50.
   c. greater than $50.
   d. impossible to determine from the information given.

4. In equilibrium, the wage rate for each factor will be equal to the marginal physical product of the factor times product price if the firm is
   a. a monopolist in its output market.
   b. a perfect competitor in its output market.
   c. both of the above.
   d. none of the above.

5. If a monopolist is producing at an output for which demand for its product is inelastic and for which marginal physical product of labor is positive, the marginal revenue product of labor for the firm must be
   a. positive.
   b. negative.
   c. zero.
   d. impossible to determine from the information given.

6. Which of the following would cause the demand curve for a factor of production to shift to the left?
   a. An increase in demand for the product.
   b. An increase in the price of a good that is a substitute for the product.
   c. An improvement in technology that increases the marginal physical product of the factor.
   d. A decrease in the price of a factor that is a substitute for the factor in question.

7. Which of the following is represented graphically by a movement along a given labor demand curve?
   a. The effects of a change in the wage rate.
   b. The effects of a change in raw materials prices.
   c. The effects of a change in output prices.
   d. None of the above.

8. The substitution effect of a wage increase, considered in isolation, causes the number of labor hours supplied by a worker per time period
   a. to increase as the wage increases.
   b. to decrease as the wage increases.
   c. first to increase, then to decrease as the wage goes higher still.
   d. first to decrease, then to increase as the wage goes higher still.

9. If leisure time were considered an inferior good by some person, that person's labor supply curve
   a. would have a positive slope at low wage levels and a negative slope at high wage levels.
   b. would have a negative slope at low wage levels and a positive slope at high wage levels.
   c. would have a negative slope at all wage levels.
   d. would have a positive slope at all wage levels.

10. The market supply curve for economics professors most likely has which of the following shapes?
   a. First slopes up, then bends back as the salary level rises.
   b. First has a negative slope, then a positive slope at high salary levels.
   c. A positive slope throughout.
   d. A negative slope throughout.

11. In equilibrium in a perfectly competitive labor market, the wage rate is equal to
   a. marginal revenue product.
   b. marginal factor cost.
   c. the height of the supply curve.
   d. all of the above.

12. The Atlas Company is a monopolist in its product market but a price taker in the market where it hires labor. In equilibrium, it sells its product for $8 per unit, and the marginal physical product of labor is 1.5 units per labor hour. The equilibrium wage rate must be
   a. $12 per hour
   b. $8 per hour.
   c. less than $12 per hour, but not necessarily $8 per hour.
   d. impossible to determine from the information given.

13. If a firm must raise its wage rate from $20 per hour to $20.05 per hour in order to increase the quantity of labor it hires from 1,000 labor hours to 1,001 labor hours, its marginal labor cost is closest to which of the following values?
   a. $20.
   b. $50.
   c. $70.
   d. $140.

14. In equilibrium, a firm that is a competitor in its output market but a monopsonist in its labor market will pay a wage rate
   a. equal to marginal revenue product.
   b. less than marginal revenue product.
   c. greater than marginal revenue product.
   d. impossible to determine from the information given.

15. Given the same marginal revenue product and supply curves, the wage rate in a monopsonistic labor market will be
   a. higher than that in a competitive labor market.
   b. equal to that in a competitive labor market.
   c. lower than that in a competitive labor market.
   d. impossible to determine from the information given.

ANSWERS TO CHAPTER 30 SELF TEST

True or False

1-T
2-F; firms are the buyers, households the sellers.
3-T
4-T
5-T
6-F; they may be backward bending.
7-T
8-F; it can be either one without being the other.
9-T
10-T

Multiple Choice

1-c
2-a
3-a
4-b
5-b
6-d
7-a
8-a
9-d
10-c
11-d
12-c
13-c
14-b
15-c

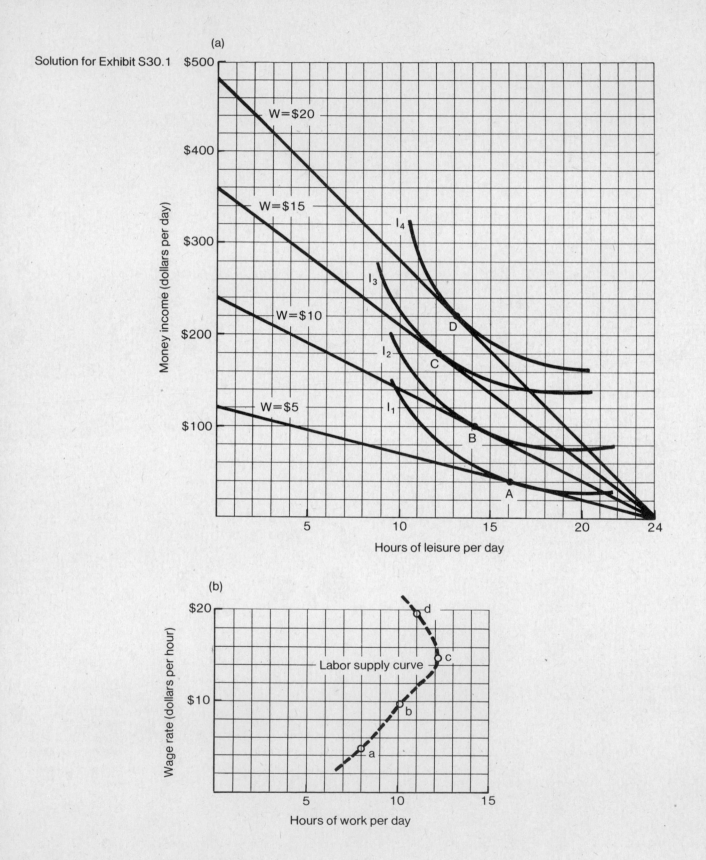

(a)

Solution for Exhibit S30.1

CHAPTER THIRTY-ONE
LABOR UNIONS AND COLLECTIVE BARGAINING

WHERE YOU'RE GOING

Here is what you will be able to do when you have mastered this chapter:

--Distinguish between craft unions and industrial unions, and explain the place of each in the history of the labor movement in the United States.

--Recount the historical origins of the AFL-CIO, the dominant U.S. labor organization today.

--List various goals that a labor union might pursue in its bargaining with employers, and explain how it might be able to achieve those goals by means of a strike or strike threat.

--Compare the effects of unionization in a monopsonistic labor market with its effects in a competitive labor market.

--Discuss the effects of unionization on the relative wages of union members, and on the average wages of all workers.

--Describe the development of public policy toward unions in the United States, and list the major pieces of union legislation.

--Explain the meaning and significance of the following additional terms and concepts:

    Featherbedding.
    Bilateral monopoly.

CHAPTER SYNOPSIS

Reading this synopsis is not a substitute for reading the chapter, but it should help you to recall the main points. If there are any you feel unsure of, refer to the full discussion in the text.

Only about 20 percent of all U.S. workers now belong to labor unions, and the percentage is falling. Nonetheless, unions retain an importance out of proportion to their membership, partly because of their importance in certain strategic industries and partly because union wages are believed to set patterns for nonunion wages.

The earliest beginnings of unionism in the United States go back as far as the eighteenth century, when local craft unions were formed. These unions were organizations of workers practicing the same trade who united to look after their mutual interests. The first labor group organized on a national scale was a post-Civil War organization, the Knights of Labor. This organization, in turn, was soon overshadowed by the emerging American Federation of Labor (AFL), which remains important today. The AFL based itself on the principle of craft unionism. It devoted most of its attention to bread-and-butter issues of pay and working conditions, and limited its political role to that of a lobbyist on labor's behalf.

As early as the late nineteenth century, attempts were made to form industrial unions, which differed from craft unions in that they included all workers in an industry, regardless of the trade they practiced. Aside from some early successes such as the United Mine Workers, industrial unions did not enjoy major success until the 1930s, when such industries as steel and automobile manufacturing were organized under the Congress of Industrial Organizations (CIO). By 1945, over a third of the nonagricultural labor force in the United States had been unionized.

After the war, union membership stagnated. The AFL and CIO merged in 1955, but that did not stem the gradual decline in the percentage of the labor force belonging to unions.

A major aim of labor unions has always been higher wage rates for union members. By threatening to strike unless at least a certain wage is paid, unions in effect change the shape and position of the labor supply curve facing employers. In a competitive labor market, unions can raise wages only at the cost of reduced employment opportunities for their members. It is theoretically possible, however, that a union formed to bargain with a monopsonistic employer could raise both wages and the quantity of labor employed, at least within limits.

Empirical studies of the effects of unions on wages indicate that unions sometimes, but not always, have been able to raise the wages of their members relative to those of nonunion workers. However, there is little evidence that unionization has had much effect on the percentage of GNP as a whole paid to workers.

Throughout most of their early history, unions were regarded with hostility by government and the courts. The legal climate facing unions changed dramatically during the 1930s, however. The Norris-LaGuardia Act of 1932 moved the government toward a neutral position in labor disputes. Then the Wagner Act of 1935 created the National Labor Relations Board and, in effect, placed government on the side of the unions. The Taft-Hartley Act of 1947 somewhat modified union privileges by listing certain unfair union labor practices, limited the closed shop, and provided for federal intervention in emergencies caused by labor disputes. The Landrum-Griffin Act of 1959 attempted to combat union corruption and to encourage internal union democracy.

WALKING TOUR

You have read the chapter at least once and have reviewed the synopsis. Now you are going to walk through the material step by step, filling in the blanks and answering the questions as you go along. After you have answered each question, check yourself by uncovering the answer given in the margin. If you do not understand why the answer given is the right one, refer back to the proper section of the text.

History of U.S. Unionism

The earliest unions in the United States were formed from

local groups of workers all practicing the same trade. Such

unions are known as _____ unions. The first   craft

national labor organization was the _____,   Knights of Labor

formed in the post-Civil War period. This union [did/did not]   did not

limit itself to craft union activities. Its membership reached

a peak of about _____ in 1886, but declined rap-   700,000

idly thereafter to be replaced by the _____. This   AFL

organization once again emphasized _____ unionism   craft

and avoided political activity not closely related to bread-

and-butter issues.

Unions made up of all workers in an industry, regardless of trade, are known as _____ unions.   industrial
The most successful early industrial union was the _____
_____, founded in _____. How-   United Mine Workers;
ever, industrial unions did not become strong until the   1890
_____. The _____ was formed at that time,   1930s; CIO
and by the end of World War II, union membership reached
an all-time peak of about _____ percent of the non-   33
agricultural labor force. Since that time, union membership
has stagnated, and now only about _____ percent of   20
the nonagricultural labor force is unionized.

Unions and Wage Rates

Exhibit S31.1 can be used to analyze the effects of union
activities on wage rates and employment in a competitive
industry. The supply and demand curves shown there indicate an equilibrium wage rate of _____ per hour $5
and an equilibrium employment of _____ labor hours   20,000
per day.

Suppose now that the workers in the industry in
question formed a union and threatened to strike if they
were not paid at least $7.50 per hour. In terms of the

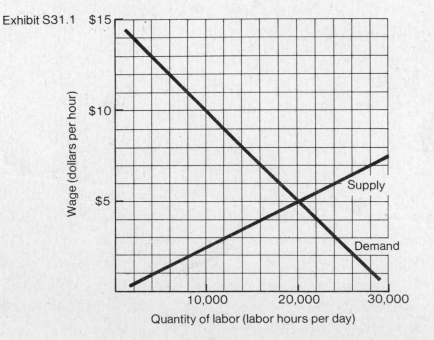

Exhibit S31.1

diagram, this action could be represented as a change in position of the [supply/demand] curve. This curve would now have a [vertical/horizontal] section at _____ up to its intersection withe the original [demand/supply] curve. Sketch in this modified supply curve. With the modified supply curve in place, the equilibrium wage rate would be

_____ per hour and the equilibrium quantity of labor would be _____ labor hours per day.

Note that the wage rate is [higher/lower] and the number of labor hours employed is [higher/lower] than without the union. At $7.50 per hour, workers would want to supply _____ labor hours per day, leaving an excess labor supply of _____ hours per day. The available work would have somehow to be _____ among the workers. Note also that total labor income with the union is _____ per day. This is [up/down] from its level of _____ without the union. However, raising the wage still higher than $7.50 would begin to reduce total labor income once again. Already at $8 per hour, for example, labor income would be back down to _____ per day. Total labor income would fall below its level in competitive equilibrium if the wage rate were forced above _____ per hour. In general, raising the wage rate will raise total labor income only so long as the demand for labor is [elastic/inelastic].

Turn your attention now to Exhibit S31.2, which can be used to show the effects of unionization in a monopsony labor market. The supply curve of labor shown there is the same as in Exhibit S31.1, and the marginal revenue product curve for this monopsonist is the same as the demand curve shown in the previous exhibit. Begin by sketching in the marginal labor cost curve for the monopsonist, as you learned to do in the last chapter; it is a straight line starting at the origin and intersecting the marginal revenue product curve at a height of _____. The quantity of labor hired in equilibrium by the monopsonist can thus be seen to be _____ labor hours per day and the equilibrium wage rate to be _____ per hour. (Note that the wage rate is given by the height of the supply curve, not the

supply
horizontal; $7.50
supply

$7.50
15,000
higher
lower

30,000
15,000
rationed

$112,500; up
$100,000

$112,000

$10

inelastic

$7.50

15,000
$3.75

270

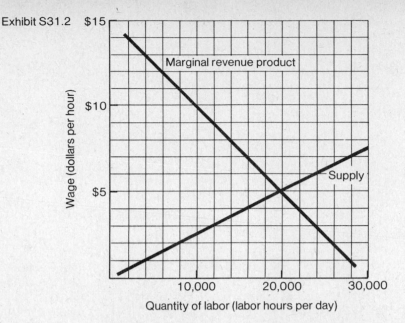

Exhibit S31.2

marginal revenue curve!) In comparison with the competitive equilibrium, the wage rate under monopsony is
[higher/lower] and the quantity of labor hired is   lower
[higher/lower].   lower

   If the labor force is unionized and refuses to work for
any wage below a certain level, the marginal labor cost curve
facing the monopsonist effectively becomes a [horizontal/
vertical] line corresponding to the wage demanded up to the   horizontal
point where it intersects the labor supply curve; beyond
that point, the marginal labor cost jumps to its previous
level. Sketching in such a marginal labor cost curve corresponding to a union demand of $4 per hour, for example,
shows that the monopsonist would hire _____ labor   16,000
hours per day at that wage. If $5 per hour were demanded,
_____ labor hours per day would be used. A   20,000
demand of $6 would cause _____ labor hours to be   18,000
hired; and $7.50 per hour, _____ labor hours. Thus   15,000
it can be seen that beginning from a monopsony equilibrium,
the union can force the wage rate as high as $7.50 per hour
without a loss of work. Maximum employment for union
members is obtained at a wage of _____ per hour. $5

271

SELF TEST

These sample test items will help you check how much you have learned. Answers and explanations can be found at the end of this chapter. Scoring yourself: One or two wrong -- on target. Three to five wrong -- passing, but you haven't mastered the chapter yet. Six or more wrong -- not good enough; start over and restudy the chapter.

True or False

Indicate whether each statement is true or false as it stands. If it is false, explain why in a few words.

T F 1. The extent of unionization is less in the United States than in many European countries.

T F 2. The earliest labor unions in the United States were local industrial unions.

T F 3. The Knights of Labor kept their activities within the bounds of traditional craft unions.

T F 4. The first successful industrial unions in the United States were founded during the 1930s.

T F 5. Union membership as a percentage of the nonagricultural labor force reached a peak in the United States at the end of World War II.

T F 6. A union operating in a previously competitive labor market is likely to end up with less work for its members if it succeeds in raising their wages.

T F 7. The competitive equilibrium wage rate always maximizes total labor income.

T F 8. Empirical evidence indicates that unions can sometimes raise the relative wage rates of their members.

T F 9. Empirical evidence shows that the share of wages in GNP has increased over the past half-century.

T F 10. Until passage of the Norris-LaGuardia Act, government policy could be considered hostile to labor unions.

Multiple Choice

1. Approximately what percentage of the nonagricultural labor force belonged to unions in the United States of as the late 1970s?
    a. 10 percent.
    b. 20 percent.
    c. 33 percent.
    d. 50 percent.

2. Which of the following labor organizations was founded at the earliest date?
    a. American Federation of Labor.
    b. Congress of Industrial Organizations.
    c. Knights of Labor.
    d. Industrial Workers of the World.

3.   Which of the following did not characterize the American Federation of Labor in its early years?
     a. Craft unionism.
     b. Business unionism.
     c. Lobbying in support of labor.
     d. Support of a national labor party.

4.   Which of the following industries was the first to be organized on industrial union principles?
     a. Coal.
     b. Steel.
     c. Tires.
     d. Automobiles.

5.   Which of the following union organizations was most radical in its political activities?
     a. American Federation of Labor.
     b. Congress of Industrial Organizations.
     c. Knights of Labor.
     d. International Workers of the World.

6.   A union formed in a previously competitive labor market, in which the competitive equilibrium lies on an elastic portion of the labor demand curve, can reasonably hope to be able to increase which of the following in the market where it operates?
     a. The wage rate.
     b. Total labor income.
     c. Total employment.
     d. All of the above.

7.   A union facing a straight-line labor demand curve maximizes the total income of its members by setting the wage at
     a. the highest possible level.
     b. the point of unit demand elasticity.
     c. the competitive equilibrium wage.
     d. b or c, whichever is the higher wage.

8.   A union formed in a monopsonistic labor market can, at least within limits, reasonably hope to raise which of the following for its members?
     a. Wages.
     b. Total employment.
     c. Both of the above.
     d. None of the above.

9.   A union formed in a previously monopsonistic labor market has already raised the wage of its members up to the equivalent of the competitive equilibrium wage. Which of the following will happen if it raises the wage further?
     a. Employment will increase and total labor income will decrease.
     b. Employment will decrease and total labor income will increase.
     c. Employment and total labor income will both decrease.
     d. Insufficient information is given for an answer to be reached.

10. In a situation of bilateral monopoly in a labor market, the equilibrium wage rate will be
     a. equal to the competitive equilibrium wage.
     b. above the competitive equilibrium wage.
     c. below the competitive equilibrium wage.
     d. impossible to determine from the information given.

11. Empirical studies indicate that unions have often been successful in raising
    a. the share of wages in GNP.
    b. the relative wages of their members.
    c. both of the above.
    d. none of the above.

12. Which of the following labor laws was passed at the earliest date?
    a. The Norris-LaGuardia Act.
    b. The Wagner Act.
    c. The Taft-Hartley Act.
    d. The Landrum-Griffin Act.

13. Which of the following pieces of labor legislation is most strongly pro-union?
    a. The Norris-LaGuardia Act.
    b. The Wagner Act.
    c. The Taft-Hartley Act.
    d. The Landrum-Griffin Act.

14. Which of the following labor laws established a list of unfair union labor practices?
    a. The Norris-LaGuardia Act.
    b. The Wagner Act.
    c. The Taft-Hartley Act.
    d. The Landrum-Griffin Act.

15. Which of the following labor laws is concerned with the rights of rank-and-file union members in internal union affairs?
    a. The Norris-LaGuardia Act.
    b. The Wagner Act.
    c. The Taft-Hartley Act.
    d. The Landrum-Griffin Act.

ANSWERS TO CHAPTER 31 SELF TEST

True or False

1-T
2-F; local craft unions.
3-F; their activities were much broader.
4-F; a few were founded earlier.
5-T
6-T
7-F; maximizes total employment.
8-T
9-T
10-T

Multiple Choice

1-b
2-c
3-d
4-a
5-d
6-a
7-d
8-c
9-d; must also know elasticity of demand.
10-d; depends on relative bargaining power.
11-b
12-a
13-b
14-c
15-d

CHAPTER THIRTY-TWO
RENT, INTEREST, AND PROFITS

WHERE YOU'RE GOING

Here is what you will be able to do when you have mastered this chapter:

--Define and give examples of pure economic rent.

--Explain how a perpetual rent can be capitalized to give the market value of the asset on which the rent is earned.

--Explain why borrowers are willing to pay interest on consumption loans and production loans.

--Demonstrate the determination of interest rates in capital markets.

--Discuss the relationship between profit, on the one hand, and risk, arbitrage, and innovation on the other.

--Explain the relationship of monopoly profits, windfall profits, and loot to pure economic profit and entrepreneurship.

CHAPTER SYNOPSIS

Reading this synopsis is not a substitute for reading the chapter, but it should help you to recall the main points. If there are any you feel unsure of, refer to the full discussion in the text.

Pure economic rent is the income earned by a factor of production that is in perfectly inelastic supply. Land is the classic example of such a factor, but other nonreproducible resources, including unique talents of individuals, can also be thought of as earning pure economic rents. If an asset capable of earning a rent is sold, the annual value of the rent is said to be capitalized into the value of the asset. In the simplest case, where an asset is expected to earn a constant rent in perpetuity, the capitalized value of the rent is simply the annual rent divided by the rate of interest.

The term "interest" is used to identify the price paid by borrowers to lenders for the use of loanable funds and the market return earned by capital as a factor of production. The interest rate is determined by the interaction between supply and demand in capital markets. The demand for loans comes partly from consumers who want to consume more than their current incomes permit and partly from firms that want to engage in roundabout production techniques based on the use of capital. The demand for production loans results from the fact that such roundabout production techniques are often more productive than more direct production techniques.

Pure economic profit is what remains to a firm after both implicit and explicit costs of production have been deducted from revenues. Over the years, economists have developed a variety of theories to explain why profits exist, that is, why costs do not, on the average, entirely exhaust revenues. According to one theory, profits are a reward that entrepreneurs receive for bearing risks. A second theory equates profits with the return to the activity of arbitrage--buying a good at a low price in one market or at one time and selling it at a higher price in another market or at another time. Still a third theory associates profits with the activity of innovation.

Because production cannot take place without entrepreneurship, and because entrepreneurs receive a reward for their efforts, entrepreneurship is sometimes spoken of as a fourth factor of production, together with labor, capital, and natural resources. However, the similarity of entrepreneurship to the three traditional factors of production is limited in that entrepreneurship is an intangible concept. Thus, while the conventional factors of production are subject to measurement, there is no way to measure the quantity of entrepreneurship used per unit of time or its price per unit.

As was shown in Chapter 25, a monopolist, unlike a competitive firm, may earn pure economic profits over a long period rather than only temporarily. On close inspection, however, some such monopoly profits might better be considered pure economic rents accruing to the monopolist as the result of its ownership of a unique asset such as a location, patent, or franchise.

Sometimes firms or individuals earn so-called windfall profits as the result of unexpected increases in the values of resources that they own. For example, owners of U.S. oil wells were said to have earned a windfall profit when the world price of oil increased sharply during the 1970s. Windfall profits, like monopoly profits, are difficult to distinguish from pure economic rents and are not an exact term of economic science.

One final type of financial gain to firms or individuals sometimes confused with profit is wealth acquired not through production and exchange but, rather, through theft or use of force. There is no widely accepted economic term for such ill-gotten gains, but the term "loot" would seem to serve as well as any to distinguish them from wages, rents, interest, and profits earned in the marketplace.

WALKING TOUR

You have read the chapter at least once and have reviewed the synopsis. Now you are going to walk through the material step by step, filling in the blanks and answering the questions as you go along. After you have answered each question, check yourself by uncovering the answer given in the margin. If you do not understand why the answer given is the right one, refer back to the proper section of the text.

Rent

Pure economic rent is the income earned by a factor of

production that is in perfectly _____ supply.   inelastic

The supply curve of such a factor is a _____ line.   vertical

The rental value of the factor is determined in a competi-

tive market by the intersection of the vertical supply curve

with the marginal _____ curve of   revenue product

the factor.

If a rent-earning factor of production, such as a parcel

of land, is sold outright, its rental value becomes capitalized

into the rental price. In the simplest case, where a resource

is expected to earn a constant annual rent in perpetuity,

the capitalized value of the resource can be calculated by

dividing the _____ by the _____   annual rent

_____. For example, given a 5 percent rate   rate of interest

277

of interest, a property producing an annual rental income
of $2,000 would have a capitalized value of _____. $40,000

Interest and Capital

Interest can be earned both on loans made for consumption
purposes and on those made for productive investment.
Investors are willing to pay interest on production loans
because of the superior productivity of _____   roundabout
methods of production. Roundabout methods of production
are those that use _____ resources to produce   present
capital equipment that, in turn, will increase the rate of
_____ output.   future

In the short run, the supply of capital equipment is
fixed and can be represented by a [vertical/horizontal]   vertical
supply curve. The intersection of this supply curve with
the demand curve for capital equipment determines the
current rental value of the capital equipment. If the current
rental value of the equipment, capitalized at the prevailing
rate of interest, is [higher/lower] than the replacement   higher
cost of the equipment, it will be profitable to invest in
more of such equipment. As the capital stock increases, the
short-run supply curve shifts to the [left/right] and the   right
current rental value [rises/falls]. Eventually, if the demand   falls
curve remained stationary, an equilibrium would be reached
in which no further investment would be profitable.

Profit and Entrepreneurship

According to one theory, profit is a reward that entrepreneurs earn for bearing risk. This theory assumes that
most people [like/dislike] risk, other things being equal,   dislike
and hence are willing to pay to avoid it. For example, an
entrepreneur starting a new business contracts to pay
workers and suppliers even if the firm fails and is thus able
to buy their labor and resources at a [higher/lower] price   lower
than would be the case if they share more of the risk.

According to a second theory, profits are earned by
buying [high/low] and selling [high/low]. This activity is   low; high
known as _____. Still another theory sees   arbitrage
profits as a reward for innovation. This theory was popu-
larized by the economist _____.   Joseph Schumpeter
In practice, it seems reasonable to take an eclectic view of

profits, considering them a reward for a mixture of risk
bearing, arbitrage, and innovation.

SELF TEST

These sample test items will help you check how much you have learned. Answers and explanations can be found at the end of this chapter. Scoring yourself: One or two wrong -- on target. Three to five wrong -- passing, but you haven't mastered the chapter yet. Six or more wrong -- not good enough; start over and restudy the chapter.

True or False

Indicate whether each statement is true or false as it stands. If it is false, explain why in a few words.

T F   1.   Pure economic rent is the income earned by a factor of production that is in perfectly elastic supply.

T F   2.   The capitalized value of a rent, in dollars per year, is determined by the intersection of the supply curve of the factor with its marginal revenue product curve.

T F   3.   Part of the income earned by uniquely talented individuals can be considered pure economic rent.

T F   4.   The term "interest" is used to express more than one thing in economics.

T F   5.   Capital-using methods of production can also be thought of as roundabout methods of production.

T F   6.   In the short run, the supply curve of capital equipment can be considered perfectly inelastic.

T F   7.   According to one major theory of profit, entrepreneurs are able to earn a profit because, other things equal, they prefer more risky to less risky situations.

T F   8.   The activity of buying high and selling high is known as arbitrage.

T F   9.   Monopoly profit is a category of income distinct from the ordinary rent, interest, and profit earned in a competitive market.

T F 10.   "Loot" is another term for "windfall profit."

Multiple Choice

1.   Which of the following might be said to earn a pure economic rent?
     a.   A parcel of farmland.
     b.   An operatic tenor with a voice of rare quality.
     c.   A cab owner in a city where the supply of cab licenses is perfectly inelastic.
     d.   All of the above.

2. A parcel of land having a perpetual rental value of $400 per year would have what capitalized value, assuming a 4 percent rate of interest?
   a. $1,000.
   b. $10,000.
   c. $1,600.
   d. $16,000.

3. Assuming a 5 percent rate of interest, what would be the capitalized value of an apartment building that produced a rental income of $100,000 per year and was expected to become worthless at the end of twenty years?
   a. $2 million.
   b. Less than $2 million.
   c. More than $2 million.
   d. Insufficient information is given for an answer to be reached.

4. The term "interest" can be used to mean
   a. the income earned from consumption loans.
   b. the income earned from production loans.
   c. the return to capital as a factor of production.
   d. any of the above.

5. Other things being equal, an increased preference by households for present rather than future consumption would mean
   a. a rightward shift in the demand curve for loanable funds.
   b. a leftward shift in the demand curve for loanable funds.
   c. a movement down along the loanable funds demand curve.
   d. a movement up along the loanable funds demand curve.

6. Other things being equal, which of the following would cause a decline in the rate of interest?
   a. An improvement in the productivity of roundabout production methods.
   b. A rightward shift in the marginal revenue product curve of capital equipment.
   c. An increase in the average life expectancy, causing households to postpone some present consumption.
   d. None of the above.

7. If household saving were the only source of loanable funds and if the only reason to save were to build up a "nest egg" of fixed nominal size for retirement, we would expect the supply curve of loanable funds to be
   a. positively sloped.
   b. negatively sloped.
   c. vertical.
   d. horizontal.

8. If an office word processor expected to last seven years (with no scrap value) has a rental value of $1,000 per year to a firm and a replacement cost of $10,000, it will not pay the firm to acquire another such machine unless the rate of interest is which of the following?
   a. At least 10 percent.
   b. Exactly 10 percent.
   c. Less than 10 percent.
   d. It will not pay no matter what the rate of interest.

9. The best explanation of why we have not reached a "steady state" in which no further capital investment of any kind is worthwhile is that
   a. the demand curve for capital is perfectly elastic.
   b. the supply curve of capital is perfectly elastic.
   c. technological progress constantly shifts the supply curve to the right.
   d. technological progress constantly shifts the demand curve to the right.

10. Pure economic profit means total revenue minus
    a. implicit costs.
    b. explicit costs.
    c. both of the above.
    d. none of the above.

11. The theory of profit as a reward for risk bearing implies that most people, given a choice between a $100 bill and a lottery ticket having one chance in a thousand of winning $100,000, would show which preference?
    a. They would prefer the lottery ticket.
    b. They would prefer the $100 bill.
    c. They would be indifferent between the two.
    d. None of the above is implied by the theory.

12. A person who, on a certain date, bought 100 ounces of gold in the London gold market at $402 per ounce and simultaneously sold 100 ounces of gold in the Zurich market at $403.50 per ounce would be said to earn an income primarily through
    a. risk bearing.
    b. arbitrage.
    c. innovation.
    d. looting.

13. The writings of Joseph Schumpeter placed particular emphasis on which of the following sources of profit?
    a. Arbitrage.
    b. Risk bearing.
    c. Innovation.
    d. Windfalls.

14. A tax on so-called windfall profits might have an effect on quantities supplied
    a. if the supply of the resource in question were perfectly inelastic.
    b. if the event giving rise to the so-called windfall was not entirely unforeseen at the time the tax was instituted.
    c. if either of the above were true.
    d. only if both a and b were true.

15. Entrepreneurship cannot be considered a true factor of production in the same sense as labor, capital, and natural resources are, because
    a. it is not necessary for production.
    b. it produces no income for the person who supplies it.
    c. it is not scarce.
    d. it is not measurable.

ANSWERS TO CHAPTER 32 SELF TEST

True or False

1-F; inelastic supply.
2-F; the current rental value is so determined.
3-T
4-T
5-T
6-T
7-F; they need not like risk, but only need be willing to bear it for a reward.
8-F; buying low and selling high.
9-F; it is hard or impossible to distinguish from the others.
10-F; loot means wealth gained by force or fraud.

Multiple Choice

1-d
2-b
3-b
4-d
5-a
6-c
7-b
8-d
9-d
10-c
11-b
12-b
13-c
14-b
15-d

WHERE YOU'RE GOING

Here is what you will be able to do when you have mastered this chapter:

--Discuss alternative definitions of poverty, including the definition used officially by the U.S. government.

--Distinguish between event-conditioned and income-conditioned transfers, and list the major programs of each variety.

--Analyze the incentive effects of income transfer programs in terms of benefit reduction rates and effective marginal tax rates.

--Explain the concept of a negative income tax, and describe recent experiments with transfer programs of this kind.

--Discuss the major job market strategies for combating poverty, distinguishing between demand-side and supply-side strategies.

CHAPTER SYNOPSIS

Reading this synopsis is not a substitute for reading the chapter, but it should help you to recall the main points. If there are any you feel unsure of, refer to the full discussion in the text.

Although everyone knows that poverty exists and has seen it, poverty remains a difficult concept to define precisely or to measure. There are at least three major points of view on how to define and measure poverty. The first view is that those people are poor whose incomes fall below some fixed level identified as the minimum needed to provide a decent standard of living. The second view is that the poor are those whose incomes fall below some level defined in relation to other incomes, say, below one-half of the median income. The third view makes poverty not so much a matter of income as a matter of culture, behavior, and lifestyle. Of these three views, the first is the one on which the official U.S. government definition of poverty is based.

Even if the conceptual basis of the official definition of poverty is accepted, however, official poverty statistics are open to criticism. The criticism most frequently made is that in counting the number of poor households, the governments takes into account only money income and ignores the value of in-kind benefits such as food stamps, Medicaid, and public housing. For this reason, government data showing more than 10 percent of U.S. households to be poor are believed to overstate the number of people actually falling below the official low-income level.

Transfer strategies aim to help the poor by supplementing their low incomes with money or in-kind benefits. Transfer programs, in turn, fall into two categories-- event-conditioned transfers and income-conditioned transfers.

Event-conditioned transfers--often referred to as social insurance programs-- are available to all citizens, regardless of income, upon the occurrence of some specific event such as retirement, unemployment, or disability. Social security is the largest single event-conditioned transfer program. Despite the many people it has benefited, the program faces a number of criticisms. Some criticisms focus on the burdensome and regressive payroll tax used to finance social security, others on the program's effects on private saving, and still others on its treatment of women.

Income-conditioned transfers are those available only to households meeting some income-related standard of need. Aid to Families with Dependent Children, Medicaid, and food stamps are the largest income-conditioned transfer programs of the U.S. government. Critics of income-conditioned transfers focus especially on the disincentive effects built into them. Under most such programs, payments are reduced according to some specified benefit reduction rate as income increases. When the benefit reduction rates of various programs are added together and allowance is also made for such explicit taxes as income and payroll taxes, the effective marginal tax rates on low-income households often exceed the tax rates imposed on earned income of even the wealthiest individuals.

Economists concerned about the disincentive effects of the current mix of transfer programs have often suggested combining them all into a single negative income tax. Under such a tax, the government would pay households falling below some specified income level an income supplement that gradually decreased as their income increased. In theory, a properly designed negative income tax could substantially reduce the adverse incentive effects of current programs. Recent experimental programs, however, have shown that details of a negative income tax must be worked out very carefully if adverse incentive effects are to be minimized.

Job market strategies seek to help the poor by helping them to become self supporting, rather than by giving them money. Supply-side programs such as education and manpower training are intended to enable poor people to supply more valuable labor services to the market. Demand-side strategies such as antidiscrimination efforts and public employment are designed to create more job opportunities for low-income families.

WALKING TOUR

You have read the chapter at least once and have reviewed the synopsis. Now you are going to walk through the material step by step, filling in the blanks and answering the questions as you go along. After you have answered each question, check yourself by uncovering the answer given in the margin. If you do not understand why the answer given is the right one, refer back to the proper section of the text.

The Nature of Poverty

The official government definition of poverty begins with a

minimum cost budget for _____, which is then   food

multiplied by _____ to get an official low-income level.   3

Part of the reason for having such an objective definition

of poverty is to be able to measure progress toward elimin-

ating poverty. During the 1960s, the percentage of the

population officially classified as poor fell from about _____   22

percent in 1959 to about _____ percent in 1969. During   12

the 1970s, this official percentage [did/did not] fall further.   did not

However, various unofficial attempts to adjust incomes for the

value of _____ transfers show that the in-   in-kind

cidence of poverty relative to the official low-income level

[did/did not] fall further.   did

284

Transfer Strategies

Transfer strategies for helping the poor fall into two groups.
Those that are available to all citizens regardless of need
upon retirement, disability, or some other occurrence are
known as _____ transfers.
Those available only to people who can demonstrate that
they are poor are known as _____
transfers.

event-conditioned

income-conditioned

    The biggest single event-conditioned transfer program
is _____. Much of the criticism
of the social security system is focused on the _____
tax used to finance it. This [regressive/progressive] tax
is believed to have serious incentive effects.

social security
payroll
regressive

    Income-conditioned programs include AFDC, Medicaid,
food stamps, and some others. Such programs are subject
to gradual reductions of benefits as income rises, and the
benefit reduction rates of various programs are additive.
For example, if each dollar of income results in a 30 cent
reduction in AFDC benefits and a 20 cent reduction in food
stamp benefits, the effective marginal tax rate on a household benefiting from both programs is _____ percent.

50

    Some economists have suggested that all income-
conditioned transfers should be combined into a single
negative income tax program. Exhibit S33.1 provides a

Exhibit S33.1

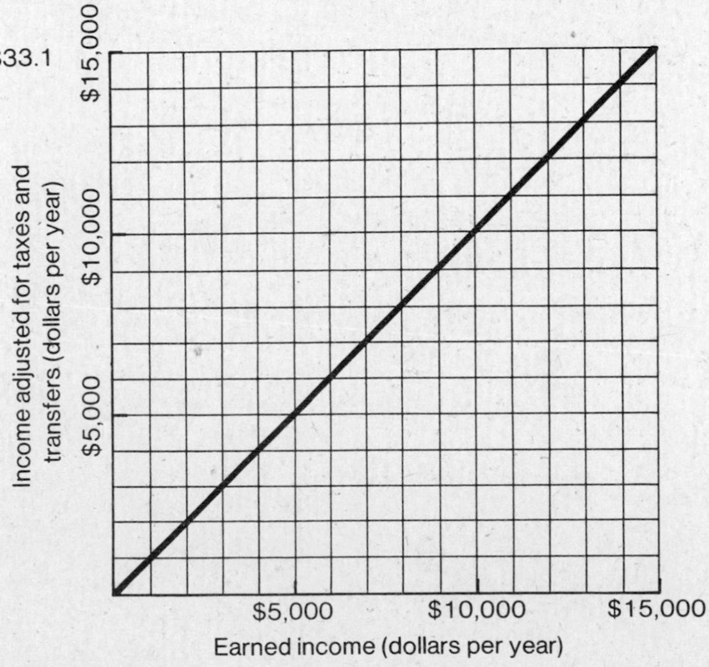

Income adjusted for taxes and transfers (dollars per year)

Earned income (dollars per year)

place for you to illustrate how a negative income tax program might work. Construct a line showing after-tax incomes at various levels of earned income assuming that the program will provide a minimum benefit of $5,000 and will incorporate a 50 percent benefit reduction rate. Assume that households not qualifying for any payments under the negative income tax pay a marginal tax rate of 20 percent. Your schedule should be a straight line intersecting the vertical axis at a height of _____ and intersecting the $5,000

45° line at a height of _____. Beyond $10,000 $10,000

of income, the schedule should continue with a slope of

_____.   0.8

        Reading now from your negative income tax schedule, you see that a family with no earned income would be paid

_____ in benefits; a family with a $5,000 earned $5,000

income would be paid _____ in benefits; a family $2,500

with $9,000 earned income would be paid _____ in $500

benefits; and so on.

SELF TEST

These sample test items will help you check how much you have learned. Answers and explanations can be found at the end of this chapter. Scoring yourself: One or two wrong -- on target. Three to five wrong -- passing, but you haven't mastered the chapter yet. Six or more wrong -- not good enough; start over and restudy the chapter.

True or False

Indicate whether each statement is true or false as it stands. If it is false, explain why in a few words.

T F 1. The wealthiest 1 percent of the U.S. population receives some 40 percent of all personal income.

T F 2. According to the official definition, a family just at the low-income level would have three times enough income to purchase an adequate diet.

T F 3. Taking in-kind transfers into account would reduce the number of poor by about half.

T F 4. Social security is the leading income-conditioned transfer program.

T F 5. Aid to Families with Dependent Children (AFDC) is the government's largest single income transfer program.

T F 6. The attraction of a negative income tax is that it reduces the benefit reduction rate for poor families to zero.

T F 7. Education and manpower training are examples of demand-side job market strategies for helping the poor.

T F 8. As a result of federal antidiscrimination efforts, the income of black families as a percentage of the income of white families increased steadily throughout the 1970s.

T F 9. Demand-side job market strategies for helping the poor are thought by some to work more quickly than supply-side strategies, because they make use of the skills that low-income people already have to offer.

T F 10. In principle, shifting just 1 percent of GNP to the poorest 20 percent of the population would eliminate all officially measured poverty.

Multiple Choice

1. Which of the following is distributed least equally among the U.S. population?
   a. Ownership of capital.
   b. Income from labor.
   c. Income from all sources.
   d. Labor in terms of hours worked per person.

2. Which of the following views of poverty is the basis of official U.S. government poverty statistics?
   a. Poverty as a matter of lifestyle.
   b. Poverty as a matter of culture.
   c. Poverty as a matter of relative income.
   d. Poverty as an objectively defined minimum living standard.

3. According to the official definition of poverty, the low-income level is calculated by multiplying the cost of an economy food plan by
   a. 1.5.
   b. 2.
   c. 3.
   d. 4.

4. The official measurements of poverty are sometimes criticized for not taking which of the following into account?
   a. Family size.
   b. Place of residence.
   c. In-kind transfers.
   d. Year-to-year changes in living costs.

5. Which of the following grew most rapidly during the 1970s?
   a. Cash transfer programs.
   b. In-kind transfer programs.
   c. The number of people officially counted as poor.
   d. The number of people counted as poor after adjustment for in-kind transfers.

6. Approximately what percentage of the U.S. population was officially classified as poor as of the late 1970s?
   a. 6.
   b. 11.
   c. 22.
   d. 33.

7. Social security is considered
   a. an income-conditioned transfer program.
   b. an event-conditioned transfer program.
   c. an in-kind transfer program.
   d. a supply-side transfer program.

8. The social security system is subject to criticism because
   a. it is financed by a regressive tax.
   b. it displaces private saving.
   c. it has traditionally failed to treat men and women equally.
   d. it does all of the above.

9. Which of the following is an income-conditioned transfer program?
   a. Aid to Families with Dependent Children.
   b. Food stamps.
   c. Medicaid.
   d. All of the above.

10. The benefit reduction rate for the AFDC program is typically
    a. 10 percent.
    b. 22 percent.
    c. 33 percent.
    d. 50 percent.

11. If a certain family benefits from Program A, which has a benefit reduction rate of 40 percent, and also from Program B, which has a benefit reduction rate of 15 percent, the effective marginal tax rate on the family (taking no other tax or transfer programs into account) is
    a. 15 percent.
    b. 25 percent.
    c. 40 percent.
    d. 55 percent.

12. A family with an earned income of $5,000 receives a total income of $6,000 after all taxes and transfers are taken into account. A similar family earning $10,000 receives no transfer payments and pays $2,000 in income and payroll taxes. The effective marginal tax rate in the $5,000–$10,000 range is thus
    a. 20 percent.
    b. 40 percent.
    c. 60 percent.
    d. 100 percent.

13. If the benefit reduction rate for a negative income tax program is reduced while the basic benefit remains the same, which of the following groups will probably work less than previously?
    a. Those with zero earned income.
    b. Those with earned incomes greater than zero but less than the basic benefit.
    c. Those made eligible for payments for the first time by the change in the benefit reduction rate.
    d. All of the above.

14. The results of the Seattle-Denver Income Maintenance Experiment indicated that
    a. the negative income tax would have no adverse incentive effects.
    b. work effort of recipients was insensitive to the benefit reduction rate.
    c. people would work more under a negative income tax than if there were no transfer programs at all.
    d. an actual negative income tax program would cost more than a hypothetical program having no effect on work effort.

15. Which of the following is considered a supply-side strategy for helping the poor?
    a. AFDC.
    b. Job training.
    c. Antidiscrimination measures.
    d. Public employment.

ANSWERS TO CHAPTER 33 SELF TEST

True or False

1-F; owns 40 percent of all capital.
2-T
3-T
4-F; it is event-conditioned.
5-F; social security is larger.
6-F; it may reduce it, but not to zero.
7-F; they are supply-side strategies.
8-F; it rose, then fell again.
9-T
10-T

Multiple Choice

1-a
2-d
3-c
4-c
5-b
6-b
7-b
8-d
9-d
10-c
11-d
12-c
13-c
14-d
15-b

CHAPTER THIRTY-FOUR
THE ECONOMICS OF POLLUTION

WHERE YOU'RE GOING

Here is what you will be able to do when you have mastered this chapter:

--Discuss environmental issues in terms of trade-offs and opportunity costs.

--Draw a marginal social cost of pollution schedule, and explain why it can be expected to have a positive slope.

--Draw a marginal cost of pollution abatement schedule, and explain why it can be expected to have a negative slope.

--Explain why the point of intersection of the marginal social cost of pollution schedule with the marginal cost of pollution abatement schedule is considered the optimum degree of pollution.

--Explain why, when firms and households can discharge wastes into the environment without charge, pollution is likely to exceed the optimal level.

--Discuss residual charges as a pollution control technique, and discuss possible weaknesses of this approach.

--Explain the relationship between pollution control and property rights.

--Discuss the debate over economic incentives versus command and control as alternative strategies of pollution abatement.

--Discuss the normative economics of pollution control.

CHAPTER SYNOPSIS

Reading this synopsis is not a substitute for reading the chapter, but it should help you to recall the main points. If there are any you feel unsure of, refer to the full discussion in the text.

Economics can contribute to the discussion of environmental issues by helping to formulate standards of wise use against which to measure the actual allocation of resources, by helping to identify the sources of past and present errors in resource use, and by helping to formulate policies to control present and future problems. In many ways, pollution is a typical problem of scarcity, in which the scarce resource is the waste disposal capacity of the environment. The problem can be thought of in terms of opportunity costs and tradeoffs--tradeoffs between one kind of pollution and another and between pollution abatement and other goods and services.

The problem of pollution control is one of balancing two margins. The first is the marginal social cost of pollution--the total additional cost to all members of society of an additional unit of pollution. The second is the marginal cost of pollution abatement--the added cost of reducing a given kind of pollution by one unit.

In graphical terms, the marginal social cost of pollution can be represented as an upward sloping curve, on the assumption that as concentrations of pollutants rise, the damage done by each additional increase in pollution becomes more severe. The marginal cost of pollution abatement curve has a negative slope on a graph where the quantity of pollution appears on the horizontal axis because the cost of each further reduction in pollution rises as the quantity of pollution falls. The intersection of the two curves represents the optimal quantity of pollution. Pollution in excess of this amount is wasteful in that the damage done by each additional unit of pollution exceeds the cost of eliminating it. But to reduce pollution below the optimal quantity is wasteful too, because the resources used for pollution abatement cost more than the benefit gained in return.

Economic strategies for pollution control can be thought of in terms of supply and demand. The demand for pollution opportunities can be represented by the marginal cost of pollution abatement curve, because the value to a firm or household of an opportunity to pollute is determined by the cost of disposing of the same waste in a nonpolluting manner. The policy problem, then, is to manipulate the supply curve of pollution opportunities so that it intersects the demand curve at the optimal quantity of pollution.

For example, if a residual charge were imposed—so much for each unit of pollution released into the environment—the supply curve for pollution opportunities would become a horizontal line at a height equal to the amount of the charge per unit. If the charge were set at a level corresponding to the intersection of the marginal social cost and marginal abatement cost schedules, the optimal degree of pollution abatement would occur.

Despite the theoretical elegance of residual charges, however, they have not been widely used in the U.S. economy. Industrialists object to the burden they impose on firms. Consumers object that part of the burden is likely to be passed along to them. And environmentalists object that they constitute a license to pollute. None of these objections has much merit as a matter of positive economics, although some may be valid from a normative point of view.

An alternative strategy for pollution control is based on the rights of property owners to enjoy their property free of pollution. If property owners could take legal action against polluters, the threat that they would do so would have to be taken into account as a cost of polluting, and pollution abatement would thereby be encouraged.

Still another strategy for pollution control—the one most widely practiced—is the command and control approach. Under this approach, the environmental authorities attempt to estimate the optimal quantity of pollution and then attempt to limit pollution to that amount by imposing specific engineering controls on individual sources. This approach has been criticized for not giving polluters sufficient incentive to adopt least-cost methods of pollution abatement.

In addition to the positive economic problem of achieving the optimal quantity of pollution, various normative issues are raised by the choice of pollution abatement strategies. One is whether polluters should compensate the victims of pollution. The property rights approach to pollution control is seen by some as superior to other methods because it forces polluters to pay victims of pollution. Another issue concerns the distribution of the costs and benefits of pollution control across income classes. Some observers suggest, for example, that the value of pollution control is less to low income groups than to high income groups.

WALKING TOUR

You have read the chapter at least once and have reviewed the synopsis. Now you are going to walk through the material step by step, filling in the blanks and answering the questions as you go along. After you have answered each question, check yourself by uncovering the answer given in the margin. If you do not understand

Alternative Strategies of Pollution Control

Exhibit S34.1 is designed to allow you to compare various
alternative strategies of pollution control in terms of supply
and demand. It contains an upward sloping marginal social
cost of pollution curve and a downward sloping marginal
cost of pollution abatement curve. Of these two, the
[social cost/abatement cost] curve can also serve as a   abatement cost
demand curve for pollution opportunities. Add that label
to the diagram. As the curves are drawn, the optimal
quantity of pollution is _____ units.   50

　　Begin by considering the situation in the absence of
any pollution control measures. If it costs nothing for firms
and households to dispose of wastes by discharging them
into the environment, the supply curve of pollution opportunities will be a _____ line at a height   horizontal
of _____ units above the horizontal axis. Sketch in   zero
this curve, and label it S_1. With this supply curve, the
equilibrium quantity of pollution will be _____ units.   100

Exhibit S34.1

Marginal cost of pollution abatement

Marginal social cost of pollution

Dollars per unit of pollution

$0.20
$0.15
$0.10
$0.05

25   50   75   100

Quantity of pollution (arbitrary units)

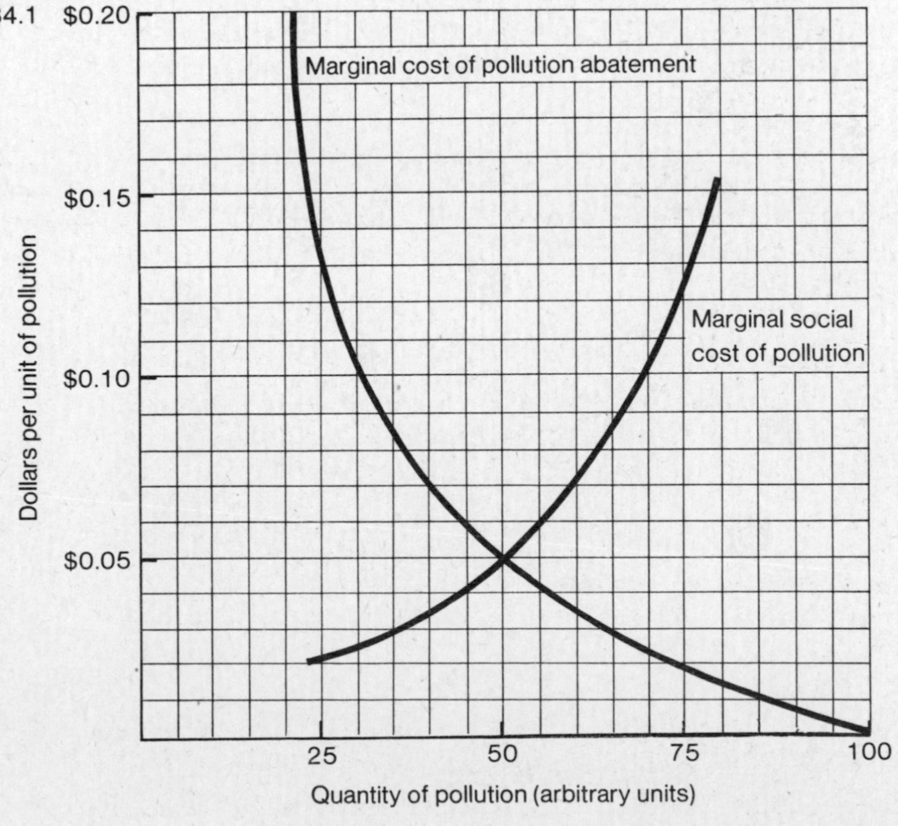

Next consider the command and control approach. Under this approach, a target level of pollution is chosen that, in principle, coincides with the optimal quantity of pollution. Below that point, firms can pollute without charge; above that point, additional pollution is (in principle) strictly prohibited. The supply curve of pollution opportunities under such a program can thus be represented by a _____ line drawn at the target level, which in this case we assume to be 50 units. Draw such a line and label it S_2.

       vertical

The third pollution control strategy to be considered is a residual charge. A constant residual charge per unit of pollution makes the supply curve of pollution opportunities a _____ line at a height equal to the charge per unit. In this case, in order to achieve the optimal degree of pollution abatement, the charge should be set at _____ per unit. Draw in the appropriate supply curve and label it S_3. Note that if the charge were set any higher, there would be too much [pollution/abatement]; if the charge were set too low, there would be too much [pollution/abatement].

       horizontal

       5 cents

       abatement

       pollution

Finally, consider the property rights approach to pollution abatement. Under this approach, each source of pollution is legally liable for all damage done by pollution that it emits. If the legal system functioned without transactions costs to impose exactly the proper burden on each pollution source, the supply curve of pollution opportunities would coincide with the marginal _____ curve. Sketch in such a supply curve, and label it S_4. If imperfections in the legal system raised the burdens on polluters above this level, for example, by adding court costs to damages paid, there would be too much [pollution/abatement]. If imperfections in the legal system prevented victims of pollution from imposing on polluters the full cost of damages suffered, there would be too much [pollution/abatement].

       social cost

       abatement

       pollution

In principle, each of the three pollution control approaches is capable of doing an optimal job; the choice among them turns on such practical considerations as incentives, measurement, and transactions costs.

SELF TEST

These sample test items will help you check how much you have learned. Answers and explanations can be found at the end of this chapter. Scoring yourself: One or two wrong -- on target. Three to five wrong -- passing, but you haven't mastered the chapter yet. Six or more wrong -- not good enough; start over and restudy the chapter.

True or False

Indicate whether each statement is true or false as it stands. If it is false, explain why in a few words.

T F 1. If the environment had a limitless capacity for absorbing and recycling human and industrial wastes, pollution would not be an economic problem.

T F 2. Most pollution control methods only turn one form of waste into another and are thus of little economic value.

T F 3. The marginal cost of pollution abatement is the total cost to all members of society of all pollution produced.

T F 4. The optimal quantity of pollution, from an economic point of view, is not always zero pollution.

T F 5. If no efforts are made to control pollution, the equilibrium quantity of pollution is infinite.

T F 6. One advantage of the residual charge approach to pollution control is that it is not sensitive to errors in measuring the marginal social cost of pollution.

T F 7. The objection that residual charges are a "license to pollute" is as much a normative as a positive objection.

T F 8. If a residual charge is imposed on pollution originating in steel mills, the price of steel is likely to rise.

T F 9. High transactions costs would be a major drawback of relying entirely on the property rights approach to controlling pollution for at least some types of pollution.

T F 10. The property rights approach probably works best when sources of pollution are relatively concentrated.

Multiple Choice

1. Economics can best contribute to the formulation of environmental policies by, among other things,
    a. telling how best to distribute the burden of pollution control among various income groups.
    b. determining the best technical means of controlling pollution from a given source.
    c. determining who should be blamed for past errors in resource use.
    d. formulating standards of efficient resource use against which to judge alternative policies.

2. Which of the following eliminates trade-offs and opportunity costs in pollution control?
    a. Incinerating solid wastes.
    b. Scrubbing pollutants out of factory gasses.
    c. Recycling industrial wastes.
    d. None of the above.

3. For most kinds of pollution, it is likely that the marginal social cost of pollution
    a. increases as the quantity of pollution increases.
    b. increases as the quantity of pollution decreases.
    c. increases as the degree of pollution abatement increases.
    d. does none of the above.

4. If a marginal cost of pollution abatement curve is drawn on a diagram with the quantity of pollution on the horizontal axis, it can normally be expected to have a slope of
    a. zero.
    b. less than zero.
    c. greater than zero.
    d. greater than 1.

5. The optimal quantity of pollution, in economic terms, is
    a. zero.
    b. the quantity that makes marginal abatement cost zero.
    c. the quantity that makes marginal social cost zero.
    d. the quantity that makes marginal abatement cost equal to marginal social cost.

6. According to Dr. Merril Eisenbud, New York's North River sewage treatment plant is an example of
    a. willingness to tolerate excessive pollution.
    b. excessive pollution abatement.
    c. optimal pollution control policy in action.
    d. correct application of marginal analysis.

7. The demand curve for pollution opportunities is
    a. a horizontal line.
    b. coincident with the vertical axis.
    c. the same as the marginal cost of pollution abatement curve.
    d. none of the above.

8. Under the command and control strategy of pollution control, the supply curve of pollution opportunities is best represented by
    a. a horizontal line above the horizontal axis.
    b. a line coincident with the horizontal axis.
    c. a vertical line.
    d. a line coincident with the marginal social cost of pollution curve.

9. Command and control methods for controlling pollution are criticized by economists because of which of the following reasons?
    a. They do not provide incentives for finding the least-cost method of pollution abatement.
    b. In practice, they have no measurable effect on pollution.
    c. They are equivalent to a zero residual charge.
    d. None of the above.

10. Residual charges suffer from the disadvantage that they
    a. cannot be passed along by firms to consumers.
    b. cannot always be set at just the right level because of measurement difficulties.
    c. inevitably result in too little abatement.
    d. have all of the above disadvantages.

11. Of the various objections to residual charges, the most valid is the objection that residual charges
    a. impose a double burden on industry.
    b. can simply be passed along to consumers.
    c. will have no effect on the actual quantity of pollution.
    d. do not provide compensation to victims of pollution.

12. A residual charge would be entirely passed along to consumers
    a. if demand for the product were perfectly elastic.
    b. if demand for the product were perfectly inelastic.
    c. if supply of the product were perfectly inelastic.
    d. in none of the above cases; it can never be passed along entirely.

13. The most serious criticism of the property rights approach to pollution abatement is that
    a. it ignores the marginal principle.
    b. it provides no compensation to victims of pollution.
    c. it provides no penalties for polluters.
    d. it might result in too much or too little pollution abatement in situations where transactions costs were substantial.

14. The "bubble" concept in pollution control is best characterized as
    a. an improved version of the command and control approach.
    b. a variant of the residual charge approach.
    c. an attempt to implement the property rights approach.
    d. a license to pollute.

15. Suppose you did a survey of neighborhood pollution patterns and income patterns in a large city and you discovered that poor poeple tended to live in the neighborhoods that were most polluted. Which of the following might you most reasonably conclude?
    a. Poor people like bad air.
    b. Rich people are willing to pay more than poor people to avoid pollution.
    c. Poor people would benefit more from pollution abatement, in dollar terms, than would rich people.
    d. Poor people cause pollution.

ANSWERS TO CHAPTER 34 SELF TEST

True or False

1-T
2-F; it is often worthwhile to convert one form of waste into another.
3-F; it is the added cost to everyone of one more unit of pollution.
4-T
5-F; it may be larger than optimal, but not infinite.
6-F; it is sensitive to such errors.
7-T
8-T
9-T
10-T

Multiple Choice

1-d
2-d
3-a
4-b
5-d
6-b
7-c
8-c
9-a
10-b
11-d
12-b
13-d
14-a
15-b; note that c asserts the opposite of b.

CHAPTER THIRTY-FIVE
THE ECONOMICS OF ENERGY

WHERE YOU'RE GOING

Here is what you will be able to do when you have mastered this chapter:

--Use the theory of the mine to explain the basic principles of the allocation of nonrenewable resources over time.

--Compare the allocation of nonrenewable resources over time under competitive markets with their allocation under a cartel.

--Discuss, in both positive and normative terms, whether the rate of use of nonrenewable resources in competitive markets is optimal.

--Use supply and demand analysis to explain the effects of price controls on oil and natural gas in the United States.

--Discuss the pros and cons of deregulation of oil and natural gas prices.

--Discuss the relative advantages and disadvantages of coal, solar power, and nuclear power as alternatives to oil and natural gas.

CHAPTER SYNOPSIS

Reading this synopsis is not a substitute for reading the chapter, but it should help you to recall the main points. If there are any you feel unsure of, refer to the full discussion in the text.

Oil and natural gas present classic problems of allocation over time of nonrenewable resources. The ultimate stocks of these fuels cannot be increased--the economic problem is one of when to use what is available. Problems of this type belong to a branch of economics known as the theory of the mine.

The theory of the mine assumes that resource owners will be motivated primarily by financial considerations in deciding how much of their reserves to extract in a given year and how much to leave in the ground. Present and future use each have their advantages: If the resource is extracted and sold in the present, the revenue earned can be invested elsewhere at a normal rate of return and provide a source of income. On the other hand, reserves left in the ground may be sold in the future at a higher price. As a general principle, it will pay to leave resources in the ground if the expected rate of price increase exceeds the nominal rate of interest available on alternative investments. This principle puts a cap on the rate at which the resource will be depleted: the maximum rate of depletion is that which makes the expected rate of price increase equal to the interest rate. If the resource were depleted more rapidly than this, the present price would be depressed by the greater present supply and the expected future price raised by the smaller expected future supply; that would give someone an incentive to hoard reserves for the future, thus again reducing the rate of depletion.

The argument just given places a ceiling on the rate of depletion of a nonrenewable resource under competitive market conditions. If the resource is controlled by a cartel, the rate of depletion will tend to be slower than that for a competitive market. The reason is that, both in the present and in the future, the cartel will raise the price above the competitive level in order to maximize member profits.

With the price higher, the quantity consumed is initially lower, leaving greater reserves for the future.

Whether competitive or not, then, the market contains a built-in conservation mechanism that transforms predictions of future scarcity into actions to reduce current production. However, it is sometimes asked, might it not be better to be more conservational still and to use nonrenewable resources even more slowly for the benefit of future generations? The answer to this question appears to be in the negative; rather than slow the rate of depletion below the competitive market rate, future generations would benefit more if the resources were used to increase the quantity of capital passed along to the future.

During most of the 1970s, U.S. markets for oil and natural gas operated under a complex system of price controls. The effect of these controls was to reduce prices paid to U.S. producers below the world price and to reduce prices paid by U.S. consumers to an average of the prices of the imported and domestically produced product. As a result of these controls, the domestic rate of production has been lower, the domestic rate of consumption higher, and the rate of imports higher than if the domestic price had risen to the world level. By the end of the 1970s, these results of price controls were perceived as increasingly undesirable, and a gradual process of decontrol was begun. The outcome of this decontrol experiment will depend, in large part, on the price elasticity of supply and demand for the resources in question.

For the immediate future, the major energy alternatives to oil and natural gas are coal, nuclear power, and solar power. Each of them has its own economic problems and promises.

Strictly speaking, coal, as a fossil fuel, is as nonrenewable as oil and natural gas. However, coal reserves are far greater in relation to current use. Current limitations on the use of coal come more from the demand side than the supply side. The most serious demand limitation lies in the expense of burning coal in a nonpolluting manner.

Nuclear power currently faces an uncertain future. Political objections to the increased use of nuclear power center on the issue of health and safety. Economic objections center on the issue of whether the lower fuel cost of nuclear as compared to coal fired electric power plants is sufficient to offset the greater capital costs of the former. There is increasing concern even within the nuclear industry that if various hidden costs of nuclear power--including health and safety related costs-- were taken fully into account, nuclear energy might not be cost competitive with coal.

Solar power, like nuclear power, is an alternative to fossil fuels that trades off higher initial capital costs against lower fuel consumption. For small-scale applications, such as domestic hot water systems, direct solar energy is already commercially competitive in many regions of the country. So are such indirect applications of solar power as wood stoves and low-head hydroelectric generation. The commercial potential of large-scale solar energy projects, however (except for existing hydroelectric stations in favored locations), has yet to be proved.

WALKING TOUR

You have read the chapter at least once and have reviewed the synopsis. Now you are going to walk through the material step by step, filling in the blanks and answering the questions as you go along. After you have answered each question, check yourself by uncovering the answer given in the margin. If you do not understand why the answer given is the right one, refer back to the proper section of the text.

The Theory of the Mine

The theory of the mine, like most other branches of micro-economic theory, assumes that resource owners want to maximize their total income or wealth. The decision facing the mine owner is simply one of how to distribute sales of the nonrenewable contents of the mine over time.

Suppose, for example, that you own an oil well and that you want to decide whether to pump out one more barrel this year or to leave that marginal barrel in the ground until next year. Suppose you expect the price both this year and next to be $20 per barrel, and you know you can earn a 10 percent return on any funds that you invest this year outside the oil business. If you sell the barrel of oil this year and invest the proceeds, you will have _____ by next year. If you wait until next year to sell the oil, you will have _____ next year. So you will decide to sell the oil [this/next] year.

$22

$20

this

As you and your fellow oil producers decide to produce another and then another and another barrel this year, however, this year's market price will [rise/fall]; and because reserves left for next year will have been diminished, the expected future price will [rise/fall]. Suppose that this year's output is increased enough to push this year's price down to $19.10 per barrel and that in view of this greater rate of reserve depletion, next year's price is expected to rise to $21 per barrel. Now, if you extract the marginal barrel and sell it this year, investing the proceeds at 10 percent interest, you will have _____ by next year, whereas if you hold the same quantity of oil for sale until next year, you will have _____. You will decide to produce the marginal barrel [this/next] year. However, if this year's price falls by even one cent more, it will pay to produce the marginal barrel [this/next] year. A limit is thus placed on the rate of depletion: you and your fellow producers will stop producing this year and start conserving for next year as soon as the percentage increase of next year's price over this year's equals the rate of interest.

fall

rise

$21.01

$21

this

next

Effects of Price Controls

Turn your attention now to Exhibit S35.1, which shows

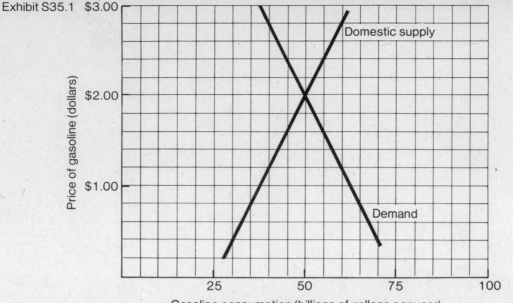

Exhibit S35.1

Price of gasoline (dollars) — $3.00, $2.00, $1.00

Domestic supply

Demand

Gasoline consumption (billions of gallons per year) — 25, 50, 75, 100

hypothetical domestic supply and demand curves for gasoline. As drawn, the equilibrium price for the domestic
market considered in isolation is _____ and the equil- $2
ibrium quantity is _____ billion gallons per year.   50
Assume, however, that gasoline can also be imported at $1.20
per gallon and that the world supply is perfectly elastic.
Add a world supply curve to the diagram. It should be a
_____ line at a height of _____.   horizontal; $1.20
With both domestic and imported gasoline available, consumers
will buy their first _____ billion gallons from domestic   40
producers, plus another _____ billion from foreign   20
producers, consuming _____ billion gallons per year   60
in all.

  Now suppose price controls are imposed on the domestic
market. The maximum price that can be paid to U.S. producers is set at 40 cents per gallon. and the price paid by
consumers is limited to the average of the domestic and imported prices, that is, 80 cents per gallon. Now domestic
producers will supply just _____ billion gallons per   30
year, while consumers will want to purchase _____   65
billion gallons. The difference will have to be made up by
importing _____ billion gallons per year. The result   35
of price controls, then, is to [reduce/increase] domestic   reduce
production, [reduce/increase] domestic consumption, and   increase
[reduce/increase] imports.   increase

302

SELF TEST

These sample test items will help you check how much you have learned. Answers and explanations can be found at the end of this chapter. Scoring yourself: One or two wrong -- on target. Three to five wrong -- passing, but you haven't mastered the chapter yet. Six or more wrong -- not good enough; start over and restudy the chapter.

True or False

Indicate whether each statement is true or false as it stands. If it is false, explain why in a few words.

T F   1.   The theory of the mine is concerned with the allocation of nonrenewable resources over time.

T F   2.   In a competitive market, it will pay a resource owner to hold a marginal unit for sale in the future whenever the future price is expected to exceed the present price.

T F   3.   According to the theory of the mine, a cartel tends to be more conservational than a competitive market.

T F   4.   Over the twenty-year period from 1950 to 1970, known reserves of most nonrenewable resources dropped substantially.

T F   5.   We of today's generation would clearly be better off, in economic terms, if past generations had depleted nonrenewable resources less rapidly than they did.

T F   6.   Price controls on domestic oil and natural gas have successfully shielded the U.S. economy from the effects of world energy price increases.

T F   7.   Throughout the 1970s, the real retail price of gasoline, adjusted for inflation, moved steadily upward.

T F   8.   One source of opposition to decontrol of natural gas prices has been that there are no known reserves of natural gas other than those that can be recovered at costs below the controlled price.

T F   9.   The main limit on coal as an energy source comes from the demand side, not the supply side, of the market.

T F 10.   A number of government programs have artificially inflated the cost of nuclear power, thus inhibiting its expansion.

Multiple Choice

1.   If this year's price of oil is $30 per barrel and the rate of interest is 10 percent, how high must next year's expected price be in order to encourage a competitive producer to conserve a marginal barrel of oil for production next year?
     a.   More than $27.
     b.   More than $30.
     c.   More than $33.
     d.   None of the above; a competitive firm will never conserve.

2. Over time in a competitive resource market, other things being equal,
    a. price will rise and the rate of use will fall.
    b. price will fall and the rate of use will rise.
    c. both price and the rate of use will rise.
    d. both price and the rate of use will fall.

3. Suppose you studied past behavior of oil prices and found that over the past
    ten years they had risen more rapidly than the rate of interest. Which of the
    following would be the most reasonable explanation?
    a. A previously competitive market had become cartelized.
    b. Oil companies do not really try to maximize profits.
    c. The demand for oil increased, as oil companies had expected it would.
    d. None of these special explanations is necessary; what happened is just
        what the theory of the mine predicts.

4. Other things being equal, a cartel
    a. sells more but charges less than a competitive industry.
    b. sells less but charges more than a competitive industry.
    c. sells less and charges less than a competitive industry.
    d. sells more and charges more than a competitive industry.

5. According to the theory of the mine, other things being equal, future gener-
    ations will best be served if
    a. today's resource markets are cartelized.
    b. today's resource markets are competitive.
    c. today's resource markets are subject to price controls.
    d. today's capital markets are subject to interest rate controls.

6. Price controls that depress both the price paid by consumers and the price
    received by domestic producers below the world price level are likely to
    a. cut domestic production.
    b. increase domestic consumption.
    c. increase imports.
    d. do all of the above.

7. In a market without other price controls, a tax on domestic but not on imported
    oil would probably not do which of the following, assuming world supply to be
    perfectly elastic?
    a. Discourage domestic production.
    b. Encourage imports.
    c. Discourage consumption.
    d. Generate any revenue.

8. U.S. gasoline consumption failed to fall during the 1970s, despite an increase
    in world oil prices. The most reasonable explanation is that
    a. the demand for gasoline is completely inelastic.
    b. the supply of domestically produced gasoline is completely elastic.
    c. real incomes of consumers increased faster than world oil prices increased.
    d. gasoline prices did not rise much relative to other prices from 1968 to 1978.

9. Which of the following is the most reasonable statement about future natural gas
    production, on the basis of what you know about U.S. reserves?
    a. Production will continue to increase even if prices continue to be controlled.
    b. Production is not likely to increase unless prices rise.
    c. Production will continue to fall no matter what happens to prices.
    d. All known reserves will be exhausted by the end of the century.

10. Which of the following would be most likely to increase the relative importance of coal as a U.S. energy resource?
    a. A ban on coal exports.
    b. A cheap technology for burning coal cleanly.
    c. Discovery of additional reserves.
    d. A reduction in the price of capital.

11. Which of the following technologies for electric power generation has the lowest capital cost per megawatt?
    a. Coal.
    b. Nuclear.
    c. Direct solar.
    d. Hydroelectric.

12. Which of the following opportunity costs of nuclear power generation is not borne entirely by nuclear power consumers?
    a. Health and safety costs.
    b. The cost of disaster insurance.
    c. The cost of dismantling existing plants when they become obsolete.
    d. None of the above costs are fully borne by consumers.

13. In which of the following respects does coal currently appear more hazardous than nuclear power?
    a. Exposure of workers to hazardous conditions.
    b. Air pollution.
    c. Both of the above.
    d. None of the above.

14. Solar energy, broadly defined, contributed about what percentage of U.S. energy needs as of 1979?
    a. 1 percent.
    b. 6 percent.
    c. 15 percent.
    d. 25 percent.

15. Net energy analysis suggests that which of the following is likely to contribute least to meeting U.S. energy needs given today's (1979) technology?
    a. Natural gas.
    b. Coal.
    c. Nuclear.
    d. Photovoltaic power.

ANSWERS TO CHAPTER 35 SELF TEST

True or False

1-T
2-F; only if the rate of price increase exceeds the rate of interest.
3-T
4-F; most expanded.
5-F; not necessarily.
6-F; they have only changed the form in which the costs have been borne.
7-F; it moved up and down, with little change on the average.
8-F; there are substantial reserves.
9-T
10-F; on balance, government programs have lowered the cost of nuclear power.

Multiple Choice

1-c
2-a
3-a
4-b
5-b
6-d
7-c
8-d
9-b
10-b
11-a
12-d
13-c
14-b
15-d

CHAPTER THIRTY-SIX
THE ECONOMICS OF POPULATION AND DEVELOPMENT

WHERE YOU'RE GOING

Here is what you will be able to do when you have mastered this chapter:

--Compare various interpretations of the process of economic development.

--Explain the conditions under which a population can grow or can achieve equilibrium.

--Describe the demographic transition, and explain the circumstances under which a country may be caught in a population trap.

--Describe the role of food production in economic development.

--Explain the meaning and significance of the following additional terms and concepts:

Depauperization.
The dual economy.
Crude birth rate.
Crude death rate.
Rate of natural increase.
Net reproduction rate.

CHAPTER SYNOPSIS

Reading the synopsis is not a substitute for reading the chapter, but it should help you to recall the main points. If there are any you feel unsure of, refer to the full discussion in the text.

Lack of economic development, like poverty, is easy to recognize but hard to define. There are at least three major viewpoints as to what constitutes economic development. One view is that economic development is synonymous with economic growth. A second view is that development means industrialization. And a third view sees the essence of development in the process of depauperization--the provision of a broadly better life for the poorest of the poor.

The choice of a definition of development influences the strategy of development. Some countries have emphasized industrialization and urbanization, even though such a strategy may create a dual economy in which a modernized, Westernized sector gains most of the benefits of development while a traditional sector remains poor. A second development strategy emphasizes land redistribution and mass education first, with growth coming later.

Whatever development strategy is chosen, most less developed countries face population problems. Population growth occurs when the number of people born per thousand of a population per year--the crude birth rate--exceeds the number who die per thousand per year--the crude death rate. The difference between the two is known as the rate of natural increase. Many less developed countries experience rates of natural increase in the range from twenty-five to thirty-five, implying population growth of 2.5 to 3.5 percent per year. A population growing at 3.5 percent per year would double each twenty years.

The size of any population is ultimately limited by the carrying capacity of its environment. Given such a limit, there is more than one way for a population to reach equilibrium. One possibility is that the poorest segment of the population may be pushed below the subsistence level, with excess deaths among the poor balancing excess births among the better off. Alternatively, if income is distributed equally, population growth can continue until everyone is living just at the subsistence level. Finally, population equilibrium can be achieved through a decline in the birth rate rather than through an increase in the death rate. However it is achieved, population equilibrium in the long run requires that the net reproduction rate--the average number of daughters born to each female child over her lifetime--be reduced to one.

Industrialized Western countries have achieved population equilibrium as the result of a process known as the demographic transition. Two centuries ago, both birth rates and death rates in these countries were high, and incomes were low. Then followed a period of economic growth, declining death rates, and rapid population growth. Eventually, as per capita income rose, birth rates too began to fall, until population equilibrium was achieved at high, and still growing, per capita incomes.

The process of demographic transition is likely to be more difficult for many of today's less developed countries than for those that underwent development in the last century. In many countries, modern medicine and public health measures have lowered death rates sharply before strong economic growth was under way, while birth rates were still very high. At the worst, countries in this situation may experience rates of population growth that exceed their rates of economic growth, so that per capita incomes fall and death rates are forced up again. This scenario is known as a population trap. The population trap can be escaped only by sustained rapid economic growth or by birth rates being brought down while per capita incomes remain low.

Underlying all problems of development is a percarious balance between population and world food production. Some observers believe that as many as two-thirds of the world's population may suffer from hunger or malnutrition in some form. The United States has long pursued a vigorous program of food aid, but food aid alone cannot solve the problem. A long-term solution to the world food problem depends on successful rural development in the less developed countries themselves.

WALKING TOUR

You have read the chapter at least once and have reviewed the synopsis. Now you are going to walk through the material step by step, filling in the blanks and answering the questions as you go along. After you have answered each question, check yourself by uncovering the answer given in the margin. If you do not understand why the answer given is the right one, refer back to the proper section of the text.

Population and Development

Immigration and emigration aside, a population can grow

only if the crude _____ exceeds the crude   birth rate

_____. The difference between the   death rate

two is known as the rate of _____.   natural increase

These measures are usually expressed in terms of births or

deaths per _____ of population. For example,   thousand

a population with a birth rate of fifty and a death rate of

thirty-six would have a rate of natural increase of _____   14

per thousand per year. This could also be expressed as a

308

population growth rate of _____ percent per year.

Still another way to express population growth is in terms of the number of years required for the population to double, were a particular rate of growth to continue. Population doubling times can be calculated by the "rule of 70" the doubling time equals 70 divided by the percentage rate of population growth. A population growth of 1.4 percent per year would thus be equivalent to a fifty-year population doubling time.

A birth rate of fifty and a death rate of thirty-five would be typical of a country at a [very low/medium/high] level of development. As such a country began to develop economically, the [birth rate/death rate] would first begin to fall. The rate of natural increase would [rise/fall] as a result. However, so long as the rate of economic growth stayed above the rate of population growth, per capita income would [rise/fall]. The eventual result of increasing per capita income would be a drop in the [birth rate/death rate], once again reducing the rate of population growth. Eventually, the country would reach a population equilibrium with a [high/low] birth rate and a [high/low] death rate. This complete sequence is known as the

_____.

> very low
>
> death rate
>
> rise
>
> rise
>
> birth rate
>
> low; low
>
> demographic transition

Suppose now that, beginning from a birth rate of fifty and a death rate of thirty-six, modern public health measures reduce the death rate of a country to fifteen over a very short period. The rate of natural increase would thus rise to _____. If the best the country could manage was a 3 percent rate of economic growth, per capita income would [rise/fall] at a rate of _____ percent per year. As per capita income fell, the [birth rate/death rate] would rise until population growth fell to the rate of economic growth. Per capita income would stagnate, and the country would be said to be in a _____.

> thirty-five
>
> fall; 0.5
> death rate
>
> population trap

Looking at a country's crude birth rate and crude death rate gives a snapshot of population dynamics at a moment in time; to predict long-term population trends, one must look at other statistics. One of the most revealing population statistics, for example, is the number of daughters born, on the average, to each female child over her lifetime.

This is known as the _____ rate.   net reproduction

If the net reproduction rate is greater than 1, population

will _____ in the long run; if it is less than 1,   grow

it will _____ ; and if it is exactly 1, it will be   shrink

_____ .   However, when the net reproduction   stable

rate of a country first falls to 1, population growth does

not stop immediately. That is because a population that

has been growing in the recent past will tend to have a

relatively [large/small] portion of its members in the prime   large

child-bearing years. Only after more than a generation with

a net reproduction rate of 1 will the age structure of the

population reach a long-run equilibrium, so that the rate of

natural increase drops to zero. Of course, if the net re-

production rate drops below 1, as it has done in West

Germany, for example, actual population growth will slow

more rapidly and even become negative.

SELF TEST

These sample test items will help you check how much you have learned.   Answers
and explanations can be found at the end of this chapter.   Scoring yourself: One
or two wrong -- on target.   Three to five wrong -- passing, but you haven't mastered the chapter yet.   Six or more wrong -- not good enough; start over and
restudy the chapter.

True or False

Indicate whether each statement is true or false as it stands.   If it is false, explain
why in a few words.

T F   1.   The poorest countries in the world have per capita incomes only a little
           over $200 per year.

T F   2.   Experience of most countries indicates that emphasis on industrialization is
           the quickest route to depauperization.

T F   3.   The crude birth rate minus the crude death rate is known as the rate of
           natural increase.

T F   4.   Population equilibrium can be achieved in a country only if the entire pop-
           ulation is reduced to a subsistence income level.

T F   5.   One way to escape the population trap is to bring birth rates down while
           per capita income is still low.

T F   6.   People are said to be malnourished if they suffer from a quantitative lack
           of calories.

T F   7.   Malnutrition operates to cut population growth chiefly through its effects
           on birth rates.

T F 8. By keeping food prices low in less developed countries, food aid can actually retard rural development.

T F 9. One major problem of economic development is how to keep people from moving to cities more rapidly than the cities can create jobs for them.

T F 10. Introduction of high-yield crop varieties increases small farmers' need for credit.

Multiple Choice

1. Emphasis on which of the following aspects of development is most likely to create a so-called dual economy?
    a. Industrialization.
    b. Rural development.
    c. Land reform.
    d. Depauperization.

2. According to research conducted by Irma Adelman and C. T. Morris,
    a. the benefits of industrialization can be counted on to trickle down to the poorest of the poor.
    b. the early experience of the Soviet Union provides a good example of the development strategy called depauperization.
    c. in many poor countries, development has been accompanied by declining living standards for the poorest segment of the population.
    d. development plans should emphasize "showcase" projects that raise national morale.

3. Depauperization is thought to be aided by
    a. land reform.
    b. mass education for literacy.
    c. development of labor-intensive industry.
    d. all of the above.

4. The number of daughters born to each female child during her lifetime is known as the
    a. crude birth rate.
    b. rate of natural increase.
    c. rate of population growth.
    d. net reproduction rate.

5. If a country's population is currently growing, it must have a net reproduction rate of
    a. 1.
    b. less than 1.
    c. greater than 1.
    d. not necessarily any of the above.

6. A country with a crude birth rate of thirty-five and a crude death rate of ten would have a rate of natural increase, per thousand per year, of
    a. thirteen.
    b. twenty-five.
    c. minus twenty-five.
    d. forty.

7. A country with a rate of natural increase of population of twenty-eight per thousand per year would have a population doubling time of approximately
   a. fourteen years.
   b. twenty-five years.
   c. twenty-eight years.
   d. forty years.

8. Which of the following patterns of birth rate (BR) and death rate (DR) would be most likely to characterize a country with a per capita income of $100 per year?
   a. BR = 25, DR = 10.
   b. BR = 10, DR = 12.
   c. BR = 20, DR = 20.
   d. BR = 45, DR = 25.

9. A population can be in equilibrium when
   a. excess births among the rich are balanced by excess deaths among the poor.
   b. everyone in the population is living just at the subsistence level.
   c. the per capita income is so high that the net reproduction rate falls to 1.
   d. any of the above is the case.

10. During the demographic transition
   a. first the birth rate falls, then the death rate.
   b. first the death rate falls, then the birth rate.
   c. first both the birth rate and death rate fall, then they both rise.
   d. first both the birth rate and death rate rise, then they both fall.

11. For a country to be caught in a population trap requires
   a. that the rate of population growth at some point exceed the rate of economic growth.
   b. that the rate of economic growth at some point exceed the rate of population growth.
   c. that the birth rate rise above its initial level at some point.
   d. that the death rate exceed the birth rate at some point

12. Population control experience in Pakistan
   a. is a major success story for modern techniques.
   b. shows that the inundation technique works.
   c. shows that availability of birth control devices is not enough without the widespread desire to use them.
   d. demonstrates the political risks of compulsory population control.

13. Protein deficiency in children, possibly leading to retarded brain development, is characteristic of populations suffering
   a. malnutrition.
   b. undernourishment.
   c. both of the above.
   d. none of the above.

14. Many development economists today emphasize the need for rural development, because
   a. food aid is not a long-term solution to the world food problem.
   b. it is nearly impossible to expand industrial jobs fast enough to keep up with urban growth in countries where the focus of development has been on the cities.
   c. rural development contributes to depauperization.
   d. all of the above are true.

312

15. Daniel Benor's experience in agricultural development demonstrates
    a. that improved technology alone can triple crop yields.
    b. that improved technology can be a boon to third-world farmers if supported by the proper organization and education.
    c. that old ways are the best ways.
    d. that modern technology can actually retard agricultural development.

True or False

1-F; the poorest are under $200.
2-F; industrialization may fail to benefit much of the population.
3-T
4-F; this is only one of several types of population equilibrium.
5-T
6-F; they are said to be undernourished.
7-F; chiefly through its effects on the death rate.
8-T
9-T
10-T

Multiple Choice

1-a
2-c
3-d
4-d
5-d; the net reproduction rate is related to long-term trends, not the growth rate at any given moment.
6-b
7-b; $70/2.8 \doteq 25$.
8-d
9-d
10-b
11-a
12-c
13-c
14-d
15-b

WHERE YOU'RE GOING

Here is what you will be able to do when you have mastered this chapter:

--Explain the difference between absolute advantage and comparative advantage.

--Demonstrate that international specialization according to comparative advantage can potentially make both trading partners better off than they would be without trade.

--Discuss several of the most important arguments for and against protectionism.

--Explain the effects of international trade on income distribution within each trading country when more than one factor of production is taken into account.

--Explain the meaning and significance of the following additional terms and concepts:

Tariffs.
Import quotas.

CHAPTER SYNOPSIS

Reading this synopsis is not a substitute for reading the chapter, but it should help you to recall the main points. If there are any you feel unsure of, refer to the full discussion in the text.

International trade in goods and services takes place because factors of production are not completely mobile among countries. Production conditions thus differ from one country to another, and these international differences can be exploited through trade to the mutual advantage of all.

Systematic study of international trade begins with the principle of comparative advantage. A country is said to have a comparative advantage in the production of some good or service if it can produce it at a lower opportunity cost, in terms of other goods and services, than its potential trading partners. Comparative advantage must be distinguished from absolute advantage, which is the ability to produce a good or service with fewer units of resources than other countries.

In international trade, it is comparative advantage rather than absolute advantage that counts. Suppose, for example, that England can produce corn for five labor hours per bushel and wine for five labor hours per gallon and that France can produce corn for four labor hours per bushel and wine for two labor hours per gallon. France thus has an absolute advantage in both products and a comparative advantage in wine; England has a comparative advantage in corn even though it has an absolute advantage in neither product. If England exports corn to France at a rate of exchange of between one and two gallons of wine per bushel of corn, both countries can end up with more of each product than they had before trade. But despite its absolute advantage in corn, France cannot profitably export corn to England (assuming that these are the only two goods and the only two countries).

Despite the demonstrable mutual advantages of trade in situations like the one just described, free international trade often encounters considerable political opposition. Protectionists favor the imposition of tariffs (taxes on imports) and quotas (quantitative limits on imports) for a variety of reasons, some more valid than others. Some argue that domestic workers need to be protected from cheap foreign labor; others that protection may be needed temporarily to aid the establishment of new industries; others that tariffs should be employed to manipulate international terms of trade; and still others that protection should be used as a tool of macroeconomic policy. Protrade economists have arguments of their own to counter each of these. The cheap foreign labor argument, taken literally, is dismissed as a contradiction of the whole theory of comparative advantage. Infant industries can be assisted by other, more efficient means, say credit subsidies. Manipulation of the terms of trade is a dangerous game, because it invites mutually damaging retaliation. And there are said to be better tools of macroeconomic policy than protectionist ones.

Perhaps the most vigorous objections to free international trade arise from the effects of trade on the distribution of income within a country. Analysis of these effects requires taking more than one factor of production into account. As a general principle, international trade raises the relative price of factors used intensively in export industries and lowers the relative price of factors used intensively in import-competing industries. Owners of factors whose relative prices fall do not necessarily suffer in terms of real income; because trade increases the total real income of a country, even their relatively smaller share of this larger total may be larger in absolute terms than their pretrade incomes. But the more specialized a factor used in an import-competing industry, the more likely that it will suffer in real terms from an increase in trade. Protrade economists do not deny this possibility; rather, they argue that there are more efficient policies than tariffs and quotas to cope with the distributional effects of trade--for example, retraining and relocation subsidies.

WALKING TOUR

You have read the chapter at least once and have reviewed the synopsis. Now you are going to walk through the material step by step, filling in the blanks and answering the questions as you go along. After you have answered each question, check yourself by uncovering the answer given in the margin. If you do not understand why the answer given is the right one, refer back to the proper section of the text.

Comparative Advantage and International Trade

Imagine two countries called, for the sake of example, England and Portugal. These are the only two countries in the world, and they produce only two products, wool and cheese. The only factor of production is labor. In England it takes six labor hours to produce a pound of wool and three labor hours to produce a pound of cheese; in Portugal three labor hours will produce a pound of wool and just one labor hour a pound of cheese. Under these conditions, England is said to have a comparative advantage in

_____ and Portugal to have a comparative ad-   wool

vantage in _____. Note, incidentally, that   cheese

Portugal has a(n) _____ advantage in   absolute

both products.

316

Suppose that each country has 1,200 labor hours available to it and that each divides these labor hours equally between the two products. That would give England a production of _____ pounds of wool and _____ pounds of cheese and Portugal a production of _____ pounds of wool and _____ pounds of cheese. Total world production of wool would be _____ pounds and total world production of cheese _____ pounds.

100; 200

200

600

300

800

In England, the opportunity cost of a pound of wool is _____ pounds of cheese, and in Portugal, the opportunity cost of a pound of wool is _____ pounds of cheese. This difference in opportunity costs is what creates a possibility of mutually advantageous trade between the two countries. England will give up a pound of wool if it can get anything more than _____ pounds of cheese in return, whereas Portugal will export up to _____ pounds of cheese if it can get a pound of wool in return. Any trading ratio between 2 for 1 and 3 for 1, then, will potentially benefit both parties.

two

three

two

three

To demonstrate this possibility of mutual advantage, suppose a trading ratio of 2.5 pounds of cheese per pound of wool is decided on. England decides to make an initial export shipment of, say, six pounds of wool. To produce the six pounds of wool for export, it must withdraw _____ labor hours from the production of cheese, which means foregoing production of _____ pounds of cheese. When it sends the six pounds of wool to Portugal, however, it receives _____ pounds of cheese in exchange, more than compensating for the loss in domestic production. To produce the fifteen pounds of cheese for export to England, Portugal must shift _____ hours of labor from producing wool to producing cheese. This means foregoing production of _____ pounds of wool. However, in return for the fifteen pounds of cheese it exports, it receives _____ pounds of wool from England, more than making up the loss in domestic production. Both countries are thus better off than before trade; England has just as much _____ and more _____ than before, whereas Portugal has just as much _____ and more _____. Note also that total world

thirty-six

twelve

fifteen

fifteen

five

six

wool; cheese

cheese

wool

317

production of both products has increased: total world
output of wool is now _____ pounds, and total   301
world production of cheese is now _____ pounds.   803
Further trade at the same ratio would bring still further
gains in production and consumption.

Trade with More Than One Factor of Production

Modify the previous example now to allow for more than
one factor of production, say land as well as labor. Suppose that production of wool uses land relatively intensively and production of cheese uses labor relatively intensively.
Now, when England begins to export wool to Portugal in
exchange for cheese, the shift in production patterns
within each country will increase demand for _____   land
relative to _____ in England and will increase   labor
demand for _____ relative to _____   labor; land
in Portugal. As a result of this shift in demand, relative
factor prices will change. In England, rents will [rise/fall]   rise
and wages will [rise/fall], while in Portugal, rents will   fall
[rise/fall] while wages will [rise/fall]. Trade will thus   fall; rise
definitely make English [workers/landowners] better off   landowners
and Portuguese [workers/landowners] better off. Whether   workers
English workers and Portuguese landowners end up better
off or worse off in real terms in uncertain. Trade raises
total real income in both countries but leaves English
workers and Portuguese landowners with a smaller relative
share of the larger total. They might gain in absolute
terms, or they might lose; the outcome would depend on
such things as the degree of difference in factor intensity
between the two production processes, the mobility of the
factors from one industry to another, and the elasticity of
demand for the factors from each type of producer.

SELF TEST

These sample test items will help you check how much you have learned. Answers
and explanations can be found at the end of this chapter. Scoring yourself: One
or two wrong -- on target. Three to five wrong -- passing, but you haven't mastered the chapter yet. Six or more wrong -- not good enough; start over and
restudy the chapter.

True or False

Indicate whether each statement is true or false as it stands. If it is false, explain why in a few words.

T F 1. A major reason for making international trade a separate branch of study in microeconomics is the fact that factors of production are not fully mobile internationally.

T F 2. The principle that a country should export goods in which it has a comparative advantage applies only to a world in which there is only one factor of production.

T F 3. International trade not only benefits consumers in both trading countries; it can also increase total world production.

T F 4. Tariffs are limitations on the quantities of goods imported into a country.

T F 5. Although certain groups of workers may suffer a loss as the result of imports from a country with low relative wages, the importing country as a whole cannot suffer a loss in real terms.

T F 6. If capital markets worked perfectly, viable "infant industries" would not need tariff barriers to get started.

T F 7. A country can improve its terms of trade by judicious use of tariffs or quotas, provided its trading partners do not retaliate with measures of the same kind.

T F 8. As a general principle, the less mobile and more specialized a factor of production, the more likely it is to be hurt by imports of the goods it is used to produce.

T F 9. As consumers, low-income groups are likely to be harmed more by imports from countries with low labor costs than are high-income groups.

T F 10. Public opinion polls show the U.S. public to be overwhelmingly in support of free trade.

Multiple Choice

1. Suppose John can sew four shirts per day or knit six caps per day, whereas Jane can sew three shirts per day or knit four caps per day. It can then be said that
   a. John has a comparative advantage in sewing shirts.
   b. John has a comparative advantage in knitting caps.
   c. both of the above are true.
   d. neither of the above are true.

2. According to international trade theory, a country should
   a. export goods in which it has a comparative advantage.
   b. never export goods in which it has an absolute advantage.
   c. never import goods in which it has an absolute advantage.
   d. import goods in which it has a comparative advantage.

3. It takes five labor hours to produce a ton of steel in Japan and three labor hours in the United States, and it requires twenty labor hours to produce a car in Japan and only fifteen labor hours in the United States. If Japan and the United States were the only two countries involved in trade, we would expect
   a. Japan to import cars and export steel.
   b. Japan to export cars and import steel.
   c. Japan to export both cars and steel.
   d. Japan to import both cars and steel.

4. Trade in meat and wheat between two countries is least likely to be profitable if
   a. one country has an absolute advantage in both goods.
   b. one country has a comparative advantage in both goods.
   c. the opportunity cost of meat, in terms of wheat, is the same in both countries.
   d. each country has an absolute advantage in one of the goods.

5. In a two-good, two-country world, international trade can increase
   a. consumer welfare in both countries, but not total output of both goods.
   b. total output of both goods, but not consumer welfare in both countries.
   c. consumer welfare only if output of both goods is increased.
   d. output of both goods and consumer welfare in both countries.

6. In Norway, it takes five labor hours to produce a ton of wheat and five to produce a ton of fish; in Greece it takes three labor hours to produce a ton of wheat and three to produce a ton of fish. If these are the only two goods and the only two trading countries, we would expect
   a. Norway to export both products.
   b. Norway to import both products.
   c. Norway to export wheat and import fish.
   d. no trade.

7. England and Germany both produce wheat and oatmeal. Oatmeal is an inferior good, and England has a comparative advantage in producing it. If the two countries begin to trade, we would expect
   a. consumer welfare in England to decline.
   b. Germans to eat more oatmeal than before.
   c. world output of oatmeal to decline.
   d. none of the above--mutually advantageous

8. The "terms of trade" argument for protectionism
   a. has no economic validity.
   b. may be valid for one country but does not suggest that all countries can gain from protection at the same time.
   c. is the one protectionist argument that is valid for all countries.
   d. is more likely to be valid for small countries than for large countries.

9. A study shows that, in the long run, Brazil could have a comparative advantage in the production of automobiles. However, it would take several years of experience to develop that advantage, and even then the advantage might be small. What should Brazil do?
   a. Forget about making its own cars.
   b. Impose tariffs on imports to give the industry a chance.
   c. Give the industry interest-free loans until it gets going.
   d. Insufficient information is given for an answer to be reached.

10. Which of the following arguments for protectionism establishes a conclusive case for tariffs?
    a. The infant industry argument.
    b. The terms of trade argument.
    c. The macroeconomic argument.
    d. None of the above.

11. If a country exports products of land-intensive industries and imports products of labor-intensive industries, we would expect that
    a. landowners will gain at the expense of workers.
    b. workers will gain at the expense of landowners.
    c. landowners will gain for sure, workers may gain.
    d. workers will gain for sure, landowners may gain.

12. It is more likely that at least some groups in a country will be hurt by trade
    a. the higher the country's initial standard of living.
    b. the lower the country's initial standard of living.
    c. the less mobile the country's factors of production.
    d. the more mobile the country's factors of production.

13. If a country exports fish and imports wheat, an interruption of trade will be likely to decrease
    a. the welfare of wheat eaters.
    b. the welfare of fishery workers.
    c. total world output of both products.
    d. all of the above.

14. Which of the following gives clear support for a policy of restricting U.S. imports of textiles from low-wage countries?
    a. Positive economics.
    b. Distributive justice.
    c. Market justice.
    d. None of the above.

15. A poll conducted in 1978 by the Wall Street Journal indicates that which of the following was most likely to favor protection?
    a. Young people.
    b. Professionals.
    c. Union members.
    d. People concerned about inflation.

ANSWERS TO CHAPTER 37 SELF TEST

True or False

1-T
2-F; to more complex worlds also.
3-T
4-F; they are taxes on imports.
5-T
6-T
7-T
8-T
9-F; they are likely to benefit more.
10-F; opinion is split with some protectionist leaning.

Multiple Choice

1-b
2-a
3-b
4-c
5-d
6-d
7-c; because world real income will rise.
8-b
9-d; depends on size of advantage, rate of interest, length of time, and so on.
10-d
11-c
12-c
13-d
14-d
15-c

CHAPTER THIRTY-EIGHT
THE BALANCE OF PAYMENTS AND THE
INTERNATIONAL MONETARY SYSTEM

WHERE YOU'RE GOING

Here is what you will be able to do when you have mastered this chapter:

--Use supply and demand analysis to explain determination of the current exchange rate in the foreign exchange market when only current account transactions are considered.

--Explain how capital account transactions contribute to determination of exchange rates.

--Explain the relationship among the current, capital, and official reserve accounts, and explain in particular why the sum of the three accounts must equal zero (statistical discrepancies aside).

--Explain the purchasing power parity theory of long-term exchange rates, and discuss the sources of short-term deviations from purchasing power parity.

--Compare fixed and floating rates as alternative bases for an international monetary system, and discuss the advantages and disadvantages of each.

--Describe the current international monetary system and its evolution from the Bretton Woods system.

--Explain the meaning and significance of the following additional terms and concepts:

> Appreciation.
> Depreciation.
> Capital inflow.
> Capital outflow.
> J-curve effect.

CHAPTER SYNOPSIS

Reading this synopsis is not a substitute for reading the chapter, but it should help you to recall the main points. If there are any you feel unsure of, refer to the full discussion in the text.

From a macroeconomic point of view, international trade differs from trade within a country in that different countries use different currencies. That means that virtually every international transaction must include a visit to the foreign exchange market--the network of banks, specialized dealers, and official government agencies through which the currency of one country can be exchanged for that of another.

The foreign exchange market, like any other market, can be understood in terms of supply and demand. The situation is complicated, however, by the great variety of international transactions that take place. To simplify things, it is best to begin by considering only current account transactions--payments for imports and exports of goods and services plus private and government transfer payments.

Consider, for example, the market in which dollars are exchanged for German marks, with the exchange rate expressed in terms of marks per dollar. The demand curve for dollars in this market is a downward-sloping line, indicating that, other things being equal (including a constant U.S. domestic price level), the more dollars Germans will demand to use for the purchase of U.S. goods, the cheaper the dollar in terms of marks. The shape of the dollar supply curve in this market is less certain--as the exchange rate rises, the United States will import a greater quantity of German goods, but whether more dollars will be needed to buy the marks to pay for those goods depends on the elasticity of U.S. demand for German goods. If U.S. demand for German goods is elastic, the supply curve of dollars in the current account foreign exchange market will have a positive slope; if the demand is inelastic, the supply curve will have a negative slope. Even with a negatively sloped dollar supply curve, however, the market will determine a stable exchange rate where the curves intersect so long as the supply curve is steeper than the demand curve.

As market conditions change, the exchange rate changes under the influence of supply and demand. If the demand for dollars increases or the supply decreases, the exchange rate, measured in marks per dollar, will rise; when this happens the dollar is said to appreciate against the mark. If the demand for dollars decreases or the supply increases, the exchange rate falls, and the dollar is said to depreciate.

In addition to current account transactions, many capital account transactions also are made each day through the foreign exchange markets. Capital account transactions include, on the one hand, purchases of U.S. assets by foreign buyers and borrowing by U.S. citizens from foreign sources, both of which are called capital inflows, and, on the other hand, purchases of foreign assets by U.S. buyers and loans by U.S. lenders to foreign borrowers, both of which are called capital outflows. To keep the two straight, remember that capital outflows are transactions that create flows of funds away from the United States, whereas capital inflows are transactions that create flows of funds into the United States.

In a world where both current and capital account transactions take place, not all imports of goods and services need be financed by current exports, nor do all exports need to be paid for by current imports. Instead, the United States can finance imports by capital inflows--borrowing from abroad or selling U.S. assets to foreign buyers. Similarly, U.S. exports can be paid for by capital outflows--loans to foreign borrowers or purchases of foreign assets by U.S. buyers.

A third section of the balance of payments accounts records official reserve transactions. These are purchases and sales of currencies made by central banks, usually for the purpose of offsetting or moderating fluctuations in exchange rates arising from current or capital account transactions. When current account, capital account, and official reserve transactions are summed, the total must be zero (aside from statistical discrepancies).

In the long run, exchange rates between currencies tend to correspond to purchasing power parities; that is, to the ratio of domestic price levels in the two countries. Thus, if 200 marks will buy the same goods in Germany as $100 will buy in the United States, the exchange rate will, according to the purchasing power parity theory, be about 2 marks per dollar. In the short run, exchange rates can be pulled above or below purchasing power parity by any of a number of causes, including changes in aggregate demand in one country or the other, international differences in interest rates, and international differences in actual and expected rates of inflation.

As noted previously, governments can, if they choose, engage in official reserve transactions to offset exchange rate fluctuations originating in current or capital account transactions. Different international monetary systems are possible according to the rules of the game that governments follow in conducting these official reserve transactions.

Under a system of fixed rates, a "par" value is determined for each currency, and official reserve sales or purchases of the currency are made to offset any changes in supply or demand that would move the exchange rate away from the par value. Under a floating rate system, governments agree to a hands-off policy, leaving exchange rates to find their own levels in the market without official intervention. Which system is better—fixed or floating rates—is the subject of a long-standing debate among economists and government officials.

The following points are made in favor of fixed exchange rates: (1) Fixed rates are said to shield the domestic economy from real effects of temporary exchange rate fluctuations. (2) In the short run, the depreciation of a country's currency can increase rather than decrease its current account deficit if demand for imports and exports is so inelastic that the negatively sloped supply curve is flatter than the demand curve; this is known as the j-curve effect. (3) Depreciation of a country's currency can cause cost-push inflation, which in turn can cause further depreciation, setting off a vicious cycle. (4) A fixed exchange rate policy amounts to an automatic anti-inflationary monetary policy, in that central bank purchases of a depreciating currency decrease that country's money supply.

Advocates of floating rates dispute each of these four points. In addition, they object to fixed rate systems because governments participating in them often refuse to play by the rules of the game. When central banks use exchange rate intervention to postpone necessary adjustments to long-term economic changes rather than just to iron out short-term exchange rate fluctuations, they end up destabilizing rather than stabilizing the international monetary system.

At the end of World War II, the world's major trading nations met at Bretton Woods, New Hampshire, to set up a new international monetary system. This sytem was fundamentally a fixed rate system, with provisions for orderly adjustments of par values when necessary. The system proved crisis-prone, however, and was abandoned in 1973 in favor of a more flexible system. The current system is some-times known as a "dirty float," because although exchange rates do fluctuate, governments continue to intervene as they see fit to steer the fluctuations in one direction or the other.

WALKING TOUR

You have read the chapter at least once and have reviewed the synopsis. Now you are going to walk through the material step by step, filling in the blanks and answering the questions as you go along. After you have answered each question, check yourself by uncovering the answer given in the margin. If you do not understand why the answer given is the right one, refer back to the proper section of the text.

Foreign Exchange Markets and the Current Account

Current account transactions--those representing payments

for current imports and exports plus transfer payments--

are only one of a number of kinds of transactions that take

place in foreign exchange markets, but assuming they are

the only kind of international transaction provides a starting

point for learning how foreign exchange markets work.

Consider Exhibit S38.1, for example. This figure shows

hypothetical current account supply and demand curves

in a foreign exchange market where U.S. dollars are traded

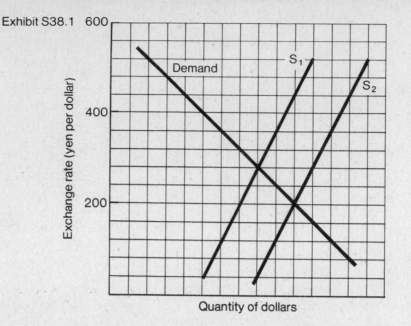

Exhibit S38.1

Exchange rate (yen per dollar)

Quantity of dollars

for Japanese yen. As the figure is drawn, the equilibrium
exchange rate is _____ yen per dollar when the   280
supply curve is S_1.

  The positive slope of this supply curve indicates that
the U.S. demand for Japanese goods is [elastic/inelastic].   elastic
As the dollar appreciates (that is, as the exchange rate in
yen per dollar [rises/falls]), the quantity of Japanese goods   rises
demanded increases [more than/less than] in proportion to   more than
the change in the dollar price of Japanese goods and
services.

  Suppose now that something happens to shift the dollar
supply curve to the position S_2--say that there is an increase in U.S. transfer payments to Japan or that U.S.
buyers develop an increased preference for Japanese goods.
The immediate result will be an excess [supply/demand] of   supply
dollars, which will cause the dollar to [appreciate/depreciate]. depreciate
As it does so, Japanese consumers will find U.S. goods
[more/less] expensive and will [increase/decrease] the   less; increase
quantity of U.S. goods they demand. This means they
must [increase/decrease] the quantity of dollars demanded   increase
in the foreign exchange markets; this increase is represen-
ted in Exhibit S38.1 as a [movement along/shift in] the   movement along
demand curve for dollars. At the same time, the lower ex-
change rate will cause U.S. buyers to [increase/decrease]   decrease

the quantities of Japanese goods demanded and thus to
[increase/decrease] the quantity of dollars they supply to

decrease

the foreign exchange market. This is shown as a movement
along the supply curve _____. A new equilibrium ex-

S_2

change rate becomes established at _____ yen per

200

dollar.

     Turn your attention now to Exhibit S38.2, which shows
the same market, but with a different possible set of supply
curves. With the supply curve S_1, the equilibrium exchange

rate is _____ yen per dollar. The negative slope of

280

this supply curve indicates an [elastic/inelastic] U.S. demand

inelastic

for Japanese goods and services.

     Again, suppose that something causes the supply of
dollars to increase, shifting the supply curve to S_2. The
immediate effect is to produce an excess [supply/demand]

supply

of dollars, causing the dollar to [appreciate/depreciate].

depreciate

As the exchange rate falls, Japanese consumers [increase/

decrease] the quantity of U.S. goods they buy and [in-

increase

crease/decrease] the quantity of dollars they demand. U.S.

increase

buyers, finding Japanese imports [more/less] expensive,

more

[increase/decrease] the quantity of those goods that they

decrease

buy, but [more/less] than in proportion to the change in

less

the dollar price of Japanese goods. As a result, the quantity of dollars they supply to the foreign exchange markets

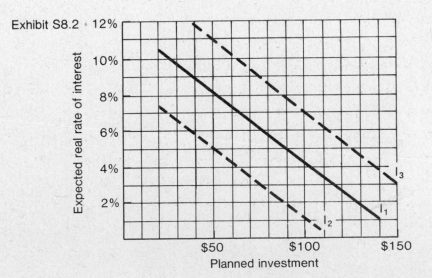

Exhibit S8.2

327

[increases/decreases]. This is shown as a [movement along/ shift in] the supply curve _____. As the dollar depreciates, the quantity of dollars demanded increases more [rapidly/slowly] than the quantity of dollars supplied; the market thus comes into a new equilibrium at an exchange rate of _____ yen per dollar.

increases
movement along; S_2

rapidly

120

Finally, turn your attention to Exhibit S38.3, which illustrates still another possible configuration of supply and demand curves for the yen/dollar exchange market. As in Exhibit S38.2, the negative slope of the supply curve S_1 indicates an [elastic/inelastic] U.S. demand for Japanese goods. Now, however, the steeper slope of the demand curve indicates a more [elastic/inelastic] Japanese demand for U.S. goods than before. The demand curve, which is now steeper than the supply curve, intersects S_1 at an exchange rate of _____ yen per dollar.

inelastic

inelastic

280

Look what happens, however, when the supply curve shifts to S_2. As before, the initial effect is an excess [supply/demand] of dollars, which causes the dollar to [appreciate/depreciate]. As it does so, Japanese buyers find U.S. goods [cheaper/more expensive], but they increase their purchases [less than/more than] in proportion to the change in the exchange rate. The quantity of dollars they demand [increases/decreases], but only slightly. On the U.S. side, [more/fewer] Japanese goods are demanded,

supply
depreciate
cheaper
less than

increases
fewer

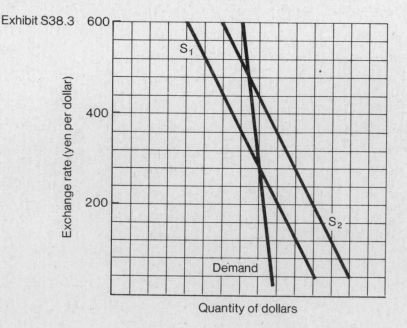

Exhibit S38.3

Exchange rate (yen per dollar)

600

400

200

S_1

S_2

Demand

Quantity of dollars

but [more/fewer] dollars are offered on the exchange mar-

more

kets. As the dollar depreciates, the quantity of dollars
supplied increases [faster/more slowly] than the quantity

faster

of dollars demanded. The excess supply of dollars thus
[increases/decreases] as the exchange rate falls, and no

increases

new equilibrium can be found.

In practice, of course, exchange rates never plunge to
zero. The reason is that current account transactions are
not the only ones that take place. The next section will
look at other kinds of international transactions.

Exchange Markets: Capital and Official Reserve Accounts

If the capital account is added to the current account,
current imports and exports need not exactly balance in
each period. Instead, an excess of imports over exports
can be paid for by capital [inflows/outflows]--that is, by

inflows

[selling assets to/buying assets from] foreigners or by

selling assets to

[borrowing from/lending to] foreigners. Similarly, there

borrowing from

can be an excess of exports over imports on current account if there is a capital [inflow/outflow]--that is, if there

outflow

is [lending to/borrowing from] foreigners or if U.S. citizens

lending to

[sell/buy] foreign assets.

buy

Upward or downward movements in exchange rates can
be initiated by changes affecting either current or capital
account transactions. For example, suppose U.S. interest
rates increase relative to interest rates abroad, other things
being equal. The effect would be to encourage the [pur-

purchase

chase/sale] of U.S. assets and to encourage borrowers to
borrow [in the U.S./abroad]--in other words, the rise in

abroad

interest rates would encourage a capital [inflow/outflow].

inflow

In the foreign exchange market, the capital inflow would
add to the [demand for/supply of] dollars and would cause

demand for

the dollar to [appreciate/depreciate].

appreciate

Alternatively, suppose the rate of inflation in the U.S.
is expected to increase, other things, including interest
rates, being equal. This would make U.S. assets [more/less]

less

attractive relative to assets denominated in more stable
foreign currencies and would thus cause a capital [inflow/

outflow]. This in turn would tend to cause the dollar to

outflow

[appreciate/depreciate].

depreciate

If the U.S. or foreign governments wish to prevent any
of the exchange rate movements described above--whether
originating in the current or capital accounts--they can
undertake _____ account trans-   official reserve
actions. For example, if the dollar begins to depreciate,
the Federal Reserve can [buy/sell] dollars in the foreign   buy
exchange markets, thus bringing supply and demand in
line at the previous exchange rate. Similarly, to prevent
an appreciation of the dollar, the Fed can [buy/sell] dollars.   sell
Such transactions must be made regularly under a [fixed/
floating] exchange rate system; under a pure [fixed/floating]   fixed; floating
rate system, they need never be made; and under the
current "dirty float" system, they are sometimes made.

SELF TEST

These sample test items will help you check how much you have learned. Answers
and explanations can be found at the end of this chapter. Scoring yourself: One
or two wrong -- on target. Three to five wrong -- passing, but you haven't mastered the chapter yet. Six or more wrong -- not good enough; start over and
restudy the chapter.

True or False

Indicate whether each statement is true or false as it stands. If it is false, explain
why in a few words.

T F 1. If the exchange rate changes from 2 marks per dollar to 1.8 marks per
         dollar, the dollar is said to depreciate and the mark to appreciate.

T F 2. The intersection of the current account supply and demand curves in the
         foreign exchange market does not, under all elasticity conditions, represent
         a stable equilibrium.

T F 3. Statistical discrepancies aside, the sum of the current, capital, and official
         reserve account balances must equal zero.

T F 4. Other things being equal, the faster a country's rate of inflation, the
         faster the rate of appreciation of its currency.

T F 5. The "j-curve" effect arises from the fact that the current account supply
         and demand curves tend to be less elastic in the short run than in the
         long run.

T F 6. One advantage claimed for a floating exchange rate system is that it forces
         central banks into an automatic anti-inflationary monetary policy.

T F 7. Under the Bretton Woods system, exchange rates were allowed to fluctuate
         within a narrow band around a fixed par value.

T F 8. A major reason for instability under the Britton Woods system was the reluc-
         tance of governments to adjust exchange rates to new par values when
         circumstances made it necessary to do so.

9. Since the institution of the floating rate system in 1973, the exchange rates of the major trading currencies have hardly changed at all.

10. A major benefit of the change to floating rates has been a marked slowdown in world inflation.

Multiple Choice

1. Foreign exchange transactions involving the U.S. dollar take place in
   a. New York.
   b. London.
   c. Zurich.
   d. all of the above places.

2. U.S. military aid to foreign countries is entered in the
   a. current account.
   b. capital account.
   c. official reserve account.
   d. intervention account.

3. If the U.S. demand for foreign goods were perfectly inelastic in the short run, the current account supply curve of dollars would
   a. have a negative slope.
   b. have a positive slope.
   c. be perfectly vertical.
   d. be perfectly horizontal.

4. Under which of the following circumstances does the intersection of the foreign exchange supply and demand curves not represent a stable equilibrium exchange rate?
   a. Supply curve vertical, demand curve negatively sloped.
   b. Demand curve vertical, supply curve negatively sloped.
   c. Supply curve negatively sloped and steeper than demand curve.
   d. The intersection is a stable equilibrium in all of the above.

5. A gasoline shortage in the United States causes an increase in demand for highly efficient Japanese cars; in the yen/dollar foreign exchange markets, the consequences would best be represented by
   a. a rightward shift in the dollar supply curve.
   b. a leftward shift in the dollar supply curve.
   c. a rightward shift in the dollar demand curve.
   d. a leftward shift in the dollar demand curve.

6. A U.S. resident sends a substantial sum of money to an elderly relative in Poland. This transaction might be offset by
   a. a slight depreciation of the dollar, encouraging exports and encouraging imports.
   b. a sale of U.S. treasury bills to a foreign buyer.
   c. a purchase of dollars by the foreign exchange desk of the Fed.
   d. any of the above.

7. A private U.S. citizen's purchase of long-term bonds issued by a British corporation would be considered
   a. a capital inflow.
   b. a capital outflow.
   c. a current account transaction.
   d. an official reserve transaction.

8. Which of the following is considered a capital inflow?
   a. A sale of U.S. assets to a foreign buyer.
   b. A loan from a U.S. bank to a foreign borrower.
   c. A purchase of foreign assets by a U.S. buyer.
   d. A U.S. citizen's repayment of a loan from a foreign bank.

9. If the United States runs a balance of payments deficit on the current account,
   a. it must run a capital account surplus.
   b. it must run an official reserve account surplus.
   c. it must do at least one of the above.
   d. it must do both a and b.

10. Which of the following would be likely to cause the U.S. dollar to appreciate relative to the French franc?
    a. An increase in French interest rates.
    b. An increase in the U.S. rate of inflation.
    c. A purchase of francs by the French central bank.
    d. None of the above.

11. According to the so-called j-curve effect, when a country's currency depreciates, its current account balance
    a. first moves toward deficit, then later toward surplus.
    b. first moves toward surplus, then later toward deficit.
    c. moves into deficit and stays there.
    d. moves into surplus and stays there.

12. According to advocates of floating exchange rates,
    a. it is usually bad to engage in restrictive monetary policy when your exchange rate is depreciating.
    b. under a fixed rate system, banks violate the rules of the game by using official reserve transactions to offset short-term exchange rate fluctuations.
    c. floating rates insulate the domestic economy from changes in exchange rates.
    d. none of the above is true.

13. Advocates of fixed exchange rates
    a. are concerned about the j-curve effect.
    b. think fixed rates help insulate the domestic economy from foreign disturbances.
    c. think fixed rates encourage central banks to pursue anti-inflationary monetary policy.
    d. agree with all of the above.

14. The Bretton Woods system is best characterized as
    a. a rigid fixed rate system.
    b. an adjustable peg system.
    c. a clean float.
    d. a dirty float.

15. The Bretton Woods system
    a. never really got off the ground.
    b. lasted more than twenty years but proved crisis prone.
    c. is still in effect.
    d. pure more emphasis on floating rates than the present system.

ANSWERS TO CHAPTER 38 SELF TEST

True or False

1-T
2-T
3-T
4-F; change appreciation to depreciation.
5-T
6-F; fixed rates do this.
7-T
8-T
9-F; they have fluctuated rather widely.
10-F; no such slowdown has taken place.

Multiple Choice

1-d
2-a
3-a
4-b
5-a
6-d
7-b
8-a
9-c
10-d
11-a
12-d
13-d
14-b
15-b

CHAPTER THIRTY-NINE
CAPITALISM VERSUS SOCIALISM

WHERE YOU'RE GOING

Here is what you will be able to do when you have mastered this chapter:

--Define capitalism, and distinguish among classical liberal capitalism, anarcho-capitalism (radical libertarianism), and state capitalism.

--Define socialism, and distinguish among centralized socialism, market socialism, and participatory socialism.

--Describe Oscar Lange's system of market socialism.

--Recapitulate the main points of the debate over the relative static and dynamic efficiency of capitalism and socialism.

CHAPTER SYNOPSIS

Reading this synopsis is not a substitute for reading the chapter, but it should help you to recall the main points. If there are any you feel unsure of, refer to the full discussion in the text.

In the branch of economics dealing with comparative economic systems, whole systems of economic institutions are the variables, rather than the givens, of analysis. The two broad classes of economic system most important in modern industrialized countries are capitalism and socialism.

Capitalist economic systems are those based on private ownership of all factors of production, with owners of capital acting as entrepreneurs and coordinating their activities through the market. A number of different types of capitalism can be distinguished. In classical liberal capitalism, the government plays only the limited role of defending personal and property rights and enforcing the rules of the game. In anarcho-capitalism (also known as radical libertarianism) even the functions of defense, police, and courts are handled by private firms, and there is no government at all. In state capitalism, the government plays a broader role in regulating, and even competing with, the private sector. The U.S. economy is a leading example of state capitalism.

Socialist economic systems are a broad family distinguished by two common tenets: (1) that some major share of nonlabor factors of production be owned cooperatively or by the government; and (2) that income be distributed more equally than under classical liberal capitalism. In centralized socialism, capital and natural resources are government owned, and economic coordination at all levels takes place according to the managerial principle (that is, according to an economic plan). The economy of the Soviet Union is the leading example of centralized socialism. Under market socialism, coordination among socialist firms takes place by means of prices and markets. Participatory socialism is a variant of market socialism under which firms are owned not by the government, but cooperatively by their own workers. The Yugoslav economy is the leading example of participatory socialism. In Western Europe, many countries are governed by social democratic parties, which place somewhat more emphasis on planning, state ownership, and redistribution than do most capitalist parties. However, the gap between European social democracy and state capitalism is often a narrow one.

The relative economic merits of capitalism versus socialism have been debated for nearly two centuries. Socialism is said by its supporters to be superior to capitalism not only in normative terms (that is, in terms of income distribution) but also in positive terms (that is, in terms of efficiency). The positive portion of the debate can be discussed under the headings of static and dynamic efficiency.

Perhaps the best-known case ever made for socialism on grounds of static efficiency was that made by Oskar Lange. Writing in the 1930s, Lange envisioned a system of market socialism in which managers were to follow marginalist rules based on the conditions for equilibrium under perfect competition. Social ownership was thus to be combined with the perfect static efficiency of capitalism at its best, while such practical problems of capitalism as monopoly and pollution were avoided. Lange's system, however, has never been put into practice. It has been criticized on grounds of administrative impractibility and also has been criticized for paying attention only to pure economizing while ignoring entrepreneurial decision making.

Socialism has been so frequently charged with failure to provide entrepreneurship that its dynamic efficiency is widely questioned. However, to some extent, planners in centralized socialist economies have been able to offset the inferior dynamic efficiency of their systems by mobilizing more resources--especially more investment--for economic growth. As the next chapter will show, though, even this superiority of socialism over capitalism in terms of growth rates has diminished in recent years.

WALKING TOUR

You have read the chapter at least once and have reviewed the synopsis. Now you are going to walk through the material step by step, filling in the blanks and answering the questions as you go along. After you have answered each question, check yourself by uncovering the answer given in the margin. If you do not understand why the answer given is the right one, refer back to the proper section of the text.

Capitalism and Socialism

Economic systems can be distinguished from one another in terms of a number of characteristics, including ownership of resources, mechanisms for coordinating economic activity, and distribution of income.

In the broadest terms, economic systems described as capitalistic emphasize [private/collective] ownership of non-labor resources. They rely primarily on the [market/managerial] principle for coordinating relationships among firms, although within firms the [market/managerial] principle is used. Distribution of income follows, in the first instance, the _____ principle.

            private

            market

            managerial

            marginal productivity

Within the broad category of capitalism, there are a number of more or less distinct possible systems. At one extreme is a hypothetical economic system in which there is no government at all; this system is known as _____ capitalism. (An-archy means "without rulers.") A capitalist system in which the government

            anarcho-

performs the limited function of protecting the property
rights and enforcing the rules of the game is known as

_____ capitalism.   In the contemporary   classical liberal

U.S. economy, the government's role in regulating private
economic activity is much more extensive; the economic
system of the United States can be described as

_____ capitalism because of this larger role   state

of government.

     Socialism too comes in a number of varieties.   The
best-known socialist economy is that of the Soviet Union,

which can be described as _____ socialism   centralized

because it relies (in principle) on [market/managerial] coor-   managerial

dination between as well as within firms.   A socialist system
in which capital and natural resources are centrally owned,
but in which the market mechanism is used to coordinate
the activities of individual firms, is referred to as

_____ socialism.   Still another variety of   market

socialism vests ownership of capital not in the state but in
the workers of individual enterprises; this is known as

_____ socialism.   An example of this   participatory

kind of system is that of _____.   Finally   Yugoslavia

many European countries are governed by parties that are
nominally socialist but which, in practice, rely on private
enterprise to nearly the same degree as does state capital.
These parties are collectively referred to as _____

_____.   social democratic

Socialism and Efficiency
The relative efficiency of capitalism and socialism has been
debated for many years.   In the 1930s, the case for the
superior efficiency of socialism was forcefully argued by

_____.   He envisioned a type of   Oskar Lange

_____ socialism that would duplicate the per-   market

formance of a perfectly competitive capitalist market in terms

of _____ efficiency, while avoiding problems   static

such as _____ and _____.   monopoly; pollution

     Lange's system was criticized as impractical, but more
fundamentally, it was criticized for paying too little attention

to _____ decision making.   Other   entrepreneurial

kinds of socialism too are criticized for being inferior to

336

capitalism in terms of _____ efficiency as   dynamic
well as static efficiency. Socialist planners have sometimes,
although not always, been able to achieve high rates of
economic growth despite low dynamic efficiency by forcing
higher rates of _____ and resource mobilization.   saving

SELF TEST

These sample test items will help you check how much you have learned. Answers
and explanations can be found at the end of this chapter. Scoring yourself: One
or two wrong -- on target. Three to five wrong -- passing, but you haven't mastered the chapter yet. Six or more wrong -- not good enough; start over and
restudy the chapter.

True or False

Indicate whether each statement is true or false as it stands. If it is false, explain
why in a few words.

T F 1. Comparative economic systems is the only branch of economics that looks at
the effects of economic institutions on economic behavior.

T F 2. An economic system with private ownership and market coordination but with
all entrepreneurial functions performed by landowners would not properly
be called capitalistic.

T F 3. Under state capitalism, government and the market exist side by side as
alternative mechanisms for the performance of many economic functions.

T F 4. Soviet leaders have deviated from the original teachings of Karl Marx, who
envisioned a system of market socialism rather than centralized socialism.

T F 5. Western European social democracy is characterized by some government
ownership of industry, together with considerable emphasis on redistribution of income and wealth.

T F 6. After World War II, Oskar Lange returned to his native Poland, where he
was able for the first time to implement the principles laid down in his
famous articles of the 1930s.

T F 7. The Austrian economists von Mises and von Hayek criticized Lange's system
for inadequate attention to entrepreneurial decision making.

T F 8. To lighten the burden on central planners, Lange proposed that prices in
the socialist economy be set through a process of trial and error.

T F 9. In principle, a socialist economy can achieve rapid growth despite low
dynamic efficiency by raising its rate of saving.

T F 10. Emphasis on distributive justice over market justice automatically makes a
person a socialist of one kind or another.

Multiple Choice

1. Which of the following is not a characteristic of capitalism?
    a. Private ownership of capital.
    b. Owners of capital perform entrepreneurial functions.
    c. Market coordination between firms.
    d. All of the above are characteristics of capitalism.

2. Which of the following economic systems preserves the smallest role for government?
    a. Classical liberal capitalism.
    b. Radical libertarianism.
    c. State capitalism.
    d. All of the above are about the same with regard to the role of the state.

3. In which of the following systems can government be thought of as a referee, concerned primarily with enforcing the rules of the game?
    a. State capitalism.
    b. Classical liberal capitalism.
    c. Radical libertarianism.
    d. Anarcho-capitalism.

4. Which of the following is not characteristic of all major varieties of socialism?
    a. Nonlabor resources must be government owned.
    b. Income must be distributed more equally than under classical liberal capitalism.
    c. Private ownership of all capital is not acceptable.
    d. All of the above are true of all types of socialism.

5. Which of the following countries has an economic system best described as centralized socialism?
    a. United Kingdom.
    b. Yugoslavia.
    c. Soviet Union.
    d. United States.

6. Which of the following countries places greatest emphasis on managerial coordination in its economic system?
    a. United Kingdom.
    b. Soviet Union.
    c. Yugoslavia.
    d. Sweden.

7. Which of the following marginal rules would not be observed under Lange's form of market socialism?
    a. Marginal cost equals price.
    b. Marginal physical product per dollar's worth of each factor of production equals marginal physical product per dollar's worth of each other factor.
    c. Marginal revenue equals marginal physical product for all goods.
    d. All of the above would be observed.

8. Which of the following is characteristic of participatory socialism?
    a. Managerial coordination between firms.
    b. Government ownership of all capital.
    c. Both of the above.
    d. None of the above.

9.   Which of the following economic systems most closely resembles state capitalism?
     a. Centralized socialism.
     b. Anarcho-capitalism.
     c. Social democracy.
     d. Lange's market socialism.

10. Which of the following economic systems believes that mangerial coordination has no role to play anywhere in the economy?
     a. Radical libertarianism.
     b. Participatory socialism.
     c. Classical liberal capitalism.
     d. None of the above.

11. Which of the following economic systems is not represented by at least one country today?
     a. Anarcho-capitalism.
     b. State capitalism.
     c. Centralized socialism.
     d. Participatory socialism.

12. Which of the following is not a valid criticism of Lange's market socialism?
     a. It ignores the proper rules for pure economizing.
     b. It would be administratively impractical.
     c. It makes insufficient provision for entrepreneurship.
     d. None of the above is a valid criticism.

13. An economy with a high degree of dynamic efficiency would
     a. always operate on its production possibility frontier.
     b. necessarily have a high rate of saving.
     c. sustain a high growth rate for any given level of saving.
     d. do none of the above.

14. To the extent that socialist economies have in many periods been able to sustain high rates of economic growth, the explanation is to be found in
     a. the superior static efficiency of socialism.
     b. the superior dynamic efficiency of socialism.
     c. the ability of socialism to mobilize saving and factor inputs.
     d. none of the above--socialist economies always grow slowly.

15. Which of the following is least prominent as a normative goal of socialism?
     a. Equality.
     b. Market justice.
     c. Elimination of exploitation.
     d. A voice for workers in management.

ANSWERS TO CHAPTER 39 SELF TEST

True or False

1-F; all branches of economics pay some attention to institutions.
2-T
3-T
4-F; Marx envisioned centralized socialism.
5-T
6-F; he returned, but did not put his ideas into practice.
7-T
8-T
9-T
10-F; some people think the goals of distributive justice can be achieved under capitalism.

Multiple Choice

1-d
2-b
3-b
4-a
5-c
6-b
7-c
8-d
9-c
10-d
11-a
12-a
13-c
14-c
15-b

CHAPTER FORTY
THE SOVIET ECONOMY

WHERE YOU'RE GOING

Here is what you will be able to do when you have mastered this chapter:

--Briefly describe the ideological and historical origins of the Soviet economic system.

--Describe the formal structure of the Soviet economy, and compare it with the theoretical economic system of centralized socialism.

--Explain, with the use of examples, how the informal structure of the Soviet economy departs from the theoretical structure of centralized socialism.

--Outline the performance of the Soviet economy in terms of economic growth, explaining both the reasons for previous rapid growth rates and for currently declining growth rates.

--Briefly describe the structure and problems of the agricultural sector of the Soviet economy.

--Explain the meaning and significance of the following additional terms and concepts:

Extensive growth.
Intensive growth.
Kolkhoz.

CHAPTER SYNOPSIS

Reading this synopsis is not a substitute for reading the chapter, but it should help you to recall the main points. If there are any that you feel unsure of, refer to the full discussion in the text.

The Soviet economy represents the most extensive and ambitious experiment in socialist economics ever undertaken. A study of the Soviet economy provides some important insights not only into the economics of socialism, but also into the nature of the resource allocation problem itself.

The roots of the Soviet economic system lie in Marxist ideology and in the history of the Russian revolution. Although most of Marx's voluminous writings were devoted to the economics of capitalism, the comments that he did make on the economics of socialism suggest that it was the centralized variant he envisioned. The emphasis on centralism fit in well with the thinking of V. I. Lenin, architect of the Russian revolution, who thought of the postrevolutionary economy as being administered like one big firm. Although early experiments with an ultra-centralized economy were disrupted by civil war, the centralized model was firmly in place in the Soviet economy by the 1930s.

In principle, the Soviet economy functions as a single enterprise under the direction of Gosplan, the central planning agency. Directives, in the form of a technical-industrial-financial plan, are issued to each enterprise, specifying what is to be produced, how much is to be produced, and what methods and inputs are to be used in the production process. The plan has the binding force of law.

Incentive bonuses and penalties for enterprise managers are tied to the fulfillment of plan targets. In the labor sector, central planning determines how much of each type of labor is to be used in each sector of the economy, but market incentives (wages) are used to attract workers to particular occupations and locations in accordance with market principles.

In practice, the Soviet economy departs from the strict centralized model in several aspects of its informal structure. A good deal of informal "horizontal" communication takes place among firms, and plans are not in practice always treated as binding. Furthermore, enterprise managers do not simply wait for plans to arrive from on high, but actively negotiate with planning officials in order to achieve a safe plan. When things do not go according to plan during the year, managers typically exercise considerable initiative in obtaining necessary inputs outside official channels. Sometimes less important goals of the plan are sacrificed in order to achieve those goals upon which planners place the most emphasis. Central authorities tolerate much of this unofficial resource allocation system, apparently believing that it is the grease the keeps the wheel of central planning in rotation.

The accomplishment of which the Soviet economy is proudest has been the transformation of peasant Russia into a modern superpower. During the early years of its existence, the Soviet economy achieved rapid expansion through extensive growth-- growth fueled primarily by increased quantities of factor inputs. In the 1980s, with opportunities for extensive growth largely exhausted, the Soviet economy is experiencing slower expansion as it attempts to turn to intensive growth--growth based on better utilization of available inputs.

One of the problems facing the contemporary Soviet economy is how to make use of prices and managerial incentives to improve static and dynamic efficiency. Traditionally, the Soviet price system performs only an accounting function, not also an allocative function as in a capitalist economy. Various proposals for economic reforms have been advanced over the last two decades, but major reforms have yet to be implemented in the Soviet Union. However, the nations of Eastern Europe, whose economies were once carbon copies of the Soviet system, have experimented more widely with economic reforms.

Agriculture remains another major problem area for the Soviet economy. The basis of Soviet agriculture is the collective farm, or kolkhoz. This institution served the Soviet economy well in its early years by channeling a steady grain surplus to the cities as a basis for industrialization. Now, however, Soviet agriculture is proving inadequate as a basis for a consumer society, and the Soviet Union has had to resort increasingly to food imports.

WALKING TOUR

You have read the chapter at least once and have reviewed the synopsis. Now you are going to walk through the material step by step, filling in the blanks and answering the questions as you go along. After you have answered each question, check yourself by uncovering the answer given in the margin. If you do not understand why the answer given is the right one, refer back to the proper section of the text.

Origins and Structure

The origins of the _____ socialist econ-   centralized

omic system of the Soviet Union can be traced to the writings

of _____ and the revolutionary prac-   Karl Marx

tice of _____. For both men, the post-   V. I. Lenin

revolutionary economy was supposed to replace the "anarchy of the market" with the "planning principle," that is, to replace _____ coordination with _____ coordination at the national level.

      market

      managerial

      After the revolution, Lenin [did/did not] attempt to implement many features of a centralized system. Coming during a period of civil war, these radical measures led to chaos. They were followed by a period of increased reliance on the market known as the _____. Central planning was once again instituted at the end of the 1920s, together with a policy of _____ of agriculture. At that time, the structure of the Soviet economy took on most of the important features it retains to this day.

      did

      "new economic policy"

      collectivization

      Under current practice, the activities of each firm are guided by a technical-industrial-financial plan that determines [inputs/outputs/both inputs and outputs] for the firm. These plans, in turn, are based on a set of _____ _____ for two or three hundred of the most important goods, which are supposed to ensure the balance of supply and demand. These material balances are refined at lower levels of the planning hierarchy, and individual firms are given a chance to negotiate with central authorities about details of the plan at that time. In practice, a major objective of enterprise managers at this stage is to develop a _____ that will make it possible to fulfill the plan even if everything does not go smoothly during the year.

      both inputs and outputs

      material balances

      safety factor

Performance

During the 1930s, immediately after the introduction of comprehensive central planning, official Soviet data show growth rates of 15 percent per year or more for national output. Western observers believe that these high growth rates are somewhat exaggerated by the use of a very [early/late] base year for constructing growth indexes. Nonetheless, growth rates were clearly high at that time. The type of growth that took place is best described as [extensive/intensive] growth, because it was based largely on mobiliza-

      early

      extensive

343

tion of new factor inputs. Since World War II, the growth
rate of the Soviet economy has gradually slowed. This apparently indicates difficulties in achieving [extensive/
intensive] growth through the more efficient utilization of   intensive
available factor supplies. The declining growth rate [has/
has not yet] led to comprehensive reforms of the centralized   has not yet
planning system. As it has throughout the past fifty years,
the _____ sector continues to lag behind   agricultural
the _____ sector.   industrial

SELF TEST

These sample test items will help you check how much you have learned. Answers
and explanations can be found at the end of this chapter. Scoring yourself: One
or two wrong -- on target. Three to five wrong -- passing, but you haven't mastered the chapter yet. Six or more wrong -- not good enough; start over and
restudy the chapter.

True or False

Indicate whether each statement is true or false as it stands. If it is false, explain
why in a few words.

T F   1.   The writings of Karl Marx were devoted almost entirely to capitalism and had
           relatively little to say about socialist economic planning.

T F   2.   During the civil war that followed the Russian revolution, the Soviet econ-
           omy was guided largely by market principles.

T F   3.   Stalin referred to his introduction of comprehensive planning and collectiv-
           ization as the "new economic policy."

T F   4.   Collectivization of agriculture did not increase total agricultural output, but
           it did increase deliveries of grain to the cities.

T F   5.   Soviet enterprise managers usually respond to suggested plans by submitting
           bids for higher plan targets, because that is how the greatest bonuses can
           be earned.

T F   6.   The informal structure of the Soviet economy is much less centralized than
           the formal structure.

T F   7.   Unlike their capitalist counterparts, Soviet managers do not have to spend
           much of their time worrying about procurement of inputs.

T F   8.   Official Soviet statistics show declining economic growth rates in the period
           1950-1980.

T F   9.   Since the beginning of the 1970s, the Soviet Union has been a net importer
           of oil.

T F 10.   Because of political tensions, the countries of Eastern Europe have been
           even more timid about economic reforms than has the Soviet Union.

Multiple Choice

1. During which of the following periods did the Soviet economy rely least on central planning?
    a. War communism.
    b. The NEP.
    c. Collectivization.
    d. The postwar period.

2. Which of the following measures was not instituted by Stalin in 1928?
    a. A five-year plan for industry.
    b. Collectivization of agriculture.
    c. Abolition of the use of money.
    d. All of the above were instituted.

3. In which of the following respects can collectivization be considered a success, given the goals of the Soviet leadership?
    a. Increased grain output.
    b. Increased livestock output.
    c. Increased flow of agricultural products to the cities.
    d. All of the above.

4. Which of the following aspects of the operation of individual Soviet enterprises is detailed in the central plan?
    a. Assortment of products.
    b. Quantity of output.
    c. Timing of output deliveries.
    d. All of the above.

5. Under the Soviet planning system,
    a. plans are drawn up in final form at the center and handed down to enterprises in finished form.
    b. each enterprise draws up its own plan, which the central authorities then combine into one big plan.
    c. the planning process begins at the center, and suggestions for modifications are made by enterprises.
    d. c until the advent of computers; now a.

6. Which of the following sectors of the Soviet economy relies most on market mechanisms to move resources to their desired uses?
    a. Industry.
    b. Labor.
    c. Transportation.
    d. Energy.

7. Which of the following would be considered a "horizontal" communication channel in the Soviet economy?
    a. The plan is transmitted from Gosplan to the enterprise.
    b. A manager bargains with Gosplan for easier plan targets.
    c. A manager barters scarce inputs with the manager of another enterprise.
    d. Central authorities use the Communist Party as a check on the performance of planning system bureaucrats.

8. A "safety factor" for a Soviet manager might take the form of
    a. an easy plan.
    b. large inventories of inputs.
    c. concealed productive capacity.
    d. any of the above.

9. Which of the following best characterizes the attitude of Soviet authorities toward the informal, and sometimes illegal, actions managers take to meet plan targets?
   a. They are often tolerated if successful.
   b. They are severely punished when discovered.
   c. They are studied for a while; then, if they work, they are incorporated into the formal structure of the system.
   d. Soviet central authorities are apparently unaware of most of what goes on in this respect.

10. Which of the following, although it is not supposed to be a major concern of enterprise managers in the Soviet Union, is a major concern in practice?
    a. Meeting plan targets for assortment.
    b. Procuring inputs.
    c. Improving labor productivity.
    d. Earning bonuses.

11. Which of the following might be a likely reaction to a plan that specifies a target in tons of equipment for an agricultural equipment manufacturer in the Soviet economy?
    a. Equipment would be made so light and brittle that it would quickly break down.
    b. Managers of such firms would compete vigorously on the black market for supplies of aluminum to replace steel in such machines.
    c. Tractors would be made so heavy they would sink deep into the mud.
    d. Only small garden tractors would be produced.

12. Which of the following best characterizes the economic advances of the past fifty years in the Soviet economy?
    a. Transformation of an essentially underdeveloped country into a modern superpower with moderate living standards.
    b. Reduction of living standards once as high as those of Italy to a level lower than those of Brazil today.
    c. Achievement of true parity with the United States in terms of living standards.
    d. Transformation of a country once as poor as Nepal into one now comparable to Brazil in living standards.

13. Other things equal, an index of economic output for a country tends to grow more rapidly
    a. the earlier the base year used.
    b. the later the base year used.
    c. the less the change in relative prices as output grows.
    d. in none of the above cases--that is, none of the above affects growth indexes.

14. Which of the following does not help explain the recent slowdown in Soviet growth rates?
    a. Lagging energy production.
    b. Lagging agricultural output.
    c. Lagging population growth.
    d. Too much experimentation with economic reforms.

15. Which of the following functions of prices is emphasized in the Soviet Union?
    a. The accounting function.
    b. The allocative function.
    c. Both a and b receive equal emphasis.
    d. Prices perform neither a nor b in the Soviet Union.

ANSWERS TO CHAPTER 40 SELF TEST

True or False

1-T
2-F; central control was emphasized.
3-F; the NEP was Lenin's temporary emphasis of markets during the twenties.
4-T
5-F; they usually bargain for lower targets to gain a safety factor.
6-T
7-F; they do spend much time on procurement.
8-T
9-F; but it may become a net importer in the 1980s.
10-F; they have experimented more freely.

Multiple Choice

1-b
2-c
3-c
4-d
5-c
6-b
7-c
8-d
9-a
10-b
11-c
12-a
13-a
14-d
15-a